Sir Bernard Ingham was born and educated in Hebden Bridge, West Yorkshire. His first job was as a reporter on the *Hebden Bridge Times*, whence he moved to the *Yorkshire Post* (1952–61) and the *Guardian* (1962–67) and then into the Government Information Service. He was Director of Information in the Department of Energy before becoming Chief Press Secretary to Margaret Thatcher in 1979. The first edition of *Kill the Messenger* was published in 1991 when it was described by Nicholas Ridley in the *Sunday Times* as 'essential reading for those who want to understand the phenomenon of the Thatcher revolution'. Bernard Ingham's book on the culture of news management under New Labour, *Wages of Spin*, was published in 2003.

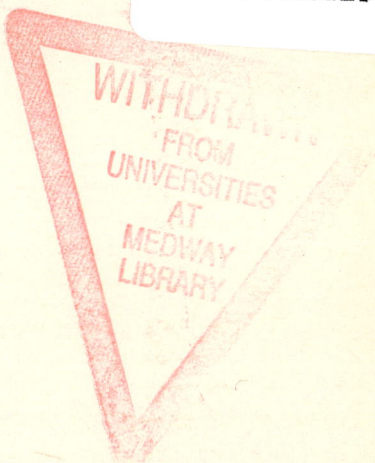

Kill The Messenger
. . . Again

BERNARD INGHAM

POLITICO'S

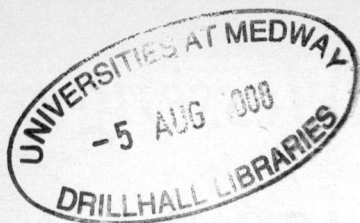

First published in Great Britain 1991 by
HarperCollins Publishers

This updated edition published in 2003 by
Politico's Publishing, an imprint of
Methuen Publishing Limited
215 Vauxhall Bridge Road
London SW1V 1EJ

1 3 5 7 9 10 8 6 4 2

A CIP catalogue record for this book is
available from the British Library

ISBN 1 84275 048 8

Typeset by Rowland Phototypesetting Limited,
Bury St Edmunds, Suffolk
Printed and bound in Great Britain by
Cox and Wyman

To Nancy

Contents

Illustrations

Four generations of Inghams (*Alice Longstaff,*
   Hebden Bridge)
Hebden Bridge (*Denis Thorpe*, Guardian)
A quiet Sunday at the *Guardian* (Guardian)

Visiting BP's production platform (*British Petroleum*)
Flying to view the Ekofisk blowout (*Army photograph*)
Outside Number 10, 17 May 1989 (Sunday Mirror)
At my desk in Number 10, 17 May 1989 (Sunday Mirror)

Welcomed by President Reagan (*White House*
   photograph)
Going native in Tbilisi
Mrs Thatcher gives the facts
I brief in Riyadh

Concentrating on President Mitterrand (*Sally Soames*,
   Sunday Times)
A happy moment (Sunday Mirror)
Mrs Thatcher in her study (Sunday Express)
Mrs Thatcher nursing my teddy

With Martin Fitzwalter
At a press conference with Gorbachev (*Press Association*)
With radio reporters in Kiev

On thin ice (*Nigel Wicks*)
Mrs Thatcher's farewell party (*Nick Taylor*)
On the quayside (Halifax Courier)
After the investiture (*Studio 'D' Photography, Blackpool*)

Introduction

Most of my friends and colleagues seemed to assume that I would write a book after eleven years with Mrs Thatcher. They gave me the impression that they rather expected it of me. Some of them said I must. Others believed that after twenty-three years in the Civil Service I would be dying to get back to writing. In fact, I wrote more in an average day in the Civil Service than I ever wrote as a journalist – and I retained all my journalistic instincts. I tried to make my Civil Service minutes interesting. I did not therefore retire a frustrated journalist from the Civil Service soon after Mrs Thatcher had resigned as Prime Minister. Instead, I left my second career much as a batsman leaves the crease after a good innings – at peace with himself, relaxed and taking some pride in his achievement while regretting that not every stroke was perfection or every run entirely merited.

I had also spent the whole of my working life up to 6 December 1990, when I left Number 10 Downing Street as a civil servant for the last time, compressing everything I wrote into its bare essentials. Government Ministers and readers of newspapers have one thing in common: they are busy people and like their information brief, simple, graphic and quick. The very idea of letting myself rip expansively in book form was truly daunting. It was a formidable challenge with little by way of personal record other than a diary of events. Giles Gordon, of Anthony Sheil Associates Ltd, the literary agents, had been determined to get me to put pen to paper for several years. He cast the die at a meeting with HarperCollins at their Hammersmith headquarters on 18 December 1990. I heroically committed myself to produce 120,000 words, according to my draft synopsis, by 31 March 1991.

I began this book the following day and by 9 p.m. had the first chapter under my belt. Giles said that if I produced 1000 words a day – like Trollope – I would be home and dry. Accordingly, I mapped out a schedule for accounting for my life and my days with

Mrs Thatcher in Number 10. This required me to be in Number 10 – in terms of the book – by 31 January 1991. I was there two days ahead of schedule. This meant that I had the most enjoyable party of my entire life on 31 January: my farewell to my colleagues in Number 10, the Government Information Service and journalists I had worked with. This was held in Number 12 Downing Street by courtesy of the Chief Whip, Richard Ryder, who had been Mrs Thatcher's first political private secretary in Number 10 and whose wife, Caroline, had been her first diary secretary as Prime Minister. Both Mrs Thatcher and John Major, her successor as Prime Minister, attended, as well as my longstanding friend in the Government, John Wakeham.

I completed the first draft of this book at 10 p.m. on Friday 22 March 1991 – six days ahead of the revised schedule. That day I wrote what for me, both as a journalist and a civil servant, is probably a record: 4500 words. The following day my wife and I flew with good conscience to Edinburgh for the annual conference of heads of information of Government departments. It was a wonderful break to meet so many former colleagues. I could not, however, have written this book, largely off the top of my head and subject to subsequent checking, without some sterling support from relatives, friends and colleagues who entered into the spirit of the challenge which the book presented. I would therefore like to record my appreciation to a rather large number of people who have made their contribution.

First, my family. My wife, Nancy, put up with the trials of an author in the house. My son, John, supported me in a constructively critical way. His wife, Christine, kept me up to scratch, organized me, taught me how to use an Amstrad PCW8256, researched facts and kept the copy flowing to Michael Fishwick, my editor, to whom I owe a great deal and probably more than I realize. My brother, Derek, verified my account of my early years. Others who contributed to the accuracy of this book as regards my relative youth are: John Shepherd, Jack Holroyd, Bryan Harwood, David J. Illingworth and Ken Dodd (of the *Guardian*).

I would also like to thank for their help Mike Devereau and Mike Hudson, of the COI; Neville Taylor, Neville Gaffin, Ian Gillis, Brian Mower, Terry Perks and Liz Drummond who are present or former members of the Government Information Service; Sir Charles Powell and Robin Catford, members of Mrs Thatcher's staff in No 10; and Sir Alex Jarratt, Sir Denis Barnes, Sir Jack Rampton and Lord Varley.

For really detailed assistance I must record my particular appreciation to Anne Allan, who was my secretary for more than two years in Number 10, and Sarah Charman, the economic press officer there. They were invaluable.

Sheenagh Wallace, head of information at the Office of Population Censuses and Surveys, also supplied me with crucial background material. I would also like to thank for their contribution to checking facts Philip Aylett and Peter Bean, press officers I left behind in Number 10, and Ian Beaumont, the manager of Number 10 Press Office; and Vera Brice, Helen Ellis, Juliet Van Oss and Annie Robertson of HarperCollins for their professional assistance.

The discipline of writing this book – for which I am entirely responsible and blameworthy – ensured that I had no withdrawal symptoms on leaving Number 10 so suddenly and earlier than planned. But I look back with some nostalgia on a thrilling period in my life serving a truly outstanding Prime Minister as one of her congenial family of staff. For the record, I would like to list all those who served with me in Number 10 Press Office from 1979 to the end of last year. They made my task much lighter and more enjoyable than it might have been.

April 1991

Getting the Drift – and the Job

It all began rather ominously. One sunny morning in May 1979, Sir Jack Rampton, Permanent Secretary of the Department of Energy, called me down from my sixth-floor office on the rear north-east corner of that shabby and highly institutional building called Thames House South on the Embankment just up-stream of Lambeth Bridge.

I gleaned little from Sir Jack's private office at the opposite end of the building with its occupants' grandstand view into the ball-room dancing club in the Millbank Tower complex. They were, I thought, singularly uninformative about the purpose of this somewhat unusual summons.

It would not have been unusual had I been the Department's director of information. As such, for three and a half years up to 1978, I had virtually daily contact with the Permanent Secretary. But, as the under-secretary in charge of the energy conservation division, I led a much more sedate, orderly and sheltered existence. I could actually plan my day's work. That was never possible in the information division, where I was at the mercy of events and at the urgent beck and call of Ministers and officials. A call to the second – Ministerial and top brass – floor was relatively infrequent except to see my immediate superior, deputy secretary Philip Jones. (He is now Sir Philip, chairman of Total Oil Marine, and was previously chairman of the old Electricity Council.)

Sir Jack was, as ever, seated behind his desk in the middle of the room with his back to the window affording a view up the Thames to Nine Elms. It was a fairly large office with a colour scheme out of the top drawer of the Property Services Agency. Mustard carpet, as I recall it, and most certainly creamy curtains spattered with rough orange crescents. The coverlet on the bed in the alcove was of the same material as the curtains. The bed was a relic – and a reminder – of the energy crisis of 1974 into which the Department was born. Sir Jack motioned me to the chair in front of his desk and, in his slightly hesitant way, asked me if I was happy at my work.

It was a good question. It was also a disturbing question. Energy conservation – the promotion of energy saving and efficiency – had been a joy while it lasted. After a very unconfident start on my conversion from director of information to an administrator with responsibility for policy, I had derived real satisfaction from trying to persuade the public to save energy – and themselves money – and more especially industry to build economy in the use of energy into its products, plant and buildings. Dr Jack Cunningham, MP for Whitehaven (now Copeland) had taken a lively and active interest in the subject as the responsible junior Minister. His Secretary of State, Tony Benn, had left him to get on with it, and he did – with a will. But, with the change of Government, morale in my division had plummeted because even informing the public and industry of how to save energy had been frowned upon and somewhat tetchily forbidden by the new Secretary of State, David Howell. Even providing basic information, which research showed consumers wanted, smacked of intervention. The new government was not interventionist. What is more, it was determined to show it. The junior Minister, John Moore, who went on to become Secretary of State for Social Services, was also an enthusiast for conserving energy, but he suffered from a temporary – as it turned out – palsy of policy.

I was therefore a little frustrated. But I tried hard to avoid giving that impression to Sir Jack. Experience in the Civil Service teaches that there are fashions in policy. What is taboo today can become the flavour of tomorrow – as indeed did energy conservation during Peter Walker's tenure as Secretary of State. I gave Sir Jack to understand that I was still enjoying the administrative position to which he had exceptionally, in a bold act of faith, promoted me.

'Could you ever conceive of returning to the Government Information Service?' he asked.

'Not really,' I replied with a firmness of tone which did not entirely represent my position. After all, if the bottom were falling out of energy conservation I might end up without a real job, bored and resentful. It was difficult to be bored or resentful for long as a Director of Information.

'Well,' I added, for the sake of clarification, 'I suppose there are two information jobs I might be interested in. One is the Director General of the Central Office of Information, but that isn't available. The other is the Chief Press Secretary's job at Number 10. And that's filled, too. And this Government aren't going to offer that to me, are they?'

Sir Jack, who knew something of my political past, smiled inscrutably behind his thick glasses. Before he terminated the meeting he secured what must have been his second objective without even putting the question directly to me. In conversation I told him that I did not believe any civil servant invited to work in No 10 could say 'No'. On reflection, I thought he seemed very pleased with himself as I left in a rather apprehensive state of mind.

'What,' I said to myself, 'was all that about?' I did not think I was falling down on the energy conservation job. Yet the Permanent Secretary did not call staff down to ask them if they were enjoying their work just to make conversation. That wasn't Sir Jack's style, either. So what was the point? I concluded that a new job of some sort was in the offing. But which? The thought that I was being propositioned for Number 10 simply did not occur to me. The reason was not just that Henry James, deputy press secretary to three Prime Ministers – Sir Alec Douglas-Home, Mr Wilson and Mr Heath – was in Number 10, which he loved, having been brought out of his retirement job advising the Vickers' board. I did not know Mrs Thatcher. I had never even met her. And failed Labour council candidates did not become Chief Press Secretaries to Conservative Prime Ministers, least of all to Mrs Thatcher.

The next move quickly followed. On 18 May Mrs Thatcher began her series of Prime Ministerial visits to Government departments in the Department of Energy. Some thirty members of the staff were selected to meet her and I correctly anticipated that I should not be among the chosen few. There were other Under-Secretaries holding far more sensitive political jobs than mine – coal, electricity, nuclear, oil or gas, for example – whom she would need to meet. I resigned myself to second-hand impressions of our

3

new Prime Minister. Then, on the very eve of her visit I was, to my surprise, invited to take tea and cucumber sandwiches with her. And I was billed not as the head of energy conservation division but as the former director of information.

The gathering was in Sir Jack's room. What Mrs Thatcher thought of the colour scheme is not recorded. The proceedings followed a typical pattern for a VIP visit: Mrs Thatcher worked her way through the invitees around the room and eventually, two minutes before she left for a vigorous argument with senior officials, in which Philip Jones was particularly vocal, she came to me. She betrayed no special interest either in me or in energy conservation. I was left wondering why on earth I had been invited to the party at the last minute. The thought that Mrs Thatcher might be giving me the once-over as her Chief Press Secretary again did not arise. I was utterly convinced that the job was closed to me by my past political affiliations.

I returned to the task of promoting energy saving as best I could in all the depressing circumstances. Then out of the blue in late June a voice came over the telephone in my office. 'Whitmore here,' the man said. 'Clive Whitmore.' Perhaps he sensed my blank face. 'You know, we met on a course in open government at Sunningdale last October.' Sunningdale is the site of the Civil Service College. I struggled to put a face to the name and congratulated myself later that I had got it right.

'Have you had a call from the Cabinet Secretary?' he asked.

'No,' I said guardedly, adding rather airily: 'I don't often talk to the Cabinet Secretary in this job.'

'Never' would have been more accurate. I had, however, met Sir Robert Armstrong and had got to know him fairly well during those taxing years of industrial strife in the first half of the 1970s when he was principal private secretary first to Mr Heath and then to Mr Wilson.

'Oh, no,' groaned Mr Whitmore. 'Not another cock-up. But I assume you are getting the drift?'

Everything immediately fell into place. I said that I assumed he was asking me if I would become Mrs Thatcher's Chief Press Secretary.

'Exactly,' he said. 'And will you?'

'Yes, of course,' I replied. 'As I told Jack Rampton, I don't think any civil servant who is asked to serve in Number 10 can refuse.'

Clive, now Sir Clive Whitmore, successively Permanent Secretary at the Ministry of Defence, his 'parent' Department, and now of the Home Office, indicated that he very much agreed with that approach.

We then went into details. I gathered that Henry James had been brought in on a six-month contract. There was, therefore, no immediate rush. It would, however, be desirable for me to meet the Prime Minister. Meanwhile, I should keep the impending appointment to myself and my immediate family. My wife, Nancy, and my son, John, who was in his second year at Durham University, shared my amazement, excitement and sense of honour that I was going to end up in Number 10 working for Mrs Thatcher. We kept the information to ourselves through July, August and part of September, including a holiday in Harrogate and the Yorkshire Dales.

It was even less easy to concentrate on energy conservation after Clive Whitmore's telephone call. Inevitably, I speculated about who had advised the Prime Minister to take me on as her spokesman and manager of her relations with the media. It remains a matter for conjecture. I assume the prime mover was Sir Robert Armstrong. Clive Whitmore had been able to size me up for two or three days at Sunningdale. And Sir Jack would have had a view. He had always treated me sympathetically and supportively – indeed, generously – through some turbulent times in the Department of Energy. I am forever grateful to him for taking a chance on me and promoting me out of the Government Information Service (GIS) at the end of 1977 to lead a new energy conservation division. This gave me twenty-one months' experience of administration and policy formulation which were to prove invaluable background in discharging my job as Chief Press Secretary.

I learned later that these top civil servants were not the only players in the recruitment game. To my astonishment I was assured by Ian Gillis, who succeeded me as the information chief at the Department of Energy and was very well informed, that a number of Conservatives had approved of my appointment. These included Derek Howe, Mrs Thatcher's political press adviser. I had come across Derek when he was a journalist on the *Yorkshire Evening*

News in Leeds where for five years I served as a reporter on the *Yorkshire Post* and then the *Guardian*. In Mrs Thatcher's early days in Number 10 he displayed an encyclopaedic knowledge of political detail. He was well aware of my Labour Party past and of my fierce contributions while I was on the politically liberal *Guardian* to a Labour Party newspaper, the *Leeds Weekly Citizen*, under the pseudonym of 'Albion'.

Derek may also have known that I was closely examined about my political attitudes by Paul Bryan, Minister of State in the Department of Employment, immediately after Mr Heath took office in 1970. Mr Bryan tried – and failed – to win Sowerby, where I was brought up, three times in 1948, 1950 and 1951. As a junior reporter on the *Hebden Bridge Times* I had covered his speeches – accurately, I trusted, as I entered his room. Within a few days of the interview the Secretary of State, Robert Carr, now Lord Carr, took me on one side and said he was not concerned about my political past. All he asked of me was professionalism and loyalty. I assured him that we all had to make choices in life and that I had made mine. I was now a civil servant, bound to serve the Government of the day to the best of my ability and he need have no doubts that I would do so. I do not recall the issue arising again until my appointment as Chief Press Secretary was announced in September 1979.

Clive Whitmore and I anticipated that my background might cause a bit of a fuss. The publicity was not the best note on which to start in Number 10 but it soon passed. It included erroneous assertions that I had been a prospective Labour Parliamentary candidate and speculation as to when I had left the Labour Party. It is likely that I could have been a Parliamentary candidate in a number of unwinnable seats in Yorkshire had I been sufficiently dedicated and prepared to cut corners with my career as a journalist. One other factor saved me from a fate which would almost certainly have blocked my passage to Number 10: I did not like the idea of union sponsorship and such political ambition as I had withered on the vine of this antipathy. The only seat I was really interested in was Douglas (now Lord) Houghton's Sowerby – my native heath. Douglas Houghton was a good friend of my father's but I never broached with him the idea of succeeding him. That interest withered, too, when the *Guardian* moved me to London, first on relief and then permanently, three days after I had lost a local election in Leeds in May 1965. I found it impossible to pinpoint when I left the Labour Party because my membership also lapsed when it became incompatible, as I saw it, with my job as a civil servant. It was probably in 1968.

My Labour Party antecedents were a talking point whenever, during Mrs Thatcher's tenure of office, controversy stimulated the diarists. They did not figure in our discussion when I was quietly paraded before her for inspection in July 1979. I was introduced to her in her study on the first floor of Number 10 looking over the garden and out over the garden wall to St James's Park. The room did not appear to be much changed from Ted Heath's days when I had been included in the Department of Employment team whom Mr Heath consulted when handling serious industrial disputes.

I approached my appointment – both my initial meeting and my job – with Mrs Thatcher more with curiosity than apprehension, notwithstanding her formidable reputation. I expected her to do most of the talking, to express herself forthrightly and to know what she wanted of me. My expectations were amply fulfilled in the course of a fascinating twenty minutes, sitting in arm-chairs on either side of the fireplace. It was to be the first in this room of many spirited gallops around the course of the subject in hand.

I had two points necessarily to get across. First, as a civil servant I was an agent of the Government and not of the Conservative Party and, as such, would have to operate within constraints with which the Prime Minister would be familiar. Second, if I were to do my job effectively I would need access both to her and to information and her authority to co-ordinate the Government information machine.

I did not have to make the first point. She recognized it herself in the course of her remarks and was always conscious of the distinction throughout her Prime Ministership. The second point I made by way of underlining her acknowledgement that, of course, I needed access both to her and to information if I were to get over the Government's messages and to explain Government policy and decisions and the thinking behind them. It was necessary for me to *understand*, and for that access and then application on my part were essential. The Government's information orchestra, she agreed, needed to be conducted.

She never asked me whether I was prepared to work for her. It was assumed that I would. All we needed to talk about was the job that needed to be done. I left stimulated, eager for the fray, impatient with the months which lay between me and my new challenge. I did not feel overawed either by Mrs Thatcher or by the impending responsibility. It would not be a novel experience for me, working for a woman Minister. In the late 1960s I had been chief information officer to that other leading woman politician of the age, Mrs Barbara Castle, when she was First Secretary and Secretary of State for Employment and Productivity. I had also been forged in many fires: prices and incomes policy; too many national strikes, including two miners' disputes; 'In Place of Strife', that failed attempt by the Labour Party to chart a new course for industrial relations; the Industrial Relations Act, 1971 – another, this time Conservative, failure to curb the abuse of union power; the development of the North Sea; a Middle East oil crisis – or two; and the attempt to preserve the nuclear power option in supplying the nation with electricity. I had run a national publicity campaign for the Government – the 'Save It' campaign. I had some experience of policy formulation; some international grounding through accompanying Ministers on visits to the USA, the Middle East, the European Community and other parts of Western Europe; and I was no stranger to Number 10 under Conservative and Labour governments because attempts to settle strikes often ended up there. This was not enough for anonymous critics, quoted in the press as saying that I lacked 'experience of central departments'. But I was fit and full of fight – rather like Mrs Thatcher.

More important, I felt an immediate rapport with her. This surprised me because I had not felt it when we met briefly and unsatisfactorily in the Department of Energy. If, as an information specialist, I had had one reaction to Mrs Thatcher as Leader of the Opposition it was that I would want to change her bossy ways and calm her down. She seemed to be a classic case of a Minister who would require lead weights rather than booster rockets. I also recall being very sceptical of the idea, advanced by Eric Varley whom I served as Secretary of State for Energy with great satisfaction and enjoyment, that Mrs Thatcher might do very well indeed if, unfortunately for him, she ever won office.

On meeting her I found I could identify with her. She was part of my north-of-Watford experience. She was a bit classier than me: her father had been in trade, mine just wove cotton; but both had led their local communities. She had also been to Oxford; I was a product of a grammar school and technical college. But we had had similar noses-to-the-grindstone upbringings. She also wanted to DO something, and something clearly needed to be done to shake Britain up and out of its accelerating decline.

As I walked back in the sunshine to the Department of Energy, up Whitehall, across Parliament Square and along Millbank, I took heart from one other fact: Mrs Thatcher had come to office without a press secretary. In this media-ridden age it was fascinating that she had had to bring the doyen of Government information officers out of retirement as a stop-gap and institute a head-hunt of the Civil Service for a longer term appointment rather than bring in a journalistic crony or party loyalist. I concluded that she was clearly going to do what she thought to be right and then think about presenting it. She was more concerned with substance than with shine. And she was more interested in reform than with being liked. It was likely to be a rough ride, but I had had it rough before.

I left the Department of Energy in September 1979 with much sadness. The Department which I had known from its formation had brought new technical, scientific, engineering, international and administrative dimensions to my professional experience, and many friends. It had been an exciting and rewarding Department in which to work.

I departed with Sir Jack Rampton's sage counsel ringing in my ears: 'Don't be afraid to give your advice. And don't be afraid to interrupt her or you'll never give that advice.'

I could not wait to interrupt.

2

Thistlebottom and All That

Hebden Bridge has a lot to answer for, according to some critics. It formed me. This small town deep in Upper Calder Valley in the West Yorkshire Pennines north-west of Halifax always calls me back. I have a deep and enduring affection for its stone mills, terraces and buttresses, its precipitous hillsides, its peaty and heathery moors, its lovely woods and brown streams which powered the early stirrings of British manufacturing, and for the decent, straightforward and upretentious natives with whom I grew up.

I was not, however, born there. My mother, née Alice Horsfall, brought my red head into this world on the morning of the longest day in 1932 in the Royal Halifax Infirmary, eight miles from home. We lived at 16 Industrial Street on the steep Birchcliffe hillside, an appropriate address for a mill family. My father, Garnet, was a cotton weaver like my mother and two of his sisters, Maud and Flo, who now live in retirement in Fleetwood next door to a third sister, Clare, the only sister to marry. The Inghams have produced a lot of corduroy in their time.

Pre-war Hebden Bridge was an industrial, chapel-going, musical, self-reliant community which remained close to the land. We had a busy blacksmith – Sowden's – in Crown Street. Steam trains puffed and shuddered their way up the valley and the Rochdale Canal was still in occasional use. At Whiteley Arches where my aunt and uncle, Clare and Alex Ackerley, lived, the LMS railway line passed over not merely one of the main Yorkshire-Lancashire turnpikes but also the canal and the River Calder. The valleys get very tight thereabouts.

They could forgive a man a lot in Hebden Bridge if he worked and supported his family. They mostly worked. The town escaped the worst of the 1930s slump, though as a child I became conscious of its threat and the anxieties it engendered when short-time working was announced. Fortunately, my father always had a job, for we were not a healthy family. The good Dr Alan Hardy Clegg attended us with a diligence and sweet temper and an understanding about his pre-NHS bills which earned our enormous gratitude and respect, for, like the rest, we paid our way.

My mother was a chronic asthmatic and I not only inherited her asthma but also suffered from the eczema which so often accompanies it. My eczema as a baby was so extensive, and the appearance of the treatment so startling, that it quite disturbed some people. According to my mother, door-to-door salesmen were apt to forget their purpose in life when she responded to their knock with the bandaged infant Ingham in her arms, his face and the rest of him under liberal applications of a black, tarry ointment. The eczema more or less cleared up by the time I was running about. The asthma and my comprehensive portfolio of allergies have remained with me, though in the mildest form compared with the trials of my childhood. In confined spaces, animals and pollen and dust, and especially that of hay, soon had my eyes running and red and my chest heaving for breath. Colds always spelled trouble, and many was the night that my despairing parents sat up with me burning the herbal Potter's asthma cure in a tin lid to try to bring me relief. When relief came it brought fearsome headaches as the brain recovered a reasonable supply of oxygen. Happily an inhaler was prescribed just before the war and this brought very quick relief, though it was a clumsy contraption for my mother to carry around for the two of us.

My brother, two years younger, contracted double pneumonia at the age of three and spent seventeen weeks in the Royal Halifax Infirmary where he was twice given up for lost. During the crisis I gathered that he might not come back home. I knew he would return when, on that tearful, joyful day for us all, we observed through the window of the children's ward this blond, round-faced child, colour restored to his cheeks, giving his Teddy a fearful shaking. 'Not much wrong with his lungs now,' I'm told a nurse remarked, sharing in the family's relief. The *Sunday Times* once called me 'the hard man'. Derek is the hard man of the family – physically and mentally; he is very tough-minded indeed. It took a singleness of purpose for a boy who determinedly left school at fourteen to become a farm hand to acquire and build up a small but thriving dairy business and farm some 800 feet up on the Pennines not far from the summit of the M62.

I never remember living in Industrial Street. The family soon moved across the narrow valley to rent 29 Albion Terrace, half a dozen doors from my mother's parents, Greenwood (Greeney) and Jane (Jenny) Horsfall. My parents never owned their own home. Architecturally the stone-built terrace was a fascinating example of how to get the most out of a hillside development. A gallery system overcame the problem of access arising from building back-to-back houses into the hill which on one side had their only doors opening into thin air two floors above the ground. Nothing was to be done about the damp in the lower houses, like ours, which backed into the earth. There was one compensation: the view down Calder Valley into and beyond Hebden Bridge.

It was from this concentrated terrace with outside toilets and its industrial, sylvan and rural aspect combined, that I was brought up, went to school and started work.

Our upbringing was Non-conformist, radical, strict, narrow-minded yet culturally mind-opening, sober – our drink was water bright – and loving in a way that avoided public and too many private demonstrations of affection. We were not a soppy lot. We were also taught to be careful: to make do and mend and to save for the future. Grandad Horsfall seemed to believe that most damage could be repaired with 'band' – heavy duty string. We had plenty of room in which to play in the Brockholes woods and quarries above the terrace where the grass smelled of soot from the mills and left bare legs blackened after cowboy games.

We went to Hope Baptist Sunday School in the town centre morning and afternoon, and attended morning service in the church. We got a new suit of clothes for each 'anniversary' Sunday in the spring. This required children to attend all three church services and to 'sit up' on a stage below the pulpit. Our social life up to leaving school centred on Hope Street under the leadership of a learned, serious but supportive pastor, the Rev. W. S. Davies BA, BD, STM. Mr Davies had one eccentricity for a Baptist minister in the 1930s: he invariably accompanied my father to Thrum

Hall where they supported Halifax Rugby League Club from the terraces. They introduced me – and later Mr Davies's son, Paul – to the game at the age of seven on a clear, freezing day with the ground deliberately left under six inches of snow to prevent the pitch from becoming hard and unplayable. I was mightily impressed by this winter sport. I subsequently covered Halifax and rugby league more generally for the *Yorkshire Evening Post* and the *Yorkshire Post* for much of the 1950s.

Derek and I went to Central Street school where we both failed our county minor examination – the forerunner to the 11-plus. There is nothing academic about Derek: his mind had been fixed on farming from an early age and my parents realized that nothing was going to shift him. My failure was regarded as a tragedy bordering on a disaster partly because I had always done well in term examinations and they wanted me to get on and partly because they feared for my health if I were forced to take my baggage of allergies into industry. They had a point at the time. This sad affair put me, a nervous wreck, in bed for a week with a massive asthma attack.

At considerable personal sacrifice my parents decided to pay for me to go to Hebden Bridge Grammar School just across the confluence of the Hebden and Calder rivers from my junior school. They did not get much encouragement from a neighbour, Mrs Edwards, who said it was a waste of time and money. Bernard, she confidently predicted, would end up in t' mill like the rest of them. My sense of failure dissolved in a series of good term results in the top 'A' form. At my best I was third and at worst sixth in the class. My asthma was also less troublesome provided I did not provoke it. My grammar school years were happy and fulfilling and my parents felt it had all been worth-while.

From an early age my maternal grandparents exercised considerable influence over us because of their proximity only six doors away. My grandmother, née Vernon, was the daughter of a Staffordshire miner from Brereton, near Rugeley. She took Derek and me back to her home village early in the war. I marvelled at the gentler, more fertile countryside. Grandma Horsfall, like her sisters, came to the West Riding 'in service' and married Greenwood Horsfall, of upland farming-weaving stock, at the turn of the century. They had but one daughter who, as a girl, was an elocutionist in some demand for the formidable programme of Sunday School concerts in the district.

My grandmother had been a beauty. She was a warm, generous person, albeit with a sharp wit in argument, and she believed strength went in at the mouth. She had an explicit faith in animal fats which would have been the despair of modern dietitians. She passed on her skills as a cook and baker to my mother with interest. We ate superbly, even during the war. I delighted in potato and onion pasty, spotted dick, ginger sponge, suet pudding with treacle and most of all bilberry pudding during the July/August season. She also made what my brother describes as Calder Valley caviar, though it has nothing to do with fish. It is dock pudding, a local delicacy made from dock leaves, nettles, onions and oatmeal, fried and served with bacon. The dock leaves are not those of the familiar cow dock, which take the sting out of nettles, but the tender, spring shoots of the sweet dock (*polygonum bistorta*). I used to earn sixpence per carrier bag of dock leaves from grateful housewives. This unique Hebden Bridge dish came to the attention of Lord Haw Haw, the propagandist for Germany, during the war. He cited it as evidence of such a critical food shortage in Yorkshire that the people were reduced to eating grass. They had been eating 'grass', probably for centuries, as a spring medicine to cleanse the blood. Dock pudding is for me gastronomic perfection.

Grandad and Grandma Horsfall loved Derek and me – and showed it. They welcomed us, indulged our cupboard love, positively spoiled us and, above all, my grandfather set out to broaden our minds in his gaslit living room reeking with pipesmoke. My other grandparents – Harry and Mary Ingham – scarcely got a look in at 23 Nutclough across the valley, though we were regular visitors. With four spinster daughters living at home during my childhood, it was a crowded, lively and welcoming household.

Grandad Horsfall was a self-taught man with a radical and irreverent turn of mind, steeped in the Co-operative and Labour movements. He was an ardent apostle of Samuel Smiles whom he never quoted; a botanist; a local historian; and a musician. He had a harmonium in his living-room which he completely failed to teach Derek and me to play over many hours of exasperation. Not to be beaten, he next encouraged us to take up the cornet in Hebden

14

Bridge brass band which my father served faithfully as a member of the committee. We sat noisily side by side among the second cornets for a time. It was even thought that all that blowing would do my asthma good. Later I took up the violin and caterwauled with the best in the school and in the Todmorden orchestra. My grandfather was also an inveterate singer of hymns and popular songs of World War I and before, and frequently conducted choral sessions with us through the living-room fog. Either my grandparents' neighbours were secretly musical or they were tolerant beyond the singing of it, as Alan Paton, the South African writer, would have put it.

My grandfather also loved walking and he was, to his own immense self satisfaction, an amateur astronomer. His mission in life was to pass on his knowledge to his beloved grandsons, to teach them and to enthuse. He could be a bit wearing and during the wartime blackout he could be shocking. The lights going out all over Europe in one sense lit up his life. The stars shone bigger and brighter and on clear, moonless nights he took us up the hill towards Heptonstall to identify and din into us the order of the heavens. These performances could cause much apprehension in lonely walkers. Our shouts of reward when, after a period of watchful silence, we caught a shooting star or thought we had a glimpse of the Northern Lights, terrified more than one passer-by into a shocked and angry response.

He walked our sturdy legs off us, up hill and down dale, through wood and field, over moor and through bog, identifying plants and trees and birds and local history from the ice age when Ted Hughes's 'death struggle of the glacier' formed the gorges and upland shelves of land. In summer these walks on Sunday had another purpose: to do the rounds of Sunday school anniversaries at hill-top chapels – Blackshawhead, Crimsworth Dean, Blakedean (where because of the steep site worshippers climbed up steps to enter the ground floor of the tiny church and walked down steps to enter the gallery), Luddenden Dean, Wainsgate and Heptonstall Slack.

My grandfather was anti-Roman Catholic, though he got no support for this from my grandmother. She could be moved to tears by the memory of a girl friend she was forced to drop because she was a 'Roman'. He also had very little time for Anglicans whom he saw as the privileged at prayer. But he moved freely in Non-conformist circles. Baptist, Methodist, Wesleyan or Congregational was not the point: what mattered were the walk to the anniversary service, the sermon and, above all, the singing. I wish I had a £5 note for every time, standing next to my grandfather, I have sung 'The day thou gavest Lord is ended' with the colours of the setting sun refracted through the bevelled windows to dapple the wooden pews.

Then one September morning after Hope chapel we learned from an acquaintance in the fields near Weasel Hall, on the hillside opposite our home, that war was about to be declared. My grandfather rushed us home, agitated and fearful, to listen on his battery-powered wireless to Mr Chamberlain.

The war brought Dad's Army practising signalling from one side of the valley to another. One lot in the field next to our terrace got into fearful trouble with their commanding officer for sending in semaphore the following message across to Old Chamber: 'Wife says dinner on table at 12. Suit yourself whether you are there.' An apoplectic CO demanded: 'Don't you know there's a war on?' This war also brought real troops, quartered in Brown's Mill, evacuees and eventually prisoners-of-war whom we eyed suspiciously. There were probing searchlights on Mount Skip to the east above our home; the occasional air raid alert and even more occasional crash landings on the moors of crippled bombers returning from raids. The toll of dead, missing and wounded servicemen was faithfully recorded in the *Hebden Bridge Times*, which was essential reading from an early age as was the *Daily Herald*. But nothing was dropped on us or fired at us in anger in Hebden Bridge. Evacuees who had known much worse thought we were insanely careless of our own safety when we stayed put as the sirens wailed. War also brought work for the many sewing shops, as Hebden Bridge's ready-made clothing works were known, to clothe the troops, and for the small engineering works into which my father, aged thirty-nine at the outbreak of war, went to work 'on munitions'. Like millions more, my aunts – my father's sisters – plotted the course of the war on a map on the wall of their Nutclough kitchen. Our knowledge of geography became precocious. The war also underlined Hebden Bridge's thrift. The townspeople invested heavily and magnificently on War Weapons savings weeks. Even the natives wondered where all that brass came from.

Hebden Bridge is, as they say in those parts, 'nobbut just' in Yorkshire, though its loyalties are sure. It tended to look west to the Lancashire coast during 'Wakes' week rather than east to the Yorkshire holiday resorts of Scarborough, Bridlington, Filey and Whitby. Blackpool gave a new dimension to the war to Hebden Bridge children. It teemed with airmen of many countries, including the smarter dressed Americans who seemed to be very well off. The sky over Blackpool Tower roared with aircraft.

Growing up in the 1939–45 war, even in safe and sheltered Hebden Bridge, with an annual trip to the coast, was a stretching experience. It was also a political education, though party politics locally were subjugated to the common purpose of defeating Hitler and later the Japanese. We also had to be careful in our family about politics. My father's side were 'Toories'. He was a renegade, presumably after exposure to Grandad Horsfall. I did not absorb much 'socialism' from either of them. They did not call themselves socialists – that would have been pretentious – though they did subscribe to nationalization and all that. 'Socialism' was a word I came to use on the Yorkshire Conservative Newspaper Company's *Yorkshire Evening Post* and the *Yorkshire Post* to discredit the Labour Party. The cause of my father and grandfather could be much more simply expressed: it was to better the lot of ordinary working people like themselves, to equalize opportunity and to curb or eliminate unearned or inherited privilege. They were not, however, envious people. I grew to regard them in my youth as appallingly accepting. 'We are only working people and we can't expect much,' my mother used to say with immense but unintended provocation, converting Sunday dinners into fierce debates. My father and grandparents tacitly agreed with her. They made no demands on others. They paid their dues and would have paid their poll tax. They observed the law and respected order. They contributed to the common weal and they did not resent the rewards of hard work and talent. Gracie Fields and Walter Widdop, the locally born operatic tenor, for example, were admired enormously. 'Hard work never hurt anyone' might have been Hebden Bridge's motto in my childhood and youth. It was the only way to get on. No wonder Mrs Thatcher mined a rich seam of support among traditional Labour voters in the 1980s. She restored common-sense values to so many people's lives. They did not recognize her as a 'Toory'. Neither did I. But that is another story.

My household rather expected a literate young chap like me to do his stuff for Labour at elections immediately after the war. I did my bit, especially as my father, a leading light in the management of Hebden Bridge Co-operative Society around which the town revolved, stood as a Labour candidate for the Hebden Royd Urban District Council. I hesitate to suggest that he was developing political ambition; it was more a case of being pressed to put his name forward. We Inghams did seem to get landed with the work, partly because of our sense of responsibility but also, I suspect, because none of us found it easy to decline. My brother, Derek, even found time to become secretary to the Calder Valley Agricultural Society – a heavy responsibility for a young farmer since it entailed helping to organize the annual show.

My father secured election in 1947 and served, with a short break in the early 1950s, until 1961. He became chairman in 1957 and the family went to support him when he made his chairman's address in the council chamber. He served his electors diligently and was helped by finding a colleague who did not like getting up in a morning. My father therefore worked permanent morning shifts, from 6 a.m., so that he could concentrate on council work in the evenings. My mother, plump and supportive, did not seem to mind in the least.

I did my bit to get my father elected, addressing envelopes, filling them with election literature and delivering them from the Labour Party headquarters in the Trades Club opposite the grammar school. Sometimes, rather shyly and hesitatingly, I took names and addresses outside the polling booth. I was anything but a brash, confident, pushy youth. Outside my home or a small circle of friends, where I could make a fool of myself more or less with impunity, I was socially insecure, lacked self-confidence and felt rather inadequate. But, given a job to do, I was reliable. Among other things, I acquired the secretaryship of the local Labour League of Youth which had, in Eric Pogson, a most formidable chairman and debater. At the age of fifteen Eric presided over a meeting addressed by Mr J. W. Belcher, MP for Sowerby and I just managed to propose a vote of thanks. How I envied Eric's gift of the gab. How I despaired of my terror in rising to contribute to the grammar school debating society. Eric, sadly dead these last few years from a massive haemorrhage in Washington, DC, where he worked for the World Bank, was an MP in the making. I seemed to be a natural backroom boy – a civil servant, perhaps? – and a committee man. Where did Eric go wrong?

The Labour League of Youth in Hebden Bridge was anything but a hotbed of revolution. It was a pretty exclusive social set – too exclusive for some who wanted to break into the clique – and it was largely sustained not by politics but by dances in the ballroom of the Trades Club. The ballroom served for a time as the grammar school's third-form classroom from which I was once expelled by Miss Barber for the rest of term – not much was left of it – for talking in class. The dances were entirely non-political, driven by enjoyment and young love and hugely successful until they fell into the hands of a band with no sense of rhythm. We could not dance to its music. It was an early lesson in market economics – they did not last long.

In the course of acquiring jobs – or having them thrust upon me – I became the extremely youthful secretary of the Hope Baptist Contact Club for the men of the church. I laid on programmes of speakers of which the predominantly middle-aged members, including my father, generally approved. I was a rather busy young chap as the school certificate – Northern Universities Joint Matriculation Board – examinations loomed in 1948. I recall feeling keyed up for them but not under intolerable pressure. My examination nerves were being conquered. I was also beginning to pace myself. I did this by working hard on my examination subjects on the living-room table until 8.30 p.m. when I went up to Mrs Gibson's yard at the top end of Albion Terrace for batting practice in the Bradman style. I had read that Bradman threw a ball against a wall and practised his shots using a wicket as his bat. I used the wall of our outside toilet and imagined that I was Arthur Morris, my Australian hero. I was a left-hander. I was also sports mad.

In summer I played cricket occasionally for the school and for Salem Methodists and the MCC – Mytholmroyd Cricket Club. In winter it was soccer, more regularly for the school than I played cricket, and consistently for Thistlebottom, a group of mostly grammar school lads whose founders – John Shepherd, Arthur Hodgson and Geoff Bamford – lived in a district of Hebden Bridge of that name where, paradoxically, the valley has no floor and consequently no space for field games. When I wasn't watching Halifax RLFC with my father and the Rev. Davies I was at Halifax Town or going over the hill to Burnley, then in the first division of the Football League, to watch real quality.

Both my cricket clubs were situated on the banks of rivers – Mytholmroyd on the Calder and Salem beside the Hebden stream. A triangular box was required in each case to retrieve the ball from the water when it was hoisted over the boundary. Mytholmroyd was higher class than Salem both in standard of cricket and ground. There were few worse grounds than Salem's Hollins Holme, nestling deep in a heavily wooded valley which rises eventually to Top Withens, or Wuthering Heights, on the Brontë Moors. It had a reasonable wicket but its outfield was very rough pasture liberally spotted with cow pats. The cattle were kept off the wicket by a movable fence. Singles did not come easily at Salem. Nor did practice. The ground was next to a small sewage works which bred midges and batting through a curtain of bloodthirsty insects did not assist concentration.

I was a reliable member of the teams: I turned up and turned out. My performances as an all-rounder were modest. While my potential was seen as a batsman, my record as a medium pace right arm bowler was probably better overall. My promise as a batsman was not complemented by self-confidence. I failed miserably to impress the professional, T. S. Worthington, when I was taken to the nets at Todmorden, the Yorkshire club which plays in the Lancashire League.

I had a brief flirtation with rugby league when efforts were made to revive the Hebden Bridge club after the war, rapidly graduating from full-back to prop forward. But the school sport was soccer and I concentrated on that. Thistlebottom was run by Levi Shepherd who seemed to us to have done – and to continue to do – most things. He was a parish councillor, a special constable, the Hebden Bridge Co-op delivery man, a leading light in the local

Conservative Party, the British Legion and at Hebden Bridge Parish Church where he was a sidesman, a worker for charities and a soccer referee. He had been with the British Army in Russia at the time of the October Revolution and was with the Black and Tans in Ireland. His only son, John, was our centre-forward – a player of such promise that he had trials with Bolton Wanderers.

Levi piloted Thistlebottom to our outstanding success as a club of sixteen-year-olds – the final of the Hebden Bridge workshops competition which we lost 1-0 to a team of grown men. Earlier teams of adults had tried to get us barred from the competition because we were all 'registered' players – that is, we were registered to play for Thistlebottom in the Halifax Red Triangle League. As a regular team we were felt to have an unfair advantage over 'scratch' sides. Common sense prevailed and as losing finalists we each won a cup – my only tin pot to show for countless hours of kicking a ball about in street, road, schoolyard, field, moor and clearings like Gypsy Flat. This competition brought a relatively high class of soccer to Hebden Bridge each spring. The quality of the football far exceeded that of the badly drained Calder Holme pitch. In wet weather its extensive puddles – nay, ponds – provided spectacular watersport.

I performed reliably at left back – solid, dependable but nothing to shout home about. I was not always the fittest, quite apart from the threat of an asthma attack. Levi showed his innate kindness before the workshops' competition semi-final by sending me at his own expense for sun ray treatment for a ricked back. After we had won he insisted I return to his home for a proper bath. The changing-room in the cellar of the Neptune Hotel about half a mile along the canal from Calder Holme had no facilities: its only water was running into a stone trough outside. At home we had only a tin bath which was used every Friday night.

My competitive sporting life was drawing to a close, though, for at sixteen I was about to start work.

3

T' Brig Times

Grammar school brings back only happy memories. Under Herbert Howarth, Hebden Bridge Grammar School was a co-educational establishment to be enjoyed. You were taught to work hard and play hard and there was a good spirit. Even during the war it catered for the sporty, the arty and the crafty and it provided a good social life for its pupils. Given the poverty of working-class ambition, it did an excellent job with the youngsters presenting themselves each August in their navy blue blazers or gym slips, white shirts and blue and gold ties. It gave me and most of my colleagues our first trip to London and abroad in 1947 when Mr Howarth led a party to Wilderswil, near Interlaken, in Switzerland. Unrationed Wilderswil was a wonderland to which many on the trip have returned over the years.

I performed well and found the arts easier than science or mathematics. Successive English teachers found my essays occasionally worth reading out to the class but my favourite subject was geography. I felt blessed with a geography teacher – Alec Jones, the deputy head, whose daughter, Barbara, was in my form – who loved his subject and had the knack, at least with me, of putting it over with a sense of humour. I won the school geography prize – 'The world's peoples and how they live' – on the strength of my distinction in that subject in the school certificate examinations. I also gained a distinction in French and credits in the other seven subjects.

But what was I going to do? There is only one thing I have ever wished to be in life: a farmer, like my brother. That avenue was closed to me by my asthma. I knew it was one thing to have spent my holidays during the war on a mixed sheep and cattle farm overlooking Hardcastle Crags in the Hebden Valley carefully nursing my allergies. It was entirely another matter to farm for a living. The owner of the farm to which my brother and I walked a couple of miles each day was Joe Davey, a distant relative by marriage and in such constant pain from a damaged nerve in a First World War leg wound that his trousers had to be reinforced on the thigh which he constantly rubbed. He walked the Gorple Moors with a leg iron, tending his sheep, and seemed to enjoy the company of my brother and me as well as his Border collies. Sometimes he cried out in pain as a spasm caught him. We stood silently and respectfully until the pain subsided. We were taught to slip out of the room when after a meal Joe managed to nod off. He needed all the sleep he could get in his ravaged life.

My imagination had been captured by journalism both by the wartime exploits of, notably, BBC correspondents and by national reporters such as Tom Park, of the *Daily Herald*, who came to cover the by-election in Sowerby following Mr J. W. Belcher's downfall as a result of the Lynskey Tribunal. Walter Marsland, the chief reporter of the *Hebden Bridge Times*, and the legendary Dent Sutcliffe who covered Calder Valley for the *Halifax Evening Courier*, were also held in respect at home. I was an avid reader of newspapers – only too avid for some customers – as one of Mrs Jones's newspaper boys. I was often asked by amused householders up the Keighley Road to 'leave some print on it for me' as I became engrossed in the day's news outside their door. Journalism certainly had its attractions. But where were the openings?

It was eventually decided that I should stay on at HBGS with the aim of becoming a geography teacher. However, just as I began to wrestle unconvincingly with calculus, the *Hebden Bridge Times* advertised a vacancy for a junior reporter. In his first year as a member of the local council my father had got to know Walter Marsland fairly well and put in a good word for me. Walter, as I came to know him, agreed that I sounded promising. So, for the first and last time (I hope) in my life, I wrote a letter applying for a job and, to my parents' delight – for this was more than they had ever dared hope for me – I was accepted. I would be paid thirty shillings a week, use my own bicycle, learn shorthand and typing at night school, and Kershaw and Ashworth, the proprietors of the mixed newspaper and jobbing printers business, would see how I 'framed', as they describe shaping up in Hebden Bridge. I reported for duty at the *Hebden Bridge Times* office in Market Street at 9 a.m. on Monday, 18 October 1948. My course in life was set.

T' Brig Times, as the weekly was universally known, occupied a distinguished building. It was the old Ebenezer Baptist Church, one of the first of its kind in the district. It is now an antique shop. We looked out from the reporters' room on to a graveyard fronting on to the main Yorkshire-Lancashire artery. The building backed into the hillside and the residents of Garnet Street at the rear looked down into the first floor printing works. A year before I began work Hebden Bridge had been severely flooded and the receding waters had left a tide-mark about four feet up the wall of the office. The mark could still be seen when I left four years later. Nor did we entirely rid ourselves of the musty smell from the residue of the mud which had penetrated air grates in the wooden floor.

The floods, incidentally, enabled Derek and me to make an invaluable contribution to the rich musical life of Hebden Bridge. The flood waters had wrecked the electric motor which pumped the organ at Hope Baptist Church. The brothers Ingham were selected to provide the necessary air manually. We occupied a small loft to the right of the organist and choirmaster, James Stansfield, and immediately behind the choir. We raised the wind by means of pumping a huge pair of bellows. A large washer at the end of a piece of 'band' was used to indicate whether we had enough air in them. On no account must the washer rise above a chalk mark while the organ was in use. Nor must we raise even the tiniest amount of puff during a sermon; otherwise the organist, in a moment of forgetfulness, might lean on his keys and shake the preacher rigid with an unexpected blast of trumpets. It happened once; the temptation was too great. It was a 'tying' – that is, it tied you down to a routine every Sunday – but undemanding job except for the annual performance of the 'Messiah' and, as we discovered, at the conclusion of a marriage service. We were reinforced for Handel's oratorio. It was exceptionally warm work, crowded in the tiny loft with Kenneth Butterworth, the well-upholstered opening batsman for Mytholmroyd, during the 'Hallelujah' chorus. The brothers only just made it when Mr Stansfield launched a happy couple into matrimony *fortissimo*. Our services were much appreciated and a wedding was worth five shillings each. Regular Sunday work was voluntary.

My first day at the *Times* office introduced me to the telephone and the typewriter. I had used neither before and was as terrified of the single telephone, which sat menacingly on the window-sill, as I was enthralled by the typewriter. I broke out into a sweaty panic answering Hebden Bridge 106 in my first few days. I endured a week of such ragging – 'Hey up, 'ere cums Garnet's lad, t' Brig Times new ace reporter' – as I was introduced to the routine and contacts by Eric Richmond, Walter Marsland's only reporter until I arrived. It ended with my laboriously writing up a Friday cricket evening at Birchcliffe Baptists on the typewriter on the living-room table. Walter sent me home at the end of the week with the portable machine to familiarize myself with the keyboard 'and practise'.

Three other matters were settled quickly. I agreed with Walter, after anticipating the point in discussion with my father, that I had better drop my party political activities because I had now to report all sides fairly and must avoid any impression of partiality. My father might be a Labour councillor but I had to play it straight and be seen to do so. It was not the last time that I made this choice. Second, I must enrol immediately at Todmorden Technical College, four miles up the valley, for the evening classes in shorthand and typing. I found, rather as expected, that I was the only lad on the course. This was not a comfortable situation in such a masculine environment, but the girls – at least – were not too difficult. I made rapid progress with my shorthand and received a certificate for it from Professor Sir John Cockcroft, the Todmorden-born atomic physicist, and soon developed a rattling speed at the typewriter. I prided myself on my neat and fast shorthand, though my ability to get it all down was often a handicap: I had too much to wade through. My shorthand remains entirely serviceable and I automatically use it for making notes. I have to reprogramme myself to write in longhand.

Typewriting class was more of a trial. The girls in the class were being prepared for commercial office work and touch-typing to perfection was required. I needed speed rather than quality and I felt more than a little impatient when so much stress was laid on centring and display. I also had to restrain myself with the texts of

25

the letters we were asked to take down in shorthand and type out: they were not written in plain English. Typing the equivalent of a column or two every day soon made me a typist for life. Third, Walter saw no reason why I should not continue to play football and cricket on Saturdays, subject to emergencies. I could at least report at first hand those matches in which I played – on the understanding, he added with a smile, that I wasn't always the star performer.

I doubt that any boy could have made a happier start to his working life. Walter and Jack Holroyd, a printer who soon followed Eric Richmond as Walter's deputy on his conversion full-time to journalism, gave me every encouragement and guidance. There was more praise than admonition, though there was one serious fall from grace. I made the cardinal mistake of revealing my source for a story, even though it was of little significance. Walter moved quickly to repair the damage. He hoped that the person I had told would not abuse the information he had gleaned from me in an unguarded moment. I was left in no doubt that there were to be no more unguarded moments of this kind. Journalists protected their sources; they did not reveal them. It was a lesson I never forgot. Walter sub-edited all the copy and, seated within a few feet of him in the small reporters' room, I quickly picked up the finer details of presentation and style which I had already absorbed as a long-standing – or as longstanding as one can be at sixteen – reader of this fine, authoritative newspaper. Like all local newspapers then, the *Hebden Bridge Times* had to be accurate and balanced or the editor and reporters got it in the neck, face to face and eyeball to eyeball, in Market Street or wherever. A reporter was never safe in his own community, least of all at the wicket. I felt that a certain veteran bowler whom I had admiringly called 'evergreen' – and who had let me know he didn't like such a liberty – put that little bit extra into his demeanour and deliveries when we met on the field.

Never have I made a better start in a new job than my first. Walter and Jack nursed me – and sometimes had to send me home when my enthusiasm outstripped my usefulness on, for example, that Wednesday in the month when Hebden Royd Council met. This was exhaustively reported and had to be written up that evening because Walter had to cover Todmorden Magistrates' Court on Thursday mornings and we went to press effectively at Thursday lunchtime. I often wondered what would happen if there were a murder or disaster on Thursday morning. Fortunately, the good Lord never put us seriously to the test. But Walter and Jack would have coped and Dent Sutcliffe would have helped, competitor though he was, out of the great goodness of his heart.

As more of my copy passed Walter's scrutiny I gained confidence and graduated from 'paragraphing' – recording, for example, the results of whist drives and charity functions and mothers' union and friendly hour meetings, if we could not find a real story in them – to parish councils, road safety committees and education executives. My parents were reassured – and delighted – to learn from Walter that 'I'd make', which is praise indeed in Hebden Bridge. But he had said it with a warmth that made them feel that, barring accidents, I was on my way in life. And what is more, I was a credit to them. Derek, as Culpan's assistant stockman, above the Colden (or Ragley) valley, was learning his trade, too, though less congenially, for he left home before 6 a.m. – a good three hours ahead of me. Christmas 1948 was a milestone in the family: the two sons were solidly embarked upon their chosen careers.

One man is curiously missing from this account of my early months in journalism: my first editor, Will Ashworth, the last remaining link with the Kershaw and Ashworth era. By the time I arrived at the *Hebden Bridge Times* the company was in transition from Kershaw and Ashworth to ownership by the Lord family, of Mytholmroyd. Will, a grey-haired, shuffling, kindly figure, remained editor until illness forced him to retire, though that did not come easily. It was my job to take proofs up to his house at Sandy Gate where he was confined. This took me up through Nutclough and a steep wood to the supposedly haunted Kittling Bridge close by Will's stone terrace house. Before he fell ill, Will sub-edited copy on Thursday mornings, when Walter was covering the magistrates' court, with a more serious prejudice against my adjectival flourishes than my chief reporter. He could be an absolute butcher, though he sometimes needed to be if we were to get anything of the late 'news' in. This was because more often than not we were 'overset', taking account of the flow of advertisements, when work began late on Wednesday to lay out the pages in formes – the metal frames within which the columns of type were locked up tightly. Anything that could wait a week was put on one side to allow the more 'perishable' material to appear. How we hated leaving anything out. Our mission in life was to inform.

Another of my jobs, usually on Thursday morning if I were not otherwise engaged in writing stories, was to 'hold copy' for my editor. This meant I read out the copy and Will corrected the proofs, having already set much of the type on one of the two linotype machines which produced the *Hebden Bridge Times*. Will was the compleat newspaperman and, though by then failing a little, used to set his reports, including council meetings, straight on to the machine. He was the most economical member of the staff. Sometimes, while he had a break for a pint of tea, he let me try my hand at setting type. The unions in Halifax would have had a collective fit had they known what was happening in this remote outpost of their empire.

A crucial part of the development of any junior reporter is how he handles specific responsibilities. I acquired one immediately: my very own district. Each Monday afternoon, whatever the weather, I cycled a good ten miles there and back to Luddenden foot and up to the village of Luddenden where Branwell Brontë caroused in the *Lord Nelson* on his way to Haworth after completing his duties as station-master. Then on further to Booth at the mouth of the loveliest and least spoiled valley in the district, Luddenden Dean. The Vicar of Luddenden, the Rev. J. A. Kings, was invariably keen to have a short debate about current affairs. The Midgley family at Booth, where I called in the summer to take down the Booth cricket club's scorecard for the previous Saturday, were enveloped in sheets. Monday was washing day. It was a good day for collecting news because people were at home. Like all journalists, I retain a particular affection for my first district and I returned to it regularly over the years, not only because my wife's sister lived there in a farm cottage at Riding Head. It was a special place in Thora Hird's heart, too. She made the television series, 'In Loving Memory', in Luddenden village and at a reception in Number 10 Downing Street in 1989 she spoke affectionately of the people I served forty years earlier.

Nothing much happened in Hebden Bridge. Locals nudged each other in surprise and pleasure whenever it was mentioned on the wireless, usually on account of the weather. For the local reporter it was none the less an endless round of calls, councils, courts and cleaning. My early routine was built around a discipline which began with a copy of the latest edition on my desk on Friday morning. I critically admired our handiwork by way of cutting up the paper for filing purposes. Then I went to collect the publicity material from the Picture House for the programme of films for the week after next which, among other things, helped me decide what to do on Saturday nights. Having put a gloss on Hollywood in the Picture House 'puff' paragraph, I set about 'Past Events', a feature about a column (1000 words) in length retailing the highlights of sixty, fifty, forty and twenty-five years ago, as recorded in past editions. This was one of the most popular features in the paper, and Grandad Horsfall, who had done so much to prepare me for a career as a Calder Valley chronicler, gave me a piece of his mind when, exceptionally, 'Past Events' had to be excluded because of pressure of space. Then I had to clean the office. This routine began with damping the bare floorboards to keep down the flood dust. It ended on four occasions with my wrecking chairs by landing too heavily on them as I stepped down from dusting the top of the high cupboard. I had a fearsome reputation as a chair-smasher, though it did not take much to demolish chairs in the reporters' room, for they were usually well past their sit-by date. There was nothing fancy about the *Hebden Bridge Times*.

Saturday mornings were usually spent on the press bench of the West Riding Court in Halifax where I prepared myself mentally for Thistlebottom's (or MCC's) next match. This court assignment considerably widened my circle of acquaintances among journalists. The *Halifax Courier* religiously covered it and reporters from the *Yorkshire Evening Post*, *Yorkshire Evening News* and *Bradford Telegraph and Argus*, who maintained offices in Halifax, looked in to see if there was anything interesting on the charge sheet. My reports of the court cases, and the Saturday afternoon matches in which I played, were typed up on Sundays after walks with my family or friends. These excursions usually yielded another story or two or ideas to be followed up. A local reporter is never off duty.

Monday took me to the Luddenden Valley and often to a meeting of Wadsworth, Heptonstall, Blackshaw or Erringden parish councils which came to be my charge, once I had found my feet. Soon after joining the *Hebden Bridge Times* the family moved a mile or so down the valley into a brand new pre-fab on the Banksfield estate at Mytholmroyd next to Fred and Joan Helliwell, newly weds who have now registered their home as a bed-and-breakfast establishment to help cope with Hebden Bridge's understandable tourist boom. The walk after tea from Mytholmroyd up Wadsworth Banks to Mount Skip and through Old Town to the school at Pecket Well where Wadsworth parish council met was idyllic in summer. Fancy being paid for this, I used to think. Parish councils tended to be informal affairs and the members were not above canvassing the views of Dent Sutcliffe, my only companion on the press bench. On one occasion Councillor McWhirter, the chairman, seeing Dent vigorously shaking his head in an argument over the precise cause of flooding, invited him to the blackboard to set out his theory. This he did by rubbing out Councillor Coneron's drawing, much to Mr Coneron's discomfiture.

Tuesday and Wednesday were the least predictable days. News gathering and writing up gathered pace and the junior had to be particularly adaptable, turning his mind from writing to proof-reading and running errands as Walter on Wednesdays and Jack on Thursdays concentrated on layout and stone subbing – that is, cutting the stories in type to fit the available space. If I could, I made an early start on 'Past Events' on Thursday before I went off to night school. I was as happy as a sandboy, as my father rather obscurely put it. I had found my niche in life.

I had no ambition, therefore, to move onwards and upwards towards Fleet Street, which is supposed to be the goal of all cub reporters. I was a fully integrated member of the local community and was entirely fulfilled helping to inform that community of what was going on within it. What was good enough for Walter Marsland and Dent Sutcliffe, who had spent their working lives in Calder Valley chronicling events, was good enough for me. Journalism – responsible, accurate, fair and unmalicious – seemed an honourable calling. It was my life and I never tired of its demands around which I wove a social life.

It was Jack Holroyd who first got itchy feet. We had an excellent working relationship and vied with each other to extract from the most inconsequential item which would normally rate only a few lines under the endless columns of district news a news story which might reasonably make the front page. Jack, as a printer by trade, also seized his chance to liven up the front page typographically when Walter went on annual holiday. In the normal course of events all the headings were set on linotype. This gave the *Hebden Bridge Times* a predictable look: only the words and pictures changed, except when Jack got to work at the type-cases upstairs on the printing floor. The results of his imagination were far from sensational – he did not have much to work with – but he always seemed a little nervous of what Walter would think of his unortho-doxy on his return from holiday.

Jack was also nine years older than me, though still single and living at home at Hawksclough, roughly half way between Hebden Bridge and my home in Mytholmroyd. We often used to walk home together down the turnpike when we had both been writing up a late story. In December 1951 he decided to take a reporter's job with the *Burnley Express*, some twelve miles over the Pennine water-shed, as his first step on a career which carried him to the *Coventry Evening Telegraph*, back with me in Halifax with the *Yorkshire Post*, to the Newcastle *Evening Chronicle*, to the South Shields *Gazette*, to the *Guardian* and then into industrial journalism with ICI in Harrogate.

His departure gave me more responsibility and at the age of nineteen I was to all intents and purposes doing a senior reporter's job for a junior's money. I felt little resentment. I was still learning my trade and I was, after all, getting the union rate. But no sooner had Jack left than the impending retirement of Dent Sutcliffe raised questions in everyone's mind as to how long Walter, for so long the heart and soul of the *Hebden Bridge Times*, would remain. He confided that he had had an approach from the *Halifax Courier*, an evening paper, and was thinking about it, though not, I judged, with much enthusiasm. Dent Sutcliffe was a hard act to follow and Walter, in early middle age, was nursing an ulcer which was eventually to kill him. On the other hand, with the retirement of Will Ashworth and the Lord family in command, commercial printing claimed prior attention. It was a weekly battle to produce a reasonable-looking newspaper. Kenneth Lord, son of the proprietor, Wilfred Lord, had a reputation for just chucking the type into the formes into which the pages were locked ready for printing. The quality of the newspaper and its appearance seemed to count for little. Commercially, this hard-headed approach could even be justified: everyone read t' Brig Times. It was compulsory reading. Why bother too much with its aesthetics? Its virtual monopoly was a source of tension between its reporters and editor/proprietor. It was this, I believe, rather than any positive desire to join the *Halifax Courier*, that caused Walter to hand in his notice early in 1952. His increase in salary would not have been huge – the *Halifax Courier* had no better reputation for 'paying' than the *Hebden Bridge Times* – and he was acquring a much larger area to cover with greater urgency yet with no greater mobility than that afforded by the *Hebden Bridge Times*: telephone, bus, train and, most of all, legs.

On the day after Walter left I called in the reporters' room with a girl friend from the grammar school – Eileen Kemp – to collect some papers. In Walter's old roll-top desk which I had now acquired Eileen found a note from Walter which said: 'It's all yours now.' And so it was. Neither Jack Holroyd nor Walter Marsland had been replaced. No one else was left to write the newspaper, except me. At the age of nineteen I succeeded Walter as editor in all bar name. My only other editorial colleague was Harold Marshall, a thirty-eight year-old compositor from Waddington's, the publishers of the *Todmorden News and Advertiser* who also printed the *Hebden Bridge Times*. He had been recruited on the strength of his desire to try his hand at journalism after covering Todmorden's cricket matches in the Lancashire League for Lancashire evening papers. The first week was uncomfortable. A mere lad was in the top job urgently knocking into shape the copy of a chap twice his age. Harold was unhappy and so was I. But I was determined that we were going to produce a good newspaper and I made it clear nothing was going to be allowed to get in the way of that. He accepted this with good grace when he saw the point of what I was doing to his copy. He put the paper before his pride and we made a good team. While no writer, he was a pleasant chap, a natural gossiper and socializer and a workmanlike news-gatherer. He could also turn his hand instantly to the linotype when setting was falling behind. He was just the man for a little local weekly in the early 1950s.

The Lords were on to a winner with me in one sense. I was exempt from National Service. I went to Bradford for my medical in August 1950 and fully expected to be in the RAF before Christmas. The doctor evidently felt I was fit enough, if a little obese – obese, indeed! – for I was passed on to the officer who was interviewing those, like myself, who had expressed an interest in flying. My ambition, if I had to do National Service, was to be a navigator. The ambition did not survive the officer's first serious question. 'Do you suffer from any permanent disability?' he asked. 'Well, not really,' I replied. 'I suffer from asthma which is set off by various things I'm allergic to. But it's a lot better than it was, and I'm OK.' I was far from OK in his eyes, I could see. 'I'm afraid,' he said, 'I shall have to refer to your own doctor for a report.' I can only imagine what Dr A. H. Clegg wrote. Very soon afterwards I received a green card through the post notifying me that I was Grade 4 and not required by His Majesty. I was a bit shaken to be considered of no use to the RAF. The *Hebden Bridge Times*, however, needed me.

The *Hebden Bridge Times* became my life just as farming was my brother's. It was effectively seven days a week for both of us. It virtually ended my active participation in sport. I threw myself into writing at least fifteen columns a week – a good 15,000 words – taking on all the most important jobs, including the thorough coverage of the affairs and meetings of two urban councils – Hebden Royd and Sowerby Bridge – and Hepton rural council; sub-editing the whole of the editorial matter and writing the headlines; writing the leader column which required me to pontificate with all the wisdom of my nineteen years on matters of concern to the good people of Calder Valley; supplying the theatrical criticism which the Hebden Bridge Little Theatre and other groups read so closely; identifying the lead story and front-page material; providing rudimentary layout sketches for the front and, if possible, other pages to try to overcome the tendency to cobble the paper together; and not least bringing order to the coverage of sport by personally laying out the page, putting the type in the forme and locking it up. The printers – Jack Winter or Clifford Oldfield – made sure it was properly locked up, shaking their heads all the time over 'what the union would think if it only knew what went on here'. The formes had to be locked up to perfection because they were put to exceptional tests. They had to be carried down the narrow stone stairs, out through the front door of the *Times* office, across the pavement and placed on the floor of a taxi which then took them four miles up to Todmorden. There the perilous carrying of the formes had to be repeated before they were safely installed in the press. One defective forme, one slip down the uneven stairs or on the pavement or one car accident and the *Hebden Bridge Times* would have been short of a page or two that week. The gods were unfailingly kind.

In retrospect, these were my halcyon days in journalism. Never again was I to derive the same enjoyment and sense of achievement in newspapers. I had less difficulty than I expected from Kenneth Lord in putting the paper to bed. Whether this was because I had a certain sanction – I was the only (still semi-) trained journalist on the staff – was never clear. Perhaps he just respected my dedication to producing as good – and as good-looking – a newspaper as was in me. On the whole, I had an amicable relationship with the readers, notwithstanding the tensions which could be generated in a small community by the reporting of court cases and other unpleasantries, one's editorial opinions and even the tiniest slip over initials in a district heavily populated with Greenwoods, Sutcliffes, Cockcrofts or Cockrofts, Helliwells or Hellowells, Crowthers or Pickles. Life was pretty tense on Thursdays, publishing day. It was rather like living on the edge of an active volcano not because I did not want a good last-minute story but because I had no idea how we would cope properly with it and get the newspaper to press. I had my trials with a number of junior reporters whom Wilfred Lord engaged because I am close to being the world's worst and most impatient teacher. But, in a district which respected experience and was always a little wary of callow youth, I was to many the personification of the *Hebden Bridge Times* and was accepted as such. Walter and his wife, Vera, told me they thought I was doing a pretty good job.

He evidently told others, too, for I was invited by the *Halifax Courier* for an interview. Like Walter, I approached this without enthusiasm. The Crapnell side of the management, father and son, conducted it very informally and probably reached the conclusion that I was not the most eager recruit to evening newspaper journalism. They found their excuse when I disclosed that Eileen was a nurse at Queen Elizabeth Hospital, Edgbaston. 'Ah, well,' they said, 'you'll be off to Birmingham before we know where we are.' They thought it unlikely that I would make my career with the *Courier*. So, that was that. It seemed a curious decision at the time. It became more curious when, later, I realized the extent to which the *Courier* reporters' room was an improvers' transit camp. I went back to Hebden Bridge rather relieved, and said nothing to the Lord family.

The episode had, however, made me wonder whether I should be moving on. I had no wish to leave home and I was under no compulsion to do so. I enjoyed my job and I seemed cut out for small-town journalism. On the evidence of my limited contacts with some national newspapermen, I doubted whether I was quite so suited to a life sustained more by imaginative presentation than close attention to the facts. Then, when I had just gone twenty, Tom Dickinson, chief reporter in the two-man Halifax district office of the *Yorkshire Evening Post* and the *Yorkshire Post*, let me know that he was looking for a replacement for his son, George, who was leaving to edit *Sea Breezes*, a journal for mariners. Tom had a substantial – and entirely merited – reputation as an all-round reporter and a congenial companion who, after finding that the *Halifax Courier* did not appreciate his talents as he thought it should, made covering the Halifax district for the *YEP* and *YP* a way of life. He arranged for me to see Frank Snape, news editor, and WLA, subsequently Sir Linton Andrews, the editor of the *Yorkshire Post*, in their Albion Street offices in the city centre. I went in my best suit, carrying a raincoat on a hot July day, and was overawed. I was offered £7.10s. a week – ten shillings more than I was earning at the *Hebden Bridge Times*. But the prospects were of a different order.

My parents had deep reservations about my giving up all – and more than – they had hoped for me for the dubious attractions of the *Yorkshire Post*. It was not that they regretted that I was joining the Yorkshire Conservative Newspaper Company. The political complexion of its newspapers did not come into the argument. Nor did they fail to acknowledge the compliment to their son that a newspaper of the *Yorkshire Post*'s reputation was interested in acquiring his services. But they were small-town people in a relatively immobile world in which a trip to Halifax by bus still represented a day out. I had reached the conclusion that the *Hebden Bridge Times* had little more to teach me and that if I were going to make a break it needed to be made soon. So, with some trepidation, I tendered my notice to Wilfred Lord. He looked shaken. Who was going to produce the paper if I went? I thought the answer was clear: Harold Marshall, with the help of juniors. Mr Lord then said that he had recognized that they might not be able to keep me and had been thinking of offering me the post of news editor. Would that and a bit more money help? I saw the title of 'news editor' as meaningless. I had already been editor in all but name for six months or so and it was clear that I was never going to be offered the editorship. In these circumstances a little bit more money – whatever that might amount to in *Times*'s terms, where weekly expenses of half a crown were a good average and five shillings an extravagance – was no reason to give up this opportunity. It might have been better had I said all this instead of just thinking it. I simply replied that my mind was made up and I just wanted him to accept my notice. Mr Lord then made me feel miserable. He said that he would regard it as disloyalty if I were to persist in wanting to leave and that I should go home for the weekend and think it over. I meekly – and foolishly – agreed to do so.

Thinking about what I should do occupied little of the weekend. My father's opposition to my leaving evaporated at Wilfred Lord's suggestion of disloyalty. There could be no question of my staying on in view of that, my father said with jutted jaw. I must go and hand in my notice first thing on Monday morning and have done with it. I did just that. A month later I put my best years in journalism behind me.

4

'Black Halifax boiled in phosphorus'

In 1952 Halifax was where people from Hebden Bridge went to hospital, to watch professional soccer or rugby league, for a day out or for a little sophistication. You had to go to Leeds for real sophistication and may still have to do so, according to the *Financial Times*. It recorded in August 1987 that when a member of its staff asked a Hebden Bridge waitress for cappuccino coffee with his breakfast she responded: 'Nay lad. You'd have to go to Leeds for that.'

Halifax was also busy working at 101, or 1001, trades, depending on the informant's enthusiasm about its varied industrial base. Up the hill from the Hebble stream at the foot of Beacon Hill climbed a forest of mill and factory chimneys. The traveller from Leeds, bursting out of Godley Cutting, had spread before him one of the classic, fuming, industrial sights of Britain. And he would invariably have the muck blown in his eyes by the prevailing south-westerly wind. Trees and vegetation on Beacon Hill fought a losing battle for life under the stream of noxious gases. No wonder Ted Hughes, now the poet laureate, who lived in Mytholmroyd when I was a lad, wrote of 'Black Halifax boiled in phosphorus'.

The *Yorkshire Post* office in Horton Street in the lower part of the town none the less represented a considerable improvement in my working conditions. We occupied the first two floors of a stone-built shops and office block. On the ground floor Harry Hill, the office manager, and Bill Riley, his assistant who had the use of a heavy delivery bike with a basket frame front, ran the advertisement and accounts office and handled the distribution of several editions of the *Yorkshire Evening Post* which were driven over from Leeds about eighteen miles away. We had our very own newspaper seller, Arthur, a cherubic, solidly built and slightly defective chap with the sweetest nature, a sales bellow which passed all understanding and a passion bordering on fanaticism for Halifax Rugby League Club which he was seldom able to watch. A machine in the centre of the workroom, screened off from the counter, ran off the stop press racing and football results telephoned to all district offices in the company from its Leeds headquarters. We also had our gambling fraternity hanging around the front door for the results.

Tom Dickinson and I had to make our way through the betting men and the workroom and up the stairs to our office which was screened off from the landing. It was light and airy with a brown linoleum floor, a couple of desks facing each other and tables on either side of the door holding our yellowing newspaper files. We each had a telephone, though there was only one line, so we had to wait for the other to finish or for the office staff down below to switch it through. There was also a dedicated line to Leeds which we had to crank to raise the central switchboard to dictate our copy. Each office was decorated in similar house style – cream above four feet of dark blue wall. The premises were mopped and dusted every day. I had never known such luxury.

Moreover, the office was within half a mile of every journalistic essential: police HQ, courts, town hall, Palace Theatre, cinemas, cafes, fish and chip shops, bus termini and umpteen pubs. On either side of the office we had a delicatessen run by a Polish refugee and a women's hair stylist, and a ballroom dancing school above. The *Yorkshire Post*'s sub-editors did not appreciate that most of our copy telephoned in the evening was inspired by Victor Sylvester. Or perhaps they did? I arrived in this relatively cosmopolitan environment in August 1952 in time to cover the Halifax connection with the Lynmouth holiday flood disaster. There was, Tom Dickinson swore, always a Halifax connection.

I swapped one Hebden Bridge routine for a much more demanding Halifax one. We wrote for the *Evening Post* all morning and afternoon until about four o'clock. Then we rewrote for the *Yorkshire Post* before tackling the late afternoon and evening jobs exclusively for the *Yorkshire Post*. Our overnight stories in the *Yorkshire Post* would then be recycled in the first, racing calendar, edition of the *Yorkshire Evening Post*. Styles were similar except that the evening paper made collective nouns singular; the morning paper insisted on the plural. Such niceties were conveniently overlooked early in the day when the first edition of the evening paper was being flung together.

We rang police (borough and West Riding forces), fire and ambulance every couple of hours between 9 a.m. and midnight, and scoured the *Halifax Courier* and our three other competitors – the *Yorkshire Evening News* and the *Bradford Telegraph and Argus* and its sister morning newspaper, the *Yorkshire Observer* – for ideas, diary dates and stories we had missed. We kept close to the town hall and council committees and our eyes and ears wide open. Nothing of importance happened, we hoped, without our recording it. The more stories in the back-page Halifax slip edition of the *Yorkshire Post* by-lined 'From our Halifax staff' the better. There was nothing Tom liked more than to beat the *Courier* which had declined to give him executive responsibility when it had the chance. Tom was self-sufficient – everyone knew him – joined no cliques and earned a bit on the side as the Halifax correspondent of the Press Association, the national news agency. I deputized for him as their representative when he took his day and alternate week-end off and he apportioned the spoils every month.

Every day was similar yet different. The regimen was monotonously the same. The stories which arose from it more or less interesting, entertaining, exciting, shocking, depressing or pathetic. 'All human life is there', as the old *News of the World* hoarding advertisement put it. It began with a bus ride into Halifax and a tour of the charge desks at the separate borough and West Riding police force headquarters about a quarter of a mile apart. At the borough force I had a chat each morning with the enormously helpful Superintendent Bill Griffiths, who became deputy chief constable, or, if he were away, his chief inspector. The more senior the officer the more confidence, generally speaking, they had to give us information, though I had some valued and reliable friends among the charge office sergeants. The friendlier the face the more confident the start to the day. If we had not telephoned the fire and ambulance stations before leaving home our first job in the office was to check on the overnight damage. Sometimes we ran into stories as, for example, when the bus carrying me down Gibbet Street to the office met the fire engines coming the other way

39

amid clouds of swirling smoke. Kumficars, manufacturers of car furnishings, were going up in flames. I dropped off the bus and quickly established the basic facts – 150 girl sewers worked at Livingstone Mills, which were well alight. I then made a quick call to Leeds to give them a flash story for the first edition and asked the picture desk to send over a photographer sharpish. By mid morning all the girls were accounted for, the factory was a wreck and the *Yorkshire Evening Post* had a big eyewitness spread with a dramatic picture. We were an edition ahead of the rest.

There were more newsworthy events in Halifax than in Hebden Bridge but not every day. Usually, by 10 a.m. Tom and I had telephoned Leeds with all our early stories and determined who would cover which event on the diary, compiled religiously by the two of us by constant application to future events during each working day and night. This left us free for the first social ritual of the day: a coffee in the Corner House Cafe with our competitors – Bryan Harwood, the *Halifax Courier*'s crime and courts man; Dennis Garvey, the *Yorkshire Evening News*; Jack Nott and David Illingworth, of the *Bradford Telegraph and Argus*; and later Alan Cooper or Stan Solomons, of the West Riding News Service, a news agency which started up soon after I arrived in Halifax. Here we checked up on each other and ran a comradely exchange and mart in running stories – and kept mum about anything we were nursing for ourselves. The Corner House served coffee and a ciga-rette for sixpence. After holding out for about twelve months, never having had more than a quick schoolboy drag before, I succumbed to cigarettes and became a slave to the weed for years. At 10.20 we all trooped off to the borough court, inquests and more of the reporter's daily diet of life's tragedies. 'Hey up', one copper on court duty used to say as there approached Alan Cooper, short and slim with a full shock of red hair and red beard, and Ingham, ginger and big and getting bigger, ''ere cums t' expanded and t' stunted Vikings'. If there were not a lunchtime engagement I had a snack; Tom often went home. In the afternoon we spent a lot of time hanging around the town hall to pick up the decisions of council committees, always keeping in touch with the office, writing fea-tures and programming ourselves for the evening's range of events, meetings and theatres.

Professionally, Halifax was merely an extension of Hebden Bridge. It added layers to my direct experience of the working of Britain – county borough council, quarter sessions, civil (county and bankruptcy) courts and professional football. It increased my knowledge of man's depravity both through the courts, which I covered daily, and the occasional murder and mayhem which came my way. It introduced me to a kind of journalism, as practised by the late Jack Nott who proceeded from the *Telegraph and Argus* to the *News of the World*, which owed more to Raymond Chandler than West Riding reality; but it read well, I despaired. When national newspapermen flooded in to cover, for example, the murder of six-year-old Mary Hackett, of Cemetery Lodge, by the caretaker of a nearby church, it exposed me to such imaginative reporting that I felt incredibly inadequate, staid and old fashioned at twenty-one. It heavily underlined the different pressures operating on the local journalist and the alien marauder who is here today and gone tomorrow, leaving the local journalist to repair the damage to his community's confidence in him. 'You're all the same', the injured people cry, unjustifiably. It toughened and coarsened me, and bred a deeper scepticism in me about human nature. After the wholesomeness of Hebden Bridge, I was learning about the wilder world outside.

The wilder world included the news desks of the two papers we served. The news editors worked normal shifts; their district men seldom less than 150 per cent, with only one week-end off in two. Relationships were never close because we seldom met. We were part of a far flung empire at the end of a line and Ken Lemmon, *YEP*, expected us to perform for him regardless of what we had been doing for Bob Greenwood, *YP*. And vice versa. We were only as good as our last story, it seemed, and only as bad as our last miss. We were the source not only of staple news and, it was hoped, exclusives but also of diary paragraphs, features and ideas for photographs in which both papers took justifiable pride. It was a treadmill. It required, apart from professionalism, a certain philosophy, a determination to pace oneself – to take it relatively easy when the opportunity presented itself – and a fundamental self-confidence. I was well-equipped professionally – at least I could take a shorthand note and read it back for my colleagues – but I still lacked self-confidence. This was not improved when I got into trouble with a man who was alleged in the West Riding court to have set his dogs on to some sheep. The police superintendent said that he had 'fastened' the sheep in the corner of a field before allowing the dogs to attack them. I took this to mean that he had 'tethered' the sheep and, without checking, foolishly said so in my report. The defendant threatened to sue. When I checked with the police, the superintendent said that by 'fastened' he had meant that the defendant had cornered the sheep by his very presence. He agreed that he might have expressed himself better and was sorry that I was in trouble. Tom and Frank Snape, the news editor, thought I had been a shade unfortunate. But the *Yorkshire Post* had to publish a correction, the sight of which haunted me for months. I found it hard going.

It became a little easier both physically and mentally when my parents, with whom I continued to live in Mytholmroyd, about seven miles away, had a telephone installed at No 1 Birchenlee Close. I had never been on the telephone at home during my four years with the *Hebden Bridge Times*, not even when I was the editorial mainstay. If anything happened I just caught up next day, though the 'bush telegraph' is very effective in getting the message through quickly in small communities. The acquisition of a telephone gave me a new security. It meant that I had not to turn out every night when I was on duty, or fifteen nights on the trot when Tom was on holiday, to walk a quarter of a mile to the bottom of the housing estate, weighed down with coppers, to put in check calls to police, fire and ambulance. More important, it meant I could work freely without running out of ready cash if, by some mischance, a serious fire was burning or there had been a fatal crash. The pressure on late duty to catch the last (11 p.m.) bus from Halifax remained; the *Yorkshire Post* did not run to many taxis.

There were compensations. There had to be. They were personal and sporting. Four journalists brought friendship and enjoyment to life. Tom Dickinson was a wise, understanding, fair, encouraging and sociable colleague. He looked after me. So did Bryan Harwood, sometimes well beyond the limits imposed by the fierce competition between newspapers. The bald, stocky son of Henry William Harwood, the grand old man of Halifax journalism, he was a dab hand at electronics, a gossip and immensely kind. David Illingworth, who shared so many late duties with me for the *Yorkshire Observer* until it closed on my wedding day, 3 November 1956, made Bryan seem taciturn. He rattled away morning, noon and night cheerfully and inconsequentially and without a grain of malice. I dug his garden at his newly built house as a wedding present. It was, they said, just what he and Marian wanted. I also sensed that George Beddoe, who was to become editor of the *Halifax Courier*, took a close interest in me personally as well as in my output which over the years gave the *Halifax Courier* plenty to follow up. He was never short of an encouraging word. And encouraging words I needed in my early years in Halifax. I sometimes wondered whether I would be better back in Hebden Bridge. But not for long because, sooner or later, I got a good show in one or other of the two newspapers I served and that lifted the spirits.

Saturdays were a bonus. I was quickly put to work to cover Halifax Rugby League Club, to which my father introduced me at the age of seven. I wrote for the *Yorkshire Evening Post* under the pseudonym 'Royd', short for Mytholmroyd where I lived.

Halifax play at Thrum Hall, where the press box was then admirable in anything but cold, blustery weather. It was situated in the roof of the main stand. It faced the east from an altitude not far short of 1000 feet. And it was necessary to open the windows if you were to see anything, let alone command a view of the touchline and near corners. Nor was the floor sealed. It channelled draughts upwards and into reporters. It was designed by the Grim Reaper to harvest the vulnerable. I survived it through eight of Halifax's best seasons with the stoic assistance of Frank Crossland, a friend from my MCC (M for Mytholmroyd) days, who telephoned my 150– 200 word 'takes' of copy to Leeds and my half-time and full-time reports to the Press Association.

Before long I was travelling all over Yorkshire, Lancashire and Cumberland covering Halifax for both my newspapers and I went on to cover RL international and Test matches.

Tom Dickinson insisted that we always had a day off each week as well as alternate Sundays. He made the point immediately by giving me my second day with the company free so that, for his convenience, he could have his day off later in the week. Those days were sacrosanct. It required a sensation – for example, a murder – to break into them, and then they had to be made up. By careful management it was possible to have a social life. In practice this amounted to a long walk, occasionally turning out ponderously for Halifax Borough police's soccer team and as makeweight for their cricket team, the cinema or a dance. Beryl Pickles, a Mytholmroyd farmer's daughter who was with me at HBGS and who worked as a secretary in a Halifax's solicitor's office, endured longest of any girl friend the disciplines imposed successively by the *Hebden Bridge Times* and the *Yorkshire Post*. For a time I devoted myself long-distance to a Newcastle-upon-Tyne girl, Shirley Dixon, whom I met on a walking holiday in Borrowdale in the Lake District. But that, hardly surprisingly, did not last either since she was up in Kenton and I was slaving away in Halifax.

Meanwhile, I had my eye on WPC2 Nancy Hoyle, of Halifax Borough Police, whom I had met in the magistrates' court where she often served as usher. She was also frequently to be seen on patrol around the town, as the police presence at functions I was reporting or when she was giving evidence in court. She also manned the police HQ switchboard on Sunday nights when the civilian telephonists had time off. In 1955 I met her near the police station as she was setting out on plain-clothes inquiries and asked her if she would like to go to the pictures. I was promptly apprehended. We – Non-conformist and Roman Catholic – married about eighteen months later at St Columcille's Church, Pellon, near Nancy's home where she lived with her widowed mother. We had a week-end honeymoon in sunny Keswick. I had got the following week off to make the small stone-built semi we had bought for £1600 at 62 Gleanings Avenue, Norton Tower, more habitable. Nancy had to return to police duty. My colleagues wryly remarked that I had chosen a good time to marry with so much news from the Hungarian uprising crowding out space in the press and with the demise of the *Yorkshire Post*'s main regional morning competitor in the West Riding, the *Yorkshire Observer*. I was sad about the *Observer*. I thought it had a particularly good agricultural correspondent in Leonard Parkin whom I was much later to meet as an ITN news presenter.

The conventional wisdom was that I was settling down as Tom Dickinson's eventual successor in charge of the office. We very much liked our home on the heights of Norton Tower, looking down on Norland Moor from the back bedroom. I was a familiar and, judging from the way I was treated, respected member of my trade on the civic scene. I thoroughly enjoyed my sports reporting. And Nancy had no illusions about the endless nature of my job. Nor I of hers when, as she often seemed to be, she was working in the CID. We tried to arrange for our days off to coincide. In June 1957 we took a holiday in the Shetlands at the peat-burning hotel converted from the old wartime airport buildings at Sullom Voe. I never suspected that later I would return there with the Prime Minister to visit Britain's principal oil terminal. On our return on a Saturday, I was busy decorating the back bedroom when WPC1 Mary Ahearne telephoned Nancy to say that an elderly woman shopkeeper had been found murdered in Gibbet Street. Could she please report for duty? A reporter married to a policewoman has to be careful not to compromise his sources. I gave it half an hour than rang Tom and offered to turn out, too. The holiday was over. In spite of the immediate reinforcement of the local police – by the immaculately dressed Detective Superintendent Herbert Hannam ('the Count of Scotland Yard') and his amanuensis, Detective Sergeant Christopher Rowe – the killer of eighty-year-old Miss Emily Pye was never found.

I was inevitably privy to the progress of the inquiry but I never compromised Nancy. I also became familiar with the strains imposed on policewomen who acted as decoys to trap sexual attackers in People's Park and with the risks they ran in handling drunks in the rougher parts of town. Nancy decided to call it a day when, with her Sergeant, Shirley Briggs, she was called upon to arrest a couple of drunks who had been thrown out of a pub in Southgate. Wrestling with drunken men on the pavement while the Black Maria is on its way is not recommended for pregnant policewomen. She left the police force with her record marked 'Exemplary' in early October. John, our only child, was born six weeks prematurely in a snowy Halifax on 16 February 1958. They kept him in the Halifax General Hospital for a month. It was snowing again when he was allowed home. I had to carry him the last quarter of a mile because the taxi driver ran out of grip and could push his car no further through the ten-inch thick carpet which covered Paddock Lane.

The birth of a son no doubt encouraged the impression that I was settling down in Halifax. Our families – Nancy had two sisters living in the district – were both physically and emotionally close. Jack Holroyd had not stayed long as our third man and had not been replaced, but Tom and I had a good understanding. And I reckoned there was always the possibility of my being called to cover rugby league full time. But I was beginning to realize that I would soon have to decide whether to settle for being the *Yorkshire Post*'s district man or to try to better myself. The more I saw of other journalists – especially those who flowed through the *Halifax Courier* gathering experience – the more I wondered why I remained. Yet the more I saw of some types of national reporter, or the unprincipled nonsense which a *Courier* reporter, an offcomer cultivating his next job elsewhere, served up on a freelance basis for a Sunday newspaper, the more certain I was that I wanted no part of that.

I was not in any way nursing political ambition. I remained Labour by upbringing and inclination but the cause did not burn in my breast. I had no qualms about working for the Yorkshire Conservative Newspaper Company. Of course, you gave the Conservatives a good run but you were expected to be fair to all sides. Political comment was for the leader column where it should be. Moreover, for ten years from leaving shcool I had necessarily abstained from party politics, covering all the parties fairly and accurately. At any rate, I got no complaints about my reports from, for example, Halifax's MP, Maurice Macmillan, whom I was later to serve when he became Secretary of State for Employment, or his Labour opponent, Peter Shore, who became a distinguished and principled member of Labour governments for which I worked. I was forced to admit in the late 1950s that Harold Macmillan, Maurice's father, wasn't doing at all badly by the workers – high praise, indeed, from a line of Yorkshiremen for whom 'fair to middling' represents just about as far as they are prepared to go in acknowledging their current well-being. I could see merit in members of all the main parties, as represented on Halifax Borough Council, even if I had reservations about a political system which packed the council with trades and professions that could do – and some apparently did – rather well commercially out of its contracts. And while I had come to realize that management left much to be desired – intelligence did not seem to be a necessary qualification for making money, still less for running professional football clubs – I was convinced that things were likely to be immeasurably worse under the workers' soviet known as the Halifax Trades and Labour Council. It wanted to run everything and manifestly could run nothing. Its meetings were the sort David Illingworth and I felt we could safely leave to the ranters and droning bores.

So what was unsettling me? I suppose, if the truth be told, it was the conviction that I had more to offer both myself and my family than the unending and often, it seemed, unappreciated round of district office work. I had been at it probably two years too long – I should have left when I got married – when I made inquiries of the Reuters and Press Association news agencies whether they were in need of a likely lad who believed in reporting the facts. They were not interested – at least, not in me. Then, when I seemed to be getting nowhere in the autumn of 1958, the *Yorkshire Post* called me over to the head office temporarily to fill in a gap as a general, all-purpose reporter. This created a number of tensions. Tom was left to fend for himself. John Bapty occasionally came down the corridor to ask me to write the lead rugby league story for the *Yorkshire Evening Post* which I did, though Bob Greenwood, the *Yorkshire Post* news editor, grumbled about the distraction. And I needed to catch the last bus to Halifax at 10.45 p.m. After a month or so of relieving the head office in Leeds, and relieving Tom of some late duties when I got back to Halifax from Leeds, I decided to bring some order to my life. It had to be either Halifax or Leeds, I told Bob, and I would prefer Leeds. And Leeds it was from the beginning of 1959. We left our semi in Halifax with much sadness and many misgivings for a first-floor company flat in Clifford House, a converted stone-built mansion on the northern outskirts of Leeds at Shadwell. We had moved a mere twenty-five miles within the same company, but it was the decisive, necessary and fateful break. I was on my way.

5

Leeds: Gateway to the World

Leeds was a release from seven years' drudgery. If that seems a harsh judgement on Halifax where I had often enjoyed my journalism, it none the less represents the reality of district office life in the 1950s when local and regional newspapers were much more journals of record and competed much more fiercely on the basis of their news coverage. For example, I find the *Hebden Bridge Times* (which I have taken consistently since I left it in August 1952) seriously deficient in obituaries, and a chap needs obituaries at my time of life. There seems to be less interest in at least the detailed coverage of local institutions such as local authorities, chambers of commerce and trade and trades councils. Changes in the law governing court reporting have substantially reduced another staple diet of the 1950s. Radio and television have swung the emphasis in local newspapers from hard news reporting to features and magazine material, some of which show the cumulative benefit in style and expression of decades of further education. But, perhaps most importantly, competition has been rationalized out of the local press. Halifax has been the preserve of the *Courier* for a couple of decades as first the *Yorkshire Evening News* died and then the *Yorkshire Post*, its sister evening paper and the *Telegraph and Argus* closed their editorial operations there. With them have gone the drive to carry today, not tomorrow, all the news that's fit to print. The availability of new technology in the 1980s, thanks partly to Mrs Thatcher, consequently did not make for later deadlines. If anything, that lethal combination of monopoly and chartered accountants brought them forward for those of us serving the media in Whitehall and Westminster.

Provincial journalism remained sober-sided and conscientious in 1959. But for a former district man embarking on a head office career his translation to Leeds was less of a culture shock, more a taste of honey. No longer was I under the tyranny of calls to the police, fire and ambulance every other hour, with the certainty that if anything serious occurred I would have to cover it – and fit everything else in, too. I had room to breathe and usually time to concentrate on the job in hand. Moreover, there was company. Instead of working often on my own I was surrounded by journalists. My immediate circle of colleagues had increased at least tenfold. I drew strength and confidence from the pack. It was the certainty, after a few weeks' experience of Albion Street in the autumn of 1958, that I could swim in this pool that drove my still unconfident self to press for a permanent move.

Once installed early in the New Year, my output increased enormously, covering anything from the plans for redesigning Leeds City Square, still dominated, I am glad to say, by a statue of the Black Prince, to the threat to cannery jobs because of a shortage of sprats. I sometimes wrote the commentary on the night's television in the absence of Peter Jackson, the TV critic. Soon I was reviewing books for W. T. Oliver, the deputy editor, writing features (both advertising and news) and thoroughly enjoying myself. I was also keeping up my rugby league connection for both papers, nominally still covering Halifax but enjoying a much wider variety of matches.

Three other factors made my first year in Leeds memorable. The first was the printers' three-month dispute which brought fewer strains than I feared it might. It was clear from the outset that many of our printers wanted nothing to do with it. It was also obvious that most of the journalists, while predominantly but not exclusively members of the National Union of Journalists like myself, were not necessarily going to respond to an NUJ instruction to restrict ourselves to normal work and do nothing to hamper the printers. There was no love lost between journalists and printers, though I had a friendly relationship with several of them, including Alan Snowden, the Halifax RL wing-threequarter. Initially we felt far from comfortable about remaining at work, but our consciences were greatly eased when we learned that the printing unions were transporting their striking members over to Manchester to help produce Northern editions of national newspapers which newsagents, understandably, were delivering to traditional readers of the *Yorkshire Post*. We grew pretty indignant when the Leeds City Council banned the purchase by libraries, reading rooms, all educational establishments and the police of the rudimentary editions of the *Yorkshire Post* and the *Yorkshire Evening Post* being produced by management and journalists. Council staff were also told not to give any information to us blacklegs.

I cannot recall any unpleasantness in going about my work, including degree days at Leeds University and the enthronement of the new Bishop of Ripon, Dr John Moorman. Nor did I encounter much distress among printers about the slimline editions we were publishing. Instead some of them hoped we might in this way be preserving their jobs. It all ended with stains on our NUJ escutcheons as the NUJ executive's Bloody Assize toured the country to try, convict and pronounce sentence. We made a sullen dock.

It was also my great good fortune to go to Leeds in an election year and to have the opportunity to draw the threads of the campaigns in Yorkshire together. The Labour leader, Hugh Gaitskell, was a Leeds MP, and the campaign by the Prime Minister, Harold Macmillan, included a tour of Yorkshire which took him to Halifax in support of his son. I was also given my home Pennine territory to assess politically. Reading between the lines, because we tried to play it straight, I expected Maurice Macmillan and Marcus Worsley to win for the Conservatives in Halifax and Keighley and Douglas Houghton to get away in dour, unpretentious Sowerby with quoting Aristophanes in his election address. He did and Messrs Macmillan and Worsley joined him in the new House of Commons. None of us were surprised that the Conservatives won. We really had never had it so good, though that was not sufficient reason to many of us for voting Tory. Privilege, unearned and unmerited, still rankled. More than just Labour voters felt sorry for the decent Mr Gaitskell.

The third benefit of moving to Leeds was that I got out of it. And Leeds, without my being in any way disparaging, is a superb city to get out of quickly: into Calderdale, Airedale, Wharfedale and Nidderdale and on to the plain of York. What more could a city dweller ask for? I frequently got to parts of Yorkshire which were new to me and so widened my narrow horizons. On the *Hebden*

Bridge Times I had been confined to Calder Valley for four years, apart from the odd trip with the disabled to the Lancashire coast. The most memorable event in that time had been my first flight, from Yeadon Aerodrome (now the Leeds/Bradford airport), over Calder Valley with the Hebden Bridge Literary and Scientific Society. In the De Havilland Rapide with me was Dent Sutcliffe. Only rugby league and, once, soccer took me out of Halifax in seven years. It was holidays, not the job, which opened my eyes then to the wider Britain. Mine had been captivated by the Lake District and the Highlands of Scotland to which I went regularly for holidays. In my first year in Leeds I flew to Dublin to cover the unveiling in Connemara of a memorial to Alcock and Brown, who made the first non-stop trans-Atlantic flight, and on the inaugural holiday air link from Yeadon to Torquay. Neither of these trips broke new ground for I had been on holiday in Torquay and I had cycled round Ireland, and to Galway, in the unremitting sunshine of June, 1953. But both were symbolic of 1959: life was opening up.

We could not have lived at Clifford House in a better year. The summer of 1959 later gave some of us a healthy scepticism about the theory of global warming. Weeks of dry weather stretched into months and Nancy spent a lot of it in the sun with John and Nicholas Edwards, the son of a future editor of the *Yorkshire Post*, playing on the Leeds Corinthians' hockey pitch next to Clifford House, the basement of which provided the club's changing-rooms and showers. We were surrounded by fields, made close friends with Dobbin, the huge Shire horse which worked on the farm of the boys' reformatory next door, and were blessed with wildlife – owls, foxes, rabbits and hedgehogs in profusion. The evening views from our first-floor balcony up the Dales and across the Vale of York were superb. It would have been idyllic had the otherwise spacious flat run to two bedrooms and been sound-proofed. It was as unsatisfactory internally as its setting was irresistible. After six months we bought a house in Greenhill Mount, Bramley, on the west side of the city nearest home in Halifax and Calder Valley, and remained there for the rest of our time in Leeds.

Sir Linton Andrews, in his last year or so before retirement as editor of the *Yorkshire Post*, gave me my head, and in 1961 I took

51

over as the *Yorkshire Post*'s Northern industrial correspondent in succession to Bob Mozley, who was leaving to join *The Times* as its Northern correspondent. It was to be an eventful year because I also had to adapt to a new editor, Kenneth Young. Mr Young, a man with Wakefield connections, had come up from the *Daily Telegraph* with a literary pedigree to edit the *Yorkshire Post*. He invented the *Yorkshire Post* literary luncheons which we thought were a bit pretentious. He also shook up Albion Street not so much by the demands he made on our journalism as by his rumbustious life-style and rather imperious ways. Senior reporters tended to resent being asked to go shopping for the Young family. The management were aghast at his alleged consumption of alcohol, though I never saw anything untoward. In fact, I escaped personal experience of what I was assured was the worse side of Mr Young. He took a sympathetic and, I thought, intelligent interest in his industrial specialist and even dropped me the occasional note in praise of my weekly industrial column. This covered issues ranging from training and various forms of efficiency to scientific developments such as the use of ultrasonics. One about inland waterways produced a family holiday on a barge in Nottinghamshire and Leicestershire. I insisted on meeting at least part of the cost to demonstrate my professional independence. Another article about 'Giving railways the personal touch' included a paragraph from a British Rail staff booklet which, had it been taken to heart thirty years ago, would have made travelling in Britain so much more pleasant. 'Attention to passengers,' it said, 'is more important than the latest football results. Sympathize with a passenger's difficulties; personal appearance DOES count; greet the passenger – we all like a "Hello" or "Good morning", and DON'T pass the buck.'

The *Yorkshire Post* had two industrial correspondents. Desmond McGimpsey, a most conscientious Ulsterman, covered the national scene from London. He concentrated on industrial and economic developments, national disputes, the activities of the TUC and the political aspects of the industrial scene which gave him a substantial foothold in covering the Labour Party. I was more heavily biased towards the economic and industrial fortunes of Yorkshire. I wrote a lot about textiles (never forgetting Ingham-produced corduroy which was then suffering from Spanish imports), engineering, transport and coal mining. Desmond had first pick of the plums, whether they were trade union annual conferences or overseas trips. But by the end of the year he had either facilitated my way or actually introduced me to a substantial part of the Labour movement. I covered the annual conferences of the National Union of Tailors and Garment Workers in Scarborough and the National Union of Mineworkers in Rothesay. I was introduced by Desmond to the Trades Union Congress in conference in Portsmouth where the Electrical Trades Union was expelled for ballot rigging and Will Paynter, general secretary of the NUM, lost his General Council seat in the consequent backlash against Communists. He inducted me into the rituals of the Labour Party's annual conference at Blackpool where I had spent so many holidays as a child. He also enabled me to go on a fascinating tour of Denmark laid on by the Danish Foreign Office. This was heady stuff for a Hebden Bridge lad so recently emerged from the confines of Halifax.

Within a few months I had been confronted first hand with most of the issues of the second half of the twentieth century: nuclear defence (on which I was never sympathetic to the CND), Anglo-American relations, Britain's place in Europe, protectionism, pay restraint, productivity and efficiency, the block vote and the Labour Party's constitution, trade union abuse of power, Britain's competitiveness and even the weakness of our industrial design.

Bob Mozley left me three legacies apart from the *Yorkshire Post*'s respect for its Northern industrial correspondent. Arguably the most important was coverage of the monthly meetings midweek of the Confederation of Shipbuilding and Engineering unions in the Royal Station Hotel at York. Each month, rather like homing pigeons, the leaders of too many, but a declining number, of manual and whitecollar unions coverged on York to flex their muscles. They arrived from London, libated and cigared by labour or industrial correspondents who had travelled up with them by rail amid, to hear some people talk, an orgy of confidential document distribution from union leaders to journalists. At all events, the various cliques of London labour correspondents set up camp in the lounge of the hotel generously dispensing drinks to thirsty union leaders and generally seeking to impress (and, possibly, depress) country yokels like Dick O'Sullivan (*Daily Express*, Manchester), Don Evans

(*Northern Echo*, Darlington), Monty Meth (*Daily Worker*, Leeds) and Ingham with their inside trackery. Once, in open court, as it were, I provocatively asked Ron Stevens (*Daily Telegraph*), of the more arrogant London tendency, what he had learned on the way up from London. 'And why,' he asked, 'should I tell you?' 'No reason, at all,' I said, 'except that if my local knowledge served your purpose you wouldn't hesitate to ask me.' A future government press officer was learning that the British media are by no means monolithic.

One man was immune from all this: he had his own sources. He was my second Mozley legacy. He is Monty Meth. This son of a Czechoslovakian emigré was at that time the Communist *Daily Worker*'s correspondent in Leeds. No one was going to make a Communist out of me after my Labour-loyalist, anti-Communist (and anti-anything in the least exotically Left) upbringing. But Monty had contacts I could never have. And I had access to a world closed to Monty, to the extent that he needed that access. That was the basis on which we operated, except that we warmed to each other as individuals and co-operated usefully. I provided the car – or at least the lift home – when our jobs coincided. He supplied the contacts and the insights on which I formed my own judgements. Not for the last time, I thought that I got more out of Monty than he got out of me. But it worked in a haphazard way. He also left me deeply impressed with the Left's organization and communications. If only, I used to sigh, this ability were used to constructive ends.

One of the passing delights of industrial reporting is the creative use of language by trade union leaders. The best example I encountered arose out of the mess in which the Yorkshire miners' executive landed themselves in August 1961 over their recommended expulsion of a young Communist, Bob Wilkinson, for his part in an expensive unofficial strike earlier in the year. When the 104 delegates to the area council met a fortnight later they narrowly reinstated Mr Wilkinson largely, so far as we could gather, because they felt he had been singled out for punishment. This rebuff made the senior officials responsible for briefing the press singularly uncommunicative. They refused to see us at lunchtime and asked us to come back later in the afternoon. Undeterred, we repaired to the pubs where we rapidly learned the facts. We also tracked down Roy Mason, now Lord Mason, Yorkshire miner and Barnsley MP. He eventually became expansive. He said Sam Bullough, the amiable, decent president, had banged the table at the end of the meeting and appealed to the delegates' better nature: 'Instead of spending all dinner time boozing wi' t' press, you should give them reporters a wide berth and keep mum. This matter's sub-juice.' This injunction was immediately reinforced by Fred Collindridge, area secretary, who had a sharper edge to him. 'Now think on what Sam's said,' he told the council. 'Don't go boozing and leaking with them press lads. This matter's got to fruitify.' Fred did not disappoint us when we went to learn the outcome of the meeting. 'Well,' he said. 'It's like this. We've decided not to dismember 'im.'

The third Mozley legacy was the *Yorkshire Post*'s annual review of industry. This was the elaborate forerunner of contemporary newspaper supplements and was designed to take stock of the Yorkshire industrial scene in profitable association with the advertising department. My job, as editor, was to produce it – commissioning articles, sub-editing the contributors' execrable prose, writing the headlines and picture captions, laying it out with the printer assigned to me and generally putting it to bed. In and among, as they say in the Yorkshire Pennines, I maintained the *Yorkshire Post*'s daily coverage of industrial news and features. It made for an extremely busy but rewarding first – and only – spring as Northern industrial correspondent.

It was in laying out the annual review of industry on the stone that I came to realize just how bad relations were between top management and the editor. Top management used to take me on one side to inquire about the temper of the editorial staff. Not half so short, it seemed, as top management's. Were they (the journalists) likely to go out on strike? I was asked. If they were, the general manager, Harold Clough, suggested, that would be all that was required to get rid of the editor. He could not survive a strike by journalists, bearing in mind their loyalty during the printers' strike in 1959. I told him frankly that I did not see the *Yorkshire Post*'s editorial staff pulling management's chestnuts out of the fire. The management had appointed Mr Young. They would have to live with him as much as the company's journalists. This is not to suggest that in my relatively privileged position as industrial correspondent I was unaware of tensions between the editor and the wider editorial staff. There was a feeling that the newspaper was becoming too populist, especially on race, too permissive and too risqué. I did not like some of the trends, but I had no personal complaint about Kenneth Young other than that too much of my working time was taken up by staff – both members of the NUJ and the Institute of Journalists – grumbling about the editor. I should have resisted being made deputy father of the NUJ chapel.

I doubt whether, after less than a year as Northern industrial correspondent, I would have entertained any approach from another newspaper had the atmosphere been better. I had earlier toyed with the idea of becoming editor of the *Pudsey News*, part of the Ackrill Group in Harrogate. Fortunately, that had not worked out. It would have been a retrograde step. The *Guardian* was, however, looking to strengthen their Leeds office where Michael Parkin, a former *Yorkshire Evening Post* writer, was their sole representative. Was I interested in joining the big league? I did not jump at the opportunity, though such a distinguished and reputable newspaper was tempting. The salary was a little better and it was another step up the ladder. But I had some reservations about giving up a specialism and going back to general reporting. I was also a little in awe of the *Guardian* as a writer's paper. On the other hand the unhappy distractions of the *Yorkshire Post* were becoming a bit wearing. I arranged to go over to Manchester for an interview with the editor, Alastair Hetherington.

On the appointed day Mr Young dropped a bombshell. He fired two sub-editors, one of whom, Walter Chuck, a former editor of the *Pudsey News*, was highly respected both for his accuracy and for his capacity to shift copy. I left for my interview in Manchester with the office in turmoil. The editor wanted to see me on my return in the evening. He seemed disconcerted by the staff's rallying behind Walter Chuck. He claimed to have dismissed him on advice from executives. I was able to say that those self-same executives had confirmed my good impression of Walter. He wondered how the staff were likely to respond. I said that I had no idea what they would do. But in Walter Chuck's case it was academic. His reputation had already brought him an offer of a job which he seemed likely to accept. The editor's problems might not be immediately acute but relations were likely to be very strained for some time. This was no way to run a newspaper. And so far as I was concerned, it was the end. I told him that I would be leaving to join the *Guardian*. I sensed that I had made a point.

My interview with Alastair Hetherington had been unconventional. He seemed interested only in the books I had read and I can recall discussing only the value of the beaver in preserving the aquatic environment of North America before he offered me the Leeds job, promising a letter of confirmation immediately in the post. I was taking a chance when I told Kenneth Young I was resigning, but not much of one. Alastair Hetherington's letter duly arrived and I joined the *Guardian* early in 1962.

6

The Candidate

Writing – as distinct from reporting events or speeches – never came easily to me. Theatre notices, feature articles and even rugby league notes for the *Yorkshire Evening Post* were invariably agony. I could fill the waste paper bin with false starts. Only the deadline conquered despair. I suppose I tried too hard, and the harder I tried the more difficult it became to produce a satisfactory introduction and flowing prose. It was little consolation to me that so many other journalists, some of whom, I imagined, were never at a loss for words, confessed to the same problem. And now I had joined the writers' paper. I was overawed – more overawed than I have ever been in my life.

I was also burdened with a conscience. I needed to feel that I was earning my keep and often in my first months with the *Guardian* I doubted whether I was. It seemed such an insubstantial life, after all that had gone before, to be scrabbling through a pile of Yorkshire weekly newspapers to which we subscribed in search of the odd, the droll, the exotic and the sharp piece of social comment. My colleague, Michael Parkin, with his goatee beard, pipe, and deliberate, unhurried manner seemed to entertain no such doubts. Of course, he was often hard pressed to find the vehicle for his sardonic humour among the columns of print he and I scanned. He was loath to go through to Harry Whewell, the news editor in Manchester, without an offering for the day. But not much got in the way of his lunchtime pint or two in Whitelock's. He was a Micawber, and something usually turned up. Nothing set him up better for the evening's social round, or a quiet night at home, than 300 words of special Parkin.

Harry Whewell did not help, though he tried hard to make me feel at home in the social club that he ran from Cross Street,

Manchester. He exhibited a lively interest in the quaint. The charitable works of the feoffees of the common lands of Rotherham who were given a new constitution during the reign of Queen Elizabeth I were good for a story in his book. He was in his seventh heaven when I came up with the tale that the mine-infested rural district of Rotherham was trying to get itself designated as a holiday resort under the Shops Act so that maggots could be sold to anglers on Sunday morning before they set off for a day's fishing in Lincolnshire. The noon call to Cross Street to give Harry our story lines frequently became an extended discussion or even debate. If you did not get in early with your call you could be hanging on for ever, it seemed, for he was nothing if not a lively conversationalist. Telephonically, he was a most expensive news editor. British Telecom shareholders should mount a campaign: 'Bring back Harry Whewell OBE.'

He insisted that we go regularly over to Manchester to keep in touch with our colleagues such as his deputy Joe Minogue, Arthur Hopcraft, Dennis Johnson, George Hawthorne and Baden Hickman. We arrived in time to go to the pub for pie, peas and pints and once we missed the last train home to Leeds. He also came out on tour. Our job was to lay on an interesting visit, starting with a good pub lunch and often ending with a visit to the Leeds City Varieties where Harry delighted in beating the comics to the punchlines. After one of these outings he ended up fast asleep in Wigan sidings instead of getting out at Manchester. My brother had bought his first farm for £1100 at Ibbotroyd, above Hebden Bridge, in 1959 and Harry was then looking for a country cottage. We thought it would be a good idea to give him a close look at the Pennines. We found my brother working in the mistal (cowshed) pulling nails out of timbers. Harry was quite disturbed: how could anyone work alone like that, doing such a boring job? Harry simply could not bear the thought of being bored. Or alone.

My Non-conformist work ethic and my irrational view that everything in the *Guardian* must be beautifully written made for a neurotic rather than my usual hesitant, unconfident start to a new job. I became deeply depressed in the autumn of 1962 after I had made my customary early mistake. There is inevitably a great deal of tension between reporters and the sub-editors who prepare a reporter's copy, cut it to length and write the headlines on the story. Sub-editors can be a reporter's best friend, smoothing the flow of his often hasty prose which he has dictated off the top of his head in a rush, picking up his silly mistakes and querying apparent inconsistencies. They can save his professional life. Their rewriting can also make a reporter hang his head in shame at the stuff which appears under his name. My experience of sub-editors on the *Guardian* was mixed but it did not become known as the *Grauniad* for nothing. Some of the consequences of dictating down a bad line copy which landed in the hands of a sub who was having an off night could be hilarious. Take, for example, my coverage of the fish war off the Yorkshire coast between inshore fishermen and foreign trawlers using fine-mesh nets. There could be no doubt from my copy that I was writing about marine life. I described how the inshore fishermen believed that the constant sweeping of the seas by foreign vessels was driving herring to seek refuge near the sea bed, making them much more difficult to catch. The Herring Industry Board in Edinburgh conceded that there might be something in this though, the *Guardian* reported, 'machine biologists were at variance over the herrings' behaviour'. Reporters as lacking in self-confidence as myself did not feel there was much of a safety net under them.

Nor was there. Reporting the Communists' renewed struggle for power in the Yorkshire coalfield one week-end, I had a complete mental blockage, got my double negatives in a twist and ended up describing Sam Bullough, area president, as a right-winger and a Communist not merely in the same paragraph but in the same sentence. It appeared thus: 'The area's president, Mr S. Bullough, as the likely right-wing candidate for Mr Collindridge's national vice-presidency, is nothing if not a Communist'. It was obvious that I was not the only one with a mental blockage that week-end. Mr Bullough's solicitors threatened to sue. Harry Whewell made light of it and wondered why Sam was suing – because we had called him a right-winger? The *Guardian* apologized and, I was told, paid a token – very token – sum to Mr Bullough. and that would have been that, but for my severe loss of confidence. For weeks I put pen to paper in near terror. Harry and Joe Minogue tried to reassure me but it took me a long time to put it behind me.

My compact with Michael Parkin was that wherever possible I handled the serious stuff and he the fancy writing, or the heavy end and the fluff, as I put it. This helped me to find my feet. It meant that I continued to cover the Confederation of Shipbuilding and Engineering Unions' monthly meeting in York – the Confed – and the often troublesome Yorkshire coalfield. I also spent much of the summer in Northern resorts at the conference of employers' bodies, professional institutions and trade unions – the draughtsmen in Blackpool and Clive Jenkins' ASTMS, the building workers, the taxmen and Nalgo in Scarborough. I also responded on behalf of the press at the 1962 Great Yarmouth conference of the Confed to the curious votes of thanks which end these occasions. My commentary on the creative use of language by trade union leaders – as evidenced earlier by the leadership of the Yorkshire miners – brought the house down.

My scepticism about incomes policy was fully revealed in the introduction to a front-page lead from the NALGO conference: 'The Government's incomes policy, left in shreds by the 4 per cent pay award to 485,000 civil servants, went into the rag bag yesterday when it was announced that the Industrial Court had awarded increases ranging from 12 to 14 per cent to 1700 hospital almoners and psychiatric social workers.' This was regarded by my colleagues as a fine example of a 'committed intro'.

After fourteen years during which my political upbringing had been subordinated to the needs of the job, The *Guardian*'s radical atmosphere had not merely brought release; it had also thrown me into the Labour and trades union movement at the deep end. I went on to the Trades Union Congress and Labour Party conferences, helping to produce the conference reports, which ran to one or two pages each day, under Joe Minogue. The emphasis in my day-to-day work and my shorthand made me a natural choice for the conference teams. Joe seemed to have got it into his head that only my shorthand was up to Frank Cousins, the general secretary of the Transport and General Workers' Union. In vain did I protest that 'Big Frank', as he was called by the popular newspapers, needed an interpreter and not a shorthand writer to make sense of him.

I was also set to work to cover the hearings, from Newcastle-upon-Tyne to Sheffield, via Middlesbrough, York and Leeds, into the Local Government Commission's draft proposals for reform. This thoroughly enjoyable experience left me with the firm impression that the best defence of the status quo was our splendid sewage system which we would tamper with at our peril. It also launched me into a lasting love affair with the North-East where Dan Smith (Newcastle) and Andrew Cunningham (Durham County) were then the local political powers in the land and George Chetwynd, former Labour MP for Sedgefield, was an immensely approachable and helpful director of the North East Development Council. At last, I was firing on all cylinders.

I also had a happy home life. John had been reading since the age of four, thanks to Nancy, and was settling into Christ the King RC infants' school, across the road from our home, with the Lynch boys, Mark and Nicholas, whose father was a sales engineer for English Electric. I have tended to judge all the self-seeking nonsense said and written since then about education by Sister Monica's 3Rs achievements with a class of some forty, on balance, underprivileged children in a pre-fabricated classroom. If every teacher had a mission to teach instead of to change the world, to blame the government, local authority or parents, or to do nothing in particular, Britain might be better off. So, too, would teachers. And so would our children.

I resolved that John would also have roots. At every opportunity I drove the family some twenty miles out to Halifax, where Nancy's mother and second sister Miriam and her husband, Maurice, had their homes; to Luddenden, a little further west, where Nancy's eldest sister, Kathleen, and her husband, Tom Manley, lived in the cottage attached to Eddie Ingham's (no relation) smallholding; and to my parents who had moved to another pre-fab at Old Town to be close to Derek's farm. On Derek's precipitous farm I introduced John to the real life; the only life that matters – living and working with nature. There, at Ibbotroyd, he learned first-hand about the seasonal cycle and the stubborn, wayward nature of hens, pigs and cattle and the need for reliable machinery. Derek also bought a stallion pony which he rapidly concluded must be gelded if it were not to brain him and were to carry John safely on its back. Life again had a great deal to offer. But not for long.

On our return home from a visit to relatives on Boxing Day 1962, we found the house running with water where it was not frozen by the onset of what I subsequently described as the sixty-two-day ordeal by frost. The bitter 1962–3 winter had claimed an early victim. It transpired that a defective tap washer in the bath had chosen this, of all days, to perish. The outlet had frozen and the house was flooded. It is a miracle that we were not electrocuted. It took months of one of the coldest winters on record for the house to dry out and for the family to get back to normal.

Meanwhile, Lord Hailsham had been appointed Minister for the North-East where unemployment was rising. It fell to me to cover his five copy-laden tours of the Tyne, Wear and Tees ending with what was intended to be an image-breaking visit to Jarrow as the ice broke up on the Tyne. I was amazed at the fuss over the cloth cap and boots he wore on his first visit. His explanation that he wore boots because of his weak ankles was entirely credible. His cloth cap was understandable in the freezing circumstances, though I always went bareheaded. It was not what he wore in Andy Capp country that mattered; it was what he did. He was thorough and he was solidly backed by an office led by Ronnie McIntosh whom I was next to meet in the Department of Employment. He was also a human being. He confessed at a press conference on Durham that his brain was 'addled'. But, while I respected him as a person, I was intensely sceptical about the exercise and disappointed with his White Paper – and showed it at a North-East Development Council press conference immediately after its publication, much to George Chetwynd's embarrassment, because he saw the White Paper as a 'statement of intent and as a valuable enabling measure'. While 'woolly' over the means of financing development, he thought it was promising. His optimism was justified. The North-East owes some of its good communications to Lord Hailsham. But, as George Chetwynd always maintained, its economic fortunes depended fundamentally on national economic growth. It had to wait for Mrs Thatcher before it could take off.

I used to drive the ninety miles from Leeds to Newcastle once or twice a week to cover the area and often drove back in the evening, phoning my copy from a telephone kiosk on the Great North Road, as we knew the perilous A1. Much of it through Durham was only three lanes wide. It is a wonder I survived. Sometimes when the weather was bad – and it was often very bad during the 1962–3 winter – I felt it prudent to go by rail. I shall always be grateful to Wilf Little, the Press Association's legendary correspondent in the North-East whom I first met covering the Mary Hackett murder committal proceedings in Halifax, and Jim Beecroft, of the *Daily Mirror*, for offering me lifts when we were trying to keep up with Lord Hailsham. This travelling, and the coverage of conferences in the summer, meant that Michael Parkin and I could go for days without seeing each other. It also meant that I was spared working in the *Guardian*'s small office in Leeds, Dickensian in every particular apart from the telephone. It was in New Briggate, opposite the Theatre Royal, and was reached up a flight of bare wooden steps. It was perishing in winter, with only electric fires to take off the chill. It overlooked St John's cemetery and the only means of escape in the event of fire was out of the window into a yard several floors below. I used it as a prime example of office accommodation which should be condemned when later in London I reviewed the Chief Inspector of Factories' report for *New Society* magazine. It was not a place to which you could take contacts, but it was essential to ensure that Harry Whewell visited it on his social trips to Leeds to remind him of the need for new premises. Harry found our badgering a trifle tedious. Eventually we moved to a pleasanter backroom in the Albion Street offices of an employment agency where Ken Ridge, the proprietor, would have sat around and talked all day had we let him.

Professionally, 1963 was for me a golden year. It began with my covering the first public hearing in Edinburgh of the National Incomes Commission into the concession of a forty-hour week by the employers of 6000 Scottish plumbers. These hearings were conceived by the Government, anxious to contain costs and inflation, as a means of requiring industries to justify their actions before the bar of public opinion. It would have helped reporters like myself to record the debate if this hearing had been held in a quieter place. I felt obliged to put a health warning on my report to readers: 'if one heard correctly as vehicles skidded up the steep and slush-covered Blackfriars Street outside the university examination hall where it [the Commission] is sitting on circuit'. The year ended with my acquiring a by-line, of which I was inordinately proud, on successive articles about the state of the North-East of England and of Scotland. In between I had seldom been so fulfilled since Hebden Bridge, or Leeds in 1959.

Lord Hailsham's tours of the North-East and the hearings of the Local Government Commission were only part of it. I went from the conference of the Merchant Navy and Airlines Officers in South Shields to the Ramblers' Association in Sheffield, the Young Socialists' bear garden in Scarborough, the Housing and Town Planning Council in Filey and the NUPE and foundry workers in Bridlington. Then I covered the Stove, Grate and General Metal Workers' and the Fire Brigades Union conferences in Scarborough, the Confed in Margate and the NUM in Bournemouth. I put in a professional appearance at the Great Yorkshire Show at Harrogate before I was off to the TUC in Brighton. Harold Wilson's 'white heat of technology' speech at the Labour Party conference in Scarborough visibly moved not just Joe Minogue and myself.

I covered the dying belligerence as a separate craft of the Yorkshire Winding Enginemen who lower and lift miners into and out of pits and raise the coal; the clean air movement which was determined to kill the link in Yorkshire minds between muck and brass; Halifax Town's appeal for twenty-three footballs (cost £8 7s 6d each) to provide the necessary for another season;, the 'bomb test' on eggs which proved that the thinnest shells can be the toughest;, and the longest known crawl by a crab – a Yorkshire crab, of course – from Whitby to Aberdeen. I also recorded the accession to the throne of another weaver's son, Brian Close, as Yorkshire's cricket captain. These were great days, indeed. And then, with a booklet on the experience of firms moving out of London under my belt in association with John Cole, the Labour correspondent and subsequently the BBC's political editor, it all collapsed. The *Guardian* appointed reporters in Scotland and, more important to me, the North-East. It was back to the tinselly life of the curious and the quaint which I had entered and from which I had quickly escaped two years earlier.

I drifted into Labour Party politics in Leeds through knowing party officers both in the city and for the Yorkshire region and being on good terms with full-time regional and local trade union officials. I offered to help them with their press relations and addressed a number of week-end schools and evening meetings on how they might improve their communications with the public through the media. The *Guardian*, a lively political forum within itself, did nothing to discourage me from taking an active role in party politics. On the contrary, Harry Whewell thought I would make a good MP and said so often enough not to be teasing me. He loved egging me on in argument. I also had time – too much time for my liking – on my hands now that I was relieved of the responsibility of covering the North-East. I believe Wilf Window of the NUPE was instrumental in my striking up a relationship with the Fabian Society and my resuming in West Leeds, where I lived, my long lapsed membership of the Labour Party. I was also introduced to Solly Pearce, the elderly gentleman who ran the local Labour Party paper, the *Leeds Weekly Citizen*. And early in 1964 I began to write a regular, highly opinionated column for Solly which I more or less maintained over a period of three years.

My new found activism reflected in many ways the spirit of the time. There was an impatience with what the Conservatives, under Sir Alec Douglas-Home, represented. This, as Iain Macleod demonstrated, did not escape the Tory party itself. There was some feeling of the need for a change of government after getting on for thirteen years of Conservative rule, and Harold Wilson had fired at least some of us with enthusiasm for his leadership. It was one of those periods in political life which bring the dormant supporter, or in my case a spiritual supporter released from the constraints of previous employment, out of his or her hibernation. Quite simply, I wanted to help and I offered my help in the way I could best do so by writing a column and making available my advice to the party on how it might better project its policies and ideas. After all, a general election was approaching.

I threw myself into this new phase in my life with familiar enthusiasm, though I felt it better for the *Guardian* to write under a pseudonym. As with my *Yorkshire Evening Post* by-line, Royd, I turned to a geographical association – Albion, after the terrace where I was brought up in Hebden Bridge and the street in which I had worked for the Yorkshire Conservative Newspaper Company. I did not advertise my links with the column but my friends and colleagues were well aware I was the contributor. It was not a secret.

My technique was to seize on a speech or utterance, or a newspaper article or leader, and use it to tear the Tories to shreds and to advocate Labour Party policy. It was trenchant, rumbustious, fierce, irreverent, cheeky and loyal. It always spoke up for the serfs against the arrogance of the ruling classes. It was supposed to get the reader's blood coursing in his or her veins. I hope it did. It certainly pleased Solly Pearce. Members of the Fabian Society described it to me with a knowing look as the professional column. But it did not inspire many letters. Sir Keith Joseph, then Housing Minister and MP for Leeds North-East and now Lord Joseph, was easily the most distinguished man from whom I drew fire over housing policy. I thanked him for his interest, said it was nice to be taken seriously by a Cabinet Minister and felt such a serious man was in the wrong party. I had a soft spot for Sir Keith. 'Would all Tories were as energetic and as honest as Sir Keith,' I wrote in July 1964. I was a discerning chap. The column gave me an enormous kick and over the months was highly therapeutic. It got a lot out of my system, some of it planted there by Grandad Horsfall.

I had been affronted by Sir Alec Douglas-Home's emergence as Prime Minister and leader of the Conservative Party and I regarded him as fair, privileged game. The *Leeds Weekly Citizen* was my grouse moor and Sir Alec my bird. I had nothing against him as a person: it was what he represented that rankled. I regret now that I was so rough on him. He did not deserve it. I quoted the *Guardian*, who had described him as 'a political fossil', and referred to him as Sir Alec Strangelove after a bright young thing's banner I had seen at a demonstration in Newcastle-upon-Tyne. He was an 'incurable waffler'. But I recall being disgusted during the election later in the year when a crowd of yobs shouted him down on the steps of Leeds Town Hall. That was not my style of politics. I was also pretty rough on Reginald Maudling because of his indolence, as I saw it, as Chancellor. I called him a layabout and Reggie the Recumbent. I was idealistic, especially about the possibilities in government planning, and deeply concerned about the gap I perceived between the overcrowded South-East and the North. I was also anxious to shake Yorkshire out of its economic complacency and reported extensively in the *Leeds Weekly Citizen* on a paper I had delivered to the Leeds Fabians on the issue.

Underlying it all was a concern for the Labour Party to equip itself better, both organizationally and presentationally, as a fighting machine. I expected Labour to win the election by 36 – why 36 is lost to me in the mists of time – in spite of its inferior electoral machine and organization. Sir Alec nearly pulled it off. Labour had a lead of thirteen seats over the Conservatives but an overall majority of only four. Writing in anticipation of a Labour victory, I warned that there was a limit to what could be achieved in five years and added: 'A lot of loyal Labour workers have not had it easy for twelve months. But now they cannot expect to have it easy again for with power comes responsibility. And one of the responsibilities that the Labour Party must accept in the flush of victory is that of looking after itself a lot better than it has done in the past.' There are three pointers to my future career in that brief extract: loyalty to a Government one has chosen, or chosen to serve; an interest in political organization; and an emphasis on the need for power to be complemented by responsibility by all who exercise it and seek to benefit from it.

I was still prepared to defend the trade unions and to hope that they would reform themselves. But I had no doubt – as I wrote in February 1964 – that they 'really do need sorting out'. I also took care to include in a report for the *Leeds Weekly Citizen* of a speech in Leeds by George Brown, deputy leader of the Labour Party, the following:

'Whatever alibis the trade unions think they now have about "We" and "Them", let us remember that after October there will be no "Them". It will be "Us". And if we fail all of us fail – not "They", not somebody else.'

I thought that the real test of any future Labour government would be its ability to govern for the good of the country and not for the benefit of vested interests. Whether the trade unions, as one of the biggest vested interests in the land, would permit it to do so nagged me but I did not make an issue of it. I just signalled the point from time to time in the *Leeds Weekly Citizen*. Meanwhile, I offered whatever help I could give to the cause of securing a Labour government. This included helping to produce an election newspaper, the *Sowerby Herald*, for Douglas Houghton. I wrote the sort of leader that could be used in similar publications throughout Yorkshire, with only the place and candidate's names changed. I was far from overworked by the *Guardian* – except on finding something Guardianish to write about – now that I was substantially confined to Yorkshire. Moreover, in an election year most of the trade union conferences were covered from London. I plugged away at the Confed and a crop of strikes. The Yorkshire coalfield was infected with them and I needed to keep my eye on a year-long dispute over the closed shop at William Denby and Sons' dyeworks at Baildon, Bradford, where 240 employees had been dismissed after a stoppage. Baildon was a bitter place as the unavailing struggle in the face of an intransigent management set family against family and union against union.

Perhaps as some consolation for losing my beloved North-East, Harry Whewell sent me on two wonderfully entertaining and instructive trips, first to the Alsace wine fair and then with Freddie Laker on British United Airways' proving flight for the VC10 to Brazil, Uruguay, the Argentine and Chile. The first must have appealed to his sense of humour, throwing Ingham, the beer drinker, in with the wine snobs. It did not work out like that, however, because Bill Sternberg, the *Yorkshire Evening Post*'s political editor, was also on the trip. As a martyr to gout, Bill saw the tour of the vineyards, and more important the caverns, as a challenge. Suitably dosed with drugs, he insisted that he and I should pronounce every wine we tasted as absolutely divine and not in the least presumptuous and down the lot. No spitting it out, he said firmly. Twenty-three rieslings, traminers and gewürtztraminers before a meal in Riquewihr leave the same sense of achievement and headiness that, I imagine, comes with a century before lunch. They also require a long snooze in the afternoon sun followed by an evening on Vittel to quench the thirst. I returned to write an extremely learned advertising feature on Alsatian wines. My offering after a wonderful trip to Lisbon, Las Palmas, Rio, Montevideo, Buenos Aires, Santiago and Valparaiso was chosen for the *Bedside Guardian*, the annual selection in book form of work by *Guardian* writers. Freddie Laker described the VC10 as 'potentially the safest aircraft every built'. Neither of us was to know then that I was going to prove it, travelling 500,000 miles with the Prime Minister and RAF Strike Command.

I wrote election specials for the *Guardian* on the Halifax, Brighouse and York constituencies and a reasonably accurate election round-up for the whole of Yorkshire, and then resumed the quiet life. I suppose three factors propelled me towards a shot at securing political office. Harry Whewell gave every indication that he would not mind in the least if one of his charges – that is, me – turned up in Parliament. I had time on my hands, even spending a day a week with John on Derek's farm. And political parties have always tried to persuade young, active, energetic supporters to stand for the council. I have no recollection of the process by which I came to be selected as the candidate for the utterly hopeless Moortown Ward of Leeds City Council where anybody who was anybody in Leeds, and had the money to go with it, tended to live. I simply turned up, along with other candidates, for interview by the local worthies, said my piece, answered their questions and was told I was their man. I do know that I did not think it would be the end of the world if I failed. Consequently, I probably gave a good account of myself. I would have been much less impressive had I been desperate to get my foot on the first rung of the political ladder. One thing held me back: my need to look after my livelihood. I recall making this point after selection to a meeting of women helpers in the ward. They were amazingly understanding. 'Aye, lad,' they said. 'You mun look after that first.' They had a proper appreciation of my chances in Moortown. But they were very pleased to have me fighting for them.

Before fighting a determined campaign I shared in the *Guardian*'s excitement over the appointment of regional economic planning councils. At the same time I wondered how well local government and industry would go along with a regional approach in such an intensely parochial area. There was no reason why co-operation should come easily to Yorkshire and Humberside, I wrote, kicking off a series on the state of the nation for the *Guardian*. After all, it did not recognize itself as a region until George Brown made it one on 10 December 1964. My two articles from this 'unnatural region', as I described it, illustrated how the professional reporter in me eclipsed the amateur propagandist. I reported that a lot of scepticism, confusion and undermined confidence were around in Yorkshire in January 1965. The sense of urgency which the new Labour Government seemed likely to generate had been lost. And I felt that the claim made, rather sadly, by a Sheffield industrialist that the Government had put itself across 'extraordinarily badly' began to ring true. I was to hear that complaint against governments I served in a presentational capacity many times in years to come.

I never expected to win Moortown. But the ebb and flow of a hard fought campaign, and the candidate's need to present himself both to his supporters and the voters as eternally confident, can generate hope in even the most realistic heart. I was no exception. There were a number of reasons for this. We had, by general consent, a professional election campaign leaflet for the whole of the city council elections. I had written it and was on the whole pleased with it, with one reservation. As always, I had tried to cram too much in and I felt it looked overcrowded. I reckoned I had as much to offer as most candidates, apart from experience. I set out my three main reasons for standing in a personal note in my election address:

'1 As a journalist I have served an adequate apprenticeship for membership of a local authority;

'2 I have something to offer Moortown, Leeds and Yorkshire through my broad understanding of their problems;

'3 The Labour Party should be supported in its effort to bring about radical – and much needed – changes in our society'.

If every Labour voter in Moortown took the trouble to vote, I added, 'Labour can take this so-called Tory citadel by storm. Give me five minutes of your time on May 13 and I will give you many hours' service in return. My object is to serve you by securing imaginative, efficient and socially just local government.'

The photograph of the chubby chap who believed he had something to offer showed how much weight I had piled on in Leeds. I threw my bulk into the fray with hope as well as enthusiasm because I had a good, small campaign team. I was on good terms with the local activists who were amazingly undogmatic – good, old-fashioned Labour people – and were not fighting each other. I was also formidably reinforced by Harry Whewell from Manchester.

71

On the pretext – for that is what it was – of mounting a circulation drive in Leeds he dispatched R. W. (Bill) Shakespeare and Victor Keegan across the Pennines in support of Michael Parkin who, generously for a Liberal, or so he said he was, toured the streets with a microphone urging people to vote for Ingham. He pulled out of one heavily Jewish area when he realized that his red Volkswagen might do me more harm than good. We had a thoroughly enjoyable time trying to pull in votes and decided on one last push on polling day. I had a single-sheet leaflet printed in red type. It conveyed a simple message: 'If everyone who THINKS Labour VOTES Labour we can WIN.' Bill Shakespeare, who went on to work for *The Times* and later as public relations adviser for the Channel Tunnel, and Victor Keegan, who still writes for the *Guardian*, joined me before anybody had let the cat in. At a trot we shoved this message through the letter-boxes on every floor of the most promising tower block territory we could cover before breakfast. There was also method in our madness. We started at the top of the blocks and ran down.

I never formally met my Conservative opponent, Mrs L. E. Henson, who looked altogether too motherly, not even on the night of the count. In a bad year for Labour she crushed me by more than 4000 votes. The figures were:

Mrs L. E. Henson (Conservative) 5532

Mr B. Ingham (Labour) 1485

Mr K. R. Dunn (Liberal) 561

Mr P. Boyles (Communist) 190

The vultures were waiting on the steps of Leeds Town Hall. 'Well,' said Bert Ramelson, the Communist Party organizer in Leeds, whom I had seen at his intellectual bullying in trades council meetings in my cub reporter's days in Hebden Bridge, 'what have you to say for yourself now?' Quick as a flash, for I was in good training, I retorted that I thought I had served my purpose by keeping the enemy resources which might otherwise have been thrown into vulnerable Labour seats tied down in Moortown. Bill Shakespeare pronounced himself deeply impressed with my fast footwork. He thought I really might make a politician.

Next day I was asked to relieve the *Guardian* labour staff in

London, where the newspaper was now established having moved down from Manchester. Peter Jenkins, the Labour correspondent, was abroad on sabbatical and Eric Jacobs was leaving immediately to become press and public relations adviser to Aubrey Jones, chairman of the newly established National Board for Prices and Incomes. After seeing little of my family for several weeks because of the election campaign, I packed my bags and took the first train from Leeds to King's Cross on Monday 17 May. Another episode in my life – this time a crucial, disillusioning but far from unhappy one – was opening up. It was to change my outlook and my career.

7

On the Labour Beat

Any disappointment that I felt over my failure to become a Leeds City councillor – and I was perhaps more relieved than frustrated – evaporated in the Labour correspondent's busy day into which I was immediately plunged. Before polling day I had warned *Leeds Weekly Citizen* readers that Labour's main problem would be in getting its supporters to bother to make a brief visit to the booth to cast their vote. Afterwards, I saw Labour's 'hammering' at the polls as partly the product of a stunning apathy on the part of its supporters and partly an organizational *malaise* within the Labour Party overall. There was, I wrote, a limit to the amount of work which women's sections, the real foundation of many election campaigns, could undertake. I was to discover other political *malaises* in London.

I had never worked in the capital before, though I was familiar with both the TUC and the Labour Party from the several rounds of annual conferences I had attended. I also knew a substantial number of the union leaders who populated my baileywick from my coverage of the Confed and my attendance at trade union conferences. For the same reason, I knew most of the members of the Labour and Industrial Correspondents' Group who were to be my colleagues for the next two years and some of them later my clients for the rest of my working life. The *Guardian*'s offices in Gray's Inn Road were the most sumptuous I had yet experienced – mostly open plan but with parquet-floored rooms for specialists like Peter Jenkins and myself who shared one, conveniently opposite the accounts department where we drew our expenses. Tubes and taxis made my inner London parish highly convenient to cover and I began to lunch – in posh restaurants with trade union leaders and politicians – consistently better than since Hebden Bridge where I had been able to go home for meals. My regular haunts were the Au Savarin in Charlotte Street and the Old Budapest in Greek Street.

I was also mightily impressed with the service I received. Most people I needed to talk to actually wanted to talk to me. More than that, they rang me up and even entertained me. As I remarked in a talk I subsequently gave as Chief Press Secretary at Number Ten: 'After seventeen years of straining blood out of millstone grit I found that government, considered in its widest sense, not merely served it up on a plate in London but often washed it down, too.' The media were part of the act in London. Individuals or organizations needed to get their point of view over, and they spared no effort to do so. (Which was exactly what I had been telling the Labour Party, through the *Leeds Weekly Citizen*, if only they would listen). So the media had to be catered for in every way. They were never catered for better than at the Ministry of Labour where Charles Birdsall was in charge of relations with the media. Charlie, as he was known with genuine affection, had long experience of government press relations – both local and national – and a noble concept of service to his Minister, Department and media. Short, bald, grey with a bristly moustache, he looked like a retired major – Light Infantry, of course, because he did everything at a trot. He was the very embodiment of a civil servant. My colleagues who telephoned him in the early hours of the morning used to swear that he invariably responded: 'How nice of you to ring'. He also rang you back if he was not available when you called. This made him an example to all press officers, even when some of his calls at 8.30 p.m. caused you frantically to rewrite your first edition story. He spoiled many hot dinners.

I was also impressed with most of my fellow Labour reporters. They took their jobs seriously. Their conscientiousness was severely tested by the endless hanging around that 'doorstepping' meetings entails. To make life tolerable they helped each other and arranged informal rotas for patrolling meetings so that those who wanted to go to the nearest pub or cafe could enjoy a break safe in the knowledge that a runner would summon them when the talks ended. At the Ministry of Labour everyone could safely repair to the Red Lion, with its marvellous Victorian decorated glass partitions, because Charles himself would ensure that we were given early warning of movement. My fellow correspondents were, I judged, mostly well disposed to the trades unions and the Labour Party. Those of us who considered the trade union movement not without blemish never questioned the need for trade unions and saw their links with the Labour Party, which they substantially financed, as a consequence of history and a fact of life. Moreover, newspapers did not appoint Labour correspondents progressively to destroy their contacts by taking the movement apart. That was left to general reporters.

This was the congenial environment I entered – temporarily, I thought – on 17 May 1965. It was steeped in incomes policies and 3½ per cent pay norms; in the first references to the National Board for Prices and Incomes; in pay claims and leapfrogging, and in pay vetting by the TUC; in the monthly paranoia, which continues to this day, about the nation's economic health with the release of the unemployment figures and the index of retail prices; and in meetings of the TUC's 'inner cabinet' – its finance and general purposes committee – and general council and the monthly gatherings of the Labour Party's national executive. It saw the development of indicative planning, culminating in the publication of George Brown's National Plan in September. It provided example after example of the hard road to the reform of restrictive practices.

And, above all, it provided the Labour reporter's staple post-war diet: strikes. Over the five months between my arrival in London and settling my wife and son there in October my cuttings show I covered a dozen actual stoppages, and threats of many more. Battersea power workers, colliery deputies, ICT service engineers, baggage loaders at London Airport who wrecked Whitsun for many people to the ripe disgust of Ray Gunter, the Minister of Labour, scientists and technicians in the engineering industry and universities, London bus drivers, Bristol dockers, bread deliverymen, building workers on the Barbican site and, of course, car workers. They were all at it. And so were engine drivers – otherwise known as motormen – on Southern Region. They were at their disruptive worst for months over bonuses. My fellow Labour reporters thought I was mad to settle on Southern Region in Purley, Surrey.

This professional Yorkshireman, this dedicated provincial,

decided to move south after only a few weeks on relief in London. John Cole, a distinguished former Labour correspondent of the *Guardian* and then the news editor, asked me what I wanted to do and seemed a shade surprised, as he was entitled to be, when I said that I would like to stay in London. After all, I was rough hewn compared with the glitterati who sparkled in the *Guardian*'s London office. I had little social grace and even less time for some of the poseurs who inhabited the office. I had, however, swum not sunk in Gray's Inn Road and I felt it was perhaps about time that I had my share of the good life. In any case, where else was there to go? I felt that I would live to regret going back to the confines of Yorkshire. What is more, a move south would not damage my chances of a political career, if I wanted one. My reservations were solely on account of my family. I wondered how Nancy would settle and whether John's education would suffer. On the other hand, I argued with myself, others had made the move and lived to enjoy the much broader horizons. A *Guardian* pal of mine, Ken Dodd, formerly of the *Halifax Courier* and Newcastle *Evening Chronicle*, who had welcomed me to London, particularly encouraged me to move South. John Cole did not argue, though I suspect I did not fit in with his plans. So far as he was concerned I was now a member of the London Labour staff. I was to look for a house and move my family south, as he had done. Meanwhile, the *Guardian* would meet my hotel bills and fares home at week-ends for a reasonable period.

When it became known that I was moving south the clique moved in. Journalism is a highly competitive trade. But it is not as competitive as editors like to kid themselves or their readers that it is. In fact, it is riddled with cartels. As a craft practised by human beings, it exhibits all the failings adumbrated by Adam Smith. 'People of the same trade,' he wrote in the *Wealth of Nations*, 'seldom meet together, even for merriment and diversion, but the conversation ends in a conspiracy against the public, or in some contrivance to raise prices.' My conversation was in the basement of Congress House, the TUC's headquarters in Great Russell Street, where the designers had sensibly provided a row of public telephones. John Cole's elevation to news editor of the *Guardian* had left a gap in the defences of the major cartel among labour and industrial correspondents. He had worked closely with Geoffrey Goodman

(*Daily Mirror*), Ron Stevens (*Daily Telegraph*) and Keith McDowall (*Daily Mail*) who collectively had a singular ability to secure confidential documents out of Congress House. Peter Jenkins, my Number 1 on the *Guardian*, to his great credit, chose to remain a free agent. He was sufficiently well informed to make the major cartel feel uneasy, so the cartel wanted to get an inside track. I was the way in. Keith McDowall, the cartel's shop steward, sidled up to me at a telephone in the Congress House basement and engaged me in esoteric conversation. 'You can't expect to take anything out of the pot,' he said, 'unless you put something in it.' I said 'Yer what?' He said: 'You know what I mean.' And I said: 'Yes, I bloody well do. Clear off.' Or words to that effect.

Barrie Devney, then the Number 2 on the *Daily Express* to John Grant, soon to be Labour MP successively for Islington East and Islington Central and junior Minister, saw me emerge from the basement fulminating, choleric, explosive. In short, I was upset. 'And what on earth has upset you?' Barrie said, with all his basic kindness shining through. I told him the story. He tittered, as only Barrie could. 'And what did you say?' he asked. 'I told him to eff off,' I said, with all the emphasis at my command. 'Isn't that funny?' he laughed. 'That's exactly what I told him, too.'

Over the five months before I settled in London I moved, as dictated by American tourists, from the Mount Pleasant to the Russell and to the Imperial hotels within half a mile of Gray's Inn Road. I used the hotels as bed-and-breakfast establishments. I worked from about 10 a.m. until late into the evening, and sometimes after midnight; certainly until I had a copy of the first edition of the *Guardian* to go to bed with. Over these five months I gave the *Guardian* reader a good news service which was noted approvingly over lunch by trade union leaders. Alastair Hetherington, the editor, from whom I never had a wrong word, got used to having me around. He became a little restive when I was nowhere to be found with two pages of my summary of George Brown's National Plan in type and needing urgent clearance. I turned up in Gray's Inn Road at 11 p.m., feeling extremely pleased with myself, to make sure that there were no problems, have a snack in the canteen and collect a first edition. The editor, the reception desk growled, wanted me. I rolled into Alastair's office, having only recently poured Joe Gormley, the miners' leader, into a taxi. Alastair made the mistake of asking me where I had been. 'I have been drinking with the Prime Minister,' I replied, triumphantly, and without so much as a suppressed hiccup. Alastair grinned. He was a tolerant man. I had spent my first evening in Number 10 at a party for Labour and Industrial correspondents and all who float with them. I had even talked to the Prime Minister. My family were agog. 'Whatever is he going to do next?' I heard my parents say. My aunts in Fleetwood were to repeat it many times.

I settled where I was going to live in London not by reference to the disruptive tendencies of the motormen of the electrified Southern Region but because I had secured a place for my son in the Margaret Roper Roman Catholic junior school in Purley with the opportunity to progress to the John Fisher School nearby. And then I settled down to giving the reader a good news service on the economic/industrial/political/trade union front. I also formed my own alliances. At various times I worked with John Grant and Barrie Devney, of the *Express*; Mark Gapper and John Torode (*FT*); and, more closely with Monty Meth, when Keith McDowall had left the *Daily Mail* to which Monty had made a dramatic switch, and Michael Jones, whom I had first met in Darlington in my *Guardian* days in the North-East and who was then on the *Daily Telegraph*. In a loose way we carved up the day between us and swapped notes by telephone around 5 p.m. if we were not together engaged upon one of the major news stories of the day.

The beauty of working for the *Guardian* in those days, as for the *Yorkshire Post*, was that the reporter needed only two stage directions: his newspaper's interests; and the need for accuracy, fairness and balance in his reportage. I saw my responsibility to be straight with the readers in whatever I wrote. And I had confidence in Alastair Hetherington and John Cole to print whatever I did write, always assuming that they did not think I had suddenly become a candidate for a mental institution. By the same token, I assumed that Alastair and John had confidence in my integrity and judgement; if not, why were they employing me? This attitude informed my approach to all the posturing I was to encounter about the much reviled Lobby system fifteen to twenty years later when I was working for Mrs Thatcher in Number 10.

While my home was still in Leeds I received a number of invitations from the less promising Parliamentary constituencies in Yorkshire to seek nomination as a prospective candidate. I also made inquiries of an officer of the Sowerby division constituency party – a trade union official – as to how long Douglas Houghton was likely to continue and whether I had any hope of succeeding him. He was not entirely discouraging but suggested that I needed to secure trade union sponsorship. He also added that I would be aware that prophets tended to have little honour in their own Sowerby country. I toyed with the idea of seeking a seat to nurse but I could never bring myself to pursue a trade union sponsor. I just felt it was wrong for someone who was increasingly in his own mind identifying the unions as an abuse of power to seek their money. I also shuddered at the thought of having to take directions from some of the trade union leaders I had encountered. And surely, the idealistic Ingham said to himself, there should be nothing between an MP and his constituents. The idea of pursuing a political career withered over the months and was to all intents and purposes dead by the time I joined the Department of Employment and Productivity in 1968.

My growing disillusionment with the approach of the trade unions to the Labour Government they had so much wanted can to some extent be charted by my articles in the *Leeds Weekly Citizen* which I maintained from London, though with less frequency. By early December, 1965 I was moved by the trade unions' lack of restraint to write:

'Either we Trade Unionists believe what we say when we talk about the brotherhood of man and social justice or we don't. And if we are not prepared to practise what we preach – often, I suspect, so hypocritically from conference platforms – we should shut up. We – and that goes for me as well as every other Trade Unionist – have to show that we have the humanity we so often deny to capitalists. If we don't we shall be branded by history as the biggest hypocrites since the Bible-toting Victorian (and some Elizabethan) mill owners; the Sunday saints who literally overnight became or become Monday devils.'

That was Grandad Horsfall coming out in all his glory. For all his social and choral non-conformity, he tended to regard chapels and their associated Sunday Schools as to some extent feudal relics; a recruiting ground for the employers among the congregations.

By Christmas 1965 I was taking severely to task George Elvin, general secretary of the Association of Cinematograph, Television and Allied Technicians. Mr Elvin, in a letter to *The Times*, had written:

> 'We are dismayed to see our Government – because we are lifelong Socialists – ranged on the side of big business against our tiny union.'

In reply in the *Leeds Weekly Citizen* I let rip: 'The Government was not elected by Trade Unions to serve Trade Union ends. It was elected by the nation to serve the nation and – at least in the minds of many who voted for it – the wider cause of humanity. I say this as a Trade Unionist . . . Finally to reduce the issue to cynical political terms, there is no real reason why the Labour Government should be particularly kind to Trade Unions. Many of them – including those who boasted about the amount of money they pumped into Labour's election machine – have so far done precious little of their own free will to support it in practical terms on the economic front . . . Mr Elvin is party to an active campaign by white collar technicians' Unions against the incomes policy. I think, therefore, that he has a confounded cheek to suggest that the Labour Government owes him anything. In cold political terms – and those were the terms on which he was arguing in the letter – I consider him a liability to the Labour Government. If nobody else will tell him so, I will.'

I am sure I felt better after that. For someone who was being advised to seek trade union sponsorship for a seat, it was a queer way of going about it, especially when the writer's identity was not concealed by the pseudonym from those in the know in Leeds Labour circles. But it was the way I had been brought up. My branch of the Labour Party knew the meaning of loyalty and discipline. There did not seem much of it around.

There seemed even less when a regular contributor to the *Guardian*, Richard Gott, threatened to stand for the Radical Alliance in a by-election in the Labour marginal Hull North constituency in protest against the conflict in Vietnam. I wrote: 'the unkindest cut of all is that Mr Richard Gott . . . is a member of the Labour Party. He is prepared because of what I accept is a sincere abhorrence of the conflict in Vietnam personally to bring down the Labour Government . . . As an individual he has a perfect right to seek this sort of glory, or infamy, depending on one's point of view. But as a member of the Labour Party he has no right at all. He surrendered the right to act in this way the minute he joined it . . . He is in these circumstances no better than the meanest Young Socialist who has been corrupted by that miserable bunch of intel- lectual bullies . . . which inhabits the fringes of the Labour Movement.'

Mr Gott, in the event, did not pull the temple down. But there were lots of others at it. I reported that 1966 began more peacefully than the previous year. None the less, in the run up to the April election I covered industrial stoppages of one kind or another among bakers, London busmen and Southern Region motormen, IPC printers over the introduction of webb offset at Southwark and printers in national newspapers because of union rivalries, building workers on the Commercial Union site in London, BMC and Vaux- hall car delivery drivers and Ford paint sprayers at Dagenham, among other motor workers at Standard Triumph and among Indian rubber-workers in Hayes, near London Airport. There was also a hullabulloo about kangaroo courts in the motor industry and the famous Jack Dash was in full throat about Devlin's proposed reforms in the docks.

Meanwhile, Lord Justice Donovan conducted his inquiries into the trade union movement. I enjoyed covering the public hearings – or at least writing my sketches of the appearances by trade union leaders before the Commission. Sir William Carron, president of the AEU, gave me most fun. 'The batsman did not score many runs,' I said. 'But they did not get him out either. Sir William . . . a Yorkshireman, of course, defied Lord Donovan's admittedly depleted team for two hours with the straightest – and broadest – bat so far seen in this predictable Test series.'

The trade union movement did not seem to care that it was presenting itself as one of the most entrenched of conservative elements in society, determined to preserve its power base at all costs, regardless of the mainfest damage to the country. Sometimes it appeared absurd. Alastair Hetherington warmed to my two by-lined accounts of the inter-union row between Messrs Richard Briginshaw (NATSOPA) and John Bonfield (NGA) over whose member should have his finger on the button to start the new rotary press in the *Birmingham Post and Mail*'s machine-room. This had become a matter of some moment since Princess Margaret had been invited to inaugurate the new press and she needed to be licensed to do so. Mr Briginshaw solved the problem by issuing the Princess with honorary membership of NATSOPA with gold lettering. He even had the gall to tell reporters that this honorary membership would bring Princess Margaret into 'fraternal trade union association' with her then husband, Lord Snowdon (the former Tony Armstrong-Jones), a member of the National Union of Journalists. It would not, I reported, 'qualify Brother Tony to press the button. That privilege is reserved to members of NATSOPA – and Sister Margaret, no less.' Mr Bonfield found all this in poor taste and 'for those who care a button', I added, the only people on a press who had exclusive rights were machine manager members of the NGA. Fortunately, Mr Bonfield did not press the point.

Labour reporters needed a little light relief. Far too often we were left looking for Charles Birdsall's Chinese electrician – as he described chinks of light – in peace talks at the Ministry. But worse was to come. The seamen's strike was looming. The last thing a Labour Government needed was such a self-inflicted wound upon the nation's trade. It came soon after the Government had been returned with a massively increased majority of 97. I agreed with the *Daily Mirror* that Labour now had no alibis to fall back on.

For forty-seven days I covered the strike morning, noon and late into the summer's night. From the shipowners in the City to the Clapham HQ of the National Union of Seamen, to the TUC, to the Ministry of Labour, to Number 10 and some days to the office in Gray's Inn Road to let them know I was not just a by-line at the end of a telephone. From inquiry to inquiry, from Chinese electrician and rising hopes to deadlock and despair. From Harold Wilson's 'tightly knit group of politically motivated men' – as he described an element in the National Union of Seamen – to the

TUC's 'inner Cabinet'. Early in the strike I found that the 'inner Cabinet' was far from tightly knit and apparently unconcerned. It had in fact taken off to the four corners of the earth – by air, of course. Joe O'Hagan, the TUC's chairman, who could only have been a blastfurnaceman to look at him, was in Guyana for their independence celebrations; Harry Nicholas, Transport and General, was in Utrecht; Lord Collison (agricultural workers) in Geneva; Lewis Wright (weavers) in America; Sir William Carron, Jack Cooper (GMWU) and Sir Tom O'Brien (theatrical and kine employees) at union conferences in Llandudno and Torquay; Sid Green (NUR) somewhere 'out of town'; Sir Harry Douglass was at the mayor-making of one of his steelworkers in Scunthorpe; Wilfred Beard (patternmakers) was detained in his office; and sadly George Lowthian (building workers) was in hospital. Only John Newton, tailors and garment workers, turned up for a meeting with George Woodcock, the TUC's general secretary. Not surprisingly, they decided that nothing could be done.

To be fair, a full turn-out would probably have been able to do nothing either. This was a strike which had to run its course until the seamen's union's inexperienced executive learned to compromise. I charted its relentless course as fully and as fairly as my rigorous journalistic upbringing required. And, to repeat, the beauty of pursuing this kind of running story – or any other – for the *Guardian*, as for the *Yorkshire Post*, was that was how they wanted it: full, fair, straight and accurate. I set out my opinions in the *Leeds Weekly Citizen*. Going back over my cuttings, there is not the slightest doubt that for me this was both a tremendous journalistic experience and a political nightmare. It was not a political watershed.

With the strike scarcely a week old I had sadly, almost despairingly condemned it. First, I set out the facts of the case. I quote:

'The seamen, comparing their lot with other seafarers from developed countries, think they are getting a raw deal. They have some justification. But last year they won a big increase of more than £8 a month for the ordinary AB, part of which was intended as compensation for being willing to work up to eight hours on both Saturday and Sunday when at sea.

84

'They get the money whether the work is actually performed or not. This increased their earnings 13 per cent.

'Then this year they went for a reduction in their official working week from 56 to 40 hours. And they demanded that the monthly consolidated rate, on which overtime pay is calculated, should remain the same.

'In other words, they wanted paying overtime for working at weekends while retaining the compensation given last year for week-end work . . .

'If they were to get it their earnings would be increased by a further 17 per cent this year. That would mean that over the space of two years the seamen would have achieved an average annual increase of 15 per cent.

'Even if, like George Woodcock, you regard rigid adherence to the norm of 3½ per cent as impossible, you can scarcely stretch the policy to 15 per cent without snapping it altogether.'

I then went on to analyse the situation in the industry.

'No doubt,' I wrote, 'some shipowners could afford to concede the Union's demand for a 40-hour week now. Others might very well be driven out of business if they tried to meet it. But costs would rise and our exports and imports would become dearer unless, of course, there was a corresponding increase in efficiency to absorb the increased outgoing. All these are important points.

'But so is the fact that the seamen feel disgruntled. Communists have had a big hand in forcing the strike but we cannot simply see it all as a dirty totalitarian plot. Not all the 47 members of the NUS executive are Communists – not by a long chalk. Yet they have been consistently unanimous in favour of taking on the shipowners, the Government and the State.

'They are obviously steamed up. Officially their fight is with the shipowners. But they know as well as the next man that they are also fighting the Government which they, on the whole, elected . . . They are an uncommonly frank and open crew.

'It is their realization of what they are doing that is, to me, the saddest part of this whole miserable affair. What it means is that brother has been set against brother. One brother is challenging what the other stands for.'

I concluded that the seamen were sabotaging the Government's chances of successfully applying the policies it was elected to carry out. 'They are conspiring,' I wrote, 'to set back the progressive forces which were unleashed at the general election. Not to put too fine a point on it, they are conniving at a resurgence of the doctrines which will hurtfully restrain them instead of ... them voluntarily [restraining] themselves.'

I suspected that this blast of common sense would bring a reaction in Leeds. But without knowing whether it did or not, I was firing away on all guns at the seamen the following week. I was not 'over-impressed' by the use of the doctors' £1000 a year pay increase to justify the seamen's demands when the doctors submitted their pay to inquiry and the seamen wouldn't. We should be prepared to submit our disputed claims to independent examination instead of knocking seven bells out of an already delicate economy.

Then came a cry from the heart: 'The fact that some doctors held the country to ransom – and I have no doubt that some tried to do – is no reason why we – or the seamen – should do so ... If we are all to be renegades there's not much a Government can do but hold the ring. Is that what we want for the next four years?'

When it was all over I immediately wrote two articles, one for the *Guardian* and one for the *Leeds Weekly Citizen*. In the *Guardian* I said all concerned in the strike would be able to claim a victory of sorts if they ignored the enormous and damaging costs. I tried to be fair to all sides. But I concluded that 'the militants were defeated as much as the rest by the Government's stand on the incomes policy. Their real gain beyond Pearson [an inquiry] amounts to 0.3 per cent – if the arithmetic is right. The headline on my story read: 'Biggest sea strike victory belongs to Government'. When, soon afterwards, I rang George Woodcock to ask for an interview, I had to persuade him. 'You've said it all,' he commented.

The other article was for the *Leeds Weekly Citizen*. I started it by saying that if anyone thought that the forces of moderation had enjoyed watching the progressive isolation of the NUS they had better think again. Like many distasteful things it had been necessary, 'and it has been necessary because the seamen have been wrong'. I concluded with a passage which probably encapsulates best of all my disillusionment at that time:

> 'We were told that the 1964 and 1966 intakes into Parliament were the brightest and best for many a long year. To me the events of the last few weeks have neither proved their brilliance nor their worth; merely their dumbness. Of course, they may not have wished to exacerbate feelings. If that is their only reason for not speaking out then I can excuse their reticence, however strange it is to discover that politicians can keep their mouths shut.
>
> 'But my guess is that far too many of them, with Trade Union ties, have found it difficult to speak out. If that is so – and I will be happy to be corrected – it reflects no credit on the system of sponsorship. A lot of things have needed saying over the last four weeks; and the last four weeks provided the opportunity for speaking them.
>
> 'It grieves me that I have had to say them in the *Citizen*. I expect MPs to speak out against wrongs, including Trade Union wrongs. They can't be popular all the time. But they might have been a lot more popular than they think if they had been saying the things I have been writing in this journal. I have found after (and not before) the event that many of my views are shared by sound, sane and by no means unmilitant Trade Unionists. I'd better end there before I say too much!'

If anyone wants to put a date on it, Ingham met Thatcher in heart, mind and spirit thirteen years almost to the day before they clapped eyes on each other in the flesh.

The Labour Party hierarchy in Leeds now knew they had a disaffected columnist on their hands. He did not think much of the trade unions and even less of MPs. He thought far too many of them for the party's good were a bunch of hypocrites. But if they thought they had a starry-eyed idealist on the rampage, I never got the message. Solly Pearce remained true and welcoming to my increasingly intermittent blasts. After all, he was an editor. He wanted people to read his newspaper. And controversy made for interest. But I was also loyal to what most members of the party thought they were supposed to stand for. At least their voice was heard.

The *Guardian*, which paid my wages, was just as satisfied. I had every reason to suppose that I was regarded as a good, sound, reliable and sensible reporter who covered his wapentake conscientiously, extensively and thoroughly. I got the comforting impression for one who never regarded his job as safe that I was an asset. For one thing I gave them a news service. After four years in the company's employment, I was also coming up for my month's sabbatical. For a change, I would be away while others covered the waterfront. But what would I do with the four weeks? We were supposed to use it for 'intellectual refreshment'. I decided to go fishing – to Bear Island in a Hull trawler in midwinter. After all, I told myself, whistling in the dark, I had never been seasick – not even in a force ten gale off the Isle of Skye during a Scottish National Trust cruise on which Harry Whewell had sent me in my Leeds days. During the storm the grand piano in the ballroom had broken loose causing devastation. My trade union contact promised to make all the arrangements. There would be no trouble. I would be well looked after. If my wife had any reservations she kept them to herself. By now she had got used to my dedication to journalism. And then benign fate struck in disguise. The *Guardian* which, to the scorn of fellow journalists on the *Manchester Evening News*, had always led a subsidized existence – subsidized, that is, by the *Evening News* – ran into a severe economic storm. It kept me in port.

After my service as treasurer of the Halifax branch of the NUJ, where I insisted that the rules over payment of subscriptions would be rigorously enforced – which led to the lapsing of the most self-important senior journalist on the *Halifax Courier* – I had acquired the position of deputy father of the *Yorkshire Post* NUJ chapel in Leeds when trouble with the editor brewed. Now I found myself deputy father of the *Guardian* NUJ London chapel. Would I ever have a quiet life? This time it was a lot more serious because the management were determined to cut back. I felt I simply could not take a sabbatical whether to Bear Island, Blackpool or Bognor, to keep matters within my pocket. I was reinforced in this view by the editor, Alastair Hetherington, after the first utterly disastrous meeting between Laurence Scott, the chairman, and Jim Bradley, general secretary of the NUJ.

Mr Bradley – I expected more from a chap from Keighley – had got off to a very bad start with the *Guardian*'s staff at a mass meeting in the Conway Hall. He very insensitively said that he was not going to postpone a visit elsewhere simply to fit in with the convenience of the *Guardian*'s management. This was not what his members whose jobs were at stake wanted to hear. My job was not at stake – at least not immediately – so I could tell Mr Bradley in no uncertain terms that he would do what his members who paid his salary wanted, or else. He did. It would have been better had he not. I have seen some explosive relationships in my time but Bradley and Scott were like nitro-glycerine. The detonator was a meeting between the nitrate and the glycerine. Whatever Alastair Hetherington and I (with the support of a constructive, young sub-editor, John Ryan, the father of the chapel, who went on to become part of East Midlands Allied Press management) had agreed in advance, with reasonable confidence in carrying our two sides, was almost certainly going to blow up in our faces.

Scott had a very serious problem which would have been entirely manageable had the printing unions known the meaning of the word reasonable. Bradley had an entirely justifiable complaint which both Alastair Hetherington and I recognized: the management were asking for disproportionate redundancies from journalists in order to get some cuts out of the printers. But what mattered was how to achieve an acceptable, decent and humane settlement, taking account of all the realities of power and its abuse, and save the *Guardian*. I simply do not know how we managed to conciliate our way through to a settlement. I suppose that self-interest on the part of all concerned eventually prevailed. But the episode did nothing for my already jaundiced opinions of both management and unions.

With that out of the way – along with my sabbatical – I was next presented with what has been described as the humiliating experience which drove me out of journalism. It was the refusal of the *Guardian* to promote me from being the second man on its

Labour staff – there were only two us – to become Labour correspondent in succession to Peter Jenkins who was moving upwards and onwards within the *Guardian*. The conventional wisdom, now hardened into fact, is that I was so insulted by the *Guardian*'s failure to recognize my talents that I slung my hook, as they say in Hebden Bridge; in short, that I left in a huff. That is not so.

Let us consider the evidence, as Judge Pickles used to say in Halifax Quarter Sessions where, to do justice to this home-made legal thespian, he did a better job of representing his clients than many other junior barristers. First, like an old sweat, I did my share of grumbling about Peter Jenkins's propensity for pursuing his own interests and his cavalier approach to a basic news service. But I had long seen it as my duty to keep the reader informed while Peter hunted for his earth-shattering exclusive. I got my kicks out of seeing a reliable news service, mostly written by me, each morning. Second, I was by no means impressed with the argument that exclusives sell newspapers. Most exclusives were, and remain, at best an elastic interpretation of the word and at worst a con job; a fraud upon the reader. And the fortunes of a newspaper are not built on casual sales. Exclusives are mostly written by journalists for journalists. John Cole, the news editor, also knew I took a sceptical view of his emphasis on the need for all self-respecting Labour reporters to get their hands on confidential TUC and other documents. This preoccupation with leaked documents led to nonsense in which the most extreme option for action canvassed in them became the news story – of course – to the virtual exclusion of the most likely option. Third, I was still not over-endowed with self-confidence. I saw myself as a plain, straightforward reporter; not as someone to justify Dame Rebecca West's definition of journalism as an ability to meet the challenge of filling the space. I was not a word spinner. And, fourth, I was not the evolving type of *Guardian* man: amazingly self-confident but on occasion unreliable and often malicious. They were not that bad in my day, not by a long chalk, but you could see the way things were going.

Against this background, I would have been rather surprised to be made Labour Correspondent – that is, the Number 1 in that specialism. I suppose I would have liked to be given the job, but had I been I would once again have been overawed and felt very insecure. The *Guardian* was not the easiest of newspapers on which to be Labour correspondent. Both John Anderson, an assistant editor, and John Cole had done the job themselves, and the remit to cover the Labour Party could make for a difficult relationship with the political staff. I was, to be realistic, not ready for the job after less than twelve months in London, always assuming that I would ever have fitted the *Guardian*'s bill for the post. I cannot say that I never grumbled about jobs for the boys, for Peter Jenkins was succeeded by a close friend of mine, John Torode, who was then a young member of the *Financial Times* Labour staff. But the notion that this left me with a permanent grudge against the *Guardian* and that I left it humiliated and embittered for ever against journalism and journalists is bunkum – and balderdash, too.

Again, consider the evidence. I left the *Guardian* but only after repeated and unavailing attempts to persuade the management to freeze my pension. I contemplated leaving the *Guardian* not with the intention of never returning but with a determination to try to preserve my links and a way back. In the end the management felt obliged to set out on paper, somewhat testily, their utter refusal to preserve my pension. If I had a grudge against anyone it was the management, which apparently had scant regard for my efforts to keep the ship afloat during the 1966–7 winter.

I left to join the National Board for Prices and Incomes on May Day 1967 after the intervention of Eric Jacobs whom I had succeeded two years earlier on the *Guardian*. Eric's recollection is that he rang Peter Jenkins to let him know that he was returning to journalism – to the *Sunday Times* – after fulfilling his contract with the Prices and Incomes Board and that almost immediately afterwards I rang him to inquire whether there might be an opening for me at the Board. I have no idea precisely how Eric Jacobs and I came to meet in the Marquis of Granby at Charing Cross to discuss my succeeding him. My impression is that both Peter Jenkins and Eric Jacobs thought it would be a good idea if I explored the opening because – and this was, for me, the clinching argument – I would be a much better journalist for the experience of working in Whitehall. It was for that reason, and the opportunity to work with the chairman and the Board, that I signed a two-year-contract, initially at £3500 a year, on the assumption that I would return to Fleet Street, if not necessarily the *Guardian*.

My colleagues on the *Guardian* gave me as a parting gift some cricket gear – pads, gloves and bat. I had resumed playing cricket at the instigation of Gwyn Morgan, the head of the Labour Party's international department, with Woodmansterne, a village club with a lovely sylvan ground in the North Downs near my home. Compared with others who were leaving the *Guardian* at the same time, I was told I displayed no emotion in expressing my thanks for companionship and the gifts. This may, of course, have been because I, at least, did not think I was necessarily saying good-bye.

8

My University

My scepticism in the early 1960s about incomes policies may have owed something to the colour of the Government which was administering them. I was not programmed to believe that the Conservatives had the interests of workers at heart. I was also the recipient from trade union leaders of a welter of arguments about the inherent unfairness of such policies in bearing down on the worker's pocket, while doing precious little about the rewards to others. Harry Whewell once provocatively saw incomes policy as only for the big battalions; if you were small enough – and not affiliated to the TUC – you could, he thought, probably get away with anything. Union leaders were also chronically against interference in free collective bargaining. I was more inclined to be influenced by notions of fairness than by union antagonisms to any change in their institutional arrangements, especially when those selfsame unions were in favour of revolutionizing or interfering in anything else that moved. I was wary of any argument which sought to have it both ways.

It was, however, difficult to defend the jungle of British industrial relations and their implications for costs, competitiveness and the disruption and damage inflicted on the poor bloody infantry by militants who were playing a wrecking game. While I had a romantic view of the ordinary miner which Grandma Horsfall, a miner's daughter, had helped to form, I was under no illusions about the jungle they also inhabited. The calibre of the pickets which sometimes appeared outside the Yorkshire miners' headquarters in Huddersfield Road, Barnsley, reminded me irresistibly of Marlon Brando's epic *On the Waterfront*.

In truth, I was torn between a highly developed sense of equity and loyalty to working people and a feeling that industry – both

93

management and unions – was in a mess. My own working life had been littered from the *Hebden Bridge Times* onwards with examples of the inadequacies of managements and unions and sometimes, it seemed, their perversities. I held no brief for management. I was deeply wary of so-called professional bodies on the basis of my experience on the *Yorkshire Post* where some members of the supposedly more genteel Institute of Journalists had been keener on a strike by the NUJ against the editor than NUJ members themselves. And the *Guardian*'s own industrial relations had done nothing to encourage me to a more favourable view. On the contrary, they had demonstrated just how bad a mess things could get into if a clash of personalities compounded a company's difficulties. Something needed to be done. Writing in the *Leeds Weekly Citizen* on the death of Sir Winston Churchill in January 1965, I commented:

> 'Britain self-evidently needs the sense of urgency which Sir Winston, as Mr Churchill, brought to a war-beleaguered world.'

It seemed to me, in my simple, direct, way that a Labour government opened the way to reform. It was a government which had been elected on a popular platform and with a positive desire to promote continuous growth, greater efficiency in industry, a fairer distribution of wealth and reasonable social provision. It went without saying, in view of my upbringing, that it had to be supported. But the point for me was that it deserved support. It was at least trying.

> 'Can anything be the same after Mr Gunter's forthright condemnation of the "viciousness" of BEA strikers at London Airport at Whitsuntide?' I wrote in July 1965. '. . . I may be wrong, but my guess is that after eight months in office the Labour Government has managed to bring a subtle change in attitude on this subject. Mr Aubrey Jones's Prices and Incomes Board, for example, has demonstrated that business – in this case the road hauliers – have restrictive practices as well as trade unions. And it has had the Government's backing in challenging both management and Unions about various aspects of haulage operation.

94

'What is more,' I added, hopefully, 'there is probably a lot more of this sort of "change through challenge" reporting to come from the board.'

Five months later at Christmas 1965, I was wondering why on earth the Government was persevering with a prices and incomes policy when it had been written off so many times that 'it seems to be a hopeless chase after the impossible'. I went on to answer the question, and I shall quote from the *Leeds Weekly Citizen* extensively because it is so revealing of my attitude at that time:

'The answer of course is that ... the prices and incomes policy really is working in the only way it can work, whatever the short term figures for earnings may show.

'It is working – and I state this categorically – because it is beginning to influence men's minds and perhaps their hearts.

'Anyone who thought that a voluntary incomes policy would overnight automatically restrict pay and price increases to 3.5 per cent a year was either mad or naïve. You cannot get people to give up immediately long established practices, such as a whopping annual pay claim, even if they are convinced they ought to.

'But what you can do is so to educate individuals on the inevitability of an incomes policy in one form or another that in framing their next demand – either on the customer or the employer – they bear in mind the criteria of the incomes policy.

'This is what is now happening. Of course, it doesn't restrict price increases or pay settlements to the norm of 3.5 per cent. If it did it would be freezing everything into its present highly unsatisfactory mould.

'Of course, some unions and some monopolies still try to use their power to take out of the national fund more than their fair share.

'Others who have no power – and perhaps don't deserve any because of their snobbish attitude to Trade Unionism and its measures – get less. It is still an unfair world.

'What to wage earners are huge dividends are still being

95

paid out. And prices are still going up although more slowly than they did during the latter part of Tory rule. But we have now reached a situation where everyone now thinks twice before he acts ... We are becoming more price and cost conscious. A new element in the form of the Government has entered into price and wage determination. Its effect is potentially very great. We are now beginning to see some of its potential.'

More than two years before I joined the Prices and Incomes Board I was exhibiting strong – not to say optimistic – support for the prices and incomes policy as a means to reform. I saw it as a powerful catalyst, provided the Government did not try to go too fast. Six months on – in July 1966 – I was tearing into Frank Cousins on his resignation from the Government over the Prices and Incomes Bill – five months after its first draft had appeared but with an increase, in the interim, of the Goverment's majority by ninety-four. In other words, I did not take too seriously a resignation which circumstances had made possible. As I saw it, Frank Cousins was 'hell-bent – perhaps unconsciously – on producing the very unemployment both he and Left wingers so shrilly – and justifiably – abhor. This will be an unusual service for a Trade Union leader to perform for his members.

'But not merely Frank Cousins and Left-Wingers abhor unemployment,' I added. 'All rational people do. And this is why they have flung their weight behind the Productivity, Prices and Incomes policy. Speaking for myself I would rather restrain myself voluntarily than be restrained.'

The National Board for Prices and Incomes was not merely recruiting a press and public relations adviser with two years' experience of reporting its work; it was also acquiring a strong supporter of its concept of change through challenge. On May Day 1967 I temporarily, as I thought, abandoned my role as chronicler of the prices and incomes policy and as columnist in both the *Leeds Weekly Citizen* and *Socialist Commentary*, a moderate (some would say rightwing) Labour journal, for promoting the cause of industrial and economic reform from within.

While I was very familiar with the policy, I had very little idea what to expect when I walked into Kingsgate House, a modern office block just up the road leading to Parliament Square from Victoria Station. Nor had I much idea how I fitted into the hierarchy. I discovered from my secretary, Elizabeth Capel-Dunn, that my Civil Service rank of Assistant Secretary was equivalent to that of a brigadier. I found this hilarious. I also found that I had a great deal of time to contemplate my newly elevated station in life, sitting in my well appointed office overlooking Victoria Street. Everyone was very pleasant and welcoming. Never had I been better housed. Never before had I had the services of a secretary. And never before in my life had I had so little to do. Hardly any journalists telephoned. I did not need to read myself in much since I had been covering the Board from its inception. It did not take me long to meet my three other support staff, Michael Becket, who went on to become a *Daily Telegraph* business journalist, Frank Scott and Mrs Waller. By the end of the first week I wondered what I had let myself in for. The pay was good, though I had lost my expenses account, but the boredom was immense.

After more than eighteen mostly busy years in journalism the Prices and Incomes Board came as a shock to the system. It might have been better had I immediately been called upon to help present one of its major reports. Instead the only publication in my first week there was a statistical supplement to Report No 29 on the pay and conditions of manual workers in local authorities, the National Health Service and the gas and water supply industries. Statistical supplements were dry as dust to the media. I have little doubt now that the chairman, Aubrey Jones, the secretary, Alex Jarratt, and John Woolf, who was technically my immediate boss, thought they were doing me a good turn by a allowing me to settle in. But they had a rather demoralized press and PR adviser on their hands after only five days. My spirits were not improved when I discovered that even Eric Jacobs, who was a much more leisurely type than me, had grown progressively bored with the entire operation.

With hindsight, it was silly of me to be so impatient. It was the most unrepresentative start to any job I have ever done. Within a few weeks I was working harder than ever in a post which I have since come to regard as my university. The Board gave me a twelve-month crash course not merely in press and public relations but also in politics, economics, administration and the organization and operations of central government. In some thirty reports published over this period it took me into about fourteen different industries and professions from banking to the solicitors' branch of the legal profession and through motor repair and servicing, milk distribution and brick and cement production to national newspapers. I was also grounded in a host of labour issues such as comparability, national versus local bargaining, pay structures, shift working and flexible hours, restrictive practices and productivity agreements.

And I really did try to master each report, producing a lengthy press summary on each – far too lengthy in retrospect. It would have been better for the media had I produced just a short press notice setting out the essential findings and either have allowed that to stand on its own or used it to cover a longer summary. I defended the lengthy summaries on the grounds that, since the Board's job was to educate and influence people's behaviour, we were more likely to do so if we could give inquirers a substantial summary rather than advising them to buy a copy from HMSO.

The Board had been set up in April 1965 as part of the machinery agreed, in those corporatist days, between the Government, the TUC and employers' organizations for the administration of a policy for productivity, prices and incomes. It was part of yet another attempt to find a route to overall price stability and continuous economic growth in an era of relatively full employment and trade union power. The aim of public policy, set down during World War II, to conquer chronic unemployment had been substantially secured. But it had given rise to inflation which was continually eroding our competitive position. However, with inflation then running at only 3.5 per cent or so, things were not all that bad. Inflation was to peak in less than eight years at nearly 27 per cent. I sometimes wondered in the 1970s how much good all our meddling had done, without, of course, knowing whether inflation would have peaked even higher if we had not meddled.

Previous attempts to reconcile full employment and inflation had collapsed fairly quickly, primarily because they had been imposed upon industry, commerce and trade unions. The Three Wise Men and the National Incomes Commission which, with straining ears, I had tried to cover on circuit in Edinburgh, had bitten the dust.

The Prices and Incomes Board was different. It was part of an agreed approach and its remit was to look into prices and productivity as well as incomes of all kinds – and not merely those of industrial workers. In other words, its comprehensive approach made it look fairer. It did not, however, have a licence to roam. It could only conduct inquiries at the express request of the Government.

From the outset its approach had appealed to my reformist instincts which are so amply documented by the *Leeds Weekly Citizen*. It saw itself as a catalyst for changing 'old habits, inherited attitudes and institutional arrangements' by 'conducting a continuing dialogue with managements, unions and indeed Government'. Its official handbook, of which I became the editor, gave it three functions: educative, consultancy and judicial. The explanation of these three roles had a fine ring to it:

'1 Educative: It is argued that the Board would be doing a valuable job if it merely collected, processed and published statistical information, so little do we know about what is happening in the economy. But the Board's educative function is not fulfilled simply by replacing supposition with fact. It is also concerned with bringing home to individual members of the community, or individual groups, the consequences of their actions for the community as a whole and with evoking a positive response from that deeper understanding. Thus the Board's reports are designed as far as possible to contain judgements and recommendations which will be of general as well as particular value. It is part of its philosophy that, granted the soundness of its judgement and recommendations, public opinion cannot for long remain impervious to its arguments.

'2 Consultancy: This function is inherent in the Government's decision to call in an independent outsider to examine the particular problems of an industry, company or plant. The Board is in a position to encourage change because of its status as a disinterested, independent body without bias to any particular interest. It tries to offer its advice in a constructive rather than a recriminatory spirit for it seeks to convince and persuade rather than to browbeat.

'3 Judicial: This function follows from the fact that the Board is required by law to form its own judgements in relation to the criteria for prices and incomes behaviour as set out in the White Paper governing the current phase of policy. But the Board has never conceived its task simply to be to say "Yes" or "No" to proposals which come before it. Its preoccupation has been to improve upon, or mitigate, particular proposals by stimulating further improvements in productivity.'

Few journalists, set on improving themselves within government, could have found an institution so closely in tune with their reformist instinct for what was required at the time. When I arrived the board was preparing for the move to the fourth phase of prices and incomes policy in twenty-seven months. It had been launched as a Royal Commission operating a voluntary policy with a 3–3.5 per cent pay norm. It became a statutory body when, after a sterling crisis, the Government legislated for a six-month pay and price freeze followed by another six months of 'severe restraint' during which employees could only justify pay increases on grounds of a direct contribution to higher productivity or for social reasons because of chronically low pay. We were now to enter a period of moderation which heralded a return to an essentially voluntary policy. The board's operational methods were well established, with individual inquiries led by a member of the Board and a senior civil servant. They drafted the report for approval by the Board. The chairman, Aubrey Jones, a former Conservative Minister of Fuel and Power and of Supply and former chairman of Staveley Industries and Laporte, himself led the major inquiries.

My basic task was to advise Aubrey Jones, his Board members and Alex Jarratt on their dealings with the media and how best to get over their messages both to particular audiences and the general public. To this end I attended Board meetings and thereby absorbed for future use in briefing the arguments in support of the Board's recommendations. On average, while I was with it, the Board produced three reports a month. As well as writing the press notices on each report, I arranged press conferences and briefed the chairman on how to use them to best effect. I issued speeches on important issues and generally tried to promote a wider understanding of the Board's work and its findings. I invited journalists to meet the chairman, Board members and senior officials over buffet lunches and spoke to a wide variety of outside organizations about the Board's work. At the same time I was responsible for handling general correspondence from the public and issuing the Board's briefing material. We never did get over to the public that the Board was not the place to register complaints about pay or, more usually, price increases. We had to forward thousands of letters to the various responsible government departments listed in the Board's handbook. I also began to produce a house magazine, PIB News, which gave me an outlet for commenting on the national scene, subject to Alex Jarratt's approval of the text. Not for the last time, I found a top civil servant adventurous in allowing me to liven things up and to help create a better *esprit de corps*.

Within a few weeks of my arrival my small information team was working harder than it had ever done before. When Michael Becket left I recruited Jim Nash, a moderate trade unionist, who had handled the media for the National Union of Seamen during the strike which I covered. He therefore knew the parish and our parishioners. Jim was fastidious about his working environment and seemed disconcerted by having to carve his own room out of a larger office using filing cabinets. Since it was such a big room he felt he would spread himself a bit. I was perfectly content with this arrangement but sticklers about entitlements within the Board said he qualified for only two windows instead of three or four. This led to a ludicrous and prolonged battle over the precise placing of filing cabinets which was at once hilarious and depressing. It made me again wonder what I had joined.

On the other hand, I soon discovered it was an incredibly sociable institution. Alex Jarratt, who became a close personal friend, paid a lot of attention to teamwork and morale. He was far from the popular concept of the staid civil servant. Tall, slim, prematurely grey with a full head of hair, he cut a bit of a dash. He worked incredibly hard and played hard, too. And expected everyone else to do the same. Parties were held for no better reason than that someone had got another report off his chest, or because somebody else just felt like celebrating. John Woolf, from Customs and Excise to which he returned to be a Commissioner, ran as tight a ship as was allowed by the motley collection of 250 civil servants culled from different Departments: accountants, economists, statisticians, industrial relations advisers and Ingham, the journalist devoid of any house training. The place was full of people who, if not necessarily sympathetic to the Government, seemed genuinely enthusiastic about the possibility of influencing behaviour and securing reform which would benefit the country and working people. They also ran a league table of inverted snobbery based upon parentage. The son of a weaver was virtually a member of the bourgeoisie. You scored much better if you could say 'My old man's a dustman.'

Aubrey Jones, the chairman, had no doubts about the Board's potential. This slight, fastidious and rather fussy man was not a dominating character in either Board meetings or at press conference. But his intellect -- and ambition – dominated the Board's work and his restless determination to open up the commanding heights as well as the nooks and crannies of the economy to public scrutiny and pressure for reform made for an interesting though not easy life.

For example, by the time I arrived the brewers had entered into the Board's folklore as one of the more conservative elements in our society after Report No 13 had found no justification for raising the price of the workers' beer. Brewers, it said, got a return on capital comparable to that of manufacturing and distribution generally for less risk. They could be more efficient. And they had no justification for asking the consumer to foot the bill for large increases in labour costs which had not been offset by changes in working practices. In my time the bankers' came to rival the brewers' reputation for conservatism. This was underlined by their reaction to Report No 34 on bank charges which came out with proposals for opening up the banks to the invigorating air of competition and ending collective agreements on charges. Both of these reports also revealed a technique with which I was to become very familiar in government: few inquiries put an issue to bed; instead they invariably suggest fresh fields for investigation. In the case of the brewers, Aubrey – as we called him when we did not have to call him chairman – suggested an inquiry into how control over the sale of liquor might be maintained without impeding the entry of new competitors into the industry. In the case of the banks, he reported that 'it seems to us that it may not be possible to carry out some of the recommendations to their full conclusion without a complementary study of other parts of the financial system – e.g. the discount houses'.

By then Mr Jones, the public scrutineer, had become efficiency auditor to the nationalized industries under the automatic reference to the Board of major nationalized industry price increases from September 1967. He saw himself, I am sure, as a consultant to the nation. All this created tensions within the Board as well as outside it. There were certainly fears that the Board might overreach itself. Aubrey seemed to entertain none of these doubts. He was thoroughly enjoying himself. This was not, however, necessarily so with the trade union officials who had accepted appointments as full- or part-time members of the Board. They were like fish out of water, with too little to do and no doubt subject to pressures of one kind or another from the trade union movement, which was far from universally sold on the idea of a productivity, prices and incomes policy. With time on their hands, where better to while it away than with an old Labour reporter called Ingham, especially when he was on tap just down the corridor?

Successively, Bob Willis, joint general secretary of the National Graphical Association, Ron Mathias, former South Wales regional secretary of the Transport and General Workers' Union, and W. L. Heywood, formerly general secretary of the National Union of Dyers, Bleachers and Textile Workers, claimed my time for gossip, enlightenment, companionship or reassurance. Mr Heywood was most at peace with himself. His concern was for us to keep York-shire County Cricket Club under close scrutiny and to reminisce about Yorkshire. His union was very strong in my part of the world – Calder Valley. Bob Willis, an old-fashioned buccaneering trade union baron and firebrand character, was the most tortured. He had lost an empire and never found a role at the Board. Ron Mathias was just plain lonely, both professionally and personally. His moder-ate, decent face had not fitted into the Jack Jones regime at the TGWU which had been his life. He was not the only regional or trade group secretary of that union who had felt exposed. More than one national official had felt so uncomfortable in my company at the bar of the Marquis of Granby in Smith Square, outside the

TGWU HQ, as to remark upon it when Norman Willis, now the TUC general secretary and then close to Jack Jones, came in. All this got my dander up about the TGWU. I was damned if I were going to be browbeaten, but I had also to consider the interests of my informants. Ron simply did not know what to do with himself, living in London during the week and going home to his wife and family in Cardiff at week-ends.

Thus, while Aubrey became consultant to the nation I, his press and public relations adviser, became consultant, confessor and friend to his trade union colleagues. Nobody seemed to mind, except John Bergin, the rather difficult establishments officer, who queried my drinks bill. What on earth did he expect trade union officers to drink? Tea? I was however discovering that public life, if that is the right term, can impose a severe strain on the liver, if you don't watch it. I became a firm friend of Ron Mathias who introduced me to Cardiff. And then, with shocking speed, he was gone, dying suddenly while on a cruise with his wife in the Mediterranean. We all went to his memorial service in Llandaff Cathedral and I subsequently visited his wife in Cardiff with his secretary, Grace Weinburg, with whom I keep in touch by Christmas card. It was a sad loss. A genuine man driven to his death by circumstance. Or so I thought. Who knows? I just believe that if he had been left to look after a motley of workers in South Wales he would have done more good than a thousand Jack Joneses put together.

I also had my moments with Clive Jenkins, the general secretary of ASSETT (later ASTMS), the technical white collar union. He once came in to see Aubrey Jones and I was invited to join them after they had fired each other with enthusiasm for some no doubt way-out idea. Aubrey was a sucker for new ideas. I doubted whether either the Government's policy or my chairman's interests would be well served by the notion they had been discussing and said so. My problem – which no doubt became apparent during the conversation – was that I did not trust the redoubtable Mr Jenkins. He was to me purpose-built for a rampantly capitalist society (notwithstanding his regular worship at the altar of socialism) and I told him so at a course he addressed in 1978. He smiled weakly.

The most important report published by the Board from my

point of view was No 36 on productivity agreements. In December 1965 I had reported in the *Leeds Weekly Citizen* a growing suspicion in goverment that far too many productivity deals were nothing but plausibly packaged pay increases. In the manner of all columnists, I called for an inquiry into their basis 'to determine how much they depend on the outright sale of restrictive or protective practices which can no longer be justified in a situation of full employment and social security'. I knew enough of employers and the trade union movement to recognize that, if it served their purposes, anything could be dressed up as productivity. The Board's Report No 36 gave me lift-off. I sat down and wrote the first NBPI guide which set out the guidelines for productivity agreements, their benefits and tips about the pitfalls in negotiating them. I produced it in association with Professor Hugh Clegg, Professor of Industrial Relations at Warwick University. To my surprise – and tremendous satisfaction – he cleared my draft guide with few amendments. We vigorously promoted this leaflet through the NBPI. It was very popular and I hope it did some good. It was followed in later NBPI life by leaflets on payment by results, job evaluation, efficiency and productivity and salary structures. The leaflet on productivity was one of the best things I have ever done. I poured my all into it as the NBPI's first popular guide to industry.

I worked so hard at the Board, sometimes into the early hours of the morning followed by a sleep in the office without going home, that I began to feel ill. I was plagued by headaches and dizziness and generally felt in a poor way. I feared it was a recurrence of the blood pressure which I had experienced in Leeds during my least confident, shattered days on the *Guardian*. Eventually, I saw Dr Mary Wilson, our family doctor in Foxley Lane, Purley. My blood pressure was very high indeed. She said I had to stop smoking and to reduce my weight – then more than sixteen stones – by at least three stones. I knew she spoke sense. After a late start, I had done enough to smoke myself into an early grave. One day during the Mary Hackett murder case in Halifax I had got through seventy-five cigarettes and felt awful. Another day when Tom Dickinson, who beat most to the cigarette count, and I felt we needed to spring clean our Halifax office we had to scrape a yellow-brown nicotine film off the windows of the partition to get them sparkling. I stopped smoking and eating, as I described my severe diet, on 1 January 1968. By the time my life evolved once more in the spring I was fitter and three stones lighter. I left the Prices and Incomes Board probably saved from an early grave.

I came to move on with only half my short-term public service contract fulfilled because of a remarkable evolution in the machinery of Government. On 5 April 1968, the Government announced that responsibility for the productivity, prices and incomes policy was being transferred from the ill-starred Department of Economic Affairs (DEA) to the Ministry of Labour which was to be renamed – how gimmicky! – the Department of Employment and Productivity (DEP).

Only a short time before Alex Jarratt had moved from the NBPI to the DEA. He was accordingly transferred from the DEA to the DEP, if you follow these acronyms. The old Ministry of Labour needed to be reinforced with staff to serve the dynamic Mrs Barbara Castle, its new Cabinet Minister, with a broader, more economic outlook than that steeped in the skills of conciliation and labour issues. Mrs Castle, whom I had never met, understandably wanted to take Don Bickerton with her from the Ministry of Transport as her Chief Information Officer. This far from suited the DEP's senior officials who were concerned about morale in the Department. They alighted on me as a former Labour reporter who was specializing within government on productivity, prices and incomes policy and looked like a promising successor to Charles Birdsall when he retired. It is clear that this was done without Aubrey Jones's knowledge. He was quietly furious and life was very difficult until Mark Gapper, Labour correspondent of the *Financial Times*, was recruited to succeed me at the Board. I was very uncomfortable straddling the Board and the new Department. My work rate, as football commentators describe it, was phenomenal. Journalism was always a doddle compared with the Civil Service.

9

Mr Solomon Binding

When Charles Birdsall heard that I was going to become a temporary civil servant and join the Prices and Incomes Board he professed
himself to be delighted. 'I always thought Bernard was a public
servant', he kept telling me. He would have been a saint had he not
had reservations about my joining him in his own division of the
Department at the same rank. Charles, I discovered first hand, was
a proud man who wanted to do everything himself. He had great
difficulty in delegating anything of importance and was always
impatient when his staff – and not himself – were briefing journalists
on the 'phone. No wonder he worked all hours that God sent. The
real saint was Charles's deputy, Jack McIntosh, who had laboured
long and loyally under Charles and now found me formally designated as deputy Head of Information. He confessed his own
disappointment and difficulty which I recognized. We became firm
friends. I had a difficult diplomatic job on my hands, as well as the
problems of coping with my first Cabinet Minister, Barbara Castle,
and keeping the Prices and Incomes Board operation going with a
chairman who felt I had spurned him.

In fact, I had taken no active part whatsoever in my translation.
It is true that I had picked up journalistic gossip that I was being
seen as a future Head of Information at the Ministry of Labour but
I did not take much notice of it. I knew only too well how ill-
founded such gossip could be. Moreover, I was only there for two
years. Yet, while the colt was far from broken into the more disciplined ways of the Civil Service, I had few regrets about leaving
journalism and found my new life as fascinating as it could be hard
work, if you chose to enter into it full-heartedly. And I had never
been half-hearted about work. It was therefore with some
excitement that I heard Sir Denis Barnes, the Permanent Secretary

at the new Department of Employment and Productivity, proposition me as Barbara Castle's speechwriter and reinforcement for
Charles Birdsall with this new-fangled prices and incomes policy.
There was the prospect, he added, of my succeeding Charles when
he retired in a couple of years' time or so provided I performed
well and wanted the job. Meanwhile, I would have to handle Charles
carefully and it would be helpful if I would agree to serve as his
Number 2.

I did not hesitate. This was far more than I had ever expected to
get out of my two years in government. While providing some
insight into how government worked, the Prices and Incomes Board
was peripheral. I was now being offered the chance to work in a
real, live Government Department with a real, live Information
Division (of which I had been a client just under a year earlier) and
for a real, live – indeed, larger than life – Cabinet Minister. My
only reservation was speechwriting. Of course, I could produce the
words probably faster than most if I knew what I was writing about
and had some understanding of the subject. But speeches are an
intensely personal property. As such, they can give acute difficulty.
Right from the start with Mrs Castle I never saw my speechwriter's
job as being more than to provide sparks. My view of speechwriting
over my twenty-three years in the Civil Service has never changed:
you have done your job if you provide the broad structure, a reasonable outline and a few headline phrases. No wonder after an early
effort Mrs Castle wrote in her diaries:

> 'I tried to make progress with Bernard Ingham's rough re-
> draft of my speech with very little success. Bernard has tried
> to liven up the ghastly officialese of the Department but I
> wouldn't say I have got myself a Kennedy-type speechwriter
> yet. However, he is still very new, poor man.'

Her opinion of me improved, for seven months later she wrote:

> 'Thanks to Bernard Ingham's lively draft, and a few jokes
> of my own, my speech was quite a hit.'

I did not jump at the chance of working with Barbara Castle as
a person, though she was clearly the hottest Ministerial property
then around outside Number 10 and had made history at the Depart-

ment of Transport by bringing in the breathalyser. She also came from Bradford which should have commended her to me. But even though I had in my time espoused some Left-wing causes, I was wary of her Left-wing past. She was a bit colourful for my sober, modest tastes. Perhaps it showed. Over time – some two and a half years – I grew to respect her many qualities, and not least her courage, and to worry about her frailties. Her idealism made her seem terribly vulnerable and she confessed that she found the House of Commons a trial. She said she felt the full weight of Government resting on her shoulders when she rose to speak. She was thorough by nature but she put that bit extra into Commons speeches and I often felt that she overprepared herself. It went without saying that I protected her. That is in part the job of a Chief Information Officer. I most certainly admired her and became proud to work for her. But we never became close in the way that, for example, Peter Brown seemed to become close to her when he was with her later at the Department for Social Services. Quite apart from personality, this may have been because by the time I succeeded Charles Birdsall to the top job eighteen months later she had seen the best of her days in the Department with the collapse of her 'In Place of Strife' reforms.

It is also possible that I was beginning to prepare myself for a career in the Civil Service and, because of my political past, was subconsciously adopting a more detached approach. It may have been this which caused Mrs Castle to describe me as 'a bit dull, a bit stodgy'. I spent that first eighteen months rooting around in the undergrowth of a Department which was in the process of fundamental reform. I could not have had a better grounding in its work, but my foundations in the Department were not painlessly laid. Indeed, I was one of those 'off-cumdens', as they say in Hebden Bridge, who were brought in to turn the old Ministry of Labour upside down and inside out. It was a comfort to find Alex Jarratt in charge of the productivity, prices and incomes aspects of the new Department with his secretary, Pam Taylor, an Australian who was a close friend of my secretary, Elizabeth Capel-Dunn. They had both been part of the Prices and Incomes Board's social scene.

The Civil Service is a remarkable institution which can perform wonders at the drop of a portfolio and miracles given reasonable notice (hours will do). Contrary to rumour, it is populated by people who are as human as the politicians and public they serve. Old Ministry of Labour civil servants would not have been human if they had not resented the intrusion of this caravan of productivity, prices and incomes wallahs, economic planners and other assorted artistes like Ingham into their midst. My sympathies were generally with them. But in 1968 the Government was trying yet another ploy to find a way through the union maze to price stability, full employment and continuous economic growth. And the full – and acceptable – resources of the old Ministry of Labour were being committed to the battle. The problem for Sir Denis Barnes was that his Department was not equipped for the task.

It was, in fact, a Department born of a different age. I often felt in those early days that it moved at two different speeds: those who handled the conciliation of industrial disputes at one hectic, exhausting pace and the rest at another, much more gentle tempo. The Department sought to promote industrial health and safety, the interests of the disabled who wanted to work and industrial training. It studied trends in manpower requirements. It looked after the unemployed and tried to find them work. It collected the raw material which went into the compilation of the unemployment and strike figures and the retail price index. It also performed at the International Labour Organization in Geneva an invaluable function in bringing sophistication to the whole international discussion of the betterment of the working man. It was a noble Department of State and anyone with an ounce of social conscience could be proud to serve it.

Charles Birdsall was inordinately proud to do so. He loved the Department, as he so often told me. His only problem was that, even for a chap who worked virtually twenty-four hours a day (and certainly nothing less than eighteen), he could not give the less urgent issues his personal attention. If Charles was anything he was the Cecil B. de Mille of St James's Square; the David Lean of the great British strike. I was to come to value my apprenticeship to him in the handling of conciliation. Meanwhile, I got on with beefing up the impact of health and safety at work, training, the disabled and manpower studies. I had also to cope with the Department's acquisition of responsibility for prices and incomes policy on which Charles often asked me to brief journalists who, quite rightly, first rang him. This involved my superintending the answering of a large postbag again, more often than not on prices rather than incomes. I sought to improve the quality of the Department's publications both in presentation and design and generally to make people – and not least the TUC – believe that the Government was giving new urgency to the interests of working people. It was, of course, the kind of quality bowling which is lost on a useless batsman. The trade union movement was not even playing cricket.

I could not have entered any Government department in 1968 with a more exciting prospect. The great British disease was not so much the totality of days lost through strikes as the sudden, unofficial, unconstitutional and highly disruptive nature of stoppages. Wildcat strikes were an appalling drag on the nation's performance. Hence the Donovan Royal Commission on Trade Unions and Employers' Associations whose 145,000-word report, with its empirical, voluntarist conclusions, was awaiting Mrs Castle's implementation. Britain's strike record was not improved by the pressures and strains imposed by incomes policy. A productivity, prices and incomes policy, conceived as a long-term exercise in institutional and attitudinal reform, had soon been employed – some would say prostituted – to the short term end of cost containment following a sterling crisis the previous year and eventually a 14.3 per cent devaluation. Department of Employment and Productivity conciliators led by that venerable, silver-haired figure from the North-East, Conrad Heron, were, paradoxically, the most overworked men in Britain.

Into this explosive mix had been thrown a formidable Left-winger and a woman to boot. By all accounts she was a socialist through and through who saw in the productivity, prices and incomes policy an instrument of socialist planning. She told Denis Barnes when he went to see her at her home, Hell Corner Farm in the Chilterns, that incomes policy was socialism. She wanted to make her new Department exciting. Denis Barnes replied: 'You should not have said that to me.' He, too, wanted to see change. He did not, however, harbour Mrs Castle's illusions about the unions. She thought she could persuade its leaders. She might have thought differently had she known what Victor Feather, the new TUC general secretary, was saying about her. Mr Feather had known her as a girl in Bradford. He was a male chauvinist pig and it was clear to me when I had lunch with him that he could not stand the sight of her. The feeling was probably mutual. Mrs Castle, at least, deserved better. Her process of disillusionment with the trade union movement was far faster than mine had been. But then she had to deal with them; I had merely to report what they said and did.

My first impressions of her – as I say, I had not met her before – were of a very feminine, extremely well preserved, hyperactive woman; a doer rather than a deep thinker, though she was always hot on getting the philosophy right; and with an idealistic view of the more Left-wing trade union leaders and powerbrokers such as Jack Jones and Hugh Scanlon. She had a certain style, a sense of humour and was so professional that she had her own joke book for speech purposes. I was invited to attend some of her policy discussions and meetings to prepare for speeches but Charles Birdsall handled the active day-to-day issues. Consequently, my view of the first eighteen months was bitty and unsatisfactory, especially when, at short notice, I was called upon to deputize for Charles in his fleeting absence from the office. The position of deputy Chief Information Officer is one of the hardest in the business. But I recall being deeply impressed and excited when it became clear that she had been converted to trade union reform.

I took part in a conference at the Civil Service College at Sunningdale to lay the foundations for a new approach which in return for strengthening trade unions would require them to accept obligations, notably in securing the constitutional conduct of industrial disputes. The famous White Paper 'In Place of Strife – A Policy for Industrial Relations' was published on 17 January 1969. It owed its title to Barbara Castle's husband, Ted, who devised it as a play upon Aneurin Bevan's book *In Place of Fear*. Among many other things, the White Paper proposed giving the Minister power to order a twenty-eight day 'conciliation pause' requiring a resumption of work pending inquiry and negotiation on the basis, important to unions, that the *status quo* continued; to impose a settlement in inter-union disputes where neither the Commission for Industrial Relations nor the TUC had succeeded in sorting them out; and in certain circumstances to order a strike ballot.

Everyone now knows that the unions would not touch all this with a barge-pole. After a tortured process of meetings the Prime Minister, Harold Wilson, and Mrs Castle were left largely isolated in Cabinet and Party. They were forced to drop legislation in return for 'Mr Solomon Binding', an insubstantial character based upon the TUC's solemn and binding undertaking at Number 10 Downing Street to place an 'obligation on unions to take energetic steps to obtain an immediate resumption of work including action within their rules.' Denis Barnes said that this Solomon Binding sounded like a character out of George Eliot. It was an humiliation. I reposed no confidence whatsoever in the unions' ability, or even desire, to deliver anything. They believed they could have it both ways as Lewis Wright, otherwise known as Lord Wright, CBE, chairman of the TUC General Council in 1967–68 and a member of the Prices and Incomes Board, had once told me over lunch. I had not expected this of a man I first met as a boy in Todmorden when my father delivered Amalgamated Weavers' dues to him at his office close by the Centre Vale cricket ground. My father never believed you could have it both ways. Neither did I. I am sorry to have to say it, but Lewis Wright's remark revealed to me the corruption of trade union power, linked with a refusal to accept any responsibility in exercising it. I was not the only one who felt that the Labour Government had lost the next election – and deserved to do so – after the 'In Place of Strife' *débâcle*. Or, more precisely, that the bloody trade unions deserved to lose their Government.

Sir Denis Barnes, having decided he wanted me to succeed Charles Birdsall, set about regularizing my position as a civil servant. To secure confirmation in my rank, I had to appear before a panel of the great and the good, including (curiously enough) Don Bickerton, whom Mrs Castle had wanted to import to the DEP. By all accounts I gave an alpha-plus performance and became an established civil servant. Charles, nearing sixty, left unwillingly for the Cabinet Office to assist Trevor Lloyd-Hughes in his co-ordinating role as the most senior information officer in Whitehall. Trevor had been Harold Wilson's first Chief Press Secretary from 1964. Charles told me that he never thought the Department he loved would do this to him. It was all very sad. Charles, I am afraid, was simply not conditioned for retirement and seemed unable to see that the Department was trying to ease him into it gently.

He had, however, seen the best of Barbara. She had one other great flourish in her: the introduction of the Equal Pay Act in January 1970. In characteristic fashion she described it as 'an historic day for Britain'. It was an Act, she said, 'to end a long-standing injustice to one third of the nation's labour force and ... provide a firm basis on which women can fight against discrimination'. Oh, what a sock in the eye for the trade union movement, if they did but know it. After all their endless, pious, insincere and futile demands for equal pay, a woman was actually going to require it. Serve 'em right.

I hesitate to say that working for Mrs Castle was a preparation for things to come. That was not how I regarded it at the time – and she might not like the idea. But the fact is that I started my career looking after the interests of Cabinet Ministers with the outstanding woman politician of the time, who was tough, dynamic, passionate and positive. And if I learned one thing from her it was to be positive and to present arguments in positive terms. How many more times was I to hear that injunction in Number 10? I am sure it was an advantage to have worked for such a woman before going to Downing Street. This is not a sexist point. In my substantial experience, senior civil servants – those who work closest to Ministers – are the least discriminatory of people. What they like in their Ministers is the capacity to win arguments in Government. If their winner is a woman so much the better. They are worldly enough to recognize that a winning woman has winning ways, especially with the media, who will write their work large upon the nation.

Barbara Castle took the terrors out of my working for a woman. Whatever male chauvinism was left in me, she taught me to respect women as real, formidable politicians. I regarded her not as a woman – and certainly not as a token woman – but as a top-flight Minister who was entitled to my utter commitment. There was one area where her sex inevitably intruded into my line of country: she taught me to build dressing, hair and make-up time into any presentational programme involving television. This will come as a considerable surprise to Richard Dixon, the former ITN industrial correspondent, who did not like being kept waiting by a Minister of the Crown. I did not keep him waiting half as long as Mrs Castle kept Douglas Smith, her Principal Private Secretary, and me waiting outside her boudoir on the second floor of 8 St James's Square. Yet, however much I have chafed at the cosmetic bit in my Civil Service career, I have to accept that women are judged by an entirely different standard to men and are entitled to the time to meet it. Their appearance is regarded much more critically than any man's would ever be.

But most of all Barbara Castle prepared me for the big stuff. She, like Margaret Thatcher, was a substantial politician endowed with good looks, energy, fire, intelligence, power, determination and guts. And the greatest of these is guts. Guts to do what you think is right. And guts to fight it through to a conclusion. Both Barbara and Margaret were made of sterner stuff than their Parliamentary parties and the Cabinets of which they were members.

Ted Heath's Conservative general election victory in June 1970 came as a considerable surprise to most people. But not so to Geoffrey Tucker, the Conservative Party's then Director of Publicity, whom I came to know well when I was recruited by Mrs Thatcher. He has consistently told me that he was confident of victory. And victory it was, with an overall majority of thirty, notwithstanding a large swing to Labour just over a month earlier in the local elections. Perhaps a newspaper strike during the election helped the Tories. At all events, the unions deserved Labour's defeat, as we all – at least, that was what it seemed – thought in the DEP after 'In Place of Strife' went down the drain. The nation, I hoped, had come to recognize that this internecine British industrial warfare could not go on. The mood, I felt, was not in doubt. But had we the leader to translate that mood into a saner, more constructive and prosperous future for the British working man which I essentially wanted? All that I can say as a civil servant, dedicated to serving the interests of the government of the day, is that I hoped against hope that something would come of it. I saw no future for the British working man on strike. As I told Derek Howe in 1969, if anyone was likely to make me vote Conservative it was Ted Heath.

My vote in the 1970 election was, I am sure, a triumph of hope over expectation. I wanted Labour to sort out its own mess. The nation's decision to leave it in other hands in no way mitigated the mess that prevailed. Although I was an established civil servant, Michael Wolfe, the new Prime Minister's right-hand man, gave me a hard time over the telephone before the Cabinet was announced. He gave me the impression that I was not long for this Governmental world because of my political past. I resolved to be only as awkward as a bloody-minded Yorkshireman, sitting on his bat end, can be. OK, I said to myself, if this jumped up party apparatchik wants to play games, so will I. I made it clear to anybody who would listen that I did not take kindly to this kind of treatment. Either I had been accepted as an established civil servant or I had not, but I was damned if I were going to be messed around by Michael Wolfe, whoever he may or may not be. I do not know whether this communicated itself to the appropriate places, but when Paul Bryan, Minister of State, came to examine my credentials face to face I made it clear that I expected to be judged not by history but by performance. Performance was properly given its chance. I can only say that, if it had not been, I would have created an unholy stink, especially in view of Michael Wolfe's attitude.

Robert Carr, the new Secretary of State, could not have been nicer. Nor could Denis Barnes have been more supportive. I had acquired a new Secretary of State who was, above all, a decent man who believed in the basic decency of one man to another. I think all of us thought that his belief would rapidly be put to the test in the months to come since the Government had come to office with the entirely laudable objective of reforming industrial relations. And so it proved, even though Robert Carr was, in Douglas Smith's words, as sure-footed as a mountain goat when it came to performing in the Commons, on a platform, in a press conference or on the hoof with media microphones. Nor was he anything like any senior Tory who had come anywhere near my upbringing, experience, imagination or prejudices. Sadly, none of this was enough in the face of union power. It was irresistible. But he gave the unions a good run for their money and, like Barbara Castle, was a stepping-stone across the stream to their taming.

Robert Carr inherited industrial breakdown and potentially runaway inflation and unemployment. Labour's attempts to secure, in one way or another, pay and price restraint had broken down.

Massive wage claims had built up under these forces of restraint yet the Conservatives had rejected wage restraint in any form. Early appeals by Mr Carr to the nationalized industries and the TUC to exercise restraint had little effect even though in the first six months of 1970 (before the new Government had taken office) wages had been rising at a rate of 12 per cent a year compared with 6 per cent for prices and 2 per cent for productivity.

There was a dock strike and a state of emergency within a month of the Government coming to office in July. Messrs Jones and Scanlon confirmed their opposition to any form of incomes restraint or policy and their willingness to challenge either if it emerged. At the end of September there were selective strikes by those doing what were emotively called 'dirty jobs' – dustmen, etc. They eventually settled for virtually what they had sought under the imprimatur of an inquiry by the – in the eyes of the Government – aptly named Sir Jack Scamp. Mr Heath optimistically envisaged 'a challenge so radical and reform so quiet and yet so total that it will go far beyond a programme for a Parliament'. And he later rejected calls for an incomes policy as 'absolutely nonsensical'. People, he said, must face up to their own responsibilities in a free society. These were exactly Mrs Thatcher's sentiments a decade later. It was Mr Heath's fate to play St John in the Wilderness ten years ahead of his time. I have never understood why a chap who had right on his side was touchy about someone else proving he was right after all. I suppose it was his guilty conscience about not sticking with it.

By November Robert Carr was forecasting that, on the basis of the first nine months, 1970 would prove to be the worst year for industrial stoppages since the year of the General Strike, 1926. This was borne out by events. Publication of the Industrial Relations Bill was followed almost immediately by a stoppage over pay by the electricity power workers which brought widespread power cuts, industrial disruption, a brief state of emergency and a candle-lit Commons.

Can anyone imagine a worse background against which to present an Industrial Relations Bill? Essentially this Bill confronted the trade union movement with the central issue: were they prepared to bring themselves and their operations within the ambit of the law or not? What, in the name of all that is sainted and holy, I said to myself, is wrong with the legal enforcement of collective agreements unless otherwise specified? With a sixty-day cooling-off period where a strike threatens the community? With secret ballots before a strike? The statutory right to belong, or not to belong, to a trade union? And a National Industrial Relations Court – NIRC, an acronym which invited such a sneering pronunciation that Robert Carr felt we had missed a public relations trick – to adjudicate on alleged offences under the Bill, with elaborate arrangements to try to avoid the jailing of individuals which I had always seen as a major difficulty in this area? Perhaps the unions' opposition to a ban on the closed shop gave the game away. Alternative arrangements for recognizing an 'agency shop' by which a single union would be entitled to represent all the employees in that organization interfered with the sovereignty of individual unions. And, of course, the institution had come to count for much more – infinitely more – than the poor people who kept it going with their hard-earned dues.

I came to work very closely with Robert Carr. He introduced me to the United States when he took me with Douglas Smith to New York and then on to Washington where the Administration showed not the slightest interest in us. Britain counted for nothing – so little, in fact, that at a meeting in the Department of Labour they had to rustle together some ancient mugs to give the apparently unexpected Secretary of State and his small party coffee. He also introduced me to terrorism, and its security consequences, when the 'Angry Brigade' tried to blow up him and his family at his home to the north of London. But above all I worked on the presentation of the Industrial Relations Bill – and subsequently the Act – on the reform of the Department of Employment, as it became known when the Conservatives immediately dropped the 'and Productivity' bit of Wilsonian gimmickry and, of course, on industrial disputes. I have seldom worked harder or longer – and never longer than when industrial disputes intruded, as they so frequently did, upon 8 St James's Square and Number 10.

The pattern was very familiar in those interventionist days. Assuming a dispute was official – a very big assumption – first came the threat of industrial action. To be fair to the unions, they preferred to start by demanding money with menaces rather than immediately clobbering the employer, the consumer, the Government and the nation over the head with what was euphemistically (and entirely erroneously) called industrial action. Journalists would soon ring me wanting to know when the Department was going to intervene. I would play for time saying that I thought they would have to stew in their own juice a bit. If Conrad Heron, after considerable internal discussion of the tactics, decided he should hold a peace conference and had secured the Secretary of State's approval, I would alert reporters to the impending performance. They would arrive, by now armed with microphones, cameras and trailing wires, to film the belligerents entering the portals of peace. I would ring my wife to say 'Here we go again; expect me when you see me.' The Department's Industrial Relations Division would take on supplies of drink, and especially whisky, and the extortion game would begin.

The war parties would first occupy separate smoke-filled rooms – or, at least, a fog would soon come down. Non-smokers Conrad Heron and his Chief Conciliation Officer, Andy Kerr, would brave the fug, sound out the two sides, move between the two to explore signs of an opening, consistent with the latest phase of incomes policy (assuming we had a formal one at the time), and retire to take stock with people like me, Douglas Smith and often Denis Barnes in his snug, as his office became. It was my job to report the intelligence from journalists – and they were often prime sources of news – to reflect their attitudes to the proceedings and to ensure that I was properly armed at the appropriate times to look after the Government's interests with the press, radio and television. I would carry the news of developments, or lack of them, to the waiting reporters in their own special room or, on these occasions, in the corridor so that they could keep their eye on any comings or goings. Sometimes a union official, playing for all the public sympathy he could milk from the situation, would saunter down and give forth. Employers seldom appeared or uttered a word except tersely and self-consciously on arrival and departure. It was a very one-sided media game and it used to exasperate me that the employers abdicated the field. Dammit, that is not the way to fight.

I would keep my eye on the approach of the main news bulletins and, in the evening, for the time when labour correspondents should be writing their first edition stories. As soon – and as late – as I could effectively brief I would go down to carry the news, such as it was, from Ghent to Aix. Of all the electronic citizens of Aix none were better, more intelligent or more sensible to deal with than Ian Ross (BBC) and the now well-known BBC presenter, Peter Sissons, then with ITN. Two minutes with them just before set them up admirably for their evening news bulletins live from the doorstep of 8 St James's Square. Most of the writing press were my former colleagues and the thought that I should mislead them (as distinct from not telling them the whole truth) was anathema. They wanted to know whether hopes were rising or falling, whether there was a chink of light or whether deadlock continued, and as much of the detail of the sticking point that I could give them. Atmospherics were all. They wanted, above all, to reflect in their bulletins or in their newspapers the mood and the prospects.

Of course, nothing usually started to happen until the early hours of the morning. Movement, if there was to be any, occurred only when the reporters, at least in terms of editions and bulletins, had gone to bed. This was because industrial disputes are wars of attrition. The unions knew that, come the early hours of the morning, they had the upper hand. They were sufficiently ideological to prevail in the end over employers who had an entirely rational view of their working life – namely, that midnight was late; 1 a.m. was very late; 2 a.m. was excessive; and 3 a.m. ludicrous. I used to get home in the seven-week Post Office dispute in early 1971, for example, around 4 a.m., resuming at 9 a.m. There have been no more idiotic periods in my life than in the depths of all-night conciliation. It is a world, I hope, for ever consigned to the dustbin of ignominious British failure.

It also brought curious sidelights on man's insensitivity. During the postal strike a senior press officer, Jennifer Price, who had piloted the Industrial Relations Bill in all its Parliamentary stages through the Press Gallery, began to wilt. I discovered that a chap with a mid-Atlantic accent was consistently ringing her at home around 3 a.m. to explain his solution to this conflict and to persuade her to put it to the Secretary of State. I only made my discovery when, with no sign that his ideas had registered with Mr Carr, he rang me at 5 a.m. – an hour after I had got home. I leave readers to imagine the tone of my necessarily quiet conversation with this nutter at the bottom of our stairs. Dick Seaman, my Chief Press Officer, insisted on handling this misguided individual. We heard no more from him.

When a settlement was achieved in any dispute the pattern was invariably the same: the employers said the minimum and Government allowed the unions to claim a victory even out of manifest defeat so that the militants could be given no ground for prolonging the stoppage. Once the strikers were back at work the Government, having allowed the unions to snatch triumph from the jaws of defeat, tried, through people like me, to inject some reality into reporting. But by then it was too late. It was all mad, bad, unprincipled and a sham. It did nothing longer-term for the working man. But it did give union leaders their daily dose of screen publicity.

My first and last full year – 1971 – with Robert Carr was appalling. A seven-week strike from 20 January by the post office workers ended in disaster for the union and, more especially, for the postmen who had no strike fund. In the middle of it an early Lord Justice Wilberforce inquiry found that the electricity power workers had not received adequate compensation for higher productivity. His findings, according to the unions, delivered increases of up to 15 per cent. The Government argued inconclusively that the damage to the pay bill – the crucial measurement of cost – was only 10.9 per cent. As always, the higher figure was the one for macho union negotiators to aim to beat. There were two one-day strikes against the Industrial Relations Bill. There was a go-slow by the train drivers for ten days in April and in June the blastfurnace-men struck for more money.

Ford's car production was halted for two months from February and eventually the company bought the men off with a pay increase of 33 per cent over two years in return, I solemnly swear, hand on heart, for a no-strike pledge. This was the equivalent of taking a Borgias' dinner party on trust. What is more, British Leyland and Vauxhall followed with similar deals within two or three days of Robert Carr having met the CBI to underline the Government's concern about the failure of private employers to support the Government in restraining pay increases. Perhaps it was a guilty conscience that persuaded the CBI, backed by 200 firms, to pledge in July a 5 per cent ceiling on price increases over the next twelve months as a contribution to fighting rising inflation. But inflation was not the only thing rising: so was unemployment, almost unrelentingly towards the emotive and – as it turned out the following year – the galvanizing and U-turning figure of one million. Its steady rise made not the slightest difference to union attitudes. Indeed, the increasing militancy in defiance of all classical economic theory was puzzling, unless it was a defiant reaction by an arrogant trade union movement to attempts to restrain pay increases and introduce a legal framework for the conduct of its activities. I became convinced – and remain convinced – that the unions are not interested in the unemployed, however much they may weep crocodile tears over them. Power is their business and the unemployed are not powerful, except in imagery.

In between Mrs Thatcher became known as 'the milk snatcher' by withdrawing free milk from primary schools to contribute towards a £132 million programme to improve and replace decaying schools for the youngest children. The Government at least won one battle – the historic Parliamentary debate to take Britain into the European Community. It ended in October with Mr Heath proclaiming: 'Now we stand ready to take our first step into a new world full of new opportunities.' Well, we needed cheering up. The Industrial Relations Act reached the Statute Book after 450 hours' debate in both Houses and launched me and my new deputy, Neville Gaffin, on a similarly demanding publicity campaign. I had earlier locked myself away to write the first draft of the handbook and Neville and I produced explanatory leaflets and even five films in association with the experts. It was an ill-fated effort but professionally rewarding. It gave me my first experience of a comprehensive publicity campaign, including film production. I admired the scrupulous professionalism that Graham Turner (scriptwriter) and Ian Latimer (film producer) brought to our film series as we sat hour upon hour in my room trying to reconcile presentation with legal nicety.

With the possible exception of Sir Geoffrey Howe, then the Solicitor-General working on the Bill, I doubt whether anyone queried my dedication to explaining the Government's legal framework for industrial relations, even though I was worried lest some militants pushed their opposition to the point of contempt of court and imprisonment. Sir Geoffrey used to come in each morning during the passage of the Bill with a list of what I, as a former journalist, thought were the most arcane points of corrections to detail in reportage. It would have been entirely counter-productive to raise most of them with journalists apart, possibly, from Vincent Hanna, of the *Sunday Times*, who had appointed himself Fleet Street's barrack-room lawyer to the Bill.

However much professional satisfaction I derived from doing what both Robert Carr and Denis Barnes clearly thought was a good job, the atmosphere in the Department of Employment was at once depressing and inspiring. We had a top class Cabinet Minister – and that counts for a lot – and we developed a sort of blitz spirit. But we were under continual bombardment. Denis Barnes paid much attention to my morale and frequently called me up from my ground-floor room for a pre-lunch drink. But the harsh reality so often intruded into our social hour. I recall that he once gloomily predicted that we would have to learn to live with much, much higher unemployment as a direct consequence of rising expectations and a bovine trade union movement's equal determination to ensure steady annual increases in real income and to resist changes in working practices which would help to pay for them. Steadily, we worked up to a crisis which was another two exhausting and sometimes frightening years in the making.

If 1971 had been grim, 1972 proved to be exponentially grimmer still. Looking back on it I wonder how we got through. And yet get through we had to, for if we had had any role in life over recent years it had been, in Denis Barnes' words, 'somehow to keep the system going'. It was as bad as that. It was not simply the industrial or economic mess; it was the carnage in Northern Ireland. I mention this not just because of 'Bloody Sunday' in the Bogside, Londonderry, in January and the destruction of our embassy in Dublin early in February, to instance only a couple of disasters and outrages. Denis Barnes brought it chillingly home to me. He confided that there was the possibility that he might be transferred to Belfast. If he were, he said that he would want me to join him. I felt I must. The idea vanished with Willie Whitelaw's posting to

Northern Ireland in a reshuffle which was to take Robert Carr from me early in April to become Lord President and Leader of the Commons. Monty Meth, then the *Daily Mail*'s industrial correspondent, telephoned me at home to tip me off that Maurice Macmillan was to be my new Minister.

Robert Carr left with the Government shell-shocked. First, unemployment predictably passed the one-million mark on 20 January. There was panic in the corridors of power and Selsdon Man was no more. Selsdon Man was the name given to the tougher, more market-oriented Conservative party approach deriving from a policy formulation conference at the Selsdon Park Hotel in Surrey. The great U-turn was under way. Like Napoleon from Moscow, we were in retreat – from free marketry and the abandonment of industrial 'lame ducks' to their awful fate. Man's responsibility for his own actions and salvation was not enough, not surprisingly since individual responsibility was a bit thin on the ground in the face of the trade union juggernaut. To be fair, the Government's 'lame duck' policy had taken a hammering the previous year when Rolls-Royce had been nationalized. Upper Clyde Shipbuilders, on the other hand, had been allowed to go into liquidation.

Before he left Robert Carr had also taken me through my biggest dispute yet: the miners' strike from 9 January to 28 February. It was a chilling affair in which Arthur Scargill made his first menacing appearance at Saltley cokeworks and anarchy stalked the land. I got a first-hand whiff of danger when, with Robert Carr, I visited Bolton, where the Lancashire miners had their headquarters. His party was given police protection and a hissing, teeth-grinding mob had to be held back until our car could get away. I was so mesmerized by this display of feeling – if such it was, for the Left are good at mounting a propaganda show – that I paused to wonder at it on the pavement as we were leaving the building we had visited. The exasperated police bundled me into the Ministerial car and demonstrators fell off either side of the bonnet as we drove on.

There was a lot of sympathy around for the miners – and inside Government as well as outside it. We genuinely felt that their pay had fallen behind. But the realities of trade union life meant that no Government could willingly differentiate, especially under threat of a strike. Not a lot happened for a month but then Wilberforce was wheeled in again as the miners began to picket and close power stations. Within eight days he had found that they had a just case for special treatment. The miners screwed a bit more on top of Wilberforce out of the Government at Number 10 Downing Street. And that was that until the next time.

Donald Maitland, the Prime Minister's Chief Press Secretary, involved me closely in the handling of these events. I was a regular attender at Number 10 both for meetings with other heads of information, such as Peter Middleton, now Permanent Secretary to the Treasury, on the presentation of economic policy, and to look after the labour correspondents who were in the main responsible for covering disputes. Any major dispute, such as the postmen's strike at the beginning of 1971, which involved consultations with Number 10 or ended up there, took me not merely to the Number 10 press office but also, with our Department of Employment officials, into Mr Heath's study for consultations. These were marked by long silences – seemingly endless silences – as the Prime Minister considered the situation. Mr Heath was nothing if not deliberate. As the miners' strike was drawing to a close, I contemplated with wry amusement members of the NUM executive tucking into a meal in the posh surroundings of the Number 10 State dining room. Beer did for most of them, but Lawrence Daly, the NUM general secretary, was partial to Antiquary whisky. Supplies of Antiquary were arranged.

With unemployment above one million and the miners victorious, the Prime Minister moved fast to try to restore order out of potential chaos. He began a series of talks on the economy with the TUC General Council (and occasionally with the CBI) which dragged on until the late autumn. I sat in on most of them, often at Chequers. The pattern was depressingly familiar. Mr Heath would open with a résumé of where he thought they had got to last time – which invariably put the most optimistic gloss on progress, such as it had been – and then the inconsequential talking would start. It was as obvious as a miner's lamp at the coalface that the unions were going to give nothing away, not even if they got the Crown Jewels thrown in for good will. They would, of course, negotiate – especially Hugh Scanlon (AUEW) – until the cows came home and the owls came out, safe in the knowledge that they could not deliver. Mr Solomon Binding was by then so sick a joke that he was not mentioned in polite society. The year after his entry into the language as one of the great cons of our time was the worst for industrial trouble since 1926. In the first quarter of 1971 the number of days lost through strikes was running at four times the level of the comparable period in 1970. Yet in 1972 Mr Heath still ploughed on with the TUC until by November even he had had enough.

Ray Gunter called the old Ministry of Labour a bed of nails. By the time Maurice Macmillan arrived in 1971 they were finely honed spikes, smeared with Robert Carr's blood. Few Ministers have inherited such an inevitable form of torture. And there have been even fewer Ministers more decent, more kind, more intelligent, more self-effacing and more vulnerable. He was vulnerable not merely because the unions had got their feet firmly under the Cabinet table; he was also the least fluent and confident speaker and interviewee both in the Commons and outside. He frankly confessed to me that his own self-confidence had been shattered by watching for so long his father perform so brilliantly at the dispatch box. On paper he was terrific; on his feet he was terrified. We became very near inseparable.

I could do no wrong since I came from Halifax for which, as its former MP, Maurice Macmillan had an immensely deep and abiding affection. When he was elevated he took as his title Viscount Macmillan of Ovenden, a district of Halifax. I resolved that whatever else happened he would not fail for want of my help. Whereas, for example, I would merely have discussed the presentational line before an interview with Barbara Castle or Robert Carr, I developed a technique with Maurice Macmillan of writing on a small sheet of paper five points to get over. He found this reminder invaluable since he seemed so often to freeze in front of a microphone. He was also strongly backed in his Private Office by some real high flyers in the Department – Geoffrey Holland, who is its current Permanent Secretary; Roger Dawe, now a deputy secretary there; and Kate Jenkins who spent much of the 1980s in Mrs Thatcher's efficiency unit. Kate is the sister of Simon Jenkins, editor of *The Times*. We made a very happy if embattled team.

Maurice Macmillan did not just have to cope with rising inflation, unemployment and industrial anarchy. There was a new and additional spike to spear the man: the Industrial Relations Act, which was under sustained attack. Within a month of his arrival its value was put seriously in doubt when the National Industrial Relations Court ordered a ballot of the railway workers who were threatening a strike. They duly obliged with a 6–1 vote in favour of industrial action, if only out of loyalty to their unions. It began to look even sicker when the Court of Appeal reversed the NIRC ruling that a union was answerable for the conduct of its shop stewards. No sooner had the Lords overturned this Appeal Court judgement than the hitherto obscure – so obscure that most people did not know he existed – Official Solicitor was wheeled in to secure the release of five dockers who had been jailed for contempt. Our worst fears had been realized: imprisonment did exist at the end of the line and there were 'martyrs' who craved the cell.

It was during this fraught period that I had my one and only quarrel with Denis Barnes. With 'martyrs' queuing up for the Tower, Maurice Macmillan was due to fly from Heathrow to make the Secretary of State's annual speech at the International Labour Organization in Geneva. I knew that the issue of whether he should go would arise. I was equally determined that he would not be seen to be panicking, turning back at Heathrow and cancelling a visit to, of all places, the ILO. As I expected, when he arrived at Heathrow, I had to inform him that Denis, possibly acting for Number 10, had been on the 'phone asking him to come back to the office. I also told him that I had argued against this course. Maurice Macmillan decided to carry on with the trip and very naughtily I decided not to ring the office until we were in Geneva. Subsequently, I was not the flavour of the day, the week or the month in the Department. But just before I was due to go on holiday Denis called me up and said he supposed that I knew he had been furious with me. I said I did indeed, but he wasn't half as furious as I had been with my Permanent Secretary because I felt I was right. He laughed in the sort of way that suggested I was incorrigible and gave me a drink.

Any pretence at a new approach by Government to the conduct of the nation's affairs collapsed in November, four days after the final meeting with the TUC. All told the talks had lasted sixty-four hours. As always, the main concern of the parties was to avoid responsibility for the breakdown. What an idiotic world I inhabited. The TUC could not have been surprised or dismayed at the turn of events. The day after a Ministerial re-shuffle, which cleared the decks for intervention, the Government imposed a three-months' standstill on pay, prices, rent and dividend increases. Later it poured money into the coal industry and tightened interest rates by one point to what was going to be a modest nine per cent. There was, understandably, a growing interest in money supply which was signalled to me by Sir Douglas Allen, Permanent Secretary to the Treasury, in discussions outside the Cabinet Room in Number 10. He was beside himself with anxiety about its rate of increase, in the twenty per cents. The foundation for Labour's peak inflation of twenty-seven per cent was being laid.

The United Kingdom became a member of the European Community from 1 January 1973. It is an interesting fact, but it has little to do with this narrative of British self-inflicted disaster. We just continued to knock seven bells out of each other. The gas workers struck in February and March. The hospital ancillary workers struck throughout March and most of April. There was a one-day strike organized by the TUC against, this time, the Government's counter-inflation policy which rather suggested they were bomb happy because no rational person could strike for a pro-inflation policy. In September the TUC expelled thirty-two unions for registering under the Industrial Relations Act. Mortgage rates went up to a record eleven per cent and then, after this personal disaster had struck me as a mortgage payer, I was out on my ear. Willie Whitelaw arrived from Northern Ireland as Secretary of State for Employment – an interesting commentary on the relative problems created by the IRA and the TUC – with Keith McDowall.

Denis Barnes had by then become chairman of the Manpower Services Commission as part of the break-up of the Department into bodies which removed its executive responsibility for health and safety, employment services, training and conciliation. Conrad Heron was the new Permanent Secretary and he gave me early warning that I would not long be the Department's Director of Information. I was extremely upset but to no effect. I could fully understand any Secretary of State wanting to bring back his Director of Information from the hell-hole of Northern Ireland and especially one who, I am sure, in his cunning way, had done a first-class job for him. But for Keith McDowall to contemplate this without so much as a telephone call to me or even a word of warning struck me as a bit much, to put it at its mildest. I blamed him exclusively. I was sure that Willie Whitelaw would be unhappy about the whole affair. The tradition of the Government Information Service then, as now, was not to follow a particular Minister around his Government departments. There was much sympathy for me in the Department and among Labour correspondents who rushed to calm me down over dinner or in the Red Lion over a drink. Geoffrey Goodman and John Elliott, the *FT*'s Labour editor who was as straight as he was awkward with press officers, were prominent among the consolers. But I was, quite frankly, inconsolable.

I asked for a meeting with Willie Whitelaw which took place in his room. We sat in armchairs opposite each other. I wondered whether he was in a position to reconsider my situation. He said, very sadly, that he was not. He had given his word to Keith McDowall that when he returned to Britain he would bring him back with him. It may have been misguided of him to do so but that was what he had done, and that was what he must now do. I said that, in that event, there was only one thing for me to do: to get out of the Department immediately. I was sent on what is euphemistically called 'gardening leave' but with a room available to me in the Department. I found I could not remain in 8 St James's Square. Denis Barnes came to my rescue. He invited me over to the embryonic headquarters of the Manpower Services Commission in Stratton Street, Piccadilly, and my secretary, Angie Marshall, created a new base for me there.

In fact, Willie Whitelaw could not have done me a better turn, though I could not see it at the time. He had removed me from a Department which was rapidly contracting out its executive responsibilities to various agencies. The Department had long passed its zenith. And I was rapidly becoming type-cast within the Government Information Service. I needed fresh fields in which to broaden my experience.

10

Mr Save It

Gardening leave in December has nothing to commend it. I did, in fact, work off some of my frustrations on the leaves and lawns and claimed the neatest garden in Purley by Christmas. But about the middle of the month I had received two strong – but very confidential – tips which were expressed in comforting and flattering terms. The Prime Minister, I was told separately by Conrad Heron and Robin Haydon (who had succeeded Donald Maitland as Chief Press Secretary at Number 10), wanted me for other nationally important work. I gathered that I would do myself a lot of good if I started reading about the energy crisis and especially about oil. It was obvious that Mr Heath was contemplating setting up a new Department, though I was later warned not to count my chickens because there was some resistance in the Department of Industry to losing its responsibility for energy.

I had to play dumb and depressed when journalists rang me to find out how I was getting on. The *Daily Mirror* was particularly solicitous, no doubt for political reasons, about the victim of a most curious exercise in industrial relations by the Department responsible for them. In fact, I was reading every back number of the *Economist* Angie Marshall could lay her hands on to get a feel for the world energy scene. And then at 5.15 p.m. on 8 January 1974, minutes after the formation of the Department of Energy had been announced, Lord Carrington rang me at home. Would I join him as his press chap in this new Department? I conquered the temptation to say something facetious about my not having much to do and time on my hands and said 'Yes, of course, immediately.' To my surprise, he said the next morning would do.

The Department was heir to a complex of crises. The war between Israel and the Arabs the previous October had cut supplies of oil and the international oil producers' cartel was extracting a much higher price for its product. The oil import bill of the developed countries had more than doubled in three years. Indeed, the era of cheap food and raw materials generally seemed to be coming to an end. There was growing concern about the capacity of the world's crust to meet rising demand. Waste was being seen as a sin. At home the Government was facing runaway inflation and its statutory prices and incomes policies – and the by now discredited Industrial Relations Act – were increasingly red rags to the union bull.

Threats to energy supplies and nervousness over pay restraint and other Government policies combined to put the miners in a powerful position. An overtime ban reduced coal production by 25 per cent within three weeks. And a simultaneous overtime ban by power workers' engineers soon brought power cuts. Within a fortnight of the onset of trouble in November 1973 the Government had declared a state of emergency and brought in measures to save electricity ranging from 10 per cent cuts in consumption in public organizations to bans on floodlighting and advertising. By the third week in November the Government and the NUM were shaping up for their second battle within two years. Joe Gormley, the miners' president, said that their pay fight was with the Government, no longer with the Coal Board. Mr Heath said there could be 'no surrender by the Government'. Mr Gormley challenged the Prime Minister to call an election; he was confident that the Government would be replaced by one which would repeal the Industrial Relations Act and tackle the country's economic problems in a different way. Lawrence Daly, the miners' secretary, hoped that if Mr Heath 'throws down the gauntlet the NUM executive will have the courage to pick it up'.

Thus the seeds of war – and arguably war for political as well as industrial ends – had been sown before I had been unceremoniously bundled out of the Department of Employment. Things went from bad to worse as I tended my rockery, absorbed energy as a subject into my system and felt utterly spare. The train drivers banned overtime and Sunday working from 12 December, bringing further disruption to fuel supplies to power stations. The following day, facing a 40 per cent shortfall in coal deliveries, Mr Heath made one of the gravest announcements in Britain since World War II: the country would go on little more than half time from the New Year. The three-day week was at hand. Some people deliberately advertised their sympathies by leaving the lights on in their houses.

And so, on 9 January 1974, after thirty-five days' frustration, I was back where I seemed to belong in Government: up to my neck in trouble. This time I very nearly went under.

If there is one thing to be learned from January 1974 it is not to form a new Government Department to handle a national emergency while you are in the middle of it. The chaos was unbelievable. First, I had no base or reliable telephone. Nominally, the new Department's headquarters were in the old Ministry of Power building at Thames House South. But there was no point in staying there because it took twenty-five minutes to raise the operator on the ancient, overloaded switchboard. My secretary, on her return from holiday, was reduced to tears by the frustration of hanging on the line all day. Sir Jack Rampton, the Permanent Secretary, had a serviceable line in his private office and I used that until I overstayed my welcome. My next stop was the House of Lords. Outside Lord Carrington's room was a bank of the most gorgeous, modern telephones a deprived press officer could ever wish to see. I commandeered one until I judged I should beat a tactical retreat from their increasingly quizzical Lordships. Off then to the Department of Industry across the road from Westminster Abbey. There I located what was to become my press office, carved out of that Department's information division without consultation with me.

I still do not understand how in those early weeks I ran around this circle of offices in search of a usable telephone; served four Ministers – Lord Carrington, Patrick Jenkin, David Howell and Peter Emery; coped with the presentational aspects of a major post-war crisis; kept the media reasonably well satisfied; and took responsibility for the national 'Switch Off Something' publicity campaign to help spin out fuel supplies at power stations. At the same time I had to build and bed-in an information and publicity team. I suppose I should count myself lucky that I made only one serious mistake. I only wish I had not allowed through Patrick Jenkin's 'brush your teeth in the dark' remark when he was asked on the BBC's 'World at One' programme for examples of how individuals could save energy. It was a mistake – an omission immediately rectified – not to have prepared a list of tips for Ministers. And it was a mistake with less than a minute to go before 'World at One' went on the air to let the remark pass without challenge. Robert Williams, the interviewer, gave me a fleeting opportunity – but an opportunity nonetheless – to ask for it to be cut out. I lived to regret not standing on ceremony, whatever problems it caused the programme so hard up against its dead-line. The remark brought ridicule down on Patrick Jenkin's head and his home was staked out by photographers and journalists behaving for all the world like wartime ARP wardens: 'Put that light out.' Unfortunately, they found lights plural.

No Minister has ever accepted responsibility more gracefully and decently than Patrick Jenkin. He apologized to the morning crisis meeting in the Department for letting the side down. We had one of nature's gentlemen in our midst.

The atmosphere, as I recall it, was extraordinary. Here we were into our second coal dispute in two years – though not yet a strike – with the country already on a three-day week and the lights out. At least at night you could not see how shabby Britain was becoming. I found it infinitely depressing that the increasing abuse of power by the unions was moving events to their logical conclusion. Whether we liked it or not – and a lot of people I talked to did not like to admit it – the issue was whether a democratically elected Government was to be allowed to run the country or whether a minority vested interest was to hold sway. This notion provoked much argument and, in discussion about the prospects of a general election, it was often ridiculed because British general election campaigns are seldom fought on one single issue or finish on the original reason for going to the country.

I watched Mr Heath from a distance resist the pressure for an election over 'Who governs Britain?' I viewed this from afar because I was preoccupied with the energy aspects of the crisis rather than with attempts to resolve the dispute. This fell to my old Department with which I had curiously little contact except to winkle out Jennifer Price to become my deputy in Energy.

Lord Carrington was one of the few bright spots in my life at that time. He was a joy to work for – a good-humoured, slightly self-mocking general who, having agreed the approach, left his staff, including me, to get on with it. He had the common-sense view that his director of information needed to know what was going on and be involved. This was invaluable because there are always those in Departments who try to distance a head of information from the facts. Lord Carrington also brought me two new professional experiences: catering for a Secretary of State who is in the Lords and has therefore to be represented in the Commons by a senior Minister; and handling a Cabinet Minister who is also chairman of his party – and at a time when a snap election might be called.

The first meant that I had to watch both Houses, though Lord Carrington was never in any doubt which really mattered – and it wasn't his. It was crucial to service Patrick Jenkin in the Parliamentary Press Gallery during his appearances in the Commons, yet Lord Carrington as Secretary of State and chairman of the party in office was a closely marked political player whenever he spoke. I never found any difficulty in this combined role. My job was to represent his interests as a Cabinet Minister; Conservative Central Office were responsible for him as chairman of the party. And it was my responsibility to ensure that presentationally his Department kept out of party politics and that matters which the Department could not handle were directed to Smith Square. A great deal of nonsense is talked about confusion along this border between Government and party. In my experience it is one of the easier things for a Government press officer to handle.

Among the issues which needed watching very closely was the content of the 'Switch Off Something' campaign. The clear purpose of this campaign was to prolong the nation's endurance against the miners by reducing the consumption of electricity and therefore supplies of coal and fuel oil. As such, it was vulnerable to the charge of being a political campaign. On the other hand, it was difficult for the miners to argue that and yet deny in the same breath that their strike was political. I had less trouble with the campaign than I feared, but we worked very closely with the experts, administrators and Young and Rubicam, our advertising agents, to ensure that our advice on how to economize was accurate and expressed in neutral terms. I did not, however, see how such a campaign could be continued during a general election, if only because immediately a general election is declared all Government advertising normally stops to clear newspaper space and air time for the political parties. I advised that any plan to continue 'Switch Off Something' would have to be put to the Opposition. To my surprise, its continuation was agreed, apparently without any difficulty. But the style and content of the campaign had to be no less closely vetted.

The Government and the TUC repeatedly tried to find a way out of the strike but both were prisoners – the TUC of their past performance and the Government of its experience of that performance. I was one of those who reposed no confidence whatsoever in the TUC's pledge that other unions would not use a generous settlement of the miners' claims as an excuse for high wage demands. There was everything against them in the form book and the Government was guided by form. In the run-up to a strike – as distinct from an overtime ban – and a general election, Mick McGahey, the Communist leader of the Scottish miners, brought out the political overtones of the dispute. In a speech in Scotland on 27 January he said the miners would appeal to the troops for help if the military were to be called in to move coal during a strike. Both his union and the Labour Party felt it necessary to repudiate him after Mr Heath had accused Mr McGahey of trying to use the coal dispute 'to get rid of the elected Government'.

Mr Heath dissolved Parliament on 8 February immediately the NUM called a national strike. A general election was set for 28 February. The day the strike began I flew to Washington for the Washington Energy Conference with Sir Alec Douglas-Home, the Foreign Secretary. Lord Nicky Gordon Lennox, Sir Alex's press secretary, invited me to have a meal on the 'plane with his boss who made me very welcome. I would have felt like jumping out over the Atlantic if the *Leeds Weekly Citizen* had come up! Lord Carrington was able to make only a fleeting visit to the conference. It proved to be a success even though Henry Kissinger and the French representative, a thin-lipped chap by the name of Jobert who introduced me to the egocentric manner of French diplomacy, seemed to spend most of their time rowing. The conference, in fact, created the International Energy Agency which, oddly enough, came to be stationed in Paris even though the French refused to join it. The main value of the conference to me – apart from the experience in energy terms – was to form a lasting friendship with Mohsin Ali, Reuters' diplomatic editor.

Mr Heath laid the election on the line in terms of which I could only approve: 'There are some people involved in this mining dispute who have made it clear that what they want to do is to bring down the elected Government – not just this Government but any Government. They have made it clear they want to change our whole democratic way of life. You have seen them on television and I have seen them in action at first hand. The great majority of you are fed up to the teeth with them and the disruption they cause. The election gives you a chance to make clear how you feel . . .'

The electorate did not take their chance. Nor did the issue remain simple. Events enabled Labour to raise other matters closer to voters' pockets. Indeed, the latter part of the campaign was a catalogue of disaster for the Government – food prices up 20 per cent in twelve months; the biggest ever monthly trade deficit three days before polling; the call by Campbell Adamson, the CBI's director-general, for the repeal of the Industrial Relations Act because of the way, he said, it had sullied relations at national level between employers and unions – a remark which, I should say, proved conclusively to me that the CBI was not much better than the TUC; and an appallingly embarrassing claim, which turned out to be entirely unfounded, that the Pay Board had discovered that the miners were badly underpaid after all. Nothing would persuade Ministers I encountered that this was other than a leak with malice aforethought. Who could blame them? But I was assured by Neville Gaffin, head of information at the Pay Board and my former deputy at the Department of Employment, that this was not so; it was another of those cases of media over-interpretation in an hysterical atmosphere.

We swapped a Conservative Government under siege for a minority Labour Government bent on reversing everything the Conservatives had stood for in return for a social contract with the unions who were supposed to exercise restraint under it. As usual, the Government did its stuff and the unions stuffed the Government.

Eric Varley became the fourth Secretary of State whom I was not conscious of having previously met. In his case it is just possible that we had encountered each other, without knowing it, at NUM, TUC or Labour Party conferences I had covered as a journalist. I warmed to him as a thoroughly decent and honest man. He was a modest, self-effacing, erstwhile Left-winger who applied his innate commonsense to practical problems. He held on to his roots in the village of Poolsbrook, known locally as 'Spike Island', amid the pit heaps to the north-west of Markham colliery beside the M1 in Derbyshire where he had worked. He spoke of his miner-father coughing up his pneumoconiosis in the next bedroom to himself at home and of the eighteen constituents who had died when their cage crashed in carnage to the bottom of Markham shaft the previous August. We were of an age and each had a single son. We had a lot in common. Our friendship continues to this day and he and his wife, Marjorie, used to invite us regularly to Ladies' Day at Royal Ascot when he was chairman of the Coalite Group after leaving politics.

It fell to Eric Varley, now Lord Varley, to get Britain back to work in 1974. He put Britain on full time from midnight on 8 March – three days after the Government had taken office. The state of emergency came to an end three days after that. The NCB's deficit was written off. Progressively the statutory incomes and industrial relations regimes were dismantled by others. The social contract was all.

It also fell to Eric Varley to build up the new Department. I spent the summer in the run-up to the second election of the year, in October, helping to develop and present a whole new energy infrastructure – a plan for coal, designed as much as anything to keep the miners at work; a framework for the development of offshore oil and gas resources announced on 11 July; arrangements through the Offshore Supplies Office for maximizing the British industrial and commercial contribution to the development of our own Continental shelf; the search for a way forward on nuclear power; the creation of an energy research and development programme under Walter Marshall, the brilliant but ill-fated Lord Marshall of Goring, covering 'the winds, the waves, the tides, the sun [solar power], the stars and all who dwell therein', as I used to put it in talks; and a comprehensive approach to energy conservation – the promotion of the efficient and economical use of energy. It was a wonderfully creative period in my life. Under a benevolent Secretary of State and Permanent Secretary, I discovered a whole new fascinating world.

It soon became clear that I would not conserve much of my own energy in this Department – however much energy of various kinds I might persuade the nation to save. And it was into energy conservation – and, indeed, into the education of the nation about the need to save energy – that I threw myself with most enthusiasm. I recruited my publicity chief, Garfield Meredith, from the Department of Employment as I had Jennifer Price. Together we converted the 'Switch Off Something' campaign of the dark days of January and February, in association with the Department's administrators, engineers and scientists, Young and Rubicam, the advertising agents, and the COI, into a comprehensive energy-saving appeal to the nation in the form of the 'Save It' campaign. Eric Varley launched it on 9 December 1974. It was a subject which claimed much of my time and in the twenty-one months immediately before I joined Mrs Thatcher in 1979 it dominated my life. My friends even began to call me 'Mr Save It'.

It brought the energy manager movement throughout the country, with its own national conference and authoritative *Energy Management* newspaper. I spent a great deal of time visiting energy managers' clubs and speaking at energy-saving conferences. We sought to address and motivate every section of the community and to this end even produced an energy teaching pack for schools. We formed a remarkably co-operative, if argumentative, team in Graham Campbell, the formidably able energy policy co-ordinator who used to take my son birdwatching; Tim Coles and David Montgomery, of Y & R; Nic Phillips (COI) and Liz Nelson, the market researcher; and from my own Information Division Garfield Meredith, Geoff Clarke, editor of *Energy Management*, Irene Lally and later Jim Coe, a real publicist who was to become my deputy at Number 10. I also brought the fuel industries into our campaign planning. We had some fascinating sessions with Geoff Kirk (NCB), Tony Vinegrad (British Gas), Alan Wheatley, the former BBC industrial correspondent who had joined the Electricity Council, and John Collins, of BP. Of all the campaigns I have run in Government none has given me greater satisfaction, or been as comprehensive, as the 'Save It' campaign with the distinctive thud of the 'Save It' stamp as its sign-off signal in TV commercials.

If there was a fly in the Ministerial ointment in the Department of Energy it was Lord Balogh. He was widely regarded as the Minister of State inserted into the Department to keep an eye on Eric Varley just as first John Smith and then Dickson Mabon were later seen as balancing Tony Benn. Lord Balogh was one of the two economists originally from Hungary – the other was Nicholas Kaldor – who advised Harold Wilson in the 1960s. He seemed to distrust – a mild way of putting it – anyone who did not instantly fall in with his ideas and had a habit of personalizing any dispute. He also accused me of taking too much upon myself when I was carrying out Departmental policies of which he did not approve. For my part, I took the view that no one with a Middle European accent as thick as his was entitled to imply that he was more patriotic than a chap with an accent as thick as mine, especially when my accent was undeniably British. We did not get on.

One Monday morning I found a front page spread in *The Times*'s business section, under an unfamiliar by-line, suggesting that oil and gas riches beyond the dreams of avarice were waiting to be tapped under the South-Western approaches. If they exist, they have yet to be found. Within the hour I had received a telephone call saying that Lord Balogh had just had a discussion over the 'phone with a public relations chap with whom he was known to consort, expressing his satisfaction with the story. I promptly asked for a meeting with Lord Balogh. I told him there could be only one director of information in the Department and that I did not intend to put up with this freelance activity, especially when I believed it to be misleading. It had either to stop or I would go. He thought that it would be a good idea if I did depart. I retorted that there was one problem: Eric Varley was responsible for the Department, not him. Things went from bad to worse. It ended with him ordering me from his room and me staring him out. I then left slamming the door with such force that I could have done its hinges no good.

I immediately reported the row to Jack Rampton who groaned about yet another official crossing swords with the noble Lord. I also asked for a meeting with Eric Varley who was not available until just before lunch. I saw him in his room at the House. He offered me a drink and I declined. 'So it's that bad?' he said. I told him the tale, which he had already heard. He told me not to fuss about Lord Balogh and then, almost as an afterthought, asked me not to shout at the Minister of State when I had a row with him in future because he had a weak heart. My eyes obviously lit up as I said, with some surprise, 'Has he?' Eric Varley laughingly told me not to be such a nasty so-and-so, and we had a drink. I cannot recall any more serious problems with Lord Balogh.

Eric Varley introduced me to conspicuous consumption in a big way when he took me to the energy show in Houston, Texas, and also to Scandinavia before he departed in a puff of smoke for the Department of Industry. Soon after a referendum had confirmed our membership of the European Community, Harold Wilson swapped him with Tony Benn whose Left-wing industrial policies had been causing increasing concern within Government. I heard about the exchange from the radio at home and laughed long and bitterly. What, I wondered, had I done to deserve this?.

Tony Benn arrived in Thames House South with his pipe, tin mug and his portable office contained in a briefcase of arm-breaking weight, a bitter and disappointed man. He had lost the only job he said he had ever wanted: the Cabinet Minister for Industry. He was entirely distrustful of journalists – as he was no doubt entitled to be – and highly suspicious of anyone and everyone's motives in the Civil Service. He probably had more goodwill than he suspected because, in spite of his record in the Department of Industry, some senior members of the staff had enjoyed working with him in his Ministry of Technology days. I am afraid that he did not set out to cultivate the Department. Instead he tended to shut himself off in his green-upholstered room with its distinctive black furniture – a legacy from Lady Carrington – and drink seventeen pint pots of tea a day with Frances Morrell and Francis Cripps, his political and economic advisers. The Department settled down for a period of readjustment after the even tenor of Eric Varley's ways. I also got early indications that Number 10 would be watching Mr Benn's antics very closely indeed and that my life could be rather fraught.

I was not in the least surprised to discover from Mr Benn's diaries that I was 'a very difficult man' during this period. Superficially, we had a civil working arrangement. I would see him at 9 a.m. with my account of the morning press and the problems and opportunities the newspapers presented and get my steer as to how to handle them. I also alerted him to the awkward questions which would be coming my way that morning about his approach to various policy issues. He would not have been in the Department of Energy had the Prime Minister not regarded him as a maverick, and one of the facts of Government life is that journalists display an inordinate amount of interest in rebels, especially if they remain in Cabinet. I was determined that, whatever else he might say about me, Tony Benn would have no cause to complain that I had abandoned him to his fate. This could also partly explain why he regarded me as 'very difficult'.

Because of the latent pressures from Number 10 I was concerned to know as much as I could of how Mr Benn was going to play his hand, for example, on the economy. I did not want to get into a position of briefing against the Government but equally I was anxious to avoid becoming a director of information who lacked credibility with reporters because I manifestly did not know what was going on. It was also my job to protect my Minister from avoidable trouble. Life was an elaborate balancing act and I count this period as one of the most testing but ultimately one of the more successful episodes in my career as a Government press officer. Whatever I may have thought of Tony Benn at times – and being one of the great wasted talents of British politics was always one of them – he could never claim that I let him down. If he had not chosen to blow it on Bennery he would have been a press officer's perfect Minister – open, courteous, funny, sure-footed and one of God's gifts to easy communication. He might have become something else, too.

In short, Mr Benn was an exasperating man to someone, like me, who did not believe in throwing gifts away. But our blow-up was several months in the making. I would still be surprised if Frances Morrell had anything to do with the ultimate cause. She arrived in the Department a tall, willowy Yorkshire rose who became trendier as the months went by. She was supposed to be as Left and daft as they come, but she wasn't. She was well to the left of centre but, as compared with Stephen Bundred, the long-haired political adviser from Liverpool with whom Eric Varley was landed, she had some experience of the world. I came to see her as someone who could smooth life's road with Wedgie, as he was universally known.

Looking back on it, I suppose there are three main elements to the confrontation which I eventually had to have with Tony Benn if we were to remain a team. The first was my utter distrust of the trade unions to deliver anything and my certain knowledge that if they could take him to the cleaners they would. This did not fit well with his office decoration in the form of TGWU and NUM banners which, while passing as colourful historical works of art, rather advertised his prejudices. My resolve on a visit to the NUM conference on the Yorkshire coast in July 1975 to alert him, in the company of his junior Minister, Alex Eadie, a Scottish miners' MP, to the risks he ran on pay policy may not have gone down too well. The Secretary of State, however, went to great lengths in the back of a car from York to Bridlington to give me my say.

The second was an operation behind my back, as I have always seen it, by an anti-nuclear team comprising Tony Benn, Frances Morrell (who temporarily fell from her state of grace with me as a result of it) and Bryn Jones, a labour reporter I had known on the *Daily Mirror* and subsequently with most of the campaigning environmental groups such as Friends of the Earth. They succeeded in hi-jacking the *Daily Mirror*'s front page with a story about a plan to make Windscale (later Sellafield) the world's 'nuclear dustbin'. I regarded this as outrageous, especially as it was the Government's policy to retain nuclear power as an option in the supply of electricity. But it was all of a piece with Tony Benn's courtship of the environmental groups, which I thought was rather misguided in its approach for a Secretary of State for Energy. No one in the Department could have been in any doubt about my attitude to the Sellafield stunt since I went on the rampage about it. And no one ever convinced me that it was other than a plot to discredit nuclear power. The Secretary of State's consultations with Frances Morrell took altogether too long to handle my complaint about the story, which must have come from inside the Department. His own approving comments about the *Mirror*'s report in the following day's edition as opening up a discussion of the nuclear issue rather gave the game away. There had, of course, been no obstacle to such discussion before the *Mirror*'s stunt. Indeed, Mr Benn was already assiduously discussing the 'problems' of nuclear power with environmentalists. He went on discussing the problems of nuclear power for the whole of his period in the Department.

The third – and terminal – element was ludicrous. Tony Benn conceived the idea of a Ministerial broadcast, without right of Opposition reply, on the development and significance of North Sea oil. It was at this point that I concluded that he must have taken leave of his senses. Given his position in the political spectrum, his reputation for wanting to nationalize anything in the North Sea that moved – or preferably stayed still – the Government's problems in keeping its head above water as a minority administration and the intensely political nature of offshore oil, which was seen as the key to eternal political life in Britain, I had to tell him that the broadcast simply was not on. There was no way, I said, that he could get away with a Ministerial broadcast which denied the Opposition right of reply. Disconcertingly, he exhibited no doubts and told me to write him a draft. I devoted a whole Sunday to a task comparable with that allotted to Sisyphus – except that Sisyphus was not playing with words. I delivered my copy on Monday morning and awaited the detonation. Nothing happened. Instead, I had to force the pace.

Two days later I told Ronnie Custis, the unforthcoming principal private secretary, that he had better concentrate his Secretary of State's mind on the broadcast text since we needed both BBC and Number 10 approval that evening if the air waves were to be cleared for 6 p.m. the following day, 13 November 1975. With less than twenty-four hours to go Tony Benn began to re-write my draft in such a way that I knew it would kill any possibility of the broadcast he sought stone dead. I duly delivered the text to Number 10 and the BBC who immediately said 'No way'. I conveyed the news to Tony Benn who took it better than I had expected. I was foolish enough to add that I was bound to say that I agreed with the BBC. And Ronnie Custis was honest enough to say that he agreed with me. Mr Benn duly noted our opinions. There was no Ministerial broadcast, but Mr Benn did give an interview to the 'Financial World Tonight' on the Petroleum and Submarine Pipelines Act.

Overnight two identical notes to the Permanent Secretary came out of the Secretary of State's red box. He wanted neither Ronnie Custis nor me to accompany him on his forthcoming visit to the United States. Ronnie Custis immediately asked for – and was given – a new job. I was in a much more difficult position. No head of information can do his job without his Secretary of State's confidence. But, as a specialist, I was not as easy to move around as an administrator. There were only a limited number of slots for a director of information. Moreover, I had already done one spell of 'gardening leave'. I did not want to acquire a reputation as the head of information Ministers are prone to lose. I mentioned my problem to John Smith, Minister of State for Energy and the man now often seen as a future leader of the Labour Party. He gave me the sort of excellent advice upon which it is difficult to act. 'Have a row with him,' he said, simply. 'Wedgie does not like rows.'

It is all very well for Ministers of State to have rows with the boss. It is another thing for the Department's director of information to make a profession of it. Instead, I asked for a private meeting with Tony Benn 'to try to clear the air'. I approached the occasion with some fatalism and prepared myself for it as I had prepared Maurice Macmillan for broadcasts. I set down my points to get over on a sheet of paper. We sat in arm-chairs, me with my points to get over on my knee. I began by saying that of all the people in the Department of Energy I had a vested interest in his success. If he were not successful, I would have a great deal of nasty clearing up to do with the media, and I would prefer he was a success. Almost immediately he said that he had treated me badly. He had suffered a trauma in being moved from the Department of Industry and he recognized that he had been unfair to me. From that moment we got on – so much so that, when Jack Rampton wanted to promote me to Under-Secretary two years later, Tony Benn said that, while he did not want to stand in my way, he would prefer me to remain with him as his director of information. I said that I felt I could not pass up this opportunity. A relationship which began so shakily ended on good terms.

If the Department of Energy was never a happy place under Tony Benn, it was never a dull one for me. The tensions between

Minister and Department were seldom far below the surface. One insight into these was given by Brian Sedgemore MP, Mr Benn's Parliamentary Private Secretary, in his book *The Secret Constitution*, a highly conspiratorial account of the machinations of the political establishment. Reviewing the book in the *Daily Telegraph*, Lord Harris of Greenwich, a Labour peer, commented:

> 'Having read it all, and the details of the "10 power struggles" in the Department of Energy, I concluded that I could not think of a fate more awful than to have been one of Mr Wedgwood Benn's officials. The sheer nastiness of it all comes spilling out of these pages. Mr Wedgwood Benn and his associates appear to have developed an obsessive suspicion of nearly all their officials and of all Ministers who did not belong to the Left.'

The tensions were seldom greater than over nuclear power. I cannot say, however, that the nuclear industry helped itself with a Minister who made no secret of his reservations about all matters nuclear. The industry was all over the shop – an utter shambles. The fact is that as a country we took the wrong turning in Eric Varley's day by plumping for the Steam Generating Heavy Water Reactor (SGHWR) system and then under Tony Benn for the Advanced Gas Cooled Reactor (AGR) system. It took some ten years and Mrs Thatcher to make the most hesitant of starts with the American-based Pressurized Water Reactor (PWR) on which the French (those well-known Americanophiles) had long since gone a bundle. Throughout, the Department of Energy had never been in any doubt about the right route: PWR.

If there is one area of British policy which demonstrates how much we deserve to fail as a nation it is nuclear energy. We may have been the first to beat nuclear swords into nuclear ploughshares, but we proved pretty conclusively in my time that we were politically and industrially incapable of tilling the soil. It wasn't that we couldn't break a straight furrow. It was quite simply that we could not get the right bullock pulling the plough. Meanwhile, Arthur Scargill made hay in the undisturbed grass.

I mention this only because of Dr Walter Marshall who has had a stormy career in the service of the public. He was fired by Tony

Benn in 1977 as the Department's Chief Scientist and subsequently resigned over nuclear power as chairman of National Power in the run up to privatization in the last months of Mrs Thatcher. While in the Department of Energy he was also deputy chairman of the Atomic Energy Authority and was advising the Shah of Iran on the development of nuclear power. I have no doubt that Walter was working for huge industrial contracts in Iran for Britain, but these were dependent on our adopting the PWR system as well. It was never very clear why Tony Benn got rid of him. I sometimes suspected it was because Walter made my Secretary of State feel an inadequate member of the human race. Walter's problem was that he made nearly everyone feel intellectually inferior. Unfortunately, not everyone accepted it as a fact as I did. He was exactly the same kind of adviser as Sir Alan Walters, Mrs Thatcher's economics guru. He displayed such an utter certainty – such a lack of doubt – that he made people who had to take decisions very uncomfortable. Both also had the utterly damaging (in Britain) track record of being more often right than wrong.

There is no doubt that Walter's lateral thinking and knowledge had made an immense contribution to the Department and it was widely felt that he had been badly treated by the Secretary of State. I felt sorry for him, which placed me in a very difficult position. All I could do, out of common decency, before he left the Department, was guide him in his handling of journalists who sought his views. He managed to get his point of view across in the scientific magazine *Nature*.

The European Community caused me far less trouble than I ever expected under Tony Benn. His first visit to an Energy Council soon after his arrival in the Department in 1975 probably won me a lot of brownie-points which were to stand me in good stead when the going later became hard between us. I briefed him extensively on what he could expect from the Europhiliacs who generally comprise the British 'Brussels' press corps and, appropriately armed, he did not put a foot wrong in interviews on the Luxembourg lawns. He confided in me later how valuable my briefing had been in the face of a press corps who were doubly hostile – first, because he was not exactly known as the most enthusiastic European; and, second, because, as Mrs Thatcher was to become, he was a target for those journalists whose hobby is collecting celebrated Ministerial scalps.

When Britain took its first turn as president of the European Community in 1977 I warned Tony Benn that his every omission would be noted and reported in a big way. He went out of his way to be thorough, assiduous and open so that not even the most prejudiced could accuse him of neglecting his responsibilities. He was also devastating on his feet – in the way that only British Ministers with their Parliamentary training can be in the EC – in reporting on his activities to the Community. But not even I had bargained for his ultimate idea: a record of his presidency. He set me to work in mid June to produce a thorough printed account of all his works in the Energy Council. He slyly noted that my short-hand note of all his appearances before committees and his press conferences as well as Hansard would make for interesting reading. The very idea gave the Department's cautious Civil Servants litters of kittens. They underestimated Tony Benn: he was not going to let himself down, and I was not going to let Tony Benn down. In any case, given his open way of reporting, he had already cleared his text, as it were. The rest of June was largely devoted to my producing this impressive record. I cannot recall its causing any adverse reaction after publication.

My nightmare with Tony Benn came in Whitehaven, Cumbria, in March 1977. The cause was unofficial action over pay at British Nuclear Fuels' plant at Windscale. The allegation was that the whole place was going to erupt in a puff of irradiated smoke if someone did not do something quickly because the strikers were stopping the import of nitrogen to provide an inert gas for the processes there. It was a ludicrous proposition and I never believed a word of it. For me, it was one of those elaborate nonsenses that occur almost as a natural law of industrial disputes. It is known in the trade as the 'panic in the streets syndrome' – that is, the more you can persuade the public, and more especially politicians, that the end of the world as they know it is nigh, the sooner you will see action on your behalf.

Inevitably, my boy scout Secretary of State felt impelled to fly to the seat of the trouble. In doing so he nearly killed the lot of us. In that event he would have saved Britain – indeed, the world, if you listen to some people – a lot of trouble because not only were the two of us on board but also Frances Morrell and Brian Sedgemore. Suffice it to say that in the howling, black, evening gale the 'plane hit the runway at Carlisle with such a hammering thud that I felt we were doomed. Thank God, I had tanked up Frances Morrell with gin and tonic; she was an appalling flyer at the best of times.

I leave it to Brian Sedgemore in his book, *The Secret Constitution*, to supply from his own diaries his account of what followed. I will merely quote one passage from the morning of 11 March 1977:

'When we have a quiet moment Bernard Ingham tells Tony he is now being used. Frances and John Cunningham (the junior Minister) tell him he must not start tripartite discussions.'

The fact is that Mr Benn got carried away. He offered, according to Brian Sedgemore, tripartite talks over which he would preside. I cannot recall any such detail. All I know is that he was getting himself into the position, as a senior Minister of the Crown – though seniority was not germane to the argument – of busting wide open the Government's incomes policy and social contract. I asked his private secretary, James Bretherton, to take him on one side and arrange a private meeting with his staff in the Waverley Hotel. I then told him in the bluntest, most uncomplicated terms in front of the Ministerial party that if he wanted to go down in history as the Cabinet Minister who single-handedly blew up the Government's pay policy then he should proceed exactly as he had been doing all morning. On the other hand, if he wished to leave Whitehaven in one Ministerial piece he had better extricate himself fast. And that is what he did with his usual skill, leaving the details of negotiation, as I recall it when he addressed a mass meeting, to the constituent parties to the negotiation. I still find it difficult to believe that we reached this point with a member of the Cabinet.

On the other hand, Tony Benn was one of the most engaging companions with whom to travel. There were two contrasting trips: one to Norway for Sunday talks with the Norwegian Government when the Ekofisk oilfield blew out; and one to Saudi Arabia for discussions with the Saudi Government on oily matters. There was absolutely no reason whatsoever – other than political, on which Tony Benn was right – to fly to Norway after Ekofisk had blown a gasket. There was even less reason why we had, at his request, a military photographer on board. We never got low enough, because of the flight restrictions, to photograph anything in detail. Quite apart from his determination to show that he was looking after Britain's maritime interests, he caught us all up in his enthusiasm and fascination for the complex technical details of an offshore blowout.

Saudi Arabia was different. It is, of course, the 'swing oil producer' which determines the price of oil. As such, it was – and is – crucial to the whole world. We stayed in an inevitably dry hotel, with only non-alcoholic beer for our comfort. This was of no inconvenience to the strictly teetotal Mr Benn. But then we received a summons to Sheikh Yamani's residence, the home of the then oil Minister. An elaborate spread was laid before us as we watched Arab workmen on the security television screens struggling in the heat to take on board boxes of booze for the Sheikh's guests. Not a drop passed the lips of our distinguished Arabian hosts or Mr Benn. Jack Rampton and I did our best to uphold the British tradition of enjoying hospitality.

Earlier in the visit we had the pleasure of visiting the Turf Club in Riyadh for lunch. This introduced me to the groaning tables of Arab hospitality I was to come to face as the Prime Minister's press secretary. How, I wondered, did the desert produce all these gastronomic experiences? The Foreign Office languidly said it was all imported, apart possibly from the sheep. It was the sheep that caused Tony Benn and his company most difficulty. What did we do with the carcases, eyes and mostly all, occupying huge plates on the tables? A friendly (and hungry?) sheikh soon showed us how: carve it up with the dagger in your left hand and tear away the succulent flesh with your right hand. These days television – if I did not stop them – would have it all on film.

One source of pride to me as director of information in the Department of Energy was my turning round my relationship with the Secretary of State. I received a great deal of help in doing so from a fellow Yorkshireman, Bryan Emmett, who had been Lord Balogh's private secretary at the time of my problem with his private PR enterprise about the still undiscovered oil reserves of the South-Western approaches. Bryan managed Tony Benn very well indeed. Occasionally we took him out for lunch which is probably the only time our Minister got a square meal during the day outside his own home. He was notoriously uninterested in food, though he did eat a hearty breakfast. The privations of his lunch table were a by-word among journalists. His innocence, if that is the right term, about alcoholic drinks was reflected in the prodigious slugs of whisky or gin he poured for his guests, fit to take the top off your skull. His sole drink was tea for which he was prepared, with Chinese enamel mug and tea bags, at all times; whether wandering down the aisle of Concorde or roaming the first class cabin of a 747 or on a train to Cambridge where the British Rail buffet attendant charged him 20p for hot water.

He was not in the least interested in energy conservation. Neither he nor Frances Morrell, who attended a presentation about the Department's campaign, sparked with anything remotely approaching enthusiasm when Young and Rubicam and the COI and I ran the gamut of the 'Save It' appeal to the public. He saw my regular visits to the International Energy Agency in Paris to chair an energy conservation presentation group as a swan. After Eric Varley, the good times in energy conservation had to await Harold Wilson's retirement and the appointment in 1976 by Jim Callaghan of his former Parliamentary Private Secretary, Dr Jack Cunningham, as junior Energy Minister and fortuitously MP for Whitehaven in which Sellafield is situated. I agree with Brian Sedgemore that Dr Cunningham was exceptionally able. His contribution to energy conservation was outstanding both while I was head of information and from 1978 when I took charge of the new energy conservation division.

As head of this division, my twenty-one months in policy, as distinct from presentation, were extremely agreeable. I even had a social life. I read books, listened to music and had time for walking as well as my garden. I still got in early – at 8 a.m. – because I could do a day's work before the telephone began to ring. But I was home for 7.30. The pressure was off after my usual extremely hesitant start in a new job, primarily in this case because I did not understand the details of economic analysis and discounting. I resisted attempts by others to rush me into decisions and commitments when I did not fully comprehend their implications. I would have liked to prove myself and Jack Rampton by going on to do a mainstream under-secretary's job. But it was not to be. Mrs Thatcher called.

11

To Build a Bridge

As I hiked in the Yorkshire Dales with my wife in July 1979, I inevitably did some stocktaking. I did not set it down on paper and what follows is therefore an attempt – but, I hope, an honest attempt – to summarize how I felt at the time both about the past and the future.

I had no doubts whatsoever about joining Mrs Thatcher. On the contrary, I was looking forward to it. She was the leader of the duly elected Government and as a Civil Servant it was my duty and privilege to serve her as Chief Press Secretary. But I approached the task neither starry-eyed nor committed – except to do my best. I did not believe that the nation had sent her to Number 10 because it necessarily liked the colour of her eyes or the cut of her jib. It was a triumph that a woman had reached the highest political office for the first time in our history, but her election was no more significant to me than that. By 1979 British politicians were rather discredited as a race. After the previous winter of discontent, during which even the dead went unburied in Liverpool, there was despair about the country's future. I did not subscribe to the theory, put about by the outgoing Prime Minister, Jim Callaghan, that there had been a political shift of geological proportions. If there had been, Mrs Thatcher's majority would have been greater than forty-three.

Instead, I took the view that Mrs Thatcher had been elected more in hope than in expectation. What is more, I later told her so. The British electorate had seen Mr Heath come with a new (right) approach and depart with the old (wrong) one. Why should Mrs Thatcher be any different? After all – as Mrs Thatcher was to acknowledge many times later – the prevailing attitude as she took office was that 'they' would not allow this, that or the other to be done. All too often 'they' turned out to be trade unions who were seen to be exercising a national veto. If they did not like it or want it – whatever 'it' may have been – it would not happen. Of course, Mrs Thatcher had come to office pledged to bring the unions under control. But we had heard that from a Government before. A Labour Government could not handle the unions, so why should Mrs Thatcher be able to do so the second Tory time around in the 1970s?

It followed from this that I expected to have a rough time. It would be all the rougher because of my political past. Just as I feared, though not from him, Alan Fisher, general secretary of the National Union of Public Employees, called me a traitor – 'Hello traitor' – when he sat himself down next to me at one of the very few meetings Mrs Thatcher had with the TUC in her early days. Paul Routledge, *The Times* labour editor, asked me at a Department of Energy party how I could live with myself. Much more easily than apparently he could, I retorted, after all that had happened during the 1970s. I at least had been affected by it. I did not understand those like him who had remained unmoved by the industrial mayhem. (According to my calculations, the Department of Employment recorded 25,924 strikes and 128,040,000 working days lost during the decade – an average of 500 strikes and 250,000 working days lost a week. No wonder all those German journalists I had to cope with in the Department of Employment thought we were crazy.) Meanwhile inflation had peaked at very nearly 27 per cent and unemployment had at least doubled in the latter half of the 1970s. Ignore that, Mr Routledge, and you are even less sensitive than I thought you were.

I was not in the least daunted by the prospect of a rough time, whether professionally or personally. Indeed, I thought I would enjoy the experience, provided that it was worthwhile. But it would only be worthwhile if the Government stood firm this time against extra-Parliamentary forces and won through. We simply could not go on as a democracy bowing the knee to militants. I had long since agreed with Maurice Macmillan that in the great sweep of history we had as a nation tamed the power of kings, barons and employers and that sooner or later it would be the unions' turn. I was, however, far from alone in wondering whether the new Government could possibly achieve such a breakthrough.

I also contemplated the future deeply prejudiced against any economic mumbo-jumbo, quick fixes or patent medicines peddled by so-called experts who reminded me of all those roguish travelling salesmen in deafeningly loud check suits I had seen in Saturday night Westerns in Hebden Bridge Picture House. All kinds of horse liniment had been applied to the body politic of Britain. Indeed, I had helped to apply some of it myself over the previous twelve years. And all that had happened was that Britain's joints had seized up ever more quickly and frequently. I knew next to nothing about monetarism, except that Milton Friedman had invented it and Denis Healey had applied it under duress from the International Monetary Fund with, it was claimed, some beneficial results. I did in fact share with my family in 1978 the view that Jim Callaghan was doing a remarkably good job. But it had all gone wrong after that. In the light of my experience, I had no doubt what was needed: for Britain to recover its sanity, for everyone to work and to keep at it, for managements to manage their enterprises and improve efficiency, and for workers to accept the inevitability of change and abandon restrictive practices. We could do with a lot less of 'them and us' in industry – and society generally – and a lot more recognition that we were all in the same leaking, sinking boat.

If I thought there was any one single thing that could change things it was that the unions should become a positive instead of negative force in our society. But that would require a 180-degree turn and I did not expect miracles. I also acknowledged the need for everyone to accept personal responsibility. Nothing had appalled me more about British management than a group of four managers on a train from Leeds to London in 1971 gleefully – and loudly – contemplating a life of indolence and comfort when the Industrial Relations Bill became law. To show that this belief in personal responsibility had not recently been acquired, let me recall what I wrote in the *Leeds Weekly Citizen* almost exactly thirteen years earlier in July 1966: 'We are for ever these days calling on the Government to do this, that and the other. But a Government can only do so much and so quickly. In a democracy – and a democracy is our pride and joy – it is we – the people – who have really to do the job.'

Mrs Thatcher was still entirely in ignorance of her new Chief Press Secretary's views as I roamed around Yorkshire. She also knew little, other than what she had been told, of my professional capabilities. And she was not aware that at least two other members of her Cabinet had their eyes on me. I knew of only one of them at the time myself, but it gave me a boost. While the Prime Minister was recruiting me, Jim Prior was trying to persuade me to return to the Department of Employment to handle the presentational aspects of the first Industrial Relations Bill. I could not tell his Permanent Secretary, Sir Kenneth Barnes, whom I knew well, the main reason why I could not take up his Secretary of State's invitation. But I was explicit about a subsidiary reason: I was very reluctant to return to Departmental information work, even if I could retain my under-secretary rank. Eventually, Sir Kenneth accepted that he had failed to lure me back to my first Department and later when my appointment to Number 10 was announced in September 1979 he rang me up to say that he now really understood why.

I would have been even more buoyed up had I known that another Cabinet Minister, Patrick Jenkin, wanted to recruit me to the Department of Social Services if, as was strongly rumoured in the press at the time, his head of information, Neville Taylor, had been called to succeed Henry James as Mrs Thatcher's Chief Press Secretary. I learned this from Lord Jenkin himself in the central lobby of the House of Commons on Wednesday, 16 January 1991 as I waited with the late Walter Terry and my wife to be collected by Robin Oakley (*The Times*) and John Deans (*Daily Mail*) and taken up to the Press Gallery restaurant to the Parliamentary Lobby dinner in my honour.

Perhaps what is more important, for a man going into the Government's top operational job with the media, is his own assessment of his professional capabilities. I had long since ceased to marvel how a former journalist, lacking in confidence, easily overawed and too often tongue-tied at the wrong time, had become such an ebullient, forthright and, some would say, innovative operator within the Government Information Service (GIS). I was nowhere near a satisfactory explanation of this transformation in myself. Some of the change could be put down to experience. I suppose the process would have been greatly speeded up had I gone to university, though that might have changed me as a person. Another part of the explanation was the much greater access to information and my habit of clarifying my mind – and often many other minds – on paper. That made me much more fluent in argument.

But perhaps the most important reason for my development was the way I responded to the top media job in the Departments and agency I had served. As head of information, I believed that I was entitled, as much as any head of a policy division, to my own view of my responsibilities and how they should be discharged. It became painfully clear to me from the outset of my career in the Civil Service that, with notable exceptions who as a result could be even more troublesome, there was a massive ignorance, prejudice and defensiveness about the media among administrators. That did not, however, stop some administrators from having their own pronounced views on how relations with the media should be conducted or how policies should be presented. And, since they regarded themselves rather highly, they expected us mere mechanics in the GIS to obey without argument. My early years in the Civil Service had been one long seethe, punctuated by explosions, over this condescending attitude. I gave those responsible to understand that I had no intention of allowing them to run me into serious presentational trouble, especially as my name would be on it in journalists' eyes and I would have to sort it out. So far as I was concerned, I was their media adviser and I expected them to listen to me; I did not expect to have to listen to them on media matters. I was always willing to learn about anything but I needed to be satisfied of their capacity to teach me in my own field.

I think I can safely say that I did not make my way in the Civil Service by being a nice, gentle soul who never bit back. Far from being a yes-man I was an extremely awkward cuss when I felt I had to be. I did not like having rows because the aftermath was so wearing, wondering whether I had been fair or not. But I did not mind having rows if that was what people wanted. I once had one with an under-secretary in the Department of Employment which started outside Victoria Station and proceeded merrily past Buckingham Palace, through Green Park, in front of Lancaster House and up Pall Mall to the very doors of 8 St James's Square. He simply was not prepared to accept a role for presentation that did not accord with his own prejudices about Information Division's place in the hierarchy. Whenever I walk past Buckingham Palace these days I recall this row and my thinking at the time how impressed Her Majesty would have been had she known that two of her civil servants were taking their jobs so seriously as they passed by her front door.

John Liverman, a deputy secretary in the Department of Energy, once complained that I was altogether too certain of myself. I retorted that somebody needed to be in view of all the 'on the one hand' and 'on the other' going on. I added that in the subjective world of presentation no one could be very certain of anything – that was why we press officers had to have guts – but an authoritative style was more calculated to achieve success than a palsied approach. Philip Jones, another deputy secretary in the Department of Energy, apparently felt I wanted to take over the whole Department. On the contrary, my objective was to make sure that no one – and most certainly not the blissfully ignorant and negative – took over my information division. Fair-minded people, like Ivor Manley, the Department's personnel director, immediately took my point when other officials showed in the *Financial Times*'s coverage that they were prepared to tell journalists more than they were prepared to tell me. I did not get on with that sort at all. I was a team player and I expected the team to play with me.

I assumed that Number 10 was well aware of my reputation. Perhaps it was felt that someone of this sort was needed to handle the purposive Mrs Thatcher. Certainly, members of my own staff at the Department of Energy – and most notably the late and much missed Margaret German who was then running energy conservation publicity – could not wait for Thatcher and Ingham to collide. In fact, I usually had an easier relationship with politicians – that is, with Ministers – than with officials. (Lord Balogh was, of course, no politician.) My thought processes were much more those of a politician than of an official. This remained the case even though, in July 1979, when I walked in the Dales, I had been one of those dreaded administrators for eighteen months. But, in common with any sensible politician, I had long before my promotion recognized the need to listen closely to what an administrator had to say on policy, law and fact. If an administrator is not a guardian of integrity he is nothing. As such, he is properly the elite. As an administrator, I also discovered why, apart from his background and training, he thinks he is the elite: it is because he has to be the elite. It is because he has to sort through and make a recommendation on the often conflicting, inconclusive and perhaps timid or bottom-protecting advice from lawyers, economists, statisticians, scientists and any other specialist you can name – except, I hope, from my information division. This may sound immodest but I tried to make a practice of calling a spade a bloody shovel and telling people what, in my view, they ought to do. It was the attitude that I took to Number 10 – and the attitude Jack Rampton told me to take there. 'Do not be afraid to give your advice . . .'

Another assumption I made in Yorkshire that summer was that I had been recruited to Number 10 because of my track record with the media. In fact, there was not a lot to go on in Number 10 terms. This is because in 1979 – and to a large extent now – Number 10 was a unique operation. This stems from its relationship with the Parliamentary Lobby Journalists – or the lobby, as they are known for short. My main clients in the National Board for Prices and Incomes and in the Department of Employment had been members of the Labour and Industrial Correspondents' Group. In the Department of Energy they had been energy correspondents, a much looser organization. Both groups brought together journalists specializing in a particular subject, and from time to time these groups arranged lunches to which they invited Ministers or experts. Neither were, however, as inveterate lunchers after truth as members of the lobby. The lobby, with its sub-structure of alliances and co-operative arrangements among journalists, marches on its stomach. That, I was to discover, could be one of the problems with the afternoon lobby which I came to take most days. But of that more later.

Both labour and energy correspondents groups were specialist extensions of the lobby in the sense that they operated under lobby rules – that is, press officers normally communicated with them on lobby terms. There is nothing complicated about this. Press officers speak as frankly as they feel able to members of these and other groups, either individually or collectively, on a background basis: i.e. the journalist does not identify his source precisely in writing his story or, to be more precise in these days when the purity of rules is so debased, he merely refers more generally to Government, Ministerial, official, Whitehall or Westminster sources. This method of communication with journalists is universally practised in Government and other circles the world over as a means of opening up the relationship – of enabling more information, and therefore more understanding, to be conveyed than if journalists were to identify their source and attribute their remarks to their informants. It is interesting that attendances at the average 12.30 on-the-record, entirely attributable briefing at the Foreign and Commonwealth Office are minimal because journalists rightly believe that nothing of any importance will be disclosed. Moreover, if anything does emerge, it will be disseminated by the news agencies on tape.

The lobby system is, of course, open to abuse by both press officer (or Minister) and journalist. It can encourage journalistic licence because there is no requirement to quote an informant. Equally, it can promote recklessness in Government because (theoretically, at least) unattributable remarks can be denied. In practice there are many checks and balances against abuse by Government. Not the least of these are the breakdown in respect among journalists for anyone – and especially anyone in what might loosely be termed government – and, I am sorry to say, a pervasive malice in journalism. Anyone talking to any journalist anywhere these days has to be careful unless a bond of trust exists between the two. Otherwise, he knows that if he makes the slightest slip he will be exposed. This is not because each and every journalist is nasty or malicious, but because the competitive pressures upon the best of them are formidable. Consequently, the trustworthy today are paragons. There are not, however, many sanctions against journalists who abuse the system other than for Number 10 to cut them off for a time when Number 10's guidance is most needed.

What was – and remains – unique about Number 10's relationship with the lobby is the systematic nature of their meetings with the Chief Press Secretary, or his deputy, twice a day at 11 a.m.

in Number 10 and at 4 p.m. in their own eyrie in the Palace of Westminster. No Department, apart from the Foreign Office, conducts its affairs on this regular, collective basis. This is not to suggest that heads of information in other departments do not brief journalists collectively – as distinct from individually, which they do all the time – but the occasions are much less frequent. Not even in the Department of Employment, in my strike-ridden days, did I see labour correspondents as regularly as I met the lobby in Number 10. To underline the point, Jean Caines, one of my six deputies in eleven years at Number 10, described her life there as more regimented than the fifth form.

In July 1979 I was therefore about to enter a new and trying phase in my career for which, as one whose experience had been confined to ordinary Government Departments, I was not entirely prepared. If there was anything which caused me concern it was the lobby. And if there was anything which influenced my actions in the following eleven years as a senior member of the GIS with responsibility for bringing on junior staff, it was relations with the Parliamentary Lobby Journalists. All of this was yet to come in 1979. In July all I had to show was my track record as a communicator with specialist groups. This was based on the values which I brought to the work of a Government information specialist.

My view of what press officers should be was greatly influenced by my experience of them as a journalist. It had by no means been all bad, though much better in London than in Yorkshire where, of course, everyone hears all, sees all and says nowt. To listen to some journalists you would think that all press officers are archetypal Yorkshiremen. This stems from a wholly unrealistic view of what a press officer can and should do. He cannot invent – unless his boss is happy for the ship to be piloted dangerously by public relations – not even for the convenience of journalists hard up against a deadline. Nor is he paid by news organizations. His first loyalty is to his employer. It is not his job to run his employer into trouble and still less, if you are working for Government, to run the Government out of office. Nor can he tell the truth, the whole truth and nothing but the truth, assuming he knows the ultimate truth. In my experience the basic facts of a case, for example about pay and conditions in an industrial dispute, evolve over time. I doubt whether I have ever finished briefing journalists in a dispute with the same basic fact sheet with which I started.

Equally, the press officer must not knowingly mislead. If he does – or if journalists believe, perhaps unfairly, that he has misled them – then he is professionally dead in the water. All the efforts of a lifetime to build up a reputation can be reduced to ashes by one careless or rash briefing. This means that the press officer deals in only one commodity: credibility. Either he is a credible, reliable informant or he is useless. And bear markets in useless press officers are not a pretty sight. They can empty a press-conference room faster than a stink-bomb. Nor, in my view, should a press officer leak, by which I mean he should not take it upon himself to disclose information without higher authority, especially when someone else will be required to answer for the consequences. Journalists, of course, love a leaky press officer, but not for long because leaky press officers do not last.

All sensible journalists recognize these limitations in the press officer, even if they do not always show it when they are under pressure. What they cannot stand is the brick wall press officer: the person who knows nothing; who will never be in a position to know anything useful; who either shows no inclination to try to find out or promises to do so and never rings back; or who can never be relied upon to be there when needed or melts mysteriously into the day or night when required in a crisis. The concept of the brick wall press officer has died much faster in my time in Government than in industry. I cannot say that it is stone dead, but there is now a much more positive view of the role of the press office within Government among administrators as well as Ministers. As a race, Ministers have never had any doubts about the need for a person who gets him publicity. Both now recognize that a brick wall is not the best basis for a creative relationship with journalists and that a brick wall, both in performance and reputation, cannot suddenly become an influential and potent ally when the press are massing for an attack.

No press officer of any potential likes to be a brick wall. For one thing, it is a wearing existence. These unfortunates do not occur naturally. They are man-made by a union of two abominations: an ignorant and probably arrogant chief executive and a weak, inconsequential and probably obsequious senior information or public relations official. Between them they have given press officers a bad name. But the person fundamentally responsible is the most senior official handling media relations. If he does not carry clout, his press officers are unlikely to carry conviction with the media. The relationship at the top of any organization between the chief and the chief press officer or his equivalent is crucial. The trade, craft or profession of press officer has not been well served.

One other quality among press officers had created an impression upon me as a journalist. It was a press officer's loyalty to his boss and his organization. By loyalty I do not mean a slavish, unseeing, uncritical devotion to the individual and the cause. That produces neither light nor shade nor understanding. I cannot bring myself to blame press officers for refusing to indulge in subtleties with some journalists, especially gossip columnists. But what deeply impressed me as a labour or industrial journalist was the willingness of admittedly a limited number of press officers to brief candidly about their boss and their organization while at the same time conveying an utter loyalty to both. I can cite no more distinguished example than the late Geoff Kirk, of the National Coal Board, who was a cruel victim of the 1984–5 coal strike.

There was also Charles Birdsall. Charles's forte was never deep, policy background briefing. Nor was Dick Seaman's at the Department of Economic Affairs. Both, in their very different ways, were positive, creative operators *par excellence*. Both set out to build a bridge between journalists and their Departments and to keep that bridge load-bearing and in a good state of repair. They were examples I took to heart.

I had also reached certain conclusions about my new role from my observation of and acquaintance with previous Chief Press Secretaries. I had met or worked with nine of the fourteen individuals – I was the fifteenth – who had served in this capacity. Sir Fife Clarke (with Winston Churchill from 1952–5) and Harold Evans (with Harold Macmillan from 1957–63), were before my time in the GIS but both, now dead, took a benevolent interest in me in my younger days. Harold Evans was particularly kind in inviting me up to his private dining-room which he tried out for Henry

James, my immediate predecessor at Number 10, on the top floor of the Vickers' Building, otherwise known as Millbank Tower. I used to leave after every lunch there wondering how on earth I would ever do any work if I had that view to all points of the compass overlooking the Thames. It had one deficiency: you could not actually watch a cricket match at the Oval. Otherwise, it was perfect.

The work and philosophy of Fife Clarke and Harold Evans, as well as their predecessors I had not known or met, helped to form me in my new role. We should not underestimate the power of observed and recorded performance, pragmatism and personality – and that is not just convenient alliteration – in shaping the development of government under an unwritten constitution. But the three, apart from Henry James, who had the most influence on me were Joe Haines, with Harold Wilson from 1969–70 and from 1974–6; Donald Maitland, with Ted Heath from 1970–4; and Robin Haydon, with Mr Heath in his last months at Number 10 in 1974. Joe Haines and Donald Maitland gave me negative guidance; Robin Haydon pointed the way forward positively.

I had to ask who J. T. W. Haines was when he left the pre-Murdoch *Sun* to succeed Trevor Lloyd-Hughes in 1969. I had never knowingly met 'Himmler', as he was universally known among journalists on account of a facial resemblance which not even the charitable, like myself, could discount. Joe was not a bad chap, and by all accounts was a brilliant speechwriter whose contribution as such to the Wilson years was never fully recognized. He did not harass me while Tony Benn was at the Department of Energy in the way that Tom McCaffrey, a real professional, was to do as Jim Callaghan's agent. I once had to tell Tom – if a right, Ingham bellow down the telephone is a correct description of 'tell' – that it was his job to co-ordinate a view within Government that Tony Benn would not particularly approve of, not mine. I was going home. Joe's contribution to my upbringing was to convince me that the prime job of a Chief Press Secretary is to maintain relations with the mass of British journalists, as distinct from a loopy minority. Joe pulled up the drawbridge and chose to communicate with the great British media, lobby and all, by means of written missive. That was never likely to be satisfactory. To be fair, his letter to the chairman of the lobby to this effect came in 1975 towards the end of his time in Number 10 and, no doubt, after immense provocation. But I could only regard it in July 1979 as an example not to be followed.

Donald Maitland was an entirely different animal. He was a career diplomat who had been the FCO's head of news and so had experience of handling journalists. He went on to be our man at the United Nations in New York and at the European Community in Brussels and the Permanent Secretary of the Department of Energy. He was extremely ill served by Ted Heath who, at a garden party on the lawns of Number 10, insulted representatives of the GIS there by calling Donald a professional. I heard a lot of dark muttering. Donald had to carry that burden for the rest of his days as Chief Press Secretary. It meant that the real pros were looking and waiting for every slip. In some ways Donald brought a refreshing, new mind to the Government's business of communicating with the media. He developed the concept of 'points to get over'. He exhibited a clear, concise intelligence in meetings to co-ordinate presentation which he chaired in Number 10, though by all accounts he poured words over the lobby like the sea pours water on to the shore. He was also pretty open and accommodating so far as I was concerned, involving me directly and intimately in Number 10 in major industrial disputes and in the 1972 talks with the TUC and CBI. I got on with him extremely well. He was just my kind of positive communicator. But he either ran out of patience with the lobby or became bored, or both. The result was that he started to experiment with on-the-record briefings and statements and with delegating the job of spokesman to Ronnie Hayles, his deputy. Neither went down well because journalists want to explore solid information with the champion hurdler and not with the second past the post.

Robin Haydon, another career diplomat who had also been the FCO's head of news, went on to be Ambassador in Dublin. He taught me one other thing: devotion to duty. I do not think Robin, a red-haired chap like me but with his temper under much better control, much relished Ted Heath's last months in Number 10. They must have been trying, to say the least. But one thing above all impressed me as he lugubriously pulled on his cheroots: his utter commitment to the job in hand. I liked him so much – he was, I felt, so much my kind of person – that I tried repeatedly to invite him out for lunch. But Robin sternly but kindly said that he simply could not get away. I remembered Robin when in Number 10 I had to cancel lunches at the last minute.

I therefore went to Number 10 with a clear and comprehensive view of the work of a press officer – indeed, of an information officer, to extend the role wider than the mere handling of press, radio and television journalists to the communications orchestra as a whole: advertising, films, visual aids, radio tapes, publications, conferences, seminars and so on. To summarize, my concept of the Chief Press Secretary's job was to:

1 maintain a dialogue – relations – with the media, and more particularly with the lobby; to build a bridge between Number 10 and journalists and keep it in a good state of repair. In other words I saw the job as being to manage the Government's overall relations with the media.

2 keep the communications bridge open on a basis of mutual respect; I recognized that they – the media – had a job to do, and they, I felt, must acknowledge that I had my responsibilities. I no more intended to stand any nonsense from them than I expected them to stand any from me.

3 be as open as I could with the media, taking account of all the circumstances; to give them as good a steer as I could as to the true nature of events and to avoid misleading them.

4 represent the views and interests of the media within Government and, not least, to the Prime Minister. In other words, to act not as a one-way conduit of news and views but as a bridge for the two-way flow of information between Government and media. (The very idea that I might be able to identify the media's interests, let alone represent them within Government, frequently brought hoots of incredulity when I spoke to courses, especially for BBC radio and TV trainees. But who else, did they assume, would do so? Probably no one, because by the mid 1980s young journalists were proud to consider themselves an estate apart, except, of course, when it came to their own personal

protection, whereupon they resumed their fully paid up membership of the human race.)

5 brief the lobby and other journalistic groups as often as I could myself, recognizing that journalists always want the organ-grinder, never the monkey – and recognizing, too, that my organ-grinder would be nothing as compared with that great wurlitzer in the sky called Mrs Thatcher.

6 treat everyone as equally as possible, regardless of which organization they represented. The provincial press, for example, had a legitimate claim on my time because of the extent to which they, above all newspapers in Britain, seek objectively to present the news and are read in their circulation areas. I had a horror of such institutions as the 'White Commonwealth' – a selected group of journalists who were given privileged access in Harold Wilson's days as Prime Minister – because of the disaffection it had caused.

7 ensure that I was in a position to meet the legitimate demands of journalists – as distinct from their wilder aspirations – through my access to the Prime Minister and her documentation.

We shall see in the chapters ahead how well I lived up to the prospectus I randomly brought together in my wanderings through Wharfedale, Nidderdale, Wensleydale and Swaledale in July 1979. If there is any place I can recommend for collecting your thoughts it is in the Yorkshire Dales. And the one to beat the lot for restoring sanity is the Hebden valley which leads up from Hebden Bridge to the Pennine Way and Wuthering Heights.

12

A Most Untypical Woman

My first month in Number 10 was, after the Prices and Incomes Board, the second most untypical start to any job I have done. First, I do not function properly as a deputy-in-waiting, and Henry James retained a full hold on the reins to the very end. He accompanied the Prime Minister to Bonn on 31 October before I took over the following day with a visit by Chairman Hua of the Chinese People's Republic. I gave a briefing about Hua's talks with the Prime Minister in the Chief Whip's Rooms in Number 12 Downing Street after a row with FCO officials who tried to bully this amateur called Ingham into saying nothing. Henry, who could not bear the thought of leaving Number 10, turned up for this briefing to pronounce that I would be a good Chief Press Secretary. I was not so sure. I found it a trying occasion.

Second, I spent most of October 1979 reading myself into the policy programmes of individual Departments and discussing them with their heads of information. This task gave me the opportunity to impress upon all chief information officers that I intended Mrs Thatcher's regime to be different. It was, I emphasized, going to be a looser Number 10 rein than some I had known myself. I hoped that they would not feel constrained by Number 10 Press Office. Their job was to put over Government policies and measures in a positive way. They knew their own subjects and journalists better than I did and it was up to them to devise their own presentational programmes, within the familiar conventions and constraints affecting Government publicity. They would only find me nagging them if I felt they were not getting through to the public. My job was to try to drag the overall Government story together and to ensure that the communications orchestra I was conducting was following the same score. I hoped that they would keep me informed of what they were up to so that I would be in a position effectively to co-ordinate Government presentation and ensure that the various elements of the orchestra came in on cue. By that I meant that I wanted to know of the broadcasts their Ministers were undertaking and the articles they were writing for newspapers so that I could be in a position to inform other Departments of any clash of activity.

If this was mostly standard stuff from Number 10, the message, I hoped, would be liberating. I did not want information heads to feel as inhibited as I had sometimes felt over the previous twelve years. Admittedly, my experience may not have been typical because of the nervousness which Tony Benn had generated at the centre. Even so, I thought that it would do no harm to accentuate the positive from the outset. Those who have been brought up by the media to assume that I ran the whole show with a rod of iron – that Wackford Squeers was in violent occupation of a 'Dotheboys Hall' within Number 10 Press Office to which heads of information were summoned for admonition or correction – will find this account of my initial approach to chief information officers incredible. The very idea that I sought rather than demanded co-operation and hoped heads of information would do this or that rather than instructing them to do so is so at variance with media legend as to require explanation. It is regrettably not enough to tell people not to believe a word they read in newspapers.

In a Cabinet system of Government the Prime Minister is first among equals. He or she can only go as far – or on for as long – as a majority of Cabinet colleagues allow. If Mrs Thatcher extended the frontiers of what is possible in a British system, so much more is there to be said for the quality of her leadership. The fundamental point of collective responsibility in Cabinet remains valid. But in a Cabinet system of Government both the formulation of policy and its presentation to Parliament and public is devolved on individual Cabinet Ministers who enjoy a substantial degree of autonomy. It is they who devise policies and clear them through Cabinet. And it is they – and only they – who have the detailed background knowledge properly to explain and present them.

The position of the Chief Press Secretary in relation to Departmental heads of information exactly mirrors that of the Prime Minister in relation to his or her Ministers. Of course, some Chief

Press Secretaries might try to throw their weight about but that does not provide a solid foundation on which to build co-operation. The only power that I felt I exercised as Chief Press Secretary over my information colleagues was that of persuasion. My arguments carried weight only to the extent that they carried conviction with them in terms of both their own Ministerial and Departmental interests and those of the wider Government for which they, too, had to have regard. These arguments would be more or less potent depending upon my reputation with the individual chief information officer concerned for being constructive, practical, fair, experienced and reliable – reliable, that is, as an adviser who would stand by his advice if it came to be tested or under fire. From the day I arrived in Number 10 to the day I left eleven years, one month and five days later, I knew the limits to my authority: it was bounded by my ability to persuade.

The third reason why my start in Number 10 was deceptive was that Parliament was in recess. Number 10 during a Parliamentary recess is unreal. There are three levels of unreality about it. While the House is sitting a quarter of a mile away, Number 10 has about it an air of tension and uncertainty which evaporates when the House rises. Don't anyone tell me that Parliament exercises no control over the Executive. When the Prime Minister leaves Number 10 for a trip abroad, or for Chequers, a great deal of dynamism and electricity drains out of the building even when the House is sitting. But when the Prime Minister departs from Number 10 during a recess the building becomes a haven of peace and tranquillity – unless, of course, a major crisis suddenly blows up. The differences in atmosphere have to be experienced to be believed. In October 1979 Mrs Thatcher went abroad three times – to Italy, Luxembourg and Bonn. I sometimes wondered what kind of operation I had joined. But once Parliament returned on 22 October I began to get a real feel for the place and, more importantly, for the Prime Minister's way of governance.

Mrs Thatcher's natural habitat, I soon discovered, was not the media. She regarded journalism as the haunt of the brittle, the cynical and the unreliable. She had a point, as I knew only too well even if up to 1 October 1979 I had led a relatively sheltered life as a Government press officer. Of course, she recognized that a free press was essential to a free society and that journalists had to be catered for. She also acknowledged that, like it or not, Governments in democracies must communicate with the public largely through a third party called the media – press, radio and television. Ministers cannot commandeer the air waves and the rules forbid buying space at taxpayers' expense to put over political messages. She might even like a few journalists who shared her beliefs and had on the whole treated her decently. But she was never going to be a Prime Minister who would court them or generally enjoy their company. Nor, to her enormous credit, did she do so throughout her eleven and a half years in office. She would do her duty to the Government she led by giving broadcast interviews and meeting editors and journalists to explain herself and her policies and even throw the occasional party for groups of journalists. But by and large she did what she did with the media because I asked her to do so – or, when the occasion demanded it, I advised her to do so in necessarily firm tones. 'Why,' she asked more than once, 'do I need to see them when I have a press secretary?' I used to reply: 'Because you are Prime Minister and I am only me.'

My next discovery – or rather confirmation in view of my musings after my initial 'interview' with Mrs Thatcher in June – was that she was almost entirely policy-oriented. As the world's top executive lady she breathed, drank and fed on substance. She most certainly slept on it, to the extent that she ever slept, because she was at her most dynamic at early morning meetings when all the ideas and requirements that had accumulated overnight poured out. The torrent was fearful to behold after a week-end at Chequers when she tried to get at least one decent night's sleep. I suppose that at that time she was running efficiently on no more than four hours' sleep on a good week-day night. What mattered to Mrs Thatcher was policy. If she could get the policy right she believed that presentation would more or less take care of itself. When I protested that this was going a bit over the top, she conceded that we needed to work at presentation, too. But her attitude to policy reflected her view that politics were not, in Bismarck's words, 'the art of the possible'. Politics, in Mrs Thatcher's view, were the art of making possible the impossible. First, you had to know what you wanted to do. Then you had to devise a practical policy to achieve it. Third, you had to marshal arguments in support of that policy and to meet criticisms of it. And finally you had to go out and bang over those arguments. But presentation was merely a mechanical operation. The key to achieving the impossible was sound policy. Mrs Thatcher gave her all to policy.

Against this background, it became rapidly clear to me that I was going to have to carry a heavy responsibility. If any Prime Minister was going to need a manager of her relations with the media it was Mrs Thatcher. She was quite simply not interested in the press, radio and television unless she came to feel that the Government's message was not getting over. It was not that she pretended that she did not read newspapers; she did not read them at all, except the front page of the *Evening Standard* which was left for her on the table outside her study at the bottom of the stairs leading up to her flat and possibly each morning the news digests on the front pages of the *Financial Times* and latterly the *Wall Street Journal*. I have no evidence that she secretly indulged herself in newspapers in her flat. She did race through some of the Saturday and Sunday newspapers at Chequers and she did while away some – but not much – of the time on flights reading the press. But these flights served only to demonstrate her unfamiliarity with the layout of individual newspapers. Most of her knowledge of what was going on in the world was imbibed from the BBC's 'Today' programme (except when she cut herself off from its mischief), the Press Association club tape outside her Private Office, which Mr Attlee had apparently regarded as the cricket score machine, and her staff. So far as I could ever tell, she watched television news and current affairs programmes only in snatches. And she never ever watched herself on television. 'Turn it off,' she demanded whenever she came up on the screen. Her attitude was inconvenient to say the least if you were trying to monitor the telly at the time.

The only occasion I can recall her watching herself on television was in preparing for the televising of the Commons in the autumn of 1989. She then spent some time looking at videos of the experimental coverage before the signal went out over public television. This brought two principal concerns – the danger, because of the angle of the camera, that the viewer would see only the top of her head if she read a speech, and the consequent need to inject greater bodily movement into her delivery. She dealt pretty effectivel[y] these problems but remained profoundly sceptical about the [wis]dom, in terms of the House's reputation, of televising proceedings. My consistent view was that Mrs Thatcher would score high marks because of her presence, her authority and her command. And so it proved.

My next discovery was the value which Mrs Thatcher put on loyalty. I do not know what went on in the Department of Education and Science between 1970 and 1974 when the Prime Minister was Secretary of State there. Nor have I had the temerity to inquire. Suffice it to say that in all my dealings with Mrs Thatcher the premium she put on loyalty to herself as a Minister harked back to her first Cabinet post in the DES. Terry Perks, my deputy in Number 10 when I retired, was chief press officer in the DES during that period. He passed muster with Mrs T. No higher tribute can be paid to his loyalty.

For my own part I had my own troubles with the DES. Over a period of some ten years the DES managed to lose three chief information officers for whose abilities I had some regard – Jennifer Price, Neville Gaffin and Liz Drummond. It has a lot to answer for. It may be that these three officials did not do justice to themselves in the DES, though I think that unlikely. Instead, I doubt that they were given the chance. I have met a number of senior Civil Servants in my time who were deficient in one way or another but I had to find a way of getting on with them. I do not accept that the three chief information officers I mention were deficient. Yet they did not get on in the DES, though Neville Gaffin made a very fine fist of it for four years with Sir Keith Joseph until Kenneth Baker and his blessed need for personal chemistry came along. Rather like Lady Bracknell, I think it would have been unfortunate of me to lose one chief information officer I rated from the DES. To lose two might be put down to carelessness. But to lose three suggests to me there might be something wrong with the DES, even taking into account the infusions under Mrs Thatcher of new blood at the top. I am less clear what the Department has done for children. I would merely record that while I was trying to secure agreement among twenty or so different Government Departments on the way forward on energy conservation in 1978–9, I conceived the idea of including energy studies in schools. The DES officials were adamant: the curriculum was sacred and inviolable territory and not to be tampered with. Three cheers for Mrs Thatcher's national curriculum.

In these early days in Number 10 I also formed the view that Mrs Thatcher by no means fitted the supremely sure, confident and overpowering mould of Prime Minister into which the media had poured her. Of course, she was secure in her own ideology. She broadly knew what she wanted and where she wanted to go. She was also determined to get there. But anyone who harboured not the slightest doubt about anything would never have provoked argument in the way that she did. Nor would they have argued as fiercely or in so personally provocative a way as was her habit. It was almost as if she believed in the trial of her policies by ordeal. Every step of the way, it seemed, had to be tested by the challenge of her assertions. Nor would a serenely certain Prime Minister have regarded it as her duty to work, but fortunately not to drink, every man under the table deep and far into the night. She had a disconcerting habit of getting second wind about 1 a.m. much to the distress of the assembled manhood. Absolutely confident people do not feel impelled continually to prove their stamina. Finally, by way of further example, for years we never went abroad without Mrs Thatcher wondering whether her journey was really necessary. This was her unconfident way of thinking herself into a visit. She ran a peculiarly wearing way of Government. But to me it was also endearingly revealing. She was very much a human being.

She was also the most untypical woman I had ever encountered. After Barbara Castle, she was not just a quick change artiste. She was a candidate for the *Guinness Book of Records*. She was the fastest female in the west when it came to dressing for dinner. Any evening she could beat her husband, Denis, into a cocked hat. She was also absolutely determined never to be late for anything. This meant that she was invariably early. On an endless number of occasions her driver had to saunter along or take the long route, or as occurred more than once to my certain knowledge, kill time in a lay-by to the concern of her detectives. This ability to dress and doll up quickly and this preoccupation with being on time meant that I had to take exceptional precautions. On one occasion, I recall, I finalized with her in her flat a speech for the centenary dinner of the Parliamentary Press Gallery in 1981 with about thirty minutes to go to the time of departure for the Caledonian Club. The changes to the text were minimal. I dashed downstairs and dictated them to my secretary, Stephanie Walmsley, and Jan Luke, the press officer responsible, all the while stripping off to the extent that decency allowed. I then ordered everyone out while I changed my trousers. They then rushed back in with the final text. And just as I began to check that the pages were in strict and proper numerical order – it is the private secretary's (and press officer's) nightmare that your Prime Minister's speech does not read from page to page – came the news that the Prime Minister was impatiently tapping her foot in the hall. And so she was.

Most important of all, I formed an impression which was crucial to my operations throughout the Thatcher years. It was of her constancy. It was not simply that she was clear what she stood for; many people can give an impression of certainty and yet fail to hold fast to their course. Mrs Thatcher imbued me with confidence that, although they say it is a woman's prerogative to change her mind, this one would not exercise that prerogative at least on the big issues. By the time of her tenth anniversary in Number 10 I was able to explain my ability to represent her views by making the point that she did not change her mind 'from headline to headline, hour to hour, day to day, week to week, month to month, year to year or, as we had now discovered, from decade to decade'. It was this loyalty to herself – to what she believed in – that made my task easy and made my reputation as one who could reliably read his principal's mind.

I think Mrs Thatcher knew that, after all that had gone before in Britain, the nation wanted the smack of firm Government. I think she sensed that the people wanted resolution whereas previously there had been fudge and mudge and infirmity of purpose. They wanted an end to compromise and accommodation and most of all capitulation. John Moore, then a Parliamentary Under-Secretary in the Department of Energy, told me in the summer of 1979 before I went to Number 10 that the people were ready as never before for hard times and sacrifice in order to get the country back on the right road. In October 1979 I did not know whether

Mrs Thatcher could or would get us back on track. But I was pretty certain that if anybody could she would. She struck me as someone exceptionally tough and enduring.

She also frequently made the point in conversation that she was a long-term Prime Minister in a long-term government. She had, of course, no idea how long she would last. Her point was that governments had to set their sights on long-term objectives and stop reacting to the short-term consequences of their policies every time they became politically alarming. She believed, as she said when industrial trouble erupted soon after she had taken office, that it was far better for people to be faced with the consequence of their wage claims – i.e. unemployment – than to save them from it. It was clear from my early days that I was in the service of a Prime Minister whose motto might well be that of the RAF: *per ardua ad astra*.

We also had some fun. In January 1984 Mrs Thatcher was asked to present for Mary Whitehouse the National Viewers' and Listeners' Association Award to her favourite programme 'Yes Minister'. I racked my brain for something more original for Mrs Thatcher to do than simply make a speech in presenting the award. Suddenly, I hit upon the idea of a sketch in which the Prime Minister would play herself, Paul Eddington Jim Hacker and Nigel Hawthorne Sir Humphrey. I wrote a script and then polished it with Robin Butler, now Secretary to the Cabinet, and Romola Christopherson, my deputy. Mrs Thatcher fell in with the idea like a good sport and we rehearsed endlessly with her in her study, Robin playing Jim Hacker and I Sir Humphrey.

Came the day, Number 10 staff crowded into the Press Office to hear a relay of the phenomenally successful world premiere of 'Yes, (Prime) Minister'. This is how it went:

Prime Minister	Ah, good morning Jim, Sir Humphrey. Do come in and sit down. How's your wife? Is she well?
Jim Hacker	(Puzzled.) Oh yes, fine, Prime Minister. Fine. Thank you. Yes, fine.
Prime Minister	Good. So pleased. I've been meaning to have a word with you for some time. I've got an idea.

174

Jim Hacker	(Brightening visibly.) An idea, Prime Minister? Oh, good.
Sir Humphrey	(Guardedly.) An idea, Prime Minister?
Prime Minister	Well, not really an idea. I've done quite a bit of thinking, and I'm sure you, Jim, are quite the man to carry it out. It's got to do with a kind of institution and you are sort of responsible for institutions, aren't you?
Sir Humphrey	(Cautiously.) Institutions, Prime Minister?
Jim Hacker	(Decisively.) Oh yes, institutions fall to me. Most definitely. And you want me to set one up, I suppose?
Prime Minister	Set one up? Certainly not. I want you to get rid of one.
Jim Hacker	(Astonished.) Get rid of one, Prime Minister?
Prime Minister	Yes. It's all very simple. I want you to abolish economists.
Jim Hacker	(Mouth open.) Abolish economists, Prime Minister?
Prime Minister	Yes, abolish economists – quickly.
Sir Humphrey	(Silkily.) All of them, Prime Minister?
Prime Minister	Yes, all of them. They never agree on anything. They just fill the heads of politicians with all sorts of curious notions, like the more you spend, the richer you get.
Jim Hacker	(Coming round to the idea.) I take your point, Prime Minister. Can't have the nation's time wasted on curious notions, can we? No.
Sir Humphrey	(Sternly.) Minister.
Prime Minister	Quite right, Jim. Absolute waste of time. Simply got to go.
Jim Hacker	(Uncertain.) Simply got to go?
Prime Minister	(Motherly.) Yes, Jim. Don't worry. If it all goes

	wrong I shall get the blame. But if it goes right – as it will – then you'll get the credit for redeploying a lot of misapplied resources. Probably get promotion, too.
Sir Humphrey	(Indignantly.) Resources? Resources, Prime Minister? Surely we're talking about economists.
Prime Minister	Were, Sir Humphrey. Were.
Jim Hacker	(Decisively.) Yes, Humphrey, were. We're going to get rid of them.
Prime Minister	Well, it's all settled, then. I'll look forward to receiving your plan for abolition soon. Tomorrow, shall we say? I'd like you to announce it before it all leaks.
Jim Hacker	(Brightly.) Tomorrow, then, Prime Minister.
Prime Minister	Yes, well, sort it out. Now, Sir Humphrey – what did you say your degree was?
Sir Humphrey	(Innocently.) Degree, Prime Minister?
Prime Minister	(Firmly.) Yes, Sir Humphrey, degree. Your degree. You have one, I take it – most permanent secretaries do – or perhaps two.
Sir Humphrey	(Modestly.) Er, well, actually, Prime Minister, a double first.
Prime Minister	Congratulations, Sir Humphrey, but what in?
Sir Humphrey	(Weakly.) Politics – er . . . and, er . . . economics.
Prime Minister	(Soothingly.) Capital, my dear Sir Humphrey. You'll know exactly where to start.
Sir Humphrey	(Bleakly.) Yes, Prime Minister.

EXIT JIM HACKER AND SIR HUMPHREY

Mrs Thatcher had no doubt sized me up in the one minute or so she used to say she required to take stock of a man. And she would have done that on one of the two occasions we met before

I joined her office. I remain much less clear just how much she understood how I went about my job – or even precisely what it entailed – because right up to the end she still seemed surprised when I told her about various aspects of my operations. 'You should not have to do that,' she once said when I told her I had had to face a particularly bloody-minded group of journalists. So what does the job of a Chief Press Secretary entail?

The first point to be made is that I inherited a system from Henry James who had served three previous Prime Ministers as deputy press secretary. I did not invent the job. Indeed, I took over a going concern with a long-standing routine. I also came to the job prejudiced against any fancy footwork. As I have already explained, I had seen experiments in the 1970s with on-the-record statements by Joe Haines and Donald Maitland bring neither appreciation from the lobby nor a bonus for the Government, and I was convinced that breaking relations with the lobby, as Joe Haines had done, could never be a realistic option. For the first time in my Civil Service career I was prejudiced against innovation. I recognized the need to handle the lobby as carefully and circumspectly as a cobra poised to strike. The fact is that in November 1990 I was still doing my job broadly as I had started to do it in November 1979. So much for those who suggest I changed things out of all recognition.

A Chief Press Secretary in Number 10 has three major tasks. They are to:

1 serve as spokesman for the Prime Minister and, as the occasion requires it, the Government as a whole;

2 act as adviser to the Prime Minister on his or her presentational programme and to the Government as a whole on the overall presentation of its policies and measures; and to

3 co-ordinate, at official as distinct from Ministerial level, the Government's presentational programme – to conduct the Government's communications orchestra.

In our system of Cabinet Government, subject to fierce Parliamentary control, the spokesman, whether in Number 10 or individual Government Departments, remains in the background – provided he does not hang around for eleven years as I did. The longer a Chief Press Secretary goes on and the more identified he becomes with his Prime Minister the more, inevitably, he becomes the subject of publicity, and the more he is consequently seen by some, including politicians, as a means of attacking the Prime Minister. I was never under any illusion that those who attacked me, and especially politicians, were having a go at me on my own account. It was just another way of belting away at a Prime Minister and especially one who was known to be fiercely loyal to her staff. Judging from my own case, I suspect that, given a fair wind and avoiding too many mistakes, a Chief Press Secretary drawn from the Civil Service has at the most three years in him these days before he becomes a target. If he is a party political appointee his period of grace will be perhaps a year shorter.

It follows from this that Chief Press Secretaries come in two forms – one drawn from the ranks of the Civil Service, as I was and most have been, or from among supporters of the party in office, such as Joe Haines who was recruited from journalism by Harold Wilson. If they are recruited from outside they become temporary Civil Servants, subject to its rules and conventions. Their task remains broadly the same.

It is no coincidence, in my view, that up to now Chief Press Secretaries have not become public personalities in their own right in the sense that they would be if they were seen and heard daily on television and radio and extensively quoted in the press. The reason is quite simple: the nature of our constitution. This requires Ministers rather than appointed, unelected officials to be seen and heard. I do not believe that Ministers would for long put up with an official, on-the-record, highly visible spokesman. Some apparently found it difficult to put up with my low profile – or the low profile I tried to keep and lost. Nor, for that matter, do I think that Parliament, and especially the Commons, would take kindly to the idea – at least not for long. Parliament requires Ministers to report to it in person. It likes to see the whites of a Minister's eyes. The very idea that some no doubt televisual official should be for ever popping up on our screens professionally presenting Government policies – and professionally testing the water, as it would be seen – would, I expect, prove to be anathema to our system.

Other democracies are different. My friend and former colleague, Marlin Fitzwater, successively press secretary to Presidents Reagan and Bush, is regularly seen on television making policy or other announcements. But he serves an executive President who is not required to report to Congress as a British Prime Minister must report to Parliament. When he chooses, the President himself makes announcements to the nation direct through the television screen without so much as a nod at Capitol Hill. In the rest of Europe, where there is a variety of constitutions but where Parliaments tend to play a less central role in the life of the nation than in Britain, spokesmen are generally less visible than Marlin Fitzwater. But sometimes they do admittedly have a higher profile than in Britain – for example, in Germany where Herr Hans Klein, the last but one of a line of Chancellor's spokesmen in my time, was a member of the Government. But the fact is that up to now – and, I suspect, for the foreseeable future – Chief Press Secretaries in Britain are generally neither seen nor heard at work by the public.

Another aspect of our constitution which contributes to the relative obscurity of the Chief Press Secretary is the dispersal of responsibility for policy to individual Cabinet Ministers which has already been noted. This means that, apart from responsibility for state security issues and the routine reportage to the Commons of the outcome of European and other summits, the Prime Minister makes few policy announcements. His or her role, or as it was most certainly seen by Mrs Thatcher, is to serve as the custodian of the Government's philosophy, direction, thrust and spirit. This is projected regularly, when the House is sitting, through Prime Minister's Questions which occupy fifteen minutes from 3.15 on Tuesday and Thursday afternoons. The Chief Press Secretary is thus concerned not so much with policy announcements as with bringing the work of the Government together in one presentational whole and serving as an interpreter for the media on the import for the conduct of Government of the Prime Minister's approach. Hence the Chief Press Secretary's meetings with journalists are not so much press conferences as background briefings. As such, they remain, appropriately I would argue, unattributable. And therein lies a tale which I shall tell in Chapter 13 where I deal with the lobby.

The advisory role of the Chief Press Secretary is discharged in a variety of ways – face to face with the Prime Minister, in meetings with her and other Ministers and officials, on paper and with the Minister responsible for the co-ordination of presentation to whom the Chief Press Secretary also reports. I began this aspect of the job each day with the preparation of a digest of the morning's national newspapers – all twelve of them, though I paid only cursory attention to the *Morning Star*. This Communist organ had been standard reading in the Department of Employment where industrial trouble was our middle name. To prepare this digest I got up at 6 a.m., listened to BBC Radio 4's exceptionally good ten-minute digest of the news, weather, newspaper summary and sport, shaved and showered and was in my car on the way to the office fifteen miles away by 6.30 a.m. Driving myself in from Purley I listened to the first half hour of BBC Radio 4's 'Today' programme. I myself wrote the press digest and my secretaries over the years typed it. Stephanie Walmsley (now Harris), Linda Bond (now Bidiscombe), Rose Padwick and lastly Anne Allan are the heroines of this production. They somehow managed to get up early, too, and then read my writing. Before Mrs Thatcher facilitated a revolution in Fleet Street I could just about summarize all ten national dailies between 7 and 9 a.m. After *Today* and the *Independent* had appeared I had to contract out the reading of *The Times*, the *Independent* and the *Financial Times* to press officers whose summaries I edited into my own. I caught up with my reading of these three newspapers later. By 9 a.m. I was fully prepared for the day. By then a summary of news and comment, good, bad and indifferent, and a record of the main issues ventilated throughout the 'Today' programme, were available.

On Tuesdays and Thursdays these documents, and the diary for the day which prefaced the press digest, formed the agenda for the Prime Minister's first briefing meeting at 9 a.m. in her study for her Questions in the House after lunch. The Prime Minister and her private secretaries went through the press digest systematically. This and my intelligence from the 'Today' programme provided a thoroughly reliable basis for anticipating the kind of questions which could be expected from the Leader of the Opposition and MPs when the Prime Minister faced the House. Mrs Thatcher seldom received notice of the questions she was to be asked by the Opposition and the service was far from systematic from her own side. But politicians proved to be fairly predictable since they have a symbiotic relationship with journalists. Anyone who knows the kind of trouble which journalists are stirring that day can forecast with remarkable accuracy which knives will be thrown across the floor of the House at 3.15.

These briefing sessions also enabled me to feed in other information I had gleaned from reporters. A Chief Press Secretary is not simply a one-way bridge, communicating information outwards to journalists. He is also a conduit for political intelligence into Number 10 – about, for example, trends in editorial thinking or rumours of demonstrations or stunts which the reporters expect to be pulled by MPs in the House. My objective – indeed that of all the Prime Minister's staff – was to try to ensure that she was never taken unawares on the floor of the House. This meant that we were still feeding in information we thought relevant until the Prime Minister left her room in the House to go into the chamber at 3.10 to shouts of 'Good luck' from her staff.

I had a wider objective in providing press digests and even briefly summarizing the Sunday press, dictating my account over the 'phone to Chequers or Number 10 to a Garden Room girl, as members of the secretarial pool in Number 10 are known because their room looks out on to the garden behind Downing Street. It was to ensure, as best I could, that Mrs Thatcher was aware of anything that was politically relevant – or, indeed, that I thought she needed to know if only to avoid appearing out of touch – and of trends in thinking in Britain. Of course, I took good care that her particular interests were covered – for example, child welfare and the NSPCC which also required me to summarize all too many horrendous cases of abuse; or the latest antics of far-Left councils which fair took the breath away, assuming they were true. But I also tried to make sure that she knew when she or the Government were getting a bad press. I succeeded. More than once she remarked 'But this is awful' after reading my summary. These summaries also helped to identify good news which the Prime Minister might reasonably draw to the House's attention to counteract the incessant knocking that goes on in Britain. They also served as a catalyst for remedial action with journalists, for example where a writer had got his facts wrong or was going sour on a particular policy or measure.

The more I look back on this home-produced press digest – in this form an innovation which evolved over the early Thatcher years – the more valuable an advisory tool I find it. It may appear to have been an appalling six- or seven-day chore. It most certainly felt like it on Sundays when it took me virtually three hours to read the eight and a half pounds of newspapers which hit the doormat even before I wrote and dictated my summary to Chequers. But it was invaluable. It encapsulated the day's newspapers in ten minutes' reading, identifying presentational opportunities as well as the potential trouble I was primarily looking for when I read the press. It was even useful as a means of identifying people with various achievements to their credit for the Prime Minister to invite to Number 10 to one of her general receptions.

I could be called on at any time to advise the Prime Minister or a group of Ministers on presentation and sometimes I was used as a plain man's sounding board. I was sometimes very plain indeed. If an individual Minister felt I might help him – or wanted to make sure I properly understood a crucial point he was trying to get over – he would pop into my room after a meeting with the Prime Minister for a chat. As I had made clear when I saw chief information officers in October 1979, Number 10 wanted to help, not hinder, by supplementing the communications resources of individual Departments. After all, we were in continuous dialogue with political correspondents.

My advisory role was also conducted extensively on paper. Press officers fall broadly into two categories: those who write and those who gossip. I exaggerate, of course, to make a point. I suppose the social scientist would identify two cultures: one written and the other oral. In an ideal world, I would prefer to employ press officers who are good at both, but you can't have everything. They did not have much of a gossip in me. Indeed, if I had my time to do over again I think I would devote more effort to talking to Ministers and officials and less to writing to them – or minuting them, in the jargon of the Civil Service. It was amazing how my successor at the Department of Energy, Ian Gillis – an archetypal gossip, if ever there was one – kept his finger on the Departmental pulse by wandering around the building rather like a doctor on his rounds. On the other hand the Civil Service is a writing culture and a well-argued minute can work wonders. Moreover, Mrs Thatcher was the very model of a proper administrator (except when, to judge from her unfinished scrawl, she fell asleep over my minutes at 2 a.m. or so). A note setting out a course of action or a briefing line I proposed to take would usually come out of her box overnight initialled and ticked, and set me up confidently for the future.

My conception of the job also required me to develop a presentational strategy usually for the six months ahead based upon a frank analysis of where the Prime Minister and the Government stood, how to improve their presentation and the sort of presentational programme I thought she ought to undertake. The advantage of this for me was that I set out my views in a far more ordered way than would ever come out in discussion. The advantage for the Prime Minister was that she knew what she was buying.

Of all the lessons I have learned in the service of the Government it is that Ministers expect advice from their advisers. And the clearer and blunter the advice the better. If they think it is bad or wrong advice they will say so and will not act upon it. But at least they have had it and have been able to react to it. Which takes me back to Jack Rampton's wise words: 'Never be afraid to give your advice.'

The third part of the Chief Press Secretary's job is to co-ordinate at official level the presentation of Government policy and measures. In doing this he usually, but not always, reports to a Minister who has been given specific responsibility for presentation by the Prime Minister. In my time, and until Mrs Thatcher took office, the task was often undertaken by junior Ministers – for example, Geoffrey Johnson-Smith in Mr Heath's time and William Price and John Grant under Labour Governments. All three happened to have been journalists and John Grant, as the *Daily Express* industrial correspondent, had been a fellow member of the Labour and Industrial Correspondents' Group. John Grant and I – sometimes with Ken Dodd, of the *Guardian* – assiduously took our sons to watch Crystal Palace or Charlton during the 1960s and 1970s. I think we enjoyed co-ordinating together, too. When Mrs Thatcher took office she gave the job to Angus Maude, a former distinguished editor, with a seat in the Cabinet as Paymaster General. Subsequently the post was held by Francis Pym, who was understandably tortured by the level of unemployment and therefore Government economic policy; John Biffen, who put co-ordination on what he described as automatic pilot – i.e. me; and the great powerhouses in their different ways, Lord Whitelaw, John Major, the present Prime Minister, and latterly John Wakeham. All of them, it should be noted, were senior Cabinet Ministers at the time.

I was extremely fortunate in having three such powerful and supportive Ministers responsible for co-ordination over the last seven years. There will probably never be another Willie Whitelaw. He made a very successful profession out of being a simple, noisy man. Few laughed, roared or detonated louder and few concealed more successfully an acute political brain behind a bluff exterior. He was a formidable operator and all the more so for being one on whom Mrs Thatcher could rely absolutely. John Wakeham's style was entirely different – quiet, almost self-effacing and subterranean. But he too derived his strength from his utter reliability in support of Mrs Thatcher. Like Lord Whitelaw, he had been Chief Whip and it was in that capacity that I first got to know, like and work closely with him. His genius lay in working his way through a problem to a practical solution – as evidenced particularly by his handling of electricity privatization as Secretary of State for Energy. John Major, as Chief Secretary, was my mentor after Lord Whitelaw's retirement through illness. He briefed me regularly and thoroughly after Cabinet meetings and gave me a strong and confident base on which to operate with journalists, especially in the economic and social fields. I have met few more modest, unassuming and unpretentious Cabinet Ministers and even fewer who were easier to get on with. But he is as sharp as a bag full of needles and his political acumen quickly shone through. No wonder Mrs Thatcher identified him a long way back as a likely successor. It would, however, have been unwise and probably counter-productive of Number 10 to canvass his name. I am delighted that such a congenial and talented man succeeded Mrs Thatcher. It is not always that a retiring Prime Minister's wishes are granted.

The formal instrument for co-ordination is a meeting of Departmental heads of information – M10 as it is designated – in the

Cabinet Office each Monday evening. The junior Ministers often used to preside over it under previous Governments, but only Angus Maude did so during Mrs Thatcher's tenure of office. For the rest of the eleven years it fell to me, or my deputy, to chair the gathering – curiously known in the trade as the Dodgers, apparently because of the habit among some of those attending of sloping off home early after the meeting instead of returning to their office. In essence, the objective of the meeting was briefly to review presentation during the week gone by – and to learn from our triumphs or mistakes – and then look ahead to the next week or fortnight. Each Department was invited to report expected events, announcements or developments of any political weight so that we could collectively identify potential presentational difficulties, Departmental clashes of interest or any likely overloading of newsy announcements on a particular day. We tried to satisfy ourselves that the Government's message was getting over and, if not, see what we could do to remedy the deficiency. The meeting also provided an opportunity to discuss matters of professional interest such as the experience of individual Departments in dealing with particular journals or broadcast programmes, or even the latest developments in media technology.

I reported to the responsible Minister anything which I felt they should know from the meeting and where I felt I needed their support or even personal intervention to achieve the desired result. It would have been amazing – and a serious, culpable omission – if such a regular meeting had not been held in Government, as it had been held for decades. Yet early on some sections of the media took a remarkably naive – and, in the case of The *Guardian*, an entirely juvenile – interest in it. The *Guardian*'s gossip column cast Angus Maude in the role of the Mekon, for reasons which were lost on me. I am sorry to say that the press's conspiracy theorists – suffering, as I put it in a talk to the Media Society on 20 November 1985, from a touch of the le Carrés – were from time to time over the first half of Mrs Thatcher's tenure of office encouraged in their interest in M10's meetings by a member or members of the Government Information Service either attending the meeting or briefed about its discussions. This was a disgraceful betrayal of trust which provoked fierce condemnation within the meeting by some of my friends who saw it, as I did, as a calculated attempt to destroy the effective co-ordination of presentation within Government. Things got so bad that even an entirely jocular – though, in the circumstances, unwise – remark by me expressing the hope that Judge Jeffreys would preside over the trial of Clive Ponting, a civil servant accused of leaking a document, found its way into the press, not surprisingly to my disadvantage. I fear that not even the Government Information Service was free of the virus which afflicted a tiny minority of the Civil Service during the Thatcher years: the deliberate leaking of information or papers by officials with the objective of discrediting the Government. This was a blot on the Civil Service landscape in the 1980s.

The systematic and often distorted disclosure of M10 discussions inevitably made the honest majority attending less open than they might otherwise have been about events and prone to see me afterwards to alert me to developments they were reluctant to disclose in open court, as it were. I made a number of efforts to trap the miscreant or miscreants and one leak inquiry fuelled our suspicions without coming up with conclusive evidence. But I was absolutely determined that no one, however unprincipled, would close down M10. Eventually we won through and gradually over the second half of Mrs Thatcher's tenure of office rebuilt some trust in M10 and restored its usefulness.

In retrospect, I think I could have co-ordinated presentation reasonably effectively without M10, though it would have been a pity for other reasons to deprive the almost entirely reliable heads of information a weekly get-together. This is because the real heroes – and heroines – of Government co-ordination are the deputy press secretary and the three senior information officers who work in Number 10 Press Office. They are in minute-to-minute touch with the Departments for which they are responsible. It is they, more than anyone else in the system, who co-ordinate Government presentation in a practical way. It is they who find out what is going on in Government; who ask the awkward questions which elicit illumination from Departments; who dispense advice on behalf of the Chief Press Secretary and ultimately the Prime Minister; who identify where things are going wrong or are likely to do so; who provide the Chief Press Secretary with the briefing which helps

Departments to get over their message; and who oil the wheels of relations between Departments and the centre. My deputies were typically (apart from my first, Neville Gaffin, who gave up the top job at the Department of Trade to join me in Number 10) people on the threshold of having their own command. The senior information officers were mostly hand picked by me and were on their way up the ladder. The three of them were responsible respectively for finance, economics, trade, industry and energy; the social departments such as health, welfare, education and law and order; and foreign affairs, defence and Northern Ireland where I always had someone drawn from the Diplomatic Service. I salute all who have served as press officers in Number 10 in Mrs Thatcher's time and I have listed them at the front of this book. They are a distinguished bunch.

The media always felt we were up to no good, though. This reflects the normal state of tension between the Government Information Service and journalists; indeed between journalists and press officers, however good, the world over. I shall discuss some aspects of relations with the journalists in the next chapter. Meanwhile, I would deal with only one aspect of the relationship: news management. This is a most heinous offence in journalists' eyes and is the crime – I do not jest – with which press officers, and not least Chief Press Secretaries, are most frequently charged. Journalists see us all as consummate Machiavellis. I plead utterly, completely and wholeheartedly guilty. Of course, I tried to manage the news. I tried – God knows, I tried – to ensure that Ministers spoke with one voice, if necessary by circulating a standard speaking note which I wrote myself. I was hit by all kinds of journalistic avalanche if they spoke out of turn. I tried to ensure that Ministers were aware of what each other was doing and whenever they were likely to cut across each other. Dammit, that was what I was supposed to do. And if I failed, then the media would fall like wolves upon Government and condemn it as useless. I tried – hell's teeth I tried – to make sure that the media had early, embargoed copies of important documents so that they had plenty of time to digest them and prepare their stories before publication. And what did some of these pious, sanctimonious characters do? Occasionally, they made it impossible for me to help them because they broke embargoes or,

187

more often, put opponents of the course of action in a position to issue instant, damning comment. I tried – heaven only knows, I tried – to ensure that the Government did not come out on any one day with two or three, let alone four or five, major statements of policy. If I had not done so the lobby would have complained like bears with a sore back about being overworked to no advantage to the Government. And they would have been right because the public, too, would have suffered from news indigestion.

But news management, in the sense of ensuring that nothing is allowed to get in the way of the story the Government wants to get over, is impossible in the modern world. A chief information officer can plan and plot and generally bust a gut in trying to clear the way for an important announcement. But he is not in charge of events, or journalists. Nor has he any influence over a Minister who suddenly goes ape and commands the front pages. Unfortunately, he is not in command of other events in the global village in this age of instant, telephonic and, more important, televisual communications. An earthquake here; a famine there; an horrendous aircrash elsewhere; or quite simply some appallingly visual event anywhere – and his news management cause is lost. The real news managers today are the media themselves. It is television which predominantly dictates news values for the masses: either there are pictures or there are not, and if there are no pictures there is no news. It is the editors of this world who receive the raw material in the form of reports from the journalist on the spot. Then they get to work on it: developing it, exploiting it, angling it, massaging it and eventually presenting it as polished fact and unvarnished truth. And they dare to accuse Government press officers of news management? They dare because, I regret to say, too many journalists today think they are the only thing that matters in this world; that their rights are unconfined; and that no one should even think of questioning their operations or the stance that lies behind them. Too many young products of schools of journalism I have encountered seem to be sans depth, sans breadth, sans shame, sans everything that should equip them for the objective life they are supposed to lead. Fortunately there were numerous exceptions who made my life worth living.

There is one other aspect of the Chief Press Secretary's job which should be acknowledged. It is that of helping the Head of the

Government Information Service (which I myself controversially became in 1989 in addition to my duties in Number 10) to run the GIS. Sitting at the centre of the Government's communications web, the Chief Press Secretary is in an unrivalled position to know the strengths and weaknesses of the communications efforts of individual Departments and their heads of information. As such, he is in a strong position to advise on the filling of top GIS posts. He also has to work closely with heads of information. The Chief Press Secretary chronically wants Departmental heads of information who are team players, on top of their job, in tune with their Minister, commanding the respect of their Departmental Civil Servants and on good terms with their particular, group of journalists. I think considerable strides were made during the Thatcher years in strengthening the GIS from the bottom to the top. Any future Government which kicked the GIS in the teeth would be mad.

13

Ingham's Hallelujah Chorus

While I was at Number 10 I gave about 5000 formal briefings to groups of journalists and probably six times as many as that to individual correspondents who telephoned or buttonholed me. This estimate is based on the pattern of my working life throughout the 1980s and beyond. In a full week I could do fourteen briefings: ten for the lobby; and one each for the Foreign Press Association each Monday in Gladstone's old house at 11 Carlton House Terrace; for separate groups of European journalists resident in Britain and writers for British provincial newspapers in Number 10 on Tuesday; and the Association of American Correspondents at 11.45 a.m. in Number 10 on Wednesday. I tried to give as many as possible of these briefings personally because journalists expect the top man, though my deputy usually performed with the lobby on Thursday afternoons after the Leader of the House had seen the group and on Friday mornings. Whenever possible I set aside Thursday afternoons after Prime Minister's Questions and Friday mornings to shift administrative work and write papers.

I took most of August off on holiday and we saw these various groups of journalists in September and early October only at their specific request in the event of a crisis. On the other hand, at European Councils and other summits, and while the Prime Minister was on tour abroad, I used to give at least five briefings a day from 10 a.m. until often well after midnight. In crises such as the Falklands or during visits by, for example, Mr Gorbachev I would give briefings to different groups of journalists as dictated by events. Assuming an average of ten briefings a week over a forty-six week working year – which is a conservative estimate – I clocked up getting on for 5000 Number 10 briefings before I retired along with Mrs Thatcher.

It was a quiet working day indeed if I did not brief ten journalists more informally over the telephone, or over lunch. Part of my job, I decided, long before I reached Number 10, was to dig my grave with my teeth at the journalists' table. I also made it my practice several evenings each week to see journalists and other contacts over a drink in my room at Number 10 for an hour from 6 o'clock. And a Chief Press Secretary does not stop at week-ends. Journalists who have known you – and your home telephone number – for years, and many for decades, come to rely upon your service when they think they need it. I tried not to discourage them, though sometimes I was less welcoming than others when interrupted in the garden for the fifth time on a Saturday morning. I was also a little breathless after rushing up the steps to the telephone. 'Sorry to drag you up from the bottom of your garden', they would say with great politeness, if not perspicacity. Ten briefings a day over, say, a six-day week and a forty-six-week year adds up to a good 30,000 individual briefings over my tenure. Not all journalists will remember every briefing I gave. Some of them fell asleep on my couch, especially the Sunday Lobby on Friday afternoons. A number of reporters have snored their way through my offerings and some have even fallen off the sofa. In fairness, however, I should say that I once fell asleep myself giving a briefing to European correspondents after a transatlantic overnight flight.

This sketch of a Chief Press Secretary's commitment to serving the press, radio and television – and the extent to which he is at risk – underlines two dominating factors in his working life in support of the Prime Minister. One is his need to be well informed and to keep up with the news. The other is how his working day is geared to the service of different groups of journalists each with their own specific needs and approach. For example, during the Falklands the Europeans were interested in the implications of the conflict for members of the European Community whereas the Americans, while taking the most distinctively global approach of all the groups I met, necessarily concentrated on the overt and, of course, covert role of the United States.

Whenever I gave talks about my job – and I was in heavy demand for courses – I anticipated one question: how can any one individual ever know enough in order accurately to brief the wide range of journalists who seek Number 10's guidance. There is only one answer to that: he can't. A Chief Press Secretary can religiously read Cabinet papers and minutes, the main policy and action telegrams sent out and received by the FCO, the Prime Minister's correspondence, internal Number 10 briefing papers, and bury himself deep in his Prime Minister's mind by attending lots of her meetings. But it is simply not possible to know everything that is going on in a devolved system of Cabinet Government any more than the Prime Minister does. The morning newspapers were often a voyage of discovery for her. And for me, too. Yet of all Heads of Government in the world she was probably the best informed because of the extent to which she briefed herself for Prime Minister's Questions. By the same token, her Chief Press Secretary was better prepared than most – and he had the benefit of serving a decisive, constant boss who knew her own mind.

And yet the most I could hope to do as guide and interpreter for reporters, when not speaking from a brief on a specific subject, was to read the game like a footballer. If I did not know the answer to a question, or felt less than confident in leading journalists to a conclusion, I had to have the courage to say I did not know and would try to find out. A Chief Press Secretary cannot, however, make a profession out of ignorance. He is there to offer guidance. Nor will he last long if he gets it wrong too often. But he often cannot be absolutely sure he is correct since he can clear only a tiny fraction of what he says in advance with his Prime Minister. Chief Press Secretaries are judged after the event. Few, if any, Government officials are as highly exposed – a point which, I am glad to say, both the Prime Minister and the deputy Prime Minister, Lord Whitelaw, recognized when things went wrong.

It was against this background, and that set out in the previous chapter, that my often stormy but enduring relationship with the Parliamentary Lobby Journalists was conducted. It is a fascinating organization. Its origins are not precisely known because the records of its first fifty years were incinerated by a fire which followed the bombing of Parliament in the blitz. But around the time that General Gordon was dispatched to Khartoum and Marks met Spencer, accounts describe a select bunch of journalists 'seven or eight sitting round the table talking to the Prime Minister', Mr

Gladstone. Since then the lobby has grown and grown. It is no longer select. But for decades it has conducted its relations with the Chief Press Secretary on a familiar pattern.

At 11 a.m. members of the lobby saunter over to Number 10 from their offices in the Palace of Westminster for the first briefing of the day in the Chief Press Secretary's room. My deputy and I sat in extremely comfortable arm-chairs on either side of the grand fireplace with a set of tongs on the hearth. My press officers sat with their backs to the windows looking out into Downing Street. The lobby used the settee and the black plastic chairs stacked against a wall for their convenience. I would tell them what the Prime Minister was doing that day and what Government news events, announcements or publications to expect and then I would place myself at their disposal. They could ask anything they liked and I would answer as I wished. We would each form our own conclusions. The questions could range from what the Prime Minister had had for breakfast – which would have been relevant, had she made a habit of having breakfast, during a salmonella, listeria or BSE scare – to the intricacies of Anglo-Soviet relations. Sometimes it became lively; on others the briefing died of boredom. The entire process was repeated at 4 p.m. when two of my staff and I went over to the lobby room in the roof of the Palace looking steeply down on to Westminster Bridge and the Thames and across to St Thomas's Hospital. This time, if there were no alarums or running news stories, the lobby would begin to fish for stories, testing me out against other informants. For me, it was a fascinating commentary on who, outside the lobby room, might have been saying what to whom and why.

I took with me to Number 10 a certain amount of prejudice against the lobby. Like other heads of information in Departments, I tended to regard its members as mere general reporters as compared with my own set of specialist correspondents. This is not unfair given the sheer range of subjects lobby correspondents are called upon to cover. But they write about them from a specialist viewpoint – their implications for the political scene. They are an exceptionally sharp and cynical bunch, although they were once disparaged by Jonathan Aitken MP as the 'Ingham hallelujah chorus'. They are Kremlinologists. They examine everything that is said for its political implications. They are fast on to nuance. They can spot a shading of opinion, approach or intent in a trice – even when it does not exist. As Lord Curzon told the Commons in 1898: 'I hesitate to say what the functions of the modern journalist may be; but I imagine they do not exclude the intelligent anticipation of facts even before they occur.' They are wise in the ways of the world and don't necessarily believe a word they are told. They do not kid easily. They have seen it all before and are utterly convinced they will see it all again. They just want to be the first to spot and trail it. They are the ultimate professionals in the apparently disorganized way of journalists – as they remind everyone on Budget Day when they are hit by an avalanche of information.

The first charge made against the lobby, by such short-lived lobby correspondents as Peter Hennessy, is that it is lazy, self-serving and easily manipulated. Mr Hennessy now has pretensions as an academic, though not, I trust, on the basis of an instantly-rubbished book containing this nonsense which he wrote for publication in 1984 with Michael Cockerell and David Walker entitled *Sources Close to the Prime Minister*. I would prefer Adam Raphael, the *Observer*'s former political editor and lobby member, to reply. He wrote on 17 June 1984:

> 'At risk of sounding self-defensive, this is a ludicrous mis-understanding of how the system actually works. There are about 150 [now 220 or so] members of the lobby, representing publications ranging from the far Left of the political spectrum to the far Right. The idea that such a large, disparate body can be collectively gulled by being drip-fed information from Number 10 is inherently implausible. The White House press corps, in which I have also worked, is a far tamer and more deferential group than the lobby, yet the authors frequently refer to Washington as a paradigm they would like to copy ... The authors also fail to understand that formal lobby briefings comprise only a small part of the information gathering process.'

As Ian Aitken, my former colleague on the *Guardian*, pointed out in a so-called 'Panorama' exposé of the lobby system in the early

1980s, there are before he can move a yard from the Palace of Westminster to a Number 10 briefing 650 Members of the Commons eager and willing to offer their ideas, points of view and arguments.

Mr Raphael added:

'... the Prime Minister doesn't have the temperament or the taste to be an effective manipulator. For a start, she doesn't like journalists and would gladly keep most of us as far away as she can. To the extent that the Government gets a better press than it deserves, this is partly due to the results of the pro-Tory bias of Fleet Street and partly due to the efforts of the Prime Minister's press secretary, Bernard Ingham, a bluff Yorkshireman, whose directness and ability to reflect her thinking have made him a trusted source of information.'

I should perhaps add, for the sake of completeness, that I told the Guild of British Newspaper Editors' conference in Cardiff in May 1983: 'I only wish I was as sophisticated, as devilishly clever, as Machiavellian, as some make out. Not even a combination of Einstein, backed up by the world's most advanced computer, could achieve the presentational coups with which ... I ... have been credited. It grieves me to have to confess this incompetence. All of us like to be thought better of, and all of us would like to be regarded as brilliant. But there is no way that this case can be proven.'

One of my very few misfortunes in life has been to be regarded by Anthony Bevins as superb. Yet that is how this obsessive political editor of the *Independent* and son of a former Tory Postmaster-General, Reginald Bevins, described my performance in justifying his withdrawal and that of his newspaper from the lobby from its launch in October 1986. It was nice, if conspiratorial, of him. But then Mr Bevins is one of the world's great conspiracy theorists. In his eyes, nobody in any Government can possibly be up to any good whatsoever. This is what Peter Hennesssy wrote about him in the *New Statesman* on 3 October 1986:

'Bevins is a possessed soul, a scouser who sandpapers his

rough edges not to smooth them down but to keep them raw. I've been devoted to Bevins for a decade since we shared a cramped, tatty office in the Lobby Corridor high up in the Palace of Westminster ... I'd arrive just before lunch and he'd look up with a mad gleam in his eye, wave some obscure Public Accounts Committee report on MoD [Defence] overspending on frigates and roar "I've got the bastards this time".'

It was inevitably Mr Bevins who set out to smash Number 10's traditional links with the lobby – albeit highly selectively because he needed to remain a member, as he still is, in order to do his job. This is because the lobby is primarily a convenience for the Serjeant at Arms, on behalf of the Speaker, to license those journalists with access to the Palace of Westminster and more especially the Members' Lobby. Without access to the Members' Lobby Mr Bevins would be in some difficulty. He is not the stuff that martyrs are made of – as he made amply clear to me when he first informed me in the summer of 1986 of his intention to stay away from my briefings. He then wanted to be sure that I would not withhold advance, embargoed copies of White Papers from him if he did withdraw. I still wonder what he would have done had I told him that he would not see another advance copy so long as I was in the job. Instead, I said that since he would remain a member of the lobby he was entitled to advance copies and to decide for himself whether to attend my briefings.

Superficially, Mr Bevins had a lot going for him. Observance of the lobby's own rules had been honoured only in the breach for years and the situation was steadily deteriorating. By the time I arrived in Downing Street a Chief Press Secretary could not count on their being observed. Indeed, he can be absolutely certain they won't be if it is to the advantage of some correspondents – which in turn puts pressure on the more responsible. In many ways the lobby's rules encourage ridicule because they are couched in the language of freemasonry and born of a more deferential age. Mrs Thatcher made fun of them when she addressed the centenary lobby lunch in the Savoy in January – a nice touch this – 1984. She said:

'After a century without a notebook – at worst, very discreetly and unobtrusively using the back of an Order Paper; never running after a Minister; never joining in a conversation with a Minister, MP or Peer unless invited to do so; never in any circumstances making use of anything accidentally overheard in any part of the Palace of Westminster; after averting your collective gaze for 100 years from any incident, pleasant or otherwise, in those parts of the building to which you have privileged access, today you can confess – this is your life. Today, in the Savoy, the Lobby is made flesh.'

Celestial Blue, as the leader of the Conservatives used to be known in Lobbyspeak (as distinct from Red Mantle, the Labour leader) felt this was the first time that the fourth estate had avowed its secret service. This, she said, simplified her task of 'proposing the health of an organization which otherwise would not exist and would never meet'. This was a reference to the passage in the tiny brown book *Notes on the Practice of Lobby Journalism* which says: 'Members are under an obligation to keep secret the fact that . . . meetings are held and to avoid revealing the sources of their information.'

Some journalists these days prefer to go to jail rather than to reveal their sources. Too many lobby correspondents just get on with it – or leave little to the imagination. It was not simply a matter of disclosing what I said to others. It was what they indicated to me other informants had told them. Sometimes, seated at my desk, I thought I was a sort of priest receiving confessions. This was extremely valuable to Number 10 but it was not the journalism I had been brought up to practise nor best calculated to promote the flow of information. There are, of course, old hands and other more principled reporters in the lobby who deplore all this. But it reflects a steady deterioration over the 1980s in standards of journalism. And the dirtier some journalists became – apparently believing that the end of hammering the Government (and me) justified the means – the more they presented themselves as members of the Independent Order of the White Knights of Veracity.

Indeed, Mr Bevins clothed himself in this white raiment in publicly justifying his boycott of my briefings. He wanted to avoid the 'collective pressure' which, he claimed, I exerted on correspondents when they met me for group therapy. He wanted to escape 'a system of information gathering which actually makes journalists a party to news management'. In renouncing the lobby system (which he never did) he believed that he – and others – would be 'forced to work much harder, using our own sources and resources as journalists'. He also saw journalistic advantage in standing outside my briefings because he felt he would be less inhibited. Indeed, he argued, when he first told me of his plans as political editor of the yet-to-be-launched *Independent*, that he would have done much better in covering the Westland affair earlier in the year had he then been boycotting my briefings. I assumed that he meant he would have felt freer to retail any old gossip that came his way regardless of whether I had dealt with it in lobby briefings. In fact, it is now clear that he was bent on killing my familiar briefings by importuning those attending for second-hand accounts which he would then attribute to me – sometimes inaccurately and often without nuance. In this way he presumably hoped to go down in history as the man who single-handedly, and acting out of the highest moral principle, slew the devil of Number 10 lobby briefings – not, please note, the lobby system on which he depended – and ushered in a new era of on-the-record honesty. Of course, he never told me this when he retailed his plans. Nor, in his public accounts of our meeting which have brought economy with the truth to a fine art, has he mentioned his initial tender concern that he would continue to have advance copies of White Papers. Nor has he said – as he told me – that boycotting my lobbies was a condition of his taking the *Independent* job. This suggests that Andreas Whittam Smith, his editor, was less sold on boycotting my briefings than the Messiah from the Mersey.

All this made little impression on me. Indeed, I can trace no note of the date when Mr Bevins stayed behind after an 11 a.m. lobby to let me know he was joining the *Independent*. Attempts to reform the lobby and require on-the-record briefings had long been canvassed. The Government itself had kept the lobby under review and, for reasons which I have rehearsed, had concluded that, imperfect instrument though it was, it was, like democracy, probably the best we could devise. I could not believe my luck that the ineffable Mr Bevins was intending to lead the charge. Where he led others would surely not follow. But I could not resist telling him what a blithering hypocrite I thought he was, especially as he had no objection in principle to unattributable briefing. Indeed, I gathered that he would not be averse to receiving unattributable guidance from me if I were daft enough to give it to him. I made it as clear as I have ever made anything to anyone that if he boycotted my briefings then he could expect nothing of me by way of guidance. I would neither lunch nor dine with him, nor sit in his assistance at the end of a telephone, for I was simply not prepared to allow journalists to have it both ways: to boycott collective briefings but enjoy a personal service given on exactly the same terms. Mr Bevins' built-in sneer, which is an instant slander on all Government press officers, not to mention Cabinet Ministers, relaxed sufficiently to indicate that he was confident I would have second thoughts when he had got to work on me from October.

It all began to go wrong for Mr Bevins in September when Peter Preston, the former gossip-columnist editor of the *Guardian*, realized that he was going to appear commercially inadequate in competition with the *Independent* when it launched itself on the impeccable platform of a lobby boycott.

Mr Preston, who, I know, has long outstayed the welcome of some of his staff, wrote to me on 18 September in his familiar machine-gun style. He was sufficiently unjournalistic to bury the point in Page 2. After suggesting that there was political, journalistic and reader dissatisfaction with the lobby – and how many readers of the *Guardian*, I wondered, knew anything about the lobby system that the *Guardian* didn't want them to know? – he informed me of his instruction to his staff. I now – deliciously – quote:

'Accordingly I have this week instructed my political staff that, when Westminster business recommences, they shall attend – as normal – your daily briefings, but that instead of employing any of the customary and increasingly thread-bare circumlocutions ... they shall refer openly to "a Downing Street spokesman" or "Mrs Thatcher's spokes-man" and, as relevant, quote what that spokesman says ...'

He went on, inevitably, to refer to my remarks about Mr
Pym and Mr Biffen which I shall discuss later.

Mr Preston had made the cardinal error of revealing his ignorance, not to mention his pomposity. He had tendered his
resignation from the lobby, as it were, to me. But I was in no
position to receive it. The lobby did not belong to me. Nor to
Number 10. Nor to the Government. Nor to Parliament, except as
a list kept by the Serjeant at Arms. It belonged only to its members.
Accordingly, I replied as follows:

> '. . . I can reply quite briefly since your letter is not for me.
> The Parliamentary Lobby Journalists exist as an indepen-
> dent body with their own constitution and rules. Under this
> so-called Lobby system, I do not invite political correspon-
> dents to briefings; they invite me. Their chairman, or acting
> chairman, presides and the terms under which briefings are
> given are covered by their rules.
> 'Consequently, if you wish to change the system you will
> have to find a way of addressing the Lobby, since I assume
> from your letter you wish to act constitutionally.
> 'In the meantime, I should say that I have no proposal to
> change existing practice.'

This letter did not reveal my innermost thoughts. I concluded that
Mr Preston was dafter than I thought he was. It was perfectly
clear that whatever economics he had done at university he did not
understand the concept of a monopoly. Who, I wondered, did he
think was giving Number 10 briefings? Most certainly, his political
staff, as members of the lobby, were entitled to attend my briefings.
But if they did, under his new instructions, I was perfectly at liberty
to tell them and the rest of the lobby to take a running jump at
themselves. I would say what I wanted to say, and unless I could
say them on my terms I wouldn't say a word. What is more, my
retribution would be wonderful to behold if the lobby agreed to
my terms and then dishonoured them – as they were all too likely
to do with this lot playing their games.

The solid, sensible, unpretentious, economically literate and –
more important –WISE members of the Lobby saw this immedi-

ately. And through them – and anyone who would listen – I began to communicate my absolute determination to see off the *Guardian*, the *Independent* (who had been beaten to the punch) and anyone else who cared to join them. Eventually, the *Scotsman*, under the editorship of Magnus Linklater, became the third and last newspaper to join the campaign. I had had six years to learn from Mrs Thatcher that will – the firm, unwavering application of your very fibre – was one of the most potent political commodities.

I am afraid that I was a little provocative. I described the *Guardian* and the *Independent* as 'The Stupid Tendency'. This hurt, as a leading article under that heading in the *Guardian* showed on 17 October 1986. No one could have been in any doubt that if they went over to their side they would cook their goose with Number 10. We quite simply would not be there when we were most needed, least of all at midnight and afterwards. Life was a bargain. We would either be treated fairly and decently or we wouldn't treat at all. The sensible majority appreciated this. So did the lobby officers who would have felt betrayed had I shown the slightest sign of weakness. Members of the staffs of the *Guardian* and the *Independent* – and later the *Scotsman* – outside the lobby, who did not seem to understand the background, were given the run-around by my press office. Before we had finished with them they very clearly understood that we were not to be mucked around by editors who arrogantly thought they could have it both ways. Their newspaper could not absent itself from the lobby – and try to bust it wide open – and its ordinary reporters then expect to be treated as if nothing had occurred. Yet in fact these editors were having it both ways – without, of course, confessing to their readers – because their other specialists were systematically attending unattributable collective briefings in Departments, including across Downing Street at the FCO.

The Great Lobby Revolt that flopped was widely heralded as a success almost before it had taken place. For example, Jonathan Aitken MP, with one misjudgement that was charitably overlooked by his constituents in 1987, contributed to the debate in the *UK Press Gazette* in November 1986 under the headline: 'The PM's Press Secretary – about to face the final act'. Mr Aitken, however, seemed to have as much going for him as the hapless Mr Bevins had earlier. All the Opposition party leaders – Messrs Kinnock, Steel and Owen – had pledged themselves to end unattributable briefings if they ever reached Number 10. Mr Preston had failed – according to Peter Hennessy – to get the editors of *The Times* (Charles Wilson) and *Daily Telegraph* (Max Hastings) to follow him into the wilderness ahead of the *Independent*, but the lobby officers had moved in. Or perhaps Glyn Mathias, the chairman, from ITN, had taken the initiative. Television, as well as radio and news agencies, has a vested interest in getting the Number 10 spokesman on the record and, if possible, on camera and on air. If, however, Mr Mathias had hoped to sort out the matter once and for all, the subsequent votes on various questions revealed the utter confusion among his members. They rejected by 54–31 a proposal that anyone wishing regularly to attend briefings should sign an undertaking – a 'loyalty oath', as it was widely portrayed. Curiously, they were evenly balanced (42–42) on whether an offender who broke the rules should be excluded until he gave a written oath of loyalty. They were overwhelmingly (76–8) in favour of having it both ways: they reaffirmed their long-standing commitment to on-the-record information except when it inhibited the flow of information from the Government to the public. And, since they are human and were in some difficulty, they voted even more overwhelmingly (80–5) for an inquiry to simplify and clarify the lobby's rules. So everything was still to play for.

Mr Mathias kindly invited me to give evidence. I knew Mrs Thatcher's views and temper as well as that of the Government. All the views expressed so far in this book about the lobby were familiar to Mrs Thatcher and Departments. I also cleared my evidence to Mr Mathias within Government. This note rehearsed the constitutional arguments lying behind the existing system and concluded:

'The Government has no plans for changing the relationship. It believes that:

'i the prime source of information from the Government will – and should – remain on the record statements by Ministers to Parliament and published material; the lobby system supplements this flow of information.

'ii the lobby system accordingly gives due recognition to

the primacy of Parliament as the channel for the communication of information by the Government to the nation.

'iii many journalists recognize that, within the constraints imposed by Parliament, the lobby system facilitates the flow of information and guidance.

'iv as operated by this Government, the lobby system serves without discrimination the interests of all parliamentary lobby journalists who wish to take advantage of briefings.

'The Government notes that journalists who seek to end unattributable briefings of the lobby as a group by the chief press secretary are in no way opposed to his (or others, including Ministers and MPs) briefing them individually on an unattributable basis, and seek such briefings as a matter of course. Indeed, journalists apparently consider it would be entirely impractical – and undesirable – to end the well-tried system of unattributable briefing in favour of an exclusively on-the-record relationship between informant and correspondent.

'The Government cannot accept that the lobby should seek to treat differently collective briefings with the chief press secretary.

'In a free society, journalists using their own judgement are free to accept or reject information imparted to them. In the exercise of their judgement they will take account of the credibility – the track record – of their informant, whether he is on the record or briefing on lobby terms. Their briefers are similarly guided by their perception of the integrity of the journalist or group of journalists with whom they are dealing.

'The Government considers that, properly operated according to the conventions, the lobby system can serve a useful purpose in our democracy and for that practical reason would wish to see it continue.'

And that was that. Those who wanted to Americanize the lobby within a British system of Cabinet Government controlled by Parliament were defeated. Virtually nothing changed except that in a spirit of helpfulness I made it clear that I did not object to being accurately described as a Government source. I refused to accept Peter Preston's idea that I should be described as a 'Downing Street' source. That would have opened the way to direct attribution which, in turn, would have led to the broadcasters pressing, with some justice, for rights to record briefings if not to broadcast them live. For its part, the lobby changed its rules to permit Ministers, if they so wished, to brief on-the-record. This was sensible, though far from revolutionary since Ministers in my experience had never felt inhibited from going on-the-record with the lobby. Nor did I hesitate to go on-the-record if I thought it would help the Government. I very nearly took out a protective patent on my distinctive on-the-record form of utter and absolute denial: 'Bunkum and balderdash'.

Those who set out to kill the system were routed because their case was rooted neither in practicality nor fairness. The editor of the *Mail on Sunday*, Stewart Steven, no close friend of mine, described Peter Preston's move in September 1986 as 'breathtaking in its naivety'. The result, he said, would be less open Government and not more as briefings became more and more selective and more and more secretive. And Brian Walden, in the *Sunday Times*, under the heading 'Guardian of cant' wrote:

> 'Mr Preston edits a newspaper which proclaims itself as objective and truthful, while conducting an unremitting campaign of vilification and innuendo against the Prime Minister. He is not fastidious about the sources used in the sport of Thatcher baiting. Somehow this pious concern for attribution is suspended in the hunt for any gossip, scandal or smear about Mrs Thatcher, her family and her friends.'

Moreover, the editors of the *Guardian* and the *Independent* were never secure in their own house. Peter Jenkins, of the *Independent*, had little time for his paper's self-exclusion from the lobby. It also became clear that the *Guardian*'s political staff, who had either wholeheartedly espoused or gone along with Peter Preston's ill-fated stunt, were anxious to return to the fold. Their reason was mainly self-interest. Their problem was that these paragons of journalistic virtue had never thought it through.

I got some grim pleasure out of receiving representations from the loquacious Jim Naughtie, then of the *Guardian* and now of the BBC's 'World at One', and Mr Bevins (by letter) about Mrs Thatcher's overseas trips. Since we used an RAF Strike Command VC10 there was strictly limited space on Mrs Thatcher's 'plane. I reserved spaces first for members of the lobby and then for representatives of organizations which generally observed its rules. I absolutely excluded the *Guardian*, the *Independent* and, if they had applied, the *Scotsman*. Mr Naughtie felt deprived and came to see me before Mrs Thatcher's celebrated 1987 visit to Moscow. Over a great deal of Scotch I eventually managed to get through to him that he would not be on the trip. If he was not prepared to attend my briefings at sea level, he most certainly was not going to have the benefit of them when he had no option at 35,000 feet. The message did not get through to Mr Bevins. Or perhaps it did, because when he tried a similar tack he made the point that he saw no difficulty about the confines of an aircraft. He could make himself scarce while I was conducting a collective briefing. I replied that I could see that he might lock himself in the lavatory while I was briefing. I might then bang on the door and tell him that I had finished and that, if he had, he could come out. I assumed he would then try to find out second hand what I had told his fellow travellers first hand. Sorry, I said: my efforts to cater for a journalist's idiosyncrasies do not extend to that.

The breathtaking hypocrisy of the two newspapers is ultimately exposed in the case of the *Guardian* by a letter which, as they say in the trade, mysteriously came into my possession, and in the case of the *Independent* by a quotation from its own news columns. As chairman of the British Executive of the International Press Institute, Peter Preston wrote to Kenneth Baker, then chairman of the Conservative Party, on 12 September 1989 in the following terms:

> 'At the executive meeting today, it was suggested that it may be nice if you had the time, sometime during the autumn, to come to lunch and talk on lobby terms about politics, the world and maybe the press.'

The *Independent*, following up the IRA's Remembrance Day bombing in Enniskillen, included this paragraph in its story:

'In an interview with the *Independent*, a senior IRA figure said the organization's morale, credibility and reputation had suffered badly as a result of the bombing, which killed 11 people and injured more than 60 on Sunday.'

Whereas the *Independent* insisted I should be on the record, it was prepared to waive that requirement for the IRA.

I continued to do lively business with the lobby right up to Mrs Thatcher's resignation – and the relationship continues today under Mr Major who has generally maintained the system. Mr Bevins continued to try to convert my briefings into quotes. But he was almost alone after Michael White, the *Guardian*'s new political editor, had brought a semblance of principle to the *Guardian*'s operations, though they remained outside my lobby briefings. But the entire record of his efforts show that his prime interest was not in information or understanding but in trying to embarrass me. He knew I was not going to be embarrassed. On the only occasion I broke my rule never to dine with Mr Bevins, I told his editor, Andreas Whittam Smith, who had invited the two of us to the Garrick, that while I admired his political editor as a competent reporter he had never in my experience been in the business of reporting politics; only of putting the boot in.

There is a lot of boot flying in political journalism. But it is possible to have a working relationship with the majority of journalists because they quite simply want to write stories rather than go on a crusade. Let Chris Moncrieff, the legendary political editor of the Press Association news agency, speak on their behalf: 'We are in the business to write stories to sell newspapers . . . All I can say is that those who go to the lobby get better and more accurate stories than those who don't.'

14

A Week in Number 10

In my time at Number 10 I regularly faced – and declined to facilitate – requests, from both writers and television producers, for access to the Prime Minister to prepare articles or programmes on a day or a week in her life. Quite apart from the strain that this would have placed on my slender resources in Number 10 Press Office – which was no reason not to help – there were formidable objections on grounds of confidentiality and security. Each of the Prime Minister's four principal private secretaries – the top official in Number 10 – who spanned my time there, agreed with me that we would not be able to advise her to give journalists unrestricted access. Consequently, any article or programme which emerged would be unrepresentative. Number 10 Press Office regularly sketched out a mythical yet reasonably typical day for journalists and tried to find a way, consistent with the Prime Minister's physical security, of helping television teams to film her on tour for a day either within or outside London.

The nearest we ever got to a portrait of life in Number 10 – as distinct from a period in the Prime Minister's life – was a BBC television programme to mark the 250th anniversary in 1985 of Number 10 as the official residence of the Prime Minister. This excellent production by Jenny Barraclough, fronted by Christopher Jones, the BBC's Parliamentary correspondent, preoccupied my deputy, Jean Caines, for months. Christopher also produced a book in connection with the programme *Number 10 Downing Street. The Story of a House*. I cannot think of a better example of co-operation between broadcasters and Government to produce a beautiful and informative programme, not to mention the book.

The programme was made before the Prime Minister was eventually moved in 1988 – notwithstanding her rigorous concern for the public purse – to refurbish the public parts of a house which each year receives scores of heads of state and leading statesmen. After getting on for twenty years since the last redecoration, Number 10 was beginning to look a little faded. At a cost of £1 million the Prime Minister had the rooms restored in a manner reflecting their eighteenth-century origins from the entrance, down the corridor to the ante-room to the Cabinet Room and then up the stairs, where the portraits of all former Prime Ministers are hung, to the five State rooms. The old familiar gold carpet was replaced by a beige carpet with a small all-over claret and green pattern. And now visitors can admire, among many other things, the warm, rich redness of the Cabinet ante-room; the superb plasterwork on the ceiling of the white drawing room arranged around the national floral emblems of the rose, thistle, shamrock and daffodil – sadly damaged by shrapnel from the IRA's mortar-bombing of Downing Street in February 1991; the giltwork in the green drawing-room (which used to be the – cold – blue room) and its Royal coat of arms carved in limewood; and the wood panelling in the State and small dining-rooms which has been restored to show its natural grain. For me the refurbishment heightened the sense of history which always affected me in Number 10.

Mrs Thatcher strove to make Number 10 a national display of our arts and history. Establishments were well advised to lock up their treasures when she was on the prowl. Museums, it is said, expected to have one of their better pieces commandeered for Number 10 when she visited them. She was particularly keen to recognize in artistic form our famous scientists – Priestley, Faraday and Newton, for example – and our great fighting men such as Wellington and Nelson. She was also concerned that embassies abroad should show Britain's best face to the world, though she was not averse to taking a fancy to one or two of their pieces for Number 10. She was appalled to discover that Number 10 had no silver. Consequently she made a dawn raid on Belton House, which she had known as a girl in Lincolnshire, to secure, by courtesy of Lord Brownlow, two Daimler bootloads of silver on permanent loan – or at least for as long as she was Prime Minister.

One of the perks for those who work in Number 10 is that they can share their privileged access with their relatives and close friends. During week-ends set aside for the purpose, they can show them around the public rooms. Nothing, I think, gives members of the staff greater pleasure – at least if I am any guide – than introducing their families to Number 10. If there is one thing which strikes visitors it is the size of the Prime Minister's headquarters behind the modest but world famous façade. The house is very deceptive from the outside. It was, in fact, originally two houses. Before Walpole became the first Prime Ministerial occupant, the typical late seventeenth-century town house in Downing Street was linked with a mansion at the rear with its walled garden backing on to Horseguards Parade. The other discovery which astonishes visitors, who get little impression of the office space, is the size of the staff – some seventy people all told. They work mostly in small teams of which the press office I ran was rather typical in size: me, a deputy, three press officers, two secretaries and an office manager giving, potentially at least, a twenty-four-hour service 365 days a year.

The hub of the entire office is the Prime Minister's principal private secretary, whose office is next door to, and connected with, the Cabinet Room. He is supported by a foreign affairs private secretary who shares his room; and four other private secretaries in an adjacent room covering economic, Parliamentary and home affairs and controlling the diary. Private secretaries – except the diary secretary – are recruited from the wider Civil Service and are obviously on their way upwards to the stratosphere. They are directly served by a team of young duty clerks, one of whom is always either present or on call. The private office is also supported by the Garden Room girls – the pool of super-secretaries – filing clerks, the section handling recommendations for honours of which about 1800 are processed a year, and of course the small back-up team which helps to prepare briefing for Prime Minister's Questions in the House.

Elsewhere in the building there are three other important contributors to the discharge of the Prime Minister's responsibilities. The policy unit provides the Prime Minister with an independent source of ideas and advice. The Appointments office is responsible for recommending to the Prime Minister candidates for thousands of posts which he or she fills or advises the Queen on their filling.

They cover both career and honorary jobs in, for example, the Church of England, the higher judiciary, Lord Lieutenancies and in academia. In the Church the Prime Minister is called upon to select or recommend priests ranging from the Archbishopric of Canterbury to the Vicarage of Broughton Poggs with Filkins, Bradwell with Kelmscot, Kencot, Langford and Little Faringdon which is in Oxfordshire. Or would you prefer the Vicarage of Sigglesthorne and Rise with Nunkeeling and Bewholme which is in Yorkshire? No one who has read the advisory submissions of the Appointments Secretaries in my time – Robin Catford and Colin Peterson – can fail to be impressed with the detailed work that goes into drawing up a recommendation. Nor can anyone who knew Mrs Thatcher as Prime Minister doubt the effort she put into filling posts.

Third, there are the party political offices which are distributed around the building but focus on the joint office, leading off from the ante-room to the Cabinet Room, of the Prime Minister's Parliamentary Private Secretary (PPS) – an MP – and her political secretary. The PPS and political secretary keep the Prime Minister in touch with members of the Parliamentary and wider parties. Finally, there are the security teams, the drivers and Peter Taylor, the house manager with his group of messengers and craftsmen who keep the mechanical wheels turning. It is a machine which runs smoother than most in Government because it is generally made up of positive doers rather than inventors of excuses for doing nothing.

All these people stand behind the Prime Minister. They are highly motivated and the household, if you like, is still small enough to have a family atmosphere. But, to the astonishment of most people from abroad where they are less parsimonious about their head of government, there was no cook in Number 10. Mrs Thatcher had to fend for herself in the privacy of her flat in Number 10 or rely on others to rustle up some food. Joy Robilliard, her constituency secretary, Amanda Ponsonby, her diary secretary, and Cynthia Crawford, who generally looked after Mrs Thatcher and, most importantly, her clothes, have all turned cook in their time. An outside caterer was engaged for official lunches or dinners. Otherwise Mrs Sherry Warner came in to feed us in the small

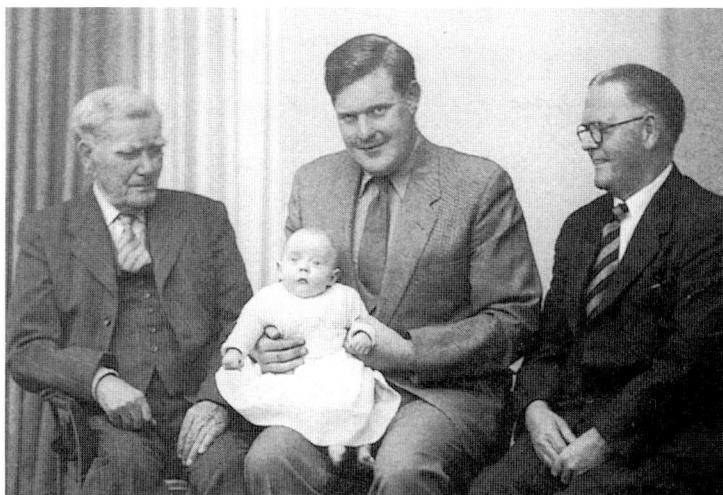

Four generations of Inghams, 1958

Hebden Bridge from Heptonstall Road, where I used to live

A quiet Sunday at the *Guardian*, Grays Inn Road, London, 1965

Visiting BP's production
platform, Graythorp 1
in the Forties Field,
North Sea, July 1975

Flying to view the Ekofisk
blowout in the North Sea
with Tony Benn, 1977

Outside Number 10,
17 May 1989

At my desk in Number 10,
17 May 1989

Welcomed by President Reagan to dinner with Mrs Thatcher
at the White House, 16 November 1988

Going native in Tbilisi, Georgia, with Charles Powell, 1 April 1987

Two press briefings:
Mrs Thatcher gives the facts to touring American correspondents
in the White Room at Number 10;
I brief in Riyadh, Saudi Arabia, April 1981

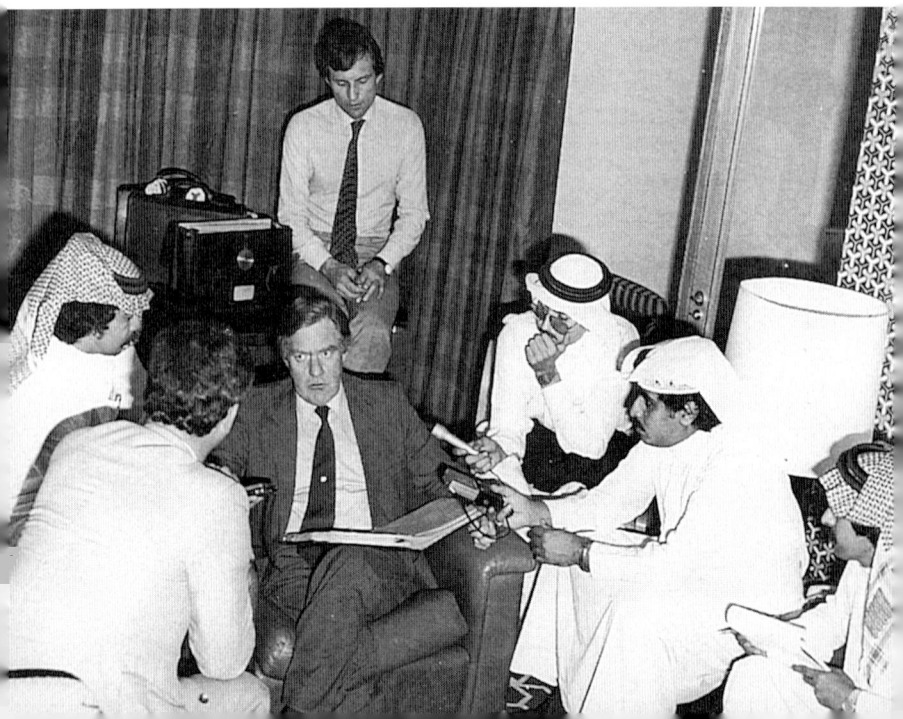

Contrasting moods:
concentrating on
President Mitterrand
at his press conference
with Mrs Thatcher,
London, 21 October 1983;
a happy moment
in my room at Number 10,
17 May 1989

Sitting in on a *Sunday Express* interview with Mrs Thatcher in her study at Number 10, March 1990

Mrs Thatcher nursing my teddy which was presented to me on my birthday at the Economic Summit in Toronto, June 1988

With Martin Fitzwalter, Press Secretary to two presidents
of the United States - Ronald Reagan and George Bush

With Mrs Thatcher in the Soviet Union, June 1990:
at a press conference with Gorbachev in Moscow, 8 June;
an interview with radio reporters in Kiev, 9 June

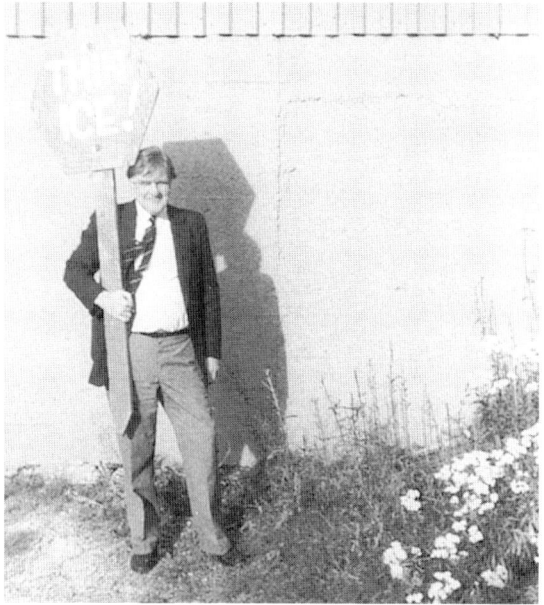

A familiar position for a press secretary - on thin ice - Grouse Mountain, Vancouver, Canada, 16 October 1987

Number 10 Press Office and colleagues with Mrs Thatcher at her farewell party in Number 10, 26 November 1990

With Charles Anson
on the canal quayside
at Hebden Bridge,
30 June 1990

After the investiture,
Buckingham Palace,
with my wife Nancy,
son John, and
daughter-in-law
Christine,
26 February 1991

dining-room on Tuesday and Thursday lunchtimes when we were expected to be on briefing standby for Prime Minister's Questions. Sherry also catered for staff parties, including the Christmas party in the Pillared Room, the largest of the reception rooms.

This, then, is the house today in which North, the younger Pitt, Wellington, Disraeli, Gladstone, Lloyd George, Winston Churchill and Attlee, to mention only a few, commanded the nation's affairs. To sketch how it was done in Mrs Thatcher's time, I have chosen at random the week beginning 22 February 1988. It was a chilly week, threatening snow which never really arrived in London. It was also before the Government fell into the usual mid-term unpopularity. At that time, it could scarcely go wrong. All this ended in December that year when Edwina Currie, a junior Minister at the Department of Health, scrambled her eggs with excessive amounts of salmonella. After that nothing went right for the Government. When reporters asked me what it was like doing my job in 1988 I compared my problems with that of the Liverpool goalkeeper: how to keep sharp and on your toes when you seldom see the opposing forwards. In 1989 and 1990 I found much in common with the goalkeeper for Halifax Town which is only too regularly at the bottom of the lowest division of ninety-two Football League soccer clubs.

MONDAY, 22 February

It had been a quiet, mild week-end and on the Sunday I had mowed the lawns for the first time. Was there something in global warming after all? Certainly, I had never before felt the need to cut the grass so early. Only the *News of the World* had disturbed the even tenor of my ways with a story – at least three months premature, as it turned out – that Mrs T was to become a granny. No wonder I thought she was being secretive when I asked her about it. The Prime Minister had returned to Number 10 from Chequers the previous evening and as usual her first appointment on Monday was a hair-do at 8.30 a.m. The hairdresser comes to her. I never met him. I keep out of these matters, which are beyond my ken.

At 10 a.m. we assemble in the Cabinet Room for WAM. This is

not, as the more paranoiac reporters might imagine, a War Alert Meeting. It is prosaically the regular Week Ahead Meeting. It brings together, under Mrs Thatcher's chairmanship, her private and press secretaries, the head of her policy unit and the chairman of the Conservative Party, Peter Brooke, his deputy, Peter Morrison (who was to become Mrs Thatcher's Parliamentary Private Secretary in her last months in office), party policy and press advisers from Smith Square and the Prime Minister's Parliamentary Private Secretary, Archie Hamilton, MP for Epsom. On Mrs Thatcher's side of the table are the Civil Servants and on Peter Brooke's the politicos. The Prime Minister is flanked, on her right, by her principal private secretary, and by me who provides the agenda. This is a suitably sanitized – that is, rendered officially non-confidential – summary, with supporting diary, of the expected highlights of the next two weeks. We concentrate on the week ahead. The object of the meeting is to ensure that both the Prime Minister's official and political machines are tuned for it.

There will, of course, be those who throw up their hands in shock and horror to learn that the Prime Minister was indulging in mixed bathing, including both Civil Servants and party apparatchiks in one discussion. They should calm down. This has taken place under every Government I have served and, far from compromising the Civil Service, enables the clear division in roles and responsibilities to be established and the subsequent action to be properly channelled, according to rules and conventions. It is a civil servant's duty to attend a meeting when summoned by a Minister of the Crown even if it is liberally sprinkled with party supporters. It is also his duty to ensure that the work he subsequently undertakes falls properly to a Government official. If it doesn't, then he must say so. Cabinet Ministers invariably know the form. Mrs Thatcher was pernickety. For example, she once asked me as we walked down the corridor to the Harcourt Room in the Commons to the launch of a couple of books about her by Aurum Press, whether I ought to be there. She was particularly sensitive because Tom Arnold MP, a vice-chairman of the Conservative Party, was chairman of the company. I said that it was perfectly reasonable for me to attend since she was going as Prime Minister to a commercial rather than a party political event.

This thirty-minute WAM has to be pretty brisk as it is to be followed immediately by a meeting of Ministers to clear the way for an announcement about the privatization of the electricity supply industry on Thursday, subject to Cabinet approval that day. There is not a lot for WAM to discuss and Mrs Thatcher is remarkably relaxed, considering she has had all week-end to find work for idle hands. The CBI has come out with an ebullient report about the economy in the very thin morning papers. The National Freight Corporation, that jewel in the crown of privatization, is to go public. And, for the party people, there is the satisfaction of reading that Roy Hattersley has said that the Prime Minister has taught the Labour Party a lot about politics. The Prime Minister is not surprised to find that the *Guardian* thinks it would be good business and common sense if we achieved reconciliation with Argentina over the Falklands.

I dash off to prepare for my first briefing of the day with the Lobby at 11 a.m. At 10.45 a.m. my deputy and press officers, standing around me at my desk, take me through all they have gleaned from their contacts with Departments and the Prime Minister's private secretaries. At 11 o'clock I open my door and in flood the twenty-five or so political correspondents who spread themselves around my room, which is the bow-fronted office to the right of the door of Number 10 as journalists and cameramen look at it from their pen in the street. All we can offer the press is news of a dinner, with the Prince of Wales representing the Royal Family, to be given by the Prime Minister this evening in honour of Cap Weinberger, the former US Secretary for Defence who, as a foreigner, has been awarded an honorary knighthood; a press notice on a new vicar of Charlesworth and Dinting Vale which slays the Lobby in the aisles (I jest); and a Parliamentary Question, for answer at 3.30, on the privatization of search and rescue services in the Solent.

I make a mental note about two of the four issues raised with me by journalists. They are massing for another assault on Paul Channon, the Secretary of State for Transport, because of an alleged near-miss air incident over Essex; and they are trying to make out that the Prime Minister has fallen out with Mr Gorbachev because of her remarks at NATO in Brussels the previous week. It was so far from a near-miss that Paul Channon had not been in touch with the Prime Minister about it. (This assault fizzles out. But it is instructive. The media seek to drag down those they think are vulnerable – and Paul Channon is vulnerable for no better reason than that he is the nicest of men and rich. What a bloody awful world I inhabit.) As for Mr Gorbachev, I emphasize that Mrs Thatcher can speak plainly about the need for the West to judge him by his actions abroad – for example, in Afghanistan and through surrogates in the Third World – without falling out with him. In any case, as I can personally testify, their relationship was founded on plain speaking.

After her Ministerial meeting on electricity privatization, the Prime Minister has her usual Monday meeting with the Ministers responsible for getting the Government's business through both Houses of Parliament – the Lord President and Leader of the Commons (John Wakeham), the Lord Privy Seal and Leader of the House of Lords (Lord Belstead) and the Chief Whip (David Waddington) and the chairman of the party. This is followed by the regular Monday lunch in the small dining room with political colleagues – a mix of Ministers and MPs. I have to cancel my lunch with Marshall Stewart, director of corporate strategy at Central TV, because the Prime Minister has called a meeting of Ministers and officials at 2.15 p.m. on a report on the inner cities programme. Rose Padwick, my secretary, gets me a salad lunch from the Cabinet Office mess and I use the free time to write a minute to the Lord President.

The Lord President seeks my views on the Government practice of making the texts of Parliamentary statements by Ministers available to members of the Press Gallery as they are being delivered. The Opposition Chief Whip, no doubt reacting to complaints from his backbenchers, is worried about this. So am I, since we never release the texts of the Prime Minister's statements until after she has made them and sat down, much to the distress of Stella Thomas, secretary to the Press Gallery. This is a difficult issue because, as a former journalist, I know how valuable it is to be able to follow a statement as it is made. On the other hand, I can imagine that Opposition (not to mention Tory) MPs feel deprived when they see journalists in the press gallery turning over the pages of a statement they do not have in front of them in unison as it is being delivered.

The Prime Minister has one of those quick, operational meetings with the Chancellor and Chief Secretary before the inner cities discussion. Inner cities – a rather inaccurate term since many of the rundown areas with which the Government is concerned are not in inner cities – land me with a lot of work to get the co-ordination of presentation right, but at least we get through the agenda in time for me to see the 4 p.m. lobby in their room at the House. In the meantime the Prime Minister successively sees the Home Secretary, the Secretary of State for Trade and Industry, the head of her policy unit, the Secretary of State for Scotland and the executive officers of the party's National Union and area chairmen.

My second meeting with the lobby is a lively encounter on the Prime Minister's relations with Mr Gorbachev on the lines of the 11 a.m. lobby; on the function of a British Budget – which, I emphasize, is to raise revenue, not to cave in on public expenditure to every lobby trying to get its hands on the public purse; and on the CBI's persistent whingeing about increases in electricity prices to industry which, as a matter of fact, have fallen by 21 per cent in real terms over the last five years. As an old energy conservation hand, I add that I would be a damned sight more impressed with the CBI if, while I was responsible for the subject, they had shown a missionary's zeal over saving electricity. It was no surprise that they hadn't; on average electricity prices represent only 2–3 per cent of a firm's total costs.

Guests for the Cap Weinberger dinner are arriving as I say farewell to Myron Belkind and Maureen Johnson, of Associated Press, the international news agency, who have been in for a drink. They convince me that the Government is not treating them equitably, especially in relation to Reuters, and I promise to try to ensure that the Government information machine as a whole changes its ways. As the Prime Minister and her guests are moving into the State dining-room I am stuffing my briefcase with work. I get home, as I always try to do when I do not have to attend a dinner, in time for the 9 p.m. news.

The newspapers remain so thin that I am ready for the Prime Minister's 9 a.m. Parliamentary Questions briefing with ten minutes to spare. Instead of my rushing into the meeting to distribute the press digests, they lie on the table awaiting the private secretaries as we foregather outside the Prime Minister's study until she comes down the stairs from her flat. She moves into the study to a litany of 'Good mornings'. We identify a number of possible Questions for her in the House: the Unionists' outrage over Dublin's inquiry into the shooting by the security forces of a man north of the Border; the press attack on Paul Channon for not ordering an immediate inquiry into a 'near-miss' over Essex which, with the 'planes twenty seconds apart, was 'unspectacular' and 'without any serious risks' in the very independent view of the *Independent*; and the Tory-dominated Treasury Select Committee's call on the Government fully to cover that part of the nurses' pay settlement it agrees to meet – that is, not to require the NHS to meet part of the cost out of higher efficiency. In terms of 'good news' that the Prime Minister might capitalize on in Questions we note that the Bedford vehicle plant at Luton is recruiting 500 more workers for double shift production after a 70 per cent increase in output through new working practices. And *Today* tells us it is no wonder members are deserting the TGWU in droves since it advised them not to buy shares in the National Freight Corporation; those members who did buy expect to make a big killing out of the company's public flotation.

After a thirty-minute briefing with me, the Prime Minister gives an hour's interview to David Montgomery, the editor of *Today*. He makes the mistake of asking a very portentous first question which absorbs fully twenty minutes of the hour set aside for the interview with a *tour d'horizon* of world politics. I can see Mr Montgomery worrying his heart out lest he loses the women's angle in which *Today* specializes. (Eventually he manages to get it.) The problem is that he doesn't know how to handle this woman – and in the rush I never managed to tell him: start simply and inconsequentially and gossip your way in. This interview means that my deputy, Terry Perks, has to see the lobby at 11 a.m. Exceptionally, he also has to do so at 4 p.m., though it is a quiet day. I cannot stay on for the afternoon lobby after attending Prime Minister's Questions because I have to write a brief on the proposed televising of the Commons for her meeting tomorrow with the Lord President and the Chief Whip. I manage to complete this in time to see a group of writers from provincial newspapers whom I meet as often as possible on Tuesday afternoons. The day ends with my meeting Peter Thornton, chief executive of Independent Radio News, and my old industrial corespondent colleague, Geoffrey Goodman, who fronts programmes for them. They are worried about maintaining political balance in their programmes because Ministers, they claim, are reluctant to appear on commercial radio, or at least in London. This surprises me. The Prime Minister and I (operating with heads of information) have always emphasized the importance of Ministers putting over the Government's case on local radio. I must crack this one, if Messrs Thornton and Goodman are right.

While I have been fully occupied the Prime Minister has in between the *Today* interview and a briefing lunch for Questions seen General Colin Powell from the White House and subsequently a backbench MP; the Foreign Secretary; our High Commissioner in Australia, John Coles, who was her foreign affairs private secretary during the Falklands war; a political supporter; and she has called on the Queen at Buckingham Palace for the weekly audience when the House is sitting. I am home for 9 p.m.

WEDNESDAY, 24 February

For the Prime Minister this is going to be a very domestic, administrative day. For me it is frantically busy. Mrs Thatcher has meetings with a group of scientists led by Professor Sir George Porter and then the Chancellor of the Exchequer (we are coming up to the Budget) before lunch with the Royal College of Surgeons. I hope she impresses upon the surgeons the need for greater efficiency in the NHS. In the afternoon she sees Sir Robin Ibbs, her Government efficiency adviser, prior to a value-for-money presentation by the Department of Employment. There then follow a succession of meetings with Nigel Wicks, her principal private secretary – on the

Honours List, I think – Paul Gray, her economics private secretary, no doubt on the economy and the Budget, and Robin Catford on recommendations for appointments. In the evening she attends a farewell party for two members of her policy unit who are leaving to return to private industry – John Whybrew and Norman Blackwell. Then she goes over to the House of Commons for a meal, to mingle with MPs and to vote at 10 p.m.; there is a three-line whip. Not much in all this for journalists – at least not much that I can tell them.

The Times and the *Daily Mail* get my blood coursing early on today because they have misinterpreted – or been allowed to do so by timid briefers – the implications of a EuroCourt judgment on VAT. I try to explain at the 11 a.m. lobby as simply as possible that this affects the interpretation of an EC directive which Britain accepted in 1977. It does NOT – repeat NOT – affect any other VAT issues and most certainly NOT the Prime Minister's pledges that VAT would not be extended to children's clothing, domestic fuel and food. I curse my fate in so often having to try to straighten out a bent story. Joe Haines was right: a lie is half way round the world before truth can get its boots on. But why can't we get it right first time round?

At 11.45 a.m. members of the Association of American Correspondents flood in for their weekly briefing. There is kneeling room only. Why the crush? Elementary, my dear Watson. We are going through one of those turbulent periods in Anglo-Irish relations when, according to the *Financial Times* this morning, even some Tory MPs who were supporters of the three-year-old Anglo-Irish Agreement now have serious reservations about its continuing value. The Americans have come to bury it – and who can blame them in view of this morning's press in Britain? I resolutely refuse to act as undertaker. Any sign of weakness on my part and the issue would catch fire. So, I put myself on auto-pilot. Rome was not built in a day. Hang it all, the Jews and the Arabs are still at each other's throats after thousands of years. What makes you chaps from Boston, Mass., think there is a quick fix in the religion-torn island of Ireland? Calm down. It's a long haul. The Anglo-Irish Agreement is still there, it is going to stay and it is obviously something that people have to take into account. What is more the inter-governmental conference is very much in business – it is, in fact, meeting today.

I have a long-arranged lunch with Sheenagh Wallace, a former Number 10 press officer, to see how she is getting on in charge of press relations at the Office of Population Censuses and Surveys. She seems to be OK. I then finish a speech I have to make in Manchester on Saturday; advise on the latest draft of the Inner Cities document; and write briefs for the Prime Minister's speech to the Marketing Club of Great Britain tomorrow night and an interview she is to give to the BBC in Yorkshire on Friday. After the 4 p.m. lobby I attend an hour-long meeting with the Prime Minister, John Wakeham and David Waddington on the televising of the Commons. John Wakeham seems likely to have the task of chairing the Select Committee which will settle the regime for broadcasting the Commons's proceedings and he wants to clear his lines within Government. I think my view is accepted that the tighter the rules with which the experiment starts the better. The House can always relax them in the light of experience. It would be very difficult to tighten them during the experimental period unless the broadcasters were extraordinarily foolish. The Prime Minister remains deeply concerned over what televising the House will do for its reputation. She may be right, but I am sure that she herself simply cannot lose. I don't think she believes that at all.

Around 10.15 p.m. I begin to get calls at home from journalists asserting that there is to be an electricity privatization statement tomorrow. As usual, politicians have been gossiping in the bars of the Commons. Geoffrey Parkhouse, *Glasgow Herald*, awakens me at midnight to gloat that he has got the privatization story even though I didn't tell him. I coldly inform him, like the rest, that I'll say what I have to say in due time and possibly when tomorrow's Cabinet is over. As I try to get back to sleep, I fervently wish that the Cabinet would mark time on privatization policy tomorrow. That would put the gossipers in their place. On the other hand, it would make my life difficult. 'Electricity privatization hits Cabinet rock' would then be the story. Imagine the crucifixion the lobby would lay on for me if I confidently trailed a statement before Cabinet which then postponed a decision. Incompetence in presentation would be the least of the charges publicly laid against me. The media have it both ways – and are bloody inconsiderate with it.

THURSDAY, 25 February

The Cabinet duly clears electricity privatization policy and Cecil Parkinson, Secretary of State for Energy, makes his statement to the Commons. It seems to go well. John Major, the Chief Secretary, who is in charge of presentation, calls on me for a coffee and gives me his usual excellent rundown on what I might say about Cabinet business. There is supposed to be a Health Alert demonstration in Westminster in support of just another £2.5 billion more for the NHS but I fail to notice it. If the Government poured into the NHS all the funds that everybody clamours for we would be the most impoverished nation of dithering hypochondriacs in the Western world. This subject seems a likely candidate for Mr Kinnock's line of questioning at 3.15 p.m., though he fell back on the old NHS faithful on Tuesday. He might, of course, try to embarrass the Prime Minister over South Africa's clampdown on black activist groups, especially as the *Independent* reports a wave of international revulsion. The Foreign Secretary has, however, rather ruined it by condemning the repression. In the event Mr Kinnock goes for South Africa rather than the NHS and another possibility – the *Daily Mirror*'s familiar claim that the poor get poorer while our millionaires and billionaires proliferate – apparently there are 200 of the blighters now alive and well in Britain.

The Prime Minister gets back late from sitting in on Cecil Parkinson's statement in the House (and the launch of Sir Philip Holland's book) and then spends an hour with the Chancellor. This means we do not get to work on her speech for the Marketing Group of Great Britain until 6 p.m. We have to leave for the Dorchester at 7.15 p.m. Another quick change is on the cards. My objective, however, is to persuade the Prime Minister to speak extempore on this more informal occasion. She carries her audience so much more with her when she speaks from the heart rather than from paper. She maps out her own speech notes quite quickly from my proposed structure. Jean Denton, the former rally driver from Wakefield who is her hostess, is obviously delighted with the way she has wowed the marketing men and women. Mrs T drops me off at Number 10 at about 11.15 p.m. and I'm home by midnight.

FRIDAY, 26 February

I am feeling acutely deprived today. Because I have to go to Manchester tomorrow, I have asked the Prime Minister to excuse me from her tour today of Salford, Milnrow and – how mortifying – Halifax. I would have loved to visit Dean Clough Mills, the old Crossley Carpet works in Halifax where Nancy's father was a joiner and which have been converted into a home for small firms and various amenities for the community. Instead, Terry Perks and Andy Bearpark, the private secretary who comes from Rochdale, enjoy themselves with Mrs Thatcher in the North. When they get back at 6.30 it has all been sweetness and light. Not a single stray protester's egg has crossed the path of her car. The main problem of the day has been Colleen's pregnancy. Colleen Harris, our lovely, bubbly coffee-coloured press officer is five months pregnant and very fit with it. Mrs Thatcher clearly feels we should not now be sending her on arduous regional visits. So she spends the day pampering her, slowing down the visit, making her sit down at every opportunity. And while the rest of the party flies home Colleen travels back to London in the back seat of the Prime Minister's car with instructions to put her feet up across the back seat. By the time they wander into my office to retail the day's successes, I have got a reasonably straight edge and the summary of the next two weeks is in the Prime Minister's box at Chequers ready for another WAM on Monday.

Charles Powell, the Prime Minister's foreign affairs private secretary, pays his usual 7.45 a.m. call on me – scorching his bottom on my radiator in the process – and we worry about the easy run the Government is having in Parliament.

It can't last, but while it does it doesn't necessarily make for an easy life for the Prime Minister's staff. We are afraid of being lulled into a sense of false security. Altogether a very uneventful day. It's funny, but I used to worry as a district office journalist when nothing was happening, wondering what I was missing. Now as press secretary I also worry when it is quiet. I suppose the truth is that I haven't time to worry about anything when I'm in the middle of a crisis. Not even much trouble from the Fishing Fleet, as the Sunday newspaper lobby is called because the six-day trawling of political waters by the dailies leaves little in the way of a Sunday catch. Murdo Maclean, the Chief Whip's splendid private secretary, pops in to say how brilliant her audience thought the Prime Minister was last night. I give him a drink. I think I can go to Manchester with good conscience.

SATURDAY, 27 February
The Prime Minister is safe and cosy at Chequers for the week-end. My wife and I drive up early to our son's home in Lymm, Cheshire. While he is covering his first Division 1 match for the *Sunday Express*, between Everton and Southampton, we go shopping in Altrincham with his wife, Christine. In the evening she drives us to the Ramada Renaissance Hotel in Manchester where, to my astonishment, a number of Ministers – Angela Rumbold, John Lee and Robert Atkins – have turned up for the Westminster Dining Club function. I comment that greater love hath no Minister for the cause of women's advancement – the purpose of this non-political club – than to listen to Ingham on a Saturday night on how he does his job for a woman Prime Minister, and what he thinks of the media. I rather enjoy myself, especially when some women journalists have a go at me. Elizabeth Peacock MP, who presides, seems well satisfied.

SUNDAY, 28 February
After a poor night worrying lest I am marooned in the North by the weather – blizzards sweeping down from the North are forecast but never materialize – I read the newspapers while Nancy is at mass in Lymm. We are home in Purley for lunch. Cecil Parkinson rings to discuss the Sundays' presentation of electricity privatization which portrays him as complacent, even gloating, over his success. He doesn't like the tone. I sympathize and say it will pass. I then

settle down to read myself in for the week ahead and the NATO Summit in Brussels on Wednesday. How long will this easy ride last?

15

Fighting and Caring

Reading again my much annotated copy of the Conservative Party manifesto for the 1979 general election – my first guide to the Government's intentions against which the lobby held it to account – both confirms my recollections and surprises me. All the themes which I came to underline for the Prime Minister in my early daily contacts with journalists are there: restoring the economy by controlling inflation and striking a fair balance between the rights and duties of the trade union movement; upholding Parliament and the rule of law; restoring incentives so that hard work pays and success is rewarded; getting Government off the backs of the people; encouraging home ownership; and strengthening Britain's defences and working with our allies to protect our interests. Such familiar Thatcher phrases as 'working with the grain of human nature', 'self reliance', 'personal responsibility' are also there. So, too, is the emphasis on the importance of small businesses. The first seeds of a privatization programme are also planted. But what surprises me is how the manifesto understates Mrs Thatcher's frustration with Britain's reduced circumstances. True, it refers to 'a great country which seems to have lost its way' and in her foreword she, herself, rejects any notion that it is too late to turn 'this once great nation' around. But it conveys nothing of her passion which I immediately encountered for making Britain great again.

The 1979 manifesto was, however, a deliberately cautious document. Mrs Thatcher says in the foreword: 'It contains no magic formula or lavish promises.' The manifesto concludes: 'The repeated disappointment of rising expectations has led to a marked loss of faith in politicians' promises. Too much has gone wrong in Britain for us to hope to put it all right in a year or so.' In between it refers to a 'disillusioned people'.

Cassius accurately summed up the mood of the Prime Minister I found in Number 10: 'The fault, dear Brutus, is not in our stars, but in ourselves, that we are underlings.'

Mrs Thatcher clearly did not intend Britons to remain underlings in the world. It was this burning love of her country and her manifest determination to restore its fortunes that inspired me. She needed all the help and support she could get if she were to have a fighting chance of achieving half of what she hoped for Britain. It was my duty as a civil servant to give her that full-hearted support. I have never had much time for those civil servants who argue that their proper duty is to withhold that last ounce from the elected Government lest they become over-committed. That, to me, could become a cover for withholding a bit more than an ounce, depending upon your preferences, if only in Ministers. Moreover, giving the last ounce implies giving the last ounce of constructive criticism as well as of positive effort. The only thing to be done in my view is to serve whomsoever you are landed with by the voters to the very best of your ability. Of course, you will get on better with some Ministers than others and, both being human, there will be good and bad days between you. But you look after them at all times.

I think my record shows that whether or not I had shared Mrs Thatcher's enthusiasm for sorting out a debilitated country I would have thrown my full weight behind her. But my account so far also shows that I shared more than her injured patriotism. I had become fed up to the back teeth with Britain's industrial performance being scorned, especially by German journalists. It would not have been so bad if they had merely been exhibiting a prejudice; unfortunately they had a powerful point. While I did not think we were endowed with the best management in the world, I believed that the British trade union movement was abusing its power and had to be curbed, and that this was a precondition for a more successful country. I had had any idea that there was a 'quick fix' for the nation's economic ills knocked out of me and had long concluded that Britons needed to accept some good old-fashioned personal responsibility and to 'buckle to' – to get stuck in – as they say in Hebden Bridge. I also recognized in the Prime Minister much of my Non-conformist upbringing. Against this background, it would be foolish to deny

225

that I shared many of her values. It should, however, be acknowledged that, giving my last ounce in her support or, as the current phrase has it, walking the last mile for her, implies I became a candid adviser and friend, too. Support comes in many forms.

Turning the economy round was clearly Mrs Thatcher's prime objective. In the light of all my experience since 1967 I thought I was in for my roughest ride yet. It would be a stern test of my nerve and resolve as well as hers. It might also be personally disagreeable. The Government's every action would be scrutinized for weakness, trimming or a change of course. I felt as if I were on my way to the Colosseum. But I also felt it was about time the Government chalked up a victory against the lions. If it were chewed up yet again I doubted whether I would want to live under the yoke of the TUC. In view of my upbringing, the last thing I wanted to see was higher unemployment. But Mrs Thatcher had not invented it. In our discussions during the late 1960s Sir Denis Barnes had gloomily forecast much higher levels of people out of work because of the country's inability, in the teeth of the unions' refusal to face facts, to contain inflation. Unemployment had roughly doubled during the 1970s. I had reached the dismal conclusion that, whatever they might say to the contrary, the unions did not care about the unemployed. All previous attempts to sort out the country had failed. Mrs Thatcher deserved her chance. I hoped that she would succeed – and that the cost would be sustainable.

It was in this grim mood that I took over responsibility for representing Mrs Thatcher's views to journalists and for co-ordinating the Government's overall economic presentation. By the time I arrived the Government, notwithstanding the honeymoon which any new administration enjoys with the press and public, had already acquired a reputation as a 'cutting' Government by slashing public expenditure by £4 billion. It had also announced a cut in direct taxation – the standard rate by 3p to 30p – but very nearly doubled the rate of indirect taxation in the form of VAT. The seeds of Mrs Thatcher's ill-deserved reputation for being 'uncaring' had therefore been sown. These reputations, for cutting and not caring, Mrs Thatcher carried with her to the end. Facts in politics seem to count for little. Perception is all. I fought perception with fact every inch of the way, and it was an uphill struggle.

This raises two interesting points about economic presentation during Mrs Thatcher's term of office. She objected less to a reputation for cutting than to one for being uncaring, though the two are interlinked. Yet however determinedly she approached public expenditure, the blunt fact is that hers was not, overall, a cutting administration whatever the rhetoric, including a 20 per cent cut in the size of the Civil Service. Mrs Thatcher's signal contribution to the management of Britain's finances was to control, as distinct from cut, public spending. That was a formidable achievement, given the number of people who were queuing up to spend your money and mine, but it meant that over time the Government was spending more, not less, of our hard earned cash. It was able to do so AND contain public spending because she brought the nation through depression into eight years of continuous economic growth. She 'cut' public expenditure as a proportion of the nation's total income but because that income was growing she spent more.

Only those who know my volcanic soul can imagine the eruptions which this continuing misrepresentation of affairs later wrought in me. I tried every way to persuade journalists to face reality, but to no avail. In journalistic terms the concept of spending more while spending less is quite complex to explain to readers, viewers and listeners. In any case, Mrs Thatcher had been poured into a 'cutting' mould by the media and there she must stay, regardless of the facts, if the image suited the story. All too often the two fitted like hand and glove. I ruefully concluded that journalists – not to mention politicians, trade union leaders, local councillors, NHS officials, teachers and all who would dip their hand into the taxpayer's pocket – had redefined the financial verb 'to cut' to mean not an actual reduction in expenditure but something less than they had demanded, desired or arbitrarily thought necessary.

As for Mrs Thatcher's being 'uncaring', she protected social security from cuts in her early years when unemployment was soaring and also the NHS while raising charges which only a minority paid. She cared more than her critics could ever imagine. But her uncaring image owed itself not merely to her leadership of a 'cutting' Government. It had, I soon concluded, something to do with her sex. Political life is particularly hard on women. They have to pay the closest attention to their appearance and clothing whereas men do not even have to be clean shaven, brushed or dressed by Savile Row. For them there may even be an advantage in appearing nondescript. A male Minister can raise his voice, thump the dispatch box and even go as red in the face as Jim Prior and me and get away with it. As a consequence, they might even be described as dominating or commanding or powerful. Let a woman raise her voice in the Commons, if only to be heard, and she immediately becomes shrill and strident and in danger of losing her cool. If your voice is high-pitched to start with, as with Dame Elaine Kellett-Bowman, MP for Lancaster, you can suffer the most disgraceful, sexist mimicking in the House. Mrs Thatcher applied formidable self-discipline to hold down the pitch of her voice in the House, even on occasions provoking shouts of 'Speak up' from the denizens of Decibel Dell who were doing their best to ensure that she could not be heard. She was regularly dubbed strident.

A woman Prime Minister's problems arising from gender do not, however, end with dress and voice. It is the lonely duty of any Cabinet Minister, not to mention a Prime Minister, to take hard decisions which can never by any stretch of the imagination be described as popular. It is also his or her duty to announce them to the House of Commons. But when you are the Prime Minister of a Government which came to office rejecting any attempt to 'gloss over the harsh facts of life' and are committed to 'substantial economies' you are a prime candidate for being labelled 'uncaring'. And when the Prime Minister of such a Government is a woman – and a Tory – you are a racing cert for such a label. God only knows what fate awaits the first Labour woman Prime Minister who has to take hard decisions. The modern process of Government requires so many of them – decisions which are incompatible with the softer image of the female – that a woman Prime Minister almost inevitably is going to be tagged 'uncaring'. So it was with Mrs Thatcher. She was, in fact, tough – very tough indeed. But she cared. If she didn't care, she once asked me challengingly, why did they think she committed every atom of her being to the job of turning Britain round? There was no answer to that – except, of course, that some journalists as well as political opponents would give her credit for nothing.

Mrs Thatcher had not merely to face the handicaps of sex and commitment in self-indulgent, slack and sad 1979; she also had to overcome an appalling defeatism. Historians will argue over her greatest achievement. I will enter my candidate now. It is NOT

- the defeat of inflation (of which the latest bout seems to have served to prove her original remedies of financial control and discipline);
- the creation of an enterprise economy;
- the spreading of the ownership of property and capital through council house sales and wider share ownership;
- the redefining of the political debate in Britain;
- the taming of the trade union barons;
- the defeat of Argentina in the Falklands war;
- the vindication of her East–West and South Africa policies;
- her progressive reform of the European Community – and I use those words advisedly; or
- her restoration of Britain's standing in the world.

For me her greatest single achievement, which made all these and other things possible, was her refusal to accept, or be daunted by, the prevailing air of defeatism which she confronted on taking office in 1979. No one should over-estimate the effect on a front line politician of attacks from the Opposition benches. Opposition from your own side is harder to take, but again not unexpected. These media-ridden days, which call for instant comment, also confront Prime Ministers with challenges which would not have occurred thirty years ago. But to overcome all the opposition you expect – and that you hope not to experience – the close attentions of the media and an all-pervasive defeatism in society requires exceptional quality. Mrs Thatcher had exceptional quality and exceptional nerve.

I deliberately go back to 1979, not for the sake of beginning at the beginning, but because the first two and a half years were crucial in the making of Mrs Thatcher and her success. Time and again she encountered the view that she would not be able to do this, that or the other because 'they' would not allow it. It was almost as if the country had become conditioned to attempting nothing in the face of vested interests of which the greatest was the trade union movement. Mrs Thatcher would have nothing of this. She had clearly set out one of her five tasks in her manifesto as 'To uphold Parliament and the rule of law'. Parliament would decide what could or could not be done; not 'they' whoever 'they' were. I had uttered similar thoughts in the *Leeds Weekly Citizen* fourteen to fifteen years earlier.

It is also germane to note that Mrs Thatcher did not think time was on her side. She repeatedly told me of her belief that this was probably the last chance to rescue Britain from the excessive power which decades of political consensus had conferred upon the State. She had stated this explicitly in the foreword to her party's 1979 manifesto: 'No one who has lived in this country during the last five years can fail to be aware of how the balance of our society has been increasingly tilted in favour of the State at the expense of individual freedom. This election may be the last chance we have to reverse that process, to restore the balance of power in favour of the people. It is therefore the most crucial election since the war.' She had won it and she was not going to waste the opportunity.

I cannot say that in 1979 I had such an aversion to the State. My upbringing saw collective action through the State as a necessary means of achieving the advancement of working people. But I had been forced to conclude that it had not worked entirely satisfactorily. There was something in Conservative criticism, with which I had grown up, that excessive reliance on the State sapped the people's will and undermined personal responsibility. Moreover, I had concluded that one of the problems in Britain was that everything was organized for the benefit of producers – and to hell with the customer. I was not however prepared to admit that nationalized industries were uniquely at fault. Service to the customer did not seem an overriding concern of many private firms either. Things are better now, but there was no point in arguing with American correspondents, even in 1990, that Britain was now a consumer society. By their standards, they made it abundantly clear – reinforced by not a few exclamations and anecdotes about the difficulty of securing simple services – that we still had a long way to go. Mr Major has acknowledged this in setting his goal of improved services to the public.

By the time I arrived in Number 10 to start spreading these

Government messages around, as circumstances afforded the opportunity, others had been added to the portfolio. Quangos – non-government (and non-elected) institutions set up allegedly to help the Government do its job but all too often to hinder it by acquiring minds and purposes of their own – were being killed. The Energy Commission, the Construction Industry Advisory Board and the eight English regional economic planning councils were among the first to go the way of a lot of quango flesh. Quango culling caught the imagination of journalists for a time. The Government was also getting out of industry and letting the public in – for example, into British Airways, British Aerospace, Cable and Wireless and British Petroleum by way of share ownership. It also prepared the way for the eventual privatization of British Telecom by splitting the Post Office into its postal and telecommunications arms. While honouring some expensive recommendations from the Clegg Commission on Comparability (which also soon died the death), it crucially stood aloof from a number of strikes. The most important were a series of one- (and later two-) day strikes in the engineering industry.

No sooner was I in post than exchange controls were lifted. The roof did not fall in and the floor did not drop out of the pound. The Prime Minister took great delight in heading a Government which had also abandoned pay, price and dividend controls. It was, she said, really getting off people's backs and restoring the right and responsibility of managers to manage their own affairs. Interest rates soared from 14 to 17 per cent. They did so to warnings from the Prime Minister that she would do whatever was necessary to control inflation. Earlier she had told employers and unions that she would not print money to finance irresponsible pay settlements. They took little notice, which tends to confirm my earlier thesis that the country was by no means convinced that Mrs Thatcher was different from those who had preceded her. There were two (deceptive) suggestions that someone might have been listening. The miners voted by a narrow majority to accept 20 per cent instead of the 63 per cent demanded by their union for faceworkers. British Leyland workers came out with a 7–1 majority in favour of accepting a programme of closures and redundancies previously rejected by shop stewards.

But then the steelworkers decided to go on strike over pay – their first national strike since 1926. The Government again stood aside in spite of the damage over very nearly a three-month stoppage both to the steel industry, which lost about 10 per cent of its British markets, and wider industry. The steelmen's decision to strike coincided with the publication of the Employment Bill – the first industrial relations measure – to predictable exclamations of anger from the unions. And as if to pile on the agony for those congenitally opposed to all its works, the Government produced Bills to break the link between rises in the level of pensions and the rise in average earnings and to strengthen the rights of parents to choose the school for their children. It also announced that it was proceeding with powers to give council tenants the right to buy their own homes. To hear some people talk, you would think I invented a tough Prime Minister. I did not invent anything about her. I reflected reality. The Iron Lady was tempered steel from the first – as this summary of her first few months shows.

Two things were clear: first, the country was going to have to learn the hard way; second, the Prime Minister could ill afford to soften her approach – otherwise her efforts to inculcate a sense of personal responsibility in the individual for his actions would be rendered ineffective. She persevered with her medicine as unemployment rose month in and month out under the influence of excessive pay settlements, tight money, a strong pound and a deep recession. Only those who sat with her in her study as bad news piled on bad news and the ITN's weekly redundancy table clocked up ever more closures can properly appreciate her nerve and her conviction that the only future for Britain lay in genuine new jobs and not in subsidized labour forces in outdated industries. It is these qualities – nerve, conviction and courage linked with her refusal to succumb to defeatism – that eventually carried us through more than 3 million unemployed to a different kind of society. But it was not until the mid 1980s that she felt confident that the enterprise she doggedly believed still existed in Britain had been unleashed. Her joy and sense of achievement came through in so many private conversations.

If there is one year in which she and her Government were truly forged it was 1981. And it was memorable not merely for her resolution in the face of adversity piled on adversity but for an occasion when her discretion became the better part of valour. She declined to take on the National Union of Mineworkers who were threatening a national strike over pit closures. The Government made more money available to the National Coal Board and the closures were cancelled. It was, however, crystal clear that that was not the end of the matter. The Government began to lay down stocks of coal at power stations and generally prepare for the eventual confrontation which Mrs Thatcher had clearly feared, but hoped to avoid, when she paid her first Departmental visit – to the Department of Energy – in May 1979. After the meeting in February 1981 at which Ministers decided not (yet) to put the Government's authority to the Scargill test, I rather got the impression that she thought I had gone soft when I told her that I felt the decision to which she was a party was right! It was not a pleasure to meet the lobby after this 'U-turn', as it was seen. Time and again journalists threw this retreat back in my face when I sought to persuade them that the Government would stand firm on other issues.

Some of the tension of 1981 was revealed by the conclusion to her speech to the CBI's annual dinner on 16 June 1981. She said: 'I can do no better than repeat the words spoken by Captain Lloyd Williams when he arrived in Northern France in June 1918 at a time when victory was almost within grasp after years of struggle but a hard fight clearly lay ahead. He said in the graphic language of a soldier: "Retreat. Hell, no! We only just got here."'

By the end of 1981 not even her severest critic among the pundits could deny that she had endured trial by ordeal and fire. Looking back on that year, I hope never to go through its like again – and I have been through some trying years in the service of the Government. Looking forward from it, I drew strength and confidence from the experience. If I could survive that I could survive anything. I imagine Mrs Thatcher felt much the same. And then came the Falklands, which is another story. Let me list what happened in 1981:

   – riots in Brixton, Toxteth (Liverpool) and Moss Side (Manchester) among other places. (News about the Brixton riots was relayed to Mrs Thatcher, via me, while she was addressing the Parliamentary Press Gallery's centenary dinner. Tom Savage, my driver for the evening, took my wife and me a roundabout route home and I recall being fearful lest he was caught in trouble on his way home in South London. I visited Upper Parliament Street in Toxteth with Mrs Thatcher immediately after the riot there and recall being shaken by the evidence in the police station of the sheer savagery of the assault on the police – for example, the top of an iron railing driven downwards into a constable's helmet. I also got a fearful hammering from some critics for allowing the Prime Minister to speak to cameras about riots at the Royal Agricultural Show wearing a pillbox hat.)

– the mounting toll of deaths among IRA hunger strikers which, for the rest of Mrs Thatcher's time in Number 10 and beyond, ended the general public's free passage through Downing Street.

– the rise of the Social Democratic Party which won three Tory seats in Warrington, Croydon NW and Crosby (and the speculation as to how many Tories would defect to it; in the end, only one MP).

– an increase of more than 500,000 over the year in the number of unemployed, with the looming certainty of 3 million out of work in 1982.

– pay strikes in the water and sewage industry (whose managers caused near despair in Government over their conduct of the dispute); seamen (again) for five weeks which seriously affected British shipping and ports; bank employees; and civil servants who claimed before they had finished to have stopped £6 billion in revenue payments, cost British Airways £40 million in lost traffic and paralysed the Scottish legal system – achievements which a union leader described as the result of 'the best organized, most beautiful and disciplined strike action there has ever been in the post-war period'. I was not part of it as I ceased to be a member of a union in 1978 when I left the NUJ on becoming an administrator.

– a very tough Budget which financed increased spending largely out of increased indirect taxation – an honest Budget,

234

as the Prime Minister so often said, in pursuit of honest money. Defending it twenty-four hours later she saw printing money instead of raising taxes to pay for agreed expenditure as 'the most immoral path of all'.

– a letter to *The Times* by 364 economists – I shall never forget the figure because it is the same as Len Hutton's record-breaking Test score against the Australians at the Oval in 1938 – who called for alternative policies as offering the 'best hope of sustained economic recovery'. The impressive list of expertise included several former chief economic advisers to the Government. Subsequently, old hands in Number 10 dated the start of the country's economic recovery under Mrs Thatcher's policies as 30 March – the date of the economists' letter. Sir Geoffrey Howe, the Chancellor, caused a fuss four months later when he announced 'we have come to the end of the recession' in the sense that output had stopped falling.

– a progressive 'drying out' over the year of her Cabinet as the 'wets' – a word, incidentally, that Mrs Thatcher was not in the habit of using but which had entered the vocabulary to indicate an individual's economic rigour – were weeded out.

Thus Mrs Thatcher came through her most testing year in the ascendant. She bluntly told her party conference in October that she would not change just to court popularity. With inflation running at 12 per cent and unemployment about to top 3 million, there was still a long way to go. But at the end of the year she felt able to tell journalists that the country was through the worst and that the fruits of her policies were being reaped. Journalists I have regularly briefed over the years know that I have no doubt that had Mrs Thatcher weakened in 1981 she would not have been in power for the whole of the 1980s. She was tried, sorely tested and did not buckle. It was in 1981 that the legend was made.

Contrary to the popular view, I played little direct part throughout Mrs Thatcher's years in the formulation of policy. This is not false modesty; it is a fact. Mrs Thatcher came to Government with a coherent philosophy and was not one to be driven solely – if at all – by presentation. In any case she did not employ me as a policymaker, except in one respect: to devise a strategy for the overall presentation of her policies and measures. Policy and its presentation are, however, closely interlinked. The administrator can submit his ideas for a policy initiative to his Minister and the head of information will express his views on how best to present it and the likely consequences of pursuing such a course. The Minister will then decide whether and how to proceed in the light of all the advice he has received. The extent to which the Chief Press Secretary influences policy is seldom clear-cut. Sometimes – as readers will discover in these pages – presentational advice can apparently be conclusive in heading off a course of action. On other occasions it may subtly rather than dramatically change the nature, if not necessarily the substance, of an announcement.

My contribution to Mrs Thatcher's policymaking lay predominantly in three areas. First, in ensuring that she was aware of any significant criticisms or comments which came my way from journalists and the public about the Government's performance and standing. Second, in monitoring the coherence of Government policies and measures as they developed and in trying to ensure that any inconsistencies or other presentational difficulties were identified, examined and dealt with. And, third, in trying to ensure that the Government's overall credibility was maintained. This last point kept me particularly on the alert for anything that might be interpreted as a U-turn. I spent roughly the first two-and-a-half years with Mrs Thatcher playing a game of 'spot the U-turn' with the lobby. If I felt that the Government's credibility was in danger of being undermined, it was my duty to say so. I did my duty, for example, when a compromise was proposed over trade union membership in the Government Communications Headquarters (GCHQ) at Cheltenham where it had been banned after industrial action. Union membership remains unacceptable.

This begs a question frequently asked of me, perhaps because I was felt to be so in tune with Mrs Thatcher; what did I do when the Government came forward with policies I did not like? The short and honest answer is that my views as a civil servant were neither here nor there once a policy had been decided. My job was to get on with its presentation regardless. I imagine that many lawyers in their time have not thought much of some of their cases but that has not prevented them from pleading professionally, and to the best of their ability, for their clients. I do not see why it cannot be allowed that a Chief Press Secretary can do the same. It is conceivable, if his critical views are known, that he will take exceptional care to ensure that his presentation of the particular case cannot be faulted.

Against this background, I was responsible both for devising a presentational strategy (and for keeping it up to date and rolling it forward) and implementing it. My dominating consideration, apart from protecting Mrs Thatcher, was whether the Government's message was getting through – and, if not, how I could remedy the situation. My main instrument for putting over the Government's message was the Prime Minister herself. My aim, therefore, was to ensure that, over and above her Parliamentary appearances and speeches elsewhere, she regularly broadcast on radio and television and gave interviews to newspapers. I also sought to preserve a balance over time between press (both newspapers and magazines, and especially women's magazines), BBC and commercial radio and television and British and foreign journalists. My claims on her time – to which she almost ritually objected often only to thank me for pressing her to give the interview – did not, if I could avoid it, extend to those who would merely come to sneer and ridicule.

Apart from my regular meetings with the Prime Minister – and my extensive reading of policy and operational papers – my crucial contacts each day were with the Prime Minister's private secretaries. Over my eleven years in Number 10 I worked with four principal private secretaries, three handling foreign affairs and defence issues; six economic; and a total of nine handling Parliamentary and home affairs. Private secretaries are the link between the Prime Minister and the rest of Government, not to mention the outside world. They are also a crucial link in the chain for formulating policy and presenting it. Between us – or my staff, according to circumstances – we would establish the facts, agree how to present them and clear our lines with the policy department.

Alternatively, the Department would provide a briefing line and, depending on its sensitivity, we would inform the responsible private secretary in Number 10 of what the Government was saying that day on the particular issue.

Mine was therefore a service industry – an industry at the service of both the Prime Minister herself and the wider Government. And part of that service was to reconcile, if not necessarily conflicting views, at least differences of emphasis between Departments. I mention this only because one popular view of my tenure seems to be that I poured oil only on fires; never on troubled waters to calm them. It also underlines the extent to which a Chief Press Secretary is at the centre of a web of negotiation within Government over what and how much is to be said to the public and how it is to be said. My inclination from first (1967) to last (1990) was to be more rather than less open, consistent with the Government's interest.

There were occasions when little could be said – for example, on the Budget and the annual public expenditure round beginning in the spring. In any case, these issues were primarily for HM Treasury who were left to handle them. My contribution to the Budget was limited over the years to minutes to the Prime Minister setting out my presentational views or relaying to her points which had been made to me by different sections of the communications industry; ensuring that the massive publication exercise associated with the Budget was on course; and reinforcing Treasury briefing on the day and subsequently. My role in relation to the public expenditure round was a little more extensive because the Cabinet came to discuss in July the economic background to the review which concluded in the autumn with individual negotiations between the Chief Secretary at the Treasury – the guardian of public expenditure – and Departmental Ministers. The familiar pattern of events was that in July Ministers, having lodged huge bids for additional spending, swore a Cabinet oath of loyalty to the cause of restraint against which, the First Lord of the Treasury hoped, they would negotiate them down in the autumn. Journalists inevitably found the review's progress interesting sport and reported it accordingly.

I myself found the separation by some four months of the announcement in the autumn of the Government's expenditure plans and the raising of revenue through the Budget in the spring presentationally less than ideal. Quite apart from divorcing expenditure from revenue, it tended to perpetuate the arithmetical nonsense of a 'cutting' Government when all that was usually happening in the autumn was that bids for much more spending were being reduced to just more public spending. At one stage I was encouraged that the

Financial Times also thought this separation left something to be desired. The case was examined within Government but no solution was found to what seemed to be an operational problem.

My supportive – as distinct from leading – role in the presentation of specific issues was underlined by the miners' strike which eventually occurred in 1984–5. Here Peter Walker, the Secretary of State for Energy and a most resourceful operator with journalists, was in charge. I attended the regular Ministerial meetings under Mrs Thatcher's chairmanship to take stock of the often violently intimidatory progress of the dispute which had been called without a national ballot. Four things were crucial: the level of coal stocks, the continued working of a substantial number of miners, the continued delivery of coal to power stations and the upholding of the rule of law to which the Prime Minister had specifically pledged herself in 1979 and again at the 1983 general election. These were preserved yet the dispute ran for very nearly a year and put the police in the front line. Throughout my aim was to support Mr Walker's presentational efforts which were not always assisted by a wayward Ian MacGregor, the NCB's chairman. Eventually constitutional forces prevailed. The miners deserved better from their leaders. The outcome – progressive closures and redundancies which Mr Scargill had confidently forecast and done his level best to bring about – could scarcely have been worse for them. I felt desperately sorry for their families whose traditional loyalty had been cruelly exploited. But the Government had to win this time and Mrs Thatcher made sure it did.

The outcome of the dispute emphasized the changed nature of Britain under Mrs Thatcher. It was, in my view, a change wrought by her grit and leadership. As we embarked on steady growth, an increase in wealth and a refurbishment of the fabric of Britain, especially that of 'inner city' areas, she might reasonably have relaxed a little in terms of workload. If so, I did not notice it. In fact, it is fair to say that she was often packing more into a working day in 1990 than she had sometimes done earlier. Relaxation for her so often seemed to mean a different kind of work at week-ends. Instead, she began to tackle the 'many things [that] will simply have to wait until the economy has been revived and we are once again creating the wealth on which so much else depends', as the 1979

239

manifesto put it. This takes me back to her reputation for being 'uncaring'.

I will quote four examples: manufacturing industry, health, education and local government. First, manufacturing. In the course of her efforts to secure genuine new jobs – and at peak well over 3 million new full- and part-time jobs were created after 1983 – Mrs Thatcher made two related points. New technology produced its own jobs – as the wheel, steam power, and the internal combustion and jet engines had so amply demonstrated. What the new jobs of the future would be she could not necessarily say but genuine new jobs there would be if the nation embraced new technology rather than sought to preserve Britain as an industrial museum. Second, genuine new jobs did not necessarily have to be in big, clanking mucky industry; they did not have to be in manufacturing at all. They were no less genuine for being in services. All this brought persistent complaints from representatives of manufacturing concerns whom I met that the Prime Minister simply did not care about manufacturing. Nothing could be further from the truth. But it was an impression that lingered, even though she took the greatest possible satisfaction in the resurgence of the motor car industry and fought tooth and nail to secure Japanese vehicle investment, especially Nissan for Washington, Co. Durham, near Sunderland.

In her early years Mrs Thatcher had not, of course, ignored education, the NHS or local government. All figured all too prominently in the annual review of public expenditure. And all three presented a similar problem: how to secure better value for the vast and increasing amounts of public money which are expended in these areas of the public service. That problem remains. For Mrs Thatcher it was unfinished business which Mr Major now sees as a priority. For me, with my upbringing, health and education were sensitive issues. For years I had wanted both to be so good that paying for those services at point of use, as distinct from through taxation and contributions, would be pointless. While Mrs Thatcher had none of my inhibitions about paying fees – I had, for example, deliberately chosen not to join BUPA – I came firmly to believe that she shared the same aspiration: publicly financed services of genuine excellence. The problem was how to achieve them. She clearly did not believe that abolishing private medicine and education was the way forward. Nor now do I. For one thing, that would reinforce a public sector monopoly. And we all know what happens even now. Instead of those working in the NHS extolling the high quality of their care and treatment they use their alleged – and I suspect usually imagined – inadequacies at every opportunity to negotiate through the television screen for more money. Everything these days is under-resourced. No winter has been complete – except perhaps this year now that Mrs Thatcher has left office –. without a campaign featuring sick and dying children because of 'the cuts'. I used to tell Romola Christopherson, a former deputy at Number 10 who became Director of Information at the Department of Health, that I would put the flag up over Downing Street when she was able to stand up, as distinct from knock down, an NHS scare story in the *Daily Mirror*. Seldom do we hear, except from Government, of the need for better management and the more efficient use of resources. Yet independent studies by the National Audit Office have shown great disparities between hospitals in the average cost of treating individual categories of patient which cannot be explained by special circumstances. Every vested interest from the British Medical Association downwards – or should it be upwards? – combined to resist reform designed to increase the power of the patient. The great lie was that Mrs Thatcher was out to kill the NHS. Yet, as a matter of simple fact, the eleven-year Government which Mrs Thatcher led spent more on the NHS, even allowing for inflation, than any previous government. There are thousands more nurses, doctors and dentists than when she took office in 1979. And when she left office the NHS was treating many more patients than ever before.

Another of the grand delusions of our time was that Mrs Thatcher did not care about education. I have no doubt that Mrs Thatcher shared with me the view that one of the greatest deprivations that can be inflicted upon a child today is to send him or her out into the world ill-educated and unproficient in the three Rs. If those who are in the education service cared as much as she did – and still does – I can state with incontestable certainty that educational standards would present no problem whatsoever. Politics' gain in Mrs Thatcher was education's great loss.

Her answer was not to privatize education. Nor was it to make it selective. Both concepts, again bearing in mind my upbringing, might have caused difficulty for me, seared as I was by my eleven-plus failure, though I would have done my duty as a civil servant. Instead, from the first in 1979, it was to strengthen the parents' right to choose the school for their children. Subsequently, it was to inform that parental choice and promote competition through the publication of school reports; to give parents the right to manage their own schools whether within or outside the local authority structure; and to prescribe a basic curriculum and to test children to see if they were coming up to scratch. Parent power and monitoring was her answer. The reply of the teaching profession and local education authorities was depressingly negative. They even queried parents' ability to manage. And yet, to hear them talk, they cared; not – never – Mrs Thatcher. All she did, you would imagine from their propaganda, was cut, cut and cut again.

If I had been as cavalier with the facts as the anti-Thatcher brigade I would have been drummed out of Number 10 inside a month. One thing is absolutely clear: they couldn't count and still can't. Current spending per pupil is about 40 per cent higher, allowing for inflation, than when she started. Of course, school rolls have fallen with the passing through of the 'bulge' but the resources available to educate the available kids shows a big increase. Capital spending (to get rid of old schools and build new ones) is up 16 per cent per pupil. And the proportion of youngsters entering higher education has risen from one in eight to approaching one in four. And still Mrs Thatcher didn't care. She was never to be allowed to care. For example, in an interview with Douglas Keay in *Woman's Own* on 31 October 1987, Mrs Thatcher was quoted as saying, 'There is no such thing as society.' In fact she did not say that. She said: 'I think we have been through a period where too many people have been given to understand that if they have a problem it is the Government's job to cope with it. "I have a problem, but I will get a grant." "I am homeless, the Government must house me." They are casting their problem on society, and, you know, there is no such thing as "society". There are individual men and women, and there are families and no Government can do anything except through people. And people must look to themselves first.' It is clear from this that what Mrs Thatcher was saying was that society is not some abstract concept; it is made up of millions of ordinary people whose individual actions are indispensable to the welfare and condition of society as a whole, which is different. Much too different, and inconvenient, for the propagandists who therefore destroyed by omission.

I covered local government as a journalist for eleven years from 1948. It taught me my first law of politics, which I have tended to observe, thereby causing some distress. Alderman John Oddy, by then eighty and in charge of Halifax parks, took me on one side one day in the Town Hall and, his hand on my shoulder and eyes narrowed in emphasis, said: 'The first law of politics, lad, is *fait accompli*. And don't you forget it.' Local government also taught me the value of elected local people being responsible for basic local services, even if the turnouts at elections were derisory. It emphasized why central government must remain in command: it provides the lion's share of the money.

The story of the Thatcher years was of the Government's efforts to recover command in the face of a political challenge which intensified with the decline of the power of the unions. In other words, the extra-Parliamentary conflict was transferred from one floor to another – from the shop floor to the floor of the Council chamber. Year in and year out local government overspent by roughly £1000 million, an average of some 5 per cent of total Government subvention over the period. No Government, and least of all one dedicated to controlling public spending, can ignore overspending on this scale. The old rating system provided no voter control over spending. It empowered the majority to oblige the minority to foot the bill. It was unfair both in terms of democratic principles and as between individual households since the elderly widow was required, in the nature of the property tax, to pay the same as a family of five adults next door who made more demands on local services. After years of Thatcher promise and no action, as the lobby never ceased to remind me, the obligatory revaluation of properties in Scotland with horrendous results for ratepayers brought action. The community charge – the poll tax of the revolutionaries who were stronger on their history than their observance of the law – was born.

Mrs Thatcher sought to end unfairness and institute democratic control. The community charge was devised as a flat rate tax on all residents of voting age. It charged every resident for the cost of local services and placed the onus on them to curb that cost through their vote. In other words, the Government was interceding on behalf of the local ratepayer who was inadequately protected within his town hall. But it did not take a genius – for I raised the point with Mrs Thatcher – to identify the charge of unfairness that would be levied against the concept: the lord in his manor would pay no more than the peasant in his hovel. Yet a flat rate Vehicle Excise Duty is readily accepted, if not universally paid. So is a flat rate VAT – now 17.5 per cent. Nor did it tax the ingenuity of local councillors, more concerned with playing party politics than with keeping the streets clean. They did what came naturally and spent more money – thereby building a platform for higher spending in the future – while they could blame the Government and politically get away with it themselves. They also complained it was costing twice as much to collect without, of course, making the point that twice as many people were paying the community charge as had paid the rates.

It may be that if a flat rate tax like the community charge is to be levied it has to be small enough for all to pay it without undue fuss. Yet I hold to the belief that had the community charge been introduced during a period of modest and stable mortgage rates it would have been accepted, even in my own Pennine country which has traditionally been lowly rated, thanks to transitional relief. It is ironic that this effort to combine financial control with equity for local residents should have, in my view, played a part in Mrs Thatcher's downfall. Yet never can the community charge be cited as an example of Mrs Thatcher's uncaring nature. If she had not cared, she would not have tried to do anything about the value for money that citizens get out of their local authority.

It was also ironic that inflation, with consequential high mortgage rates, should have helped to slay the arch-priestess of honest money and home ownership. As will have become painfully clear in this book, I am no economist. I have never pretended to be one. I have but one boast: common sense and political feel – qualities which Paul Gray, with whom I formed a particular friendship as the Prime Minister's economic private secretary, felt were more important to me than all the book learning elsewhere. I therefore leave judgements to others. As a common man, I would make just three observations:

    – Mrs Thatcher saw inflation as an enemy to be fought and refought; it was a never-ending battle. She was right.

    – she was mortified and felt ashamed by its recrudescence in the second half of her tenure from a low point of 2.4 per cent.

    – Mrs Thatcher was let down in her fight against inflation. It may be argued that she took her eye off the ball, relaxed her grip on her Government or was reluctant to impose higher interest rates on home owners whom she had encouraged to buy their own property; but have no doubt she was most certainly let down by her Chancellor, who did not take inflation seriously enough. Her earlier disciplines had to be reinstated.

That is the least I can say in defence of an honest, caring Prime Minister.

16

Turning the World Upside Down

I visited fifty-five countries with Mrs Thatcher and flew around 500,000 miles with RAF Strike Command in the process. We were superbly looked after. 'The safest airline in the world,' Lord Carrington used to say. And the softest landings, too. Charles Powell, Mrs Thatcher's foreign affairs private secretary, and I used to make a point of following the approach to see if we could detect the touchdown. It was another of the perks of Number 10 staff to be able to sit on the flight deck for landings and take-offs. Once I was quartered at the sharp end, alongside the navigator, for the whole of the journey from Cairo to Luxor, via the Aswan Dam, because so many Egyptians piled on board for the trip. I wished this would happen more often. The views were much better up front.

In the course of these travels I attended thirty-one of the thirty-two European Councils at which Mrs Thatcher represented the United Kingdom. I was at eleven of her twelve visits to the annual economic summits of the Group of Seven – the USA, Canada, Japan, France, Germany, Italy and the UK, with the European Commission looking on. I went to six of her seven Commonwealth Conferences, including the special London conference in 1986 on South Africa. And I was her *porte-parole* – as spokesman are called in diplomatic circles – at the three NATO summits which came to be held when arms control became possible and the Iron Curtain collapsed. I carried the word and just occasionally, by way of a little light relief, I carried the can. It was a tremendous privilege.

Mrs Thatcher always travelled light and Ministerially alone except when going to summits. Her party – all told around twenty-five to thirty – was invariably a fraction of the next most economical and a mere ten per cent of the American caravan. Typically she went abroad on substantial tours with two private secretaries, two press officers and a COI radio officer, Cynthia Crawford (her personal assistant and clothes-person), three Garden Room girls, a couple of duty clerks and, very occasionally, an FCO adviser. The bulk of the party was made up of security and communications staff who kept us in touch with Downing Street in flight. Mr and Mrs Thatcher had their own bunks aft of the front galley and next to a private curtained-off working and dining area with two tables, each seating four, on either side of the gangway for herself and senior staff. The rest of the party was accommodated to the rear, with the press in their own area closest to the bar at the back.

Typically in mid-Atlantic Mrs Thatcher would be sitting in her window seat, back to the pilot, reading her papers. Charles Powell might be next to her if she was checking points. Her husband would be opposite her, reading a book and having a cigarette. Across the gangway I would be reading myself in to the tour and preparing for my next briefing of the press on board. Cynthia Crawford would be working out her clothes requirements for the next stop and the other travelling private secretary would be catching up with paperwork. I would pop down to the back with the travelling press officer to brief the press over a loudspeaker system rigged up by Martin Smith, of the COI. My outline of the tour, supplemented with detailed logistics by the press officer, diverts Number 10 staff from their Trivial Pursuits, crosswords and novels. Then come the cocktails and dinner, with five-star service from the trolley for the Prime Minister's dinner party and flowers on the table all the way.

Mrs Thatcher's travels leave a kaleidoscope of impressions. Beautiful powder-green and red ochre dawns over the Australian desert and spectacular blood-red sunsets over the Sahara. Clear skies all the way over the Greenland ice-cap and the Alaskan wilderness to Anchorage where our US Air Force hosts were awaiting 'termination dust' – the first snow of the winter. Pearl Harbor under inspection by Mrs Thatcher at dead dark of night – well, at least she could say she had been there – followed by a clear, ice-cold, midwinter view of the western half of the United States from Los Angeles until night fell over Oklahoma City. A jungle drum 'welcome' from anti-apartheid demonstrators in Tromsø, deep in the Arctic Circle. A Mexican earthquake which split our hotel in Mexico City in two and cracked the swimming-pool on top of it.

247

The miracle of Shanghai during bicycle rush hour. The unutterable sadness of the waste of Gallipoli. Wonderfully welcoming crowds from Bandung (Indonesia) to Leninakan (Armenia). Ersatz coffee – and vodka for the press at £2 or $2 a shot – during a refuelling stop in Bratsk in the middle of the Siberian nowhere, en route from Tokyo to Moscow; but the leather-coated KGB were friendly. And then that memorable twenty-three-hour flight into an unsuspecting Port Stanley six months after the recapture of the Falkland Islands.

On tour with Mrs Thatcher you enjoyed your view of the world from the air. You did not see much of it once you hit the ground – running. Mrs Thatcher did not believe in enjoying herself at the taxpayer's expense. She believed in working for British interests. Consequently, the days were long, the evenings were hard and we always seemed to fly back home overnight to avoid wasting time. It was business all the way. But there were many lighter moments en route, too.

The hero of Mrs Thatcher on tour is DT, as she called her husband, Denis. DT is an officer and a gentleman. He is as decent a cove as you could wish to meet. He thinks the world of his 'lovely, lovely wife' and he knows how to back her up. He made a living as a salesman travelling to some pretty rum places. And in his seventies he did his duty flying the world to some more pretty rum places to support the Prime Minister of Great Britain and Northern Ireland. No man was more fussy over his food and ate less of it. He loves and works for sport and especially rugby union, which he used to referee, and he is entirely tolerant of this former reporter of the rival game of rugby league. He reads a lot of military history – he was a gunner during the war – and is an authority on corporate accountancy. We suspected that each week he got on the blower and dictated the 'Dear Bill' column to *Private Eye*. His baronetcy after Mrs Thatcher's resignation gave all who knew him a great deal of pleasure. Everybody loves him because he is straight and decent and loyal. With a snorterino or two inside him he develops the most extraordinary vowel sounds. Like most of us, he then becomes expansive. But never on all the Prime Minister's tours did the travelling reporters, most of them members of the lobby, ever let him down. He was off limits, out of bounds. No one on tour had a go at the Prime Minister through Denis.

The affectionate stories about him as we careered around the world are legion. I will retail just two which evoke his inimitable style. Picture him at the rear of the VC10 where the journalists are confined to what Mrs Thatcher sniffily described as 'steerage' – as, indeed, tourist class it had to be because of the invariably large demand for seats. DT is in earnest conversation with my dear friend, Michael Jones, political editor of the *Sunday Times*. We are just crossing the coast of Labrador under its first snowdusting of the autumn. 'And what,' DT says to Michael, 'do you think Northern Canada is full of?' Michael confesses ignorance. 'What,' he demands, 'is Northern Canada full of?' 'Northern Canada,' says DT, with all the whispered emphasis at his command, 'is full of eff all.' The wicked Mr Jones turns mischievous. He calls my deputy, Romola Christopherson, down to report the certainty, in view of Mr Thatcher's indiscretions, of a diplomatic incident; of a schism between Britain and Canada before we have even landed; of a veritable breach in the comity of the Commonwealth. Romola says, 'Oh, please God, no.' There is, she thinks, always a first time to be let down. Michael tells his story and roars as only he can. He has had his fun and that's that.

In Goa, during the so-called week-end 'retreat' of the New Delhi Commonwealth conference in 1983, the electricity supply proved to be unreliable. DT was at his toilet, preparing for dinner, when the latest power cut occurred. By then, exasperated beyond all measure, he appeared on the verandah of the Prime Ministerial bungalow overlooking the Fort Aguada hotel complex and addressed the entire bay in the following terms: 'This place is high on the buggeration factor.'

To the delight of Sri Lankan (and other) television viewers, DT had the utmost difficulty feeding an elephant with bananas during lunch in Kandy. The damn thing just wouldn't take them in at the mouth and insisted on flourishing its trunk in a most unhappy way. DT gave up. But at least it was cooler in Kandy. Colombo will go down in the history of Thatcher tours as the most uncomfortable place on earth. The Government guest palace had next to no air conditioning. It gave us a feel for the privations of our Empire-builders, especially when my mosquito net trapped the vampires inside. I counted fifty or so bites in the morning and spent most of the return flight home standing.

Rich or official Arabs tended to present Mrs Thatcher with horses. Tribesmen gave her sheep. Mrs Thatcher developed the sweetest line in handing back gifts. No room on board, you know. You will look after them so much better. This last seemed a dubious assertion since we gathered that the beribboned sheep presented to her up the Khyber by bearded wonders armed to the teeth should, by custom, be slaughtered immediately. I believe we put in a plea for clemency through diplomatic channels. I should add that these live tokens of welcome and respect also revealed the severe limitations of the lobby as animal sexers. Stallions in one newspaper could just as easily be mares in another. It isn't as if they didn't look. The lobby would have been decimated outside Amman if the gelding had turned frisky.

My most enjoyable riot was in Oslo. On our return from that northern outpost of the African National Congress, Tromsø, Mrs Gro Harlem Brundtland, the then Prime Minister of Norway, was due to give dinner to Mr and Mrs Thatcher in the Akershus Castle. Unfortunately IRA sympathizers got the local activists worked up. They stormed the castle (which wasn't difficult since only six policemen were guarding it, I was told). Mrs Thatcher's party were confined to the generous liquid hospitality of the British Ambassador's residence until the castle had been fumigated with tear-gas. We were eventually called to join the other guests for cocktails in far, far better spirits than I can ever recall.

Melbourne seems to have a jinx on me. Local radio managed to get through the Hilton switchboard to the Prime Minister's room at 6.30 a.m. to broadcast an instant, live interview with her about the Commonwealth conference in 1981. She had the presence of mind to say she didn't give interviews before breakfast. Bob Muldoon, the wonderfully rumbustious former Prime Minister of New Zealand, was less kind to the same early morning raider. When asked if he was ready to roll he is reported to have said over the air: 'No I am not. I don't talk to ratbags.' That same year rioting students smashed up my official car – while I was in it. The attack followed the Prime Minister's speech at Monash University, just outside the city – but not, I think, on account of the speech or because they were sure my parents weren't married, but because they identified me as a 'capitalist parasite'. (Parasite, maybe. Capitalist, not yet – unfortunately.) According to Robin Oakley, the invariably courteous political editor of *The Times*, the Grim Reaper nearly harvested me in the same city on a later visit when a police car was fast out of the blocks outside the Body Shop which the Prime Minister was visiting to the raucous disapproval of local IRA sympathizers.

I reached the conclusion in Kano, Northern Nigeria, never again to provide the lobby and television with a grandstand view of my scrummaging down with the local military or – worse still – to lay on that hitherto unheard-of facility in those parts: push-button satellite communications. We were gathered on the edge of the Sahara in a fog induced by the harmattan desert wind which fills the air with sand. Our purpose was to watch a durbar – a magnificently mediaeval display of horsemanship by menacing tribesmen armed with flintlocks which packed a man-felling recoil. The Prime Minister was ushered up to the Emir's balcony commanding a superb view of the ride. Unfortunately, the young troops guarding the approach blocked the passage of most of the Prime Minister's party. My passable imitation of human flotsam as the soldiers repelled

'Oh – By the way Bernard the Nigerians want their tribal funds'

251

all-comers, including a surging crowd of locals, was instantly flashed across the world. Michael Jones had the *Financial Times*'s account framed for me. It reads: 'The spectacle of the burly Mr Ingham, briefcase in hand, battling valiantly to reach his Prime Minister, was extraordinary. It seemed the incident could turn nasty but Mr Ingham made his way through when it dawned on the soldier that this was not a mere journalist but a person of substance.'

There was very little substance left in me by the time I reached the Emir's balcony to witness the fabulous parade. 'Are you all right?' asked Gordon Greig, who is a much kinder man than his 4 p.m. lobby assaults on me from the *Daily Mail* stable would have you imagine. 'I will be in a minute,' I replied. 'I've just had a rifle butt in my belly.' I caught the tail end of a swing – most certainly not intended for me – in the solar plexus and suffered some delayed-action winding.

Mrs Thatcher felt obliged to attend a number of working funerals which, I hasten to explain, are not fun. Tito's was the first. She wondered, as we met on the Heathrow tarmac, what possessed me to fly with her to Belgrade. There would, she assured me, be nothing to do. There was, in fact, nothing to be done but sit in my hotel room, watch the television and, in response to a torrent of calls, brief journalists all day according to my reading of the situation as revealed on screen and through my contacts with Mrs Thatcher's private secretary. Mrs Thatcher shook hands with Yasser Arafat – she could not avoid him – and conducted five bilateral meetings with other Heads of Government between the entrance to the Intercontinental Hotel and the lifts. I had never worked so hard at a funeral before – not even as a journalist taking the names of mourners at the church door. But State funerals provide an opportunity for world leaders to meet – and talk. Mrs Gandhi's tragic end also occupied the Prime Minister in a substantial round of bilateral chats, including one with George Shultz, the US Secretary of State, after the funeral pyre had produced so many hauntingly beautiful and distressing pictures for those of us who watched the ceremony on television. The funerals in quick succession of the Soviet leaders, Andropov and Chernenko, were also busy affairs. On the latter occasion Mrs Thatcher subjected Mr Gorbachev to close scrutiny. She pronounced herself satisfied that we were unlikely soon to be in Moscow again for a similar occasion.

Denis Healey represented the Labour Party at Andropov's funeral. I arrived late at the VIP suite at Heathrow. No sooner had I walked into the room than Mr Healey, who comes from Keighley just over the hill from Hebden Bridge, decided to have his bit of fun. In front of the Prime Minister he hailed me as 'another bloody Yorkshireman' and playfully thumped me in the tum as he inquired: 'Well, how are you, you old bugger?' I did not feel it necessary to explain to the Prime Minister that this is an entirely acceptable form of address where the two of us come from. But I could see that she hadn't realized I was on such informal terms with Mr Healey. Neither had I.

On these forays into the unknown – as they initially were for a Prime Minister who had little direct experience of foreign affairs before taking office – she assembled an impressive catalogue of achievement which was both a joy and a source of frustration to me. For some reason that I never fathomed, she always seemed inclined at home to underplay her role abroad. It was a curious attitude in someone who, for obvious political reasons, felt the need to trumpet her Government's domestic achievements. Yet foreign affairs successes there were aplenty:

– the Rhodesian settlement (which was well in train by the time I arrived in Number 10).

– the Hong Kong settlement with the Chinese which, for me, was all the more remarkable since the Chinese had all the aces and the trump card in the form of the expiry of our lease on the territory in 1997.

– the removal of the Argentinian invader from the Falklands, giving the clearest possible signal to the world that someone at least was prepared to stand up for a principle and international law.

– the renegotiation of Britain's contribution to the European Community and subsequently, against the odds of at least 9–1 in terms of countries benefiting financially from it, the reform of the disastrous Common Agricultural Policy (which now needs fresh attention).

– the early identification of Mikhail Gorbachev as the rising Soviet leader with whom she could do business on a basis of frankness and straight-dealing.

– her close friendship with and influence over President Reagan which subsequently President Bush came to value, especially immediately after Iraq's invasion of Kuwait.

– her straight talking on the importance of nuclear weapons and her role in keeping the peace.

– her counter-inflationary stance, adopted in 1981 by the seven nations of the Economic Summit, based on financial prudence.

– her championing of free trade in a highly protectionist world.

– the vindication of her opposition to sanctions against South Africa and her encouragement of reform to sweep away apartheid.

– her espousal of the cause of global action to protect the environment and avoid potentially disastrous climatic changes.

– her phenomenal personal achievement, in the light of history, of becoming *persona grata* not merely on both sides of the old Iron Curtain but also on both sides of the Jordan and the Limpopo.

Mrs Thatcher's influence abroad was based on three factors – her success at home, her clarity of view and her integrity. She was never a comfortable ambassador. She never will be a comfortable person. But her hosts knew where they stood. When she gave them her word they knew she meant it. And she was loyal – loyal to a cause and loyal to an ally or friend, to the exclusion of her own short-term political interests. Her fierce integrity in the confidentiality of her discussions often made difficulty for me. She was much more inclined to be secretive than open. Even after eleven years of representing her accurately across the globe I often had to persuade her to loosen up in her own interests when she debriefed me after meetings. Sometimes I had to tell her bluntly that she would lose out if she remained coy. It was all very well her being tight-lipped. But we could absolutely rely on those she had been meeting to let rip with their version of events. She needed a lot of coaxing. When she was less than forthcoming I found a way through via Charles Powell, who took a note at all her meetings. The two of us had our own little briefing afterwards to work out a line for the press. It worked. It gave journalists the essentials and seldom, if ever, brought a word of complaint from Mrs Thatcher as over breakfast (which she used to have on tour) she read her digest of British press, radio and television coverage wired to us by the Central Office of Information in London.

It is the received wisdom of Thatcher-bashers that she had a slavish devotion to Ronald Reagan, worshipped at his feet and, like some smitten schoolgirl, would do anything for him. It was not like that at all. Nor had he been her screen idol. She once told me that she could not remember ever seeing him in a film. The relationship had much more substance than that. They were philosophically in tune while she was still Leader of the Opposition and he was Governor of California. They are both fundamentally decent people who believe in the ultimate goodness of man. They believe that good will always triumph over evil, though they do not think that anything should be left to chance; you have to give the good every support at all times to ensure its eventual victory. They believe in freedom, justice, personal responsibility and individual enterprise. They are governed by the rules of a different, more disciplined age of which any Sunday School teacher would have approved. They are, if you like, old-fashioned. They hold fast to old-fashioned virtues in a self-indulgent world and, in and out of office, they were not afraid to proclaim or fight for them. Together they presented a lethal threat to the liberal establishment which consequently disparaged and dismissed them as a 'B-movie actor' and 'that bloody suburban woman'. But the Hollywood actor and Mrs Finchley made it. He went to the White House and she to Number 10. The world, thank God, was not the same again.

Together – and I emphasize the word – they turned the world upside down during their time in office by standing firm by their shared beliefs. I do not believe that this togetherness overstates Mrs Thatcher's contribution to the revolutionary changes of the 1980s. For she gave more than loyalty – the staunchness which became her watchword as an ally. She also contributed a clarity of vision and a sense of touch which were invaluable to the White House. It was a happy coincidence of history that two such soulmates came to work together in 1981.

They were not, however, much alike. President Reagan personified a relaxed form of old Western gallantry, courtesy and hospitality. Mrs Thatcher exuded drive, energy and a desire to get down to business. I often smiled to myself about the contradiction: President Reagan from the new world and Mrs T from the old. He suffered a deficiency common to politicians the world over who have not experienced the forcing house of Westminster. He was no debater. With a script he was a brilliant communicator. Mrs Thatcher admired his delivery and coveted his scriptwriter, though I do not think she could have got away with some of the American sentimentality. His professionalism was never more effectively demonstrated to the Prime Minister than when he invited her to the log cabin at Camp David where he was about to make his weekly radio broadcast to the nation. She joined him about ten minutes before he was due to go on the air. He sat there looking extremely relaxed, passing one or two inconsequential remarks and never so much as looking at his unmarked, closely-typed, five-minute script. Eventually, the Prime Minister communicated some of the nerves she was feeling for him. Didn't he feel like working on his text? Marking it up for emphasis? Just reading it? The old pro just shrugged his shoulders and rather gave me (who was looking on) the impression that it was just another in a very long line of radio scripts. Whereupon he proceeded to broadcast it flawlessly and exactly down to time – as the thumbs up producer indicated, whooping with satisfaction. We then sauntered off to Aspen Lodge, the log cabin used for summits, for lunch. Without a script Mr Reagan could appear lame, halting, uncertain and even ignorant. Across the table he was never happier than when he was anecdotal. His span of attention was limited and sometimes he looked as if he needed a nap. Mrs Thatcher was not at her best reading from paper. Moreover, it took hours to get the script right. After a broadcast she needed to wind down over a drink and chat. But extempore she was fluent, confident and fast on her feet. In meetings she fired on all cylinders. And she was open all hours to ideas and argument. An unlikely pair to change the world.

Nor, like the path of true love, was their relationship smooth. Mrs Thatcher did not believe in soppy friendship. She took her alliances seriously and felt that she owed her friends her best advice, however uncomfortable or unwelcome it might be. In their time Prime Minister Thatcher and President Reagan had a lot to argue about – the extra-territorial nature of American trade legislation; the American double-deficit – both budgetary and trade – which was a constant source of worry to her prudent soul; the American invasion of Grenada; and defence – notably the American Strategic Defense Initiative (SDI) and the concept of a non-nuclear world of which the nice, idealistic President Reagan sometimes dangerously dreamed.

He never dreamt his non-nuclear dreams more dangerously than in mid October 1986 in Reykjavik with Mr Gorbachev. It was on 12 October that year that the ground really moved for Mrs Thatcher. Indeed, she told Geoffrey Smith, of *The Times*, in January 1990 that this was 'the only time when I really have felt the ground shake under my feet politically'. President Reagan appeared to be prepared to join with the Soviet Union in giving up nuclear weapons. Fortunately, Mr Gorbachev got greedy and made his abandonment of nuclear weaponry conditional on President Reagan giving up the SDI – the American plan to block the delivery of nuclear weapons from super-tech snipers' nests in the sky. If there was one thing Mr Reagan was not going to do, it was abandon the SDI. He had what Mrs Thatcher felt were over-optimistic expectations of the SDI. She never expected this defensive system would be able to neutralize every nuclear weapon. Nothing in life is ever perfect. But she saw enormous value in establishing what such a defensive system could achieve and what promise it held out for future defence. I believe Mrs Thatcher thinks that the SDI has already served its purpose, even if it proves to be overblown, which seems unlikely in the light of the briefings she had in August 1990 at the Falcon Air Force Base in Colorado which houses the national test bed facility of the SDI. At the very least it deterred President Reagan from giving up nuclear weapons. Mrs Thatcher breathed a very deep sigh of relief in the autumn of 1986. She also hot-jetted it to Washington to clarify the way forward in a nuclear world.

While Mrs Thatcher may have been mortified on 12 October she could not exactly have been surprised. President Reagan had already revealed his aspiration of a world without nuclear weapons. She found this fundamentally misguided, and told him so. This was not her objective, though her abhorrence of nuclear weaponry is second to no woman's. Her prime objective was a world without war. Applying her hard head to the problem instead of her soft heart, she recognized that nuclear weapons were crucial to peace. Conventional weapons, which were also frightful and foul, had never deterred war. Only the unique horror of nuclear weapons had done that, for forty years and more. Winston Churchill had counselled never giving them up until we had something even more powerful. Mrs Thatcher, however, doubted whether you could give up anything once it had been invented. How can you disinvent the wheel? That being so, we had to make nuclear weapons work for peace. The way to do that, leaving aside every effort to prevent proliferation, was to secure balance at the lowest possible level of weaponry. Arms reduction – in a balanced and verifiable way – was therefore very much on the agenda after Camp David, 1986.

Mrs Thatcher had paid one previous similar visit to Camp David – two years earlier near the end of a pre-Christmas tour which took her round the world in six days via Bahrain, Bombay, Peking (where the Hong Kong accord was signed), Hong Kong, Guam, Honolulu and Washington. The purpose then was to clarify the way forward on SDI. Only a week earlier she had had her memorable first encounter at Chequers with Mr Gorbachev, as leader of an Inter-Parliamentary Union delegation. The Soviet aim was to kill SDI so that they could maintain their technological lead. Mrs Thatcher was having none of it. She was clear in her own mind that the West had at the very least to keep abreast of the Soviets in technology. She was also convinced that research and testing of SDI systems were permissible under treaty but that their production and deploy-ment would require negotiation. Against this background, her approach to Camp David 1 was instructive of her methods. She did not go to Aspen Lodge – all the log cabins at Camp David are named after trees – to argue for the sake of argument. She went to clinch. And the only way in international diplomacy to clinch it is to set out your conclusions on paper. So, in the short interval after the morning's discussion and before lunch, Charles Powell dictated a short note to an FCO official who typed it up on two sides of paper. Over lunch President Reagan said: 'I'll buy that.' What he bought, as the Prime Minister explained at a press conference at Andrews Air Force Base, near Washington, was:

– the Western aim was to maintain nuclear balance, not superiority.

– SDI deployment would be a matter for negotiation under Treaty.

– the overall objective of SDI was to enhance and not undermine deterrence.

– East–West negotiation should aim to achieve security with reduced levels of offensive weapons systems on both sides.

Thus Mrs Thatcher was twice instrumental in clarifying the way forward on defence and arms control and in stiffening opinion. She had reason to be grateful for Presidential support during the Falklands in 1982. But she was most unhappy a year later with President Reagan's invasion of Grenada, the Commonwealth island in the Caribbean, after the murder of Prime Minister Maurice Bishop by ultra-Left and, no doubt, Cuban-backed rebels. What is more, she showed it, not least to Sir David English, editor of the *Daily Mail*, to whom she gave a long-arranged interview. Her immediate reaction was visceral. So was that of the lobby who gave me a terrible time. What kind of special relationship was it that allowed the President of the United States with minimum consultation to invade a Commonwealth island? As time went by passions cooled. Mrs Thatcher came to recognize that major powers are interested in their own backyard and probably always will be. Grenada in the Caribbean was very clearly a matter of American concern in view of the potential threat which Cuba posed to the USA. She would probably have given similarly brief notice of the invasion even to an ally lest she place her servicemen's lives at risk. So what was the point of getting worked up? Her initial persuasive answer was that such invasions by the West could serve only to provide the Soviets with excuses for military adventures. She was fearful that President Reagan had legitimized the Soviet invasion of Afghanistan. The episode ended with the early withdrawal of American troops from Grenada, in contrast to the continued presence of Soviet troops in Afghanistan. This – and the success of the operation – was the best part of a bruising affair.

One of the consequences of success – and the Thatcher–Reagan partnership was a real success – is that journalists and others want to knock the shine off it. They look for signs that things are not what they were. In the Reagan–Thatcher case it extended to an analysis of the tenderness of Ronnie's kiss when Margaret arrived on American shores. I sometimes thought I was directing 'Gone with the Wind'. Mr Reagan was always gallant. Between them, they demonstrated a touching loyalty to each other through some vicissitudes. In the end I suspect that Mr Reagan felt he could always count on Mrs T, provided he was behaving reasonably, because she clearly understood that the United States is the guarantor of the free world. Everything must be done to sustain it. There is, after all, a lot of anti-Americanism around.

Then came George Bush with whom Mrs Thatcher, on tour, regularly had breakfast at his vice-presidential house just a stone's throw from the British Embassy in Massachussetts Avenue, Washington. The new President and the British Prime Minister knew each other well. Mr Bush, as a highly experienced public servant, is also more of a debater than Mr Reagan in his slow, slightly drawling kind of way. He is an eminently decent and caring family man who has, obviously without justification, had to live down a 'wimpish' image. Nothing I saw of him suggested that, but I could see how he had been saddled with it. He is a very deliberate thinker whom you can imagine agonizing over a problem. I don't think it is a bad fault in an American President to be deliberate.

Mr Bush's presidency inevitably – and nothing was more predictable in view of journalistic attitudes – brought repeated attempts to demonstrate that the special Anglo-American relationship was over. Reporters seemed to derive some of their ammunition not from the White House but from so-called 'Young Turks' in the State Department. The problem was the Germans. They had smelled unification. No wonder the American administration concentrated upon them. They needed to do so. That was manifestly not necessary with Mrs Thatcher's Government. They knew where she stood. When the going got difficult, they would soon find out who their real friends were. That was how I met the persistent efforts to write off the Brits and install the Germans as the Americans' brand new buddies. But that was not how it came out. Mrs Thatcher had to be cut down. She had to be put in her place. I found the pleasure which this task gave to some of the so-called liberal intelligentsia almost tangible.

They failed, of course. Saddam Hussein saw to that. And to think that I nearly missed the pure joy of witnessing the pundits put in their place. Much earlier in the year I had booked a motoring holiday in Austria, leaving home on 8 August. When later the Prime Minister arranged to go to Aspen, Colorado, to address the Aspen Institute, there was a possibility that I might not be back in time to start my holiday which I very much needed. I therefore resolved exceptionally to leave the trip to my deputy, Terry Perks, since it seemed unlikely to have any substantial political content. Then on Monday 30 July, Mrs Thatcher lost yet another dear friend to the IRA. Ian Gow, her former Parliamentary Private Secretary, was blown up in his car at his home in his Eastbourne constituency. There was only one thing to be done now: I must go to Aspen. Mrs Thatcher said 'Good', with feeling, when I told her I would be on the 'plane. Within three hours of installing ourselves in The Little Nell Hotel in the centre of Aspen on the afternoon of 1 August, we began to get unconfirmed reports from the press that Iraq had invaded Kuwait. Sarah Charman, the duty press officer in London, was soon ringing us in the middle of her night to find out what was going on in Aspen and to liaise with us.

The visit was instantly transformed into a major political event. It was madness for me ever to have thought of not going to Aspen. Terry Perks and I went into overdrive. It would clearly have suited the journalism fashionable at the time for President Bush to cut his visit to the Aspen Institute the following day. That would have been translated into a monumental snub for Mrs Thatcher and confirmation that the special relationship was stone-cold dead. Instead, President Bush found in Mrs Thatcher, rather than the Aspen Institute, a reason to fly to Aspen – as he told her at the end of their talk in a ranch-house 8000 feet up in the Rockies owned by Henry Catto, then the American Ambassador in London. I sat in on the talks along with Marlin Fitzwater, the President' press secretary. The exchanges exemplified two facts which were highly inconvenient for the destructive tendency among the pundits:

– George Bush had a backbone before he arrived in Aspen and did not acquire it from Mrs Thatcher;

– Mrs Thatcher made her familiar distinctive contribution to the handling of the world's problems: a clear and simply expressed analysis of the situation.

On the ranch-house lawn, with its spectacular mountain backdrop, they spoke for themselves:

PRESIDENT BUSH: 'Let me first welcome Prime Minister Thatcher back to the United States. It is a very timely visit ... Not surprisingly I find myself very much in accord with the views of the Prime Minister ... I find that Prime Minister Thatcher and I are looking at it on exactly the same wavelength: concern about this naked aggression, condemning it and hoping that a peaceful solution will be found that will result in the restoration of the Kuwaiti leaders to their rightful place and prior to that a withdrawal of Iraqi forces. Prime Minister ... if you would care to say a word ...'

MRS THATCHER: 'Thank you, Mr President, and thank you for the welcome ... Iraq has violated ... the territory of a country which is a full member of the United Nations. That is totally unacceptable and, if it were allowed to endure, then there would be many other small countries that could never feel safe ... The Security Council acted swiftly last night under United States' leadership ... and rightly demanded the withdrawal of Iraqi troops. If that withdrawal is not swiftly forthcoming we have to consider the next step ... The fundamental question is this: whether the nations of the world have the collective will effectively to see that the Security Council resolution is upheld, whether they have the collective will effectively to do anything which the Security Council further agrees to see that Iraq withdraws and that the Government of Kuwait is restored ...'

Five days later, on Monday 6 August, Mrs Thatcher called in on President Bush at the White House on her flight home. They discussed in a restricted session with General Brent Scowcroft, the President's national security adviser, and Charles Powell the reinforcement of Saudi Arabia and an oil blockade. Then they were joined by Secretary of State James Baker, the Vice-President, Dan Quayle and Governor Sununu, the White House Chief of Staff. Later Manfred Woerner, the Secretary-General of NATO, who was at the end of a holiday in North America, was called in. He announced his intention to call a NATO Foreign Ministers' meeting because of Turkey's involvement on the border with Iraq. Mr and Mrs Woerner flew home on the Prime Minister's 'plane, and we laid on a small HS125 jet to fly them on to Brussels.

If there was a bonus for me in Mrs Thatcher's being dumped by her party, it was in not having to attend my 32nd European Council in Rome in December 1990. I speak not as an anti-Marketeer, as they used to be called, but as one who voted to confirm Britain's entry in the 1975 referendum. Far from being against Europe, I made the effort to ensure that my son, as a child and youth, visited every Western European country before he went to university. Only Iceland, Andorra and San Marino remained outstanding when he went to Durham. He had also been to the Soviet Union, Hungary and Yugoslavia. I took Europe seriously and still do. Europe is my home and my heritage. It also accounts for around fifty per cent of Britain's trade. I can see every advantage in combining as one with our European partners in international trade negotiations, provided we are truly liberal in our approach. I want us to work together as willing partners in protecting and extending the frontiers of democracy and in channelling a part of our abundance to assist the development of the Third World and to relieve poverty and hardship. There is real point in Europe standing for something – as distinct from self-seeking nothing – in the enlightened councils of the world. After thousands of years of intra-European wars there should be a real sense of achievement in co-operation to positive, constructive ends. When European Councils became entirely depressing I consoled myself with the thought that it was better than making war.

I am also a realist. As Mr Stevenson, my woodwork master at

Hebden Bridge Grammar School, menacingly used to say, block of lignum vitae in hand, as we gossiped together at a bench: 'Where two or three are gathered together, I smell trouble.' I know first hand the difficulties of reconciling different interests. Energy conservation policy taught me that, both at national and international level. Europe multiplies these problems of reconciling a proliferation of both national and sub-national interests. In short, I never expected the earth.

After years of fighting for necessary reforms in the Community, Mrs Thatcher became the woman to beat. Her performance – and, if possible, her isolation – became the EC journalists' cliché. Yet – and this is the ultimate irony of Europe – Mrs Thatcher did more than the rest put together to place Europe in a position to advance. Let me explain. There was no future for the European Community when she came to office in its unfair method of financing which imposed an excessive burden on the United Kingdom. It took the Prime Minister five years until Fontainebleau, 1984, to secure justice. Even then we remained the second largest contributor, though by now the British taxpayer has benefited by some £10,000 million from the settlements she secured. Yet during this difficult and prolonged negotiation she demonstrated a positive approach to the Community by facilitating a common fisheries policy to which Britain brought a disproportionately large area of sea and fish. Having sorted out the British budget problem, she then applied herself to the reform of the profligate Common Agricultural Policy. This was truly a labour of Hercules since at least nine of the twelve Community nations benefited handsomely from its operation. Yet again, by dint of persistence and well-informed argument, she secured reforms which not merely (though sadly temporarily) laid low the outrageously expensive food mountains and drained the wine and olive oil lakes but also ended the Community's financial crisis. She warmly espoused the cause of a single internal market by 1993 – which is what the Common Market was originally supposed to be about – and ensured that Britain was second only to Denmark in the implementation of the necessary legislation. She cleared the way for the construction of the Channel Tunnel by private finance and saw the project as one which could revolutionize British attitudes to Europe. Finally, she sought to develop the

264

Community politically, economically and monetarily on flexible, pragmatic lines. The Middle East war has exposed the hollowness of more high-flown pretensions.

She received precious little thanks for all this. Instead, she suffered the abuse of small men. Mrs Thatcher's problem in Europe – and at home – was that she spent so much time fighting for necessary reforms, often in a minority of one, that her constructive approach acquired a negative image. She was also motivated by principle, knew her subject, could argue intelligently and conclusively and had, almost uniquely, a strong and secure Government behind her. She is also a woman. And she may have humiliated one or two of her colleagues by her vigorous style of knock-down argument. She was quite simply too straight, too direct, too principled and altogether too serious for them. She also believed in free trade which, for some of them, was something you talked about but did not practise. President Mitterrand, for example, was not above admitting that the point of the Community was protectionism.

Her most reliable ally was Ruud Lubbers, Prime Minister of the Netherlands, who obviously cared about her. From time to time she received support from Paul Schlüter (Denmark), Jacques Santer (Luxembourg) and, in the early days, Francesco Cossiga (Italy). But generally the European Community was an uphill struggle. Rather like domestic policy, in fact. It was another mountain to climb. Perhaps it showed too often. Perhaps Mrs Thatcher (and I reflecting her mood) were too abrasive. Perhaps too often she excused others from standing up for their beliefs by leading the debate in her usual crisp, no-nonsense fashion. Perhaps she should have learned earlier than she did not to seek perfection in a communiqué but to fight for only a limited number of essentials. Perhaps she should just have sat quiet and, where British interests were not involved, let them make fools of themselves. But she was not made like that. She was straight and played it straight. And, as a positive, practical force who did as she said she was a largely unappreciated and unexploited Community asset. They will miss her – some of them, of course, like a hole in the head. But miss her they will.

17

'We can do business together'

If like poles repel, then Mrs Thatcher's affinity with Ronald Reagan, with whom she was ideologically in tune, can only be explained by their different personalities. Her good working relationship with Mr Gorbachev must have owed itself to their clash of ideology for, as individuals, they were rather similar. Both absorbed their briefs and thrived on hard work. Both loved a debate. Both could argue with passion and force but without giving the other offence. And both were bundles of energy. Mr Gorbachev was the most untypical Russian leader Mrs Thatcher had ever met when they sat down to lunch at Chequers on Sunday 16 December 1984. He didn't have a note of the party line, let alone speak to it.

Thatcher's meeting with Gorbachev was the consequence of both good luck and good management. Both President Reagan and Mrs Thatcher spent their early years presenting a hard and determined face to the Soviet Union. Both demonstrated their utter determination to defend the Western way of life against any aggressive step across the ideological divide in Europe. President Reagan must have left no doubt in the Kremlin that he would spend them into the ground if they chose an arms race. This must have concentrated the Soviet leaders' minds wonderfully in view of the incomparably superior performance of the American economy. For her part, Mrs Thatcher set out to demonstrate her reliability as an ally of the United States and a loyal member of NATO and underlined this by taking the lead in the deployment of cruise nuclear missiles in 1983. She did so in the face of the resurgence of the nuclear disarmament campaign after the Falklands War. I had the great pleasure of working that year with Michael Heseltine, as the new Secretary of State for Defence, to win the battle for public opinion. Presentationally, he was a most resourceful Minister.

Of course, Mrs Thatcher's uncompromising line upset some people and her rhetoric was criticized for what Lord Carrington, her former Foreign Secretary who was soon to become NATO's Secretary-General, had described as 'megaphone diplomacy'. But having established her credentials, as it were, with the Soviet Union, Mrs Thatcher began to look for a positive way forward. She did it, as only she knows how, by analysing the Soviet Union and Eastern Europe through meetings and seminars. This prompted her to look for the next generation of Soviet leaders. There were a number of candidates and she chose well. But more than a year was to elapse before Mr Gorbachev led an Inter-Parliamentary Union delegation to the United Kingdom just before Christmas 1984.

In the meantime, Mrs Thatcher's rhetoric remained undiluted. Indeed, she was criticized by Opposition spokesmen back home for her 'counter-productive' remarks in accepting the Winston Churchill Foundation Award at a dinner in the British Embassy in Washington on 29 September 1983. She said: 'We are confronted by a power of great military strength which has consistently used force against its neighbours, which wields the threat of force as a weapon of policy, and which is bent on subverting and destroying the confidence and stability of the Western world. That is the threat we face.' Only twenty-eight days earlier the Soviets had shot a Korean airliner out of the skies for straying off course. Mr Healey had described that as 'a political crime'.

Mrs Thatcher's prescription was familiar: strength through NATO to defend freedom and justice and deter any aggressor. But she responded positively to Mr Andropov's challenge in June 1983 when he told the Central Committee of the Communist Party: 'A struggle is under way for the minds and hearts of billions of people on the planet, and the future of mankind depends, to a considerable extent, on the outcome of this ideological discussion.' She accepted the challenge with confidence because 'people turn to the West because we are free. It is our human values to which men aspire.'

But in a little-noticed passage in the speech she signalled her willingness to talk. She said: 'We have to deal with the Soviet Union. But we must deal with it not as we would like it to be, but as it is. We live on the same planet and we have to go on sharing it. We stand ready therefore – if and when the circumstances are right – to talk to the Soviet leadership.'

This was an early signal of the search for a new way forward on which the Americans had also embarked in the early Reagan years – coincidentally with the British and without consultation, so far as I have been able to establish. John Coles, the Prime Minister's foreign affairs private secretary, and I decided not to draw particular attention to this passage. We preferred to leave journalists to make up their own minds. Initially, the paragraph attracted little attention. But the travelling press did not thank me for leaving them to their own devices when they woke up to its significance at the end of a most exhausting tour of Canada and the United States. Some of them had fallen asleep at the table over the Embassy dinner. This illustrates the problem of looking after journalists. Another illustration was when Mrs Thatcher 'went green'. She put an enormous amount into her speech to the Royal Society in the autumn of 1988 and consulted at length on the background. This included extensive discussions with Sir Crispin Tickell, our ambassador to the United Nations in New York, who had made a particular study of climatology. (Mrs Thatcher has always stressed the importance of pursuing research in this area, given the uncertainties that surround it, and of doing everything we can in the meantime to minimize further damage to the global environment.) Again, I allowed the text of the speech to speak for itself. To my amazement television, left to its own devices, did not turn up for the dinner. Leave the media to make their own judgements and you can be accused of letting them down. Offer guidance and you can be pronounced guilty of managing the news. It's a hard life.

Mrs Thatcher emitted other signals of a willingness to talk by visiting Hungary in February 1984 and attending Mr Andropov's funeral ten days later. Ironically, she had discussed Mr Andropov extensively with Mr Kadar, the Hungarian leader, who knew him well. It could, of course, be argued that Mrs Thatcher was not being very adventurous in going to Hungary because it was not exactly typical of Eastern Europe. Mr Kadar had found a way, since his controversial assumption of the Hungarian leadership after the uprising in 1956, of liberalizing the country without provoking the USSR. None the less Mrs Thatcher made the effort by going to

Hungary, and Mr Kadar could only have relayed to the Warsaw *bloc* her lively interest in finding a better way for East and West to live together. There is some evidence that her interest was reciprocated. Certainly Mrs Thatcher felt it. She told Geoffrey Smith, of *The Times*, in 1990 '. . . if it is possible to get a welcome at a funeral, I did because they realized that it was quite something for me to go.' (She had not gone to Brezhnev's funeral in 1982.)

I had expected Mrs Thatcher's meeting with Mr Gorbachev on that rainy Sunday in December 1984 to become entangled in the miners' strike which still dragged on. To my surprise there was no reference in the *Sunday Times* to a story which they had been pursuing the previous day that the Soviets had been laundering money through a Swiss bank to the National Union of Mineworkers. This was a relief. Mrs Thatcher had more important things to talk about than the NUM, though reports of Russian financial support (which we now know occurred) worried the Government. I arrived at Chequers at lunchtime just after the Soviet party. It was a fascinating occasion. There were eighteen of us around the table including Sir Geoffrey Howe, Foreign Secretary; Michael Heseltine, Secretary of State for Defence; Michael Jopling, Minister of Agriculture; Paul Channon, Minister for Trade; and Malcolm Rifkind, Minister of State, FCO. It is a wonder Mrs Thatcher and Mr Gorbachev ate any lunch. Their interpreters were very hard worked.

I believe it was this lunch which laid the foundations for their relationship. There is no doubt that there was some plain speaking on both sides. There is no doubt either that Mr Gorbachev appreciated the Prime Minister's attitude because later in their relationship he said so. He acknowledged that she, at least, was prepared to deal with the Soviet Union on the basis of mutual respect. This was her position from the outset. She sought at Chequers to found their relationship on a clear understanding. Summarized, she made these points:

- the British and Americans are friends and allies and believe in the same values which they will defend to the hilt.

- there is no point in wasting your time, Mr Gorbachev, in trying to separate us; it simply won't work.

– I do not like Communism – it is an inhuman system which produces neither freedom, justice nor prosperity – BUT you are entitled, as we are, to your way of life and to defend it, and to enjoy security within your own borders.

– NATO is a defensive alliance which threatens no one.

– we are coming to the end of the generations who remember World War II. Those of us who have known war and so put a high premium on peace have a duty to future generations so to arrange our defences that we prevent future conflicts.

It was against this background that they adjourned to the Hawtrey Room and continued their discussions in the comfort of arm-chairs and sofas in front of a log fire. They got on so well that Mr Gorbachev stayed long after he should have been heading for the Russian Embassy down the M40. After he had left about 6 p.m. I discussed with the Prime Minister before the huge log fire in the Great Hall what I might say to the press who were restively awaiting my briefing in the Chief Whip's Rooms at Number 12 Downing Street, a seventy-five-minute drive away. The more she talked the more she seemed to be saying that she believed Mr Gorbachev was 'a man she could do business with'. Could I say that? Mrs Thatcher immediately agreed because, she said, that was how she felt. Next day she told John Cole, in an interview for the BBC, 'I like Mr Gorbachev. We can do business together.'

American correspondents who came to my briefing on the Sunday evening clearly felt that Mrs Thatcher had gone soft; that she had done a U-turn and weakened her stance. I had to work very hard to persuade them, and others, that this was not so.

For the rest Mrs Thatcher pursued a deliberate and successful policy of building up confidence with and in Mr Gorbachev. They met on about half a dozen occasions over the six years Mrs Thatcher remained in office after their first encounter. On each occasion the media looked in vain for cracks in the relationship. The foundations had been too well laid. Mr Gorbachev did not let her down. He got out of Afghanistan, for example. The gates were opened for refuseniks and Jewish emigrants. Arms control agreements, including the first to eliminate a class of nuclear weapons (short range), followed. Mrs Thatcher encouraged Mr Gorbachev down the path of reform, though with increasing scepticism, I fear, as to his grasp of free market principles. The Berlin wall came down. The flags of sovereign nations which had previously been under the heel of Moscow flew over those great European capitals of Warsaw, Prague and Budapest which Mrs Thatcher visited between 1988 and 1990. Mrs Thatcher's visit to Czechoslovakia in 1990 was in some respects a trial because she was ashamed – yes, literally ashamed – of the betrayal of Munich. She has never been to Munich and I doubt she ever will. She has an utter abhorrence of the place. (I circled it returning from Austria in 1990 in search of Dachau.) Mrs Thatcher departed from office wishing the re-emergent countries of Eastern Europe well and profoundly hoping that they – and not least Mr Gorbachev's USSR – would find their democratic, free-market feet.

The Soviet Union and Eastern Europe are, for me, full of memories. Predominant, is the apprehension and relief I felt on Mrs Thatcher's visit to the Soviet Union at the end of March 1987, a few months before her third general election victory. After all those years in Government service I did not get too many butterflies. But on this occasion I was unwontedly nervous. I was keyed up because the journalists covering the trip would have loved to write off the relationship. I knew that everything was all right when the talks, beginning in the morning in the Kremlin, went on and on. Mrs Thatcher eventually arrived at the Embassy in time for the dessert at a lunch with Russian intellectuals before resuming her talks with Mr Gorbachev at 4 p.m. I briefed the press in the Fairytale Room in the Intourist Hotel – a highly appropriate venue for my press conference in the eyes of Joe Haines, who had been most put out that I had made him carry his bags through Customs rather than make room for him, at the expense of a lobby member, on the Prime Minister's 'plane. Some people expect the earth. Other memories are many and varied and live with me:

> The deep devotion and undying commitment to their faith of the worshippers in the rich, Orthodox ornateness of a candlelit Zagorsk Monastery just outside Moscow. I had to take exceptional measures to secure the entry of the Foreign Secretary, Sir Geoffrey Howe, who had been detained outside by the

KGB. They mistook him for a photographer, which seemed reasonable since he was festooned with cameras. Later priesthood and police lunched together around the same table with the Prime Minister. I did not notice the police sing grace.

The wild enthusiasm and affection for Mrs Thatcher of the crowds in Zagorsk, Tbilisi (Georgia) and Leninakan (Armenia) where she opened a school subscribed by Britain after the earthquake of 1988. This is not to mention the covered market in Budapest, where I thought we were all goners in the 1984 crush. Nor the incredible welcome to Prague in 1990 which left members of the British Embassy staff in my car in the cavalcade from the airport shaking their heads in wonder – and me, in the centre of the city, fuming at the sheer, nasty boorishness of a handful of British students who infiltrated the enthusiastic crowd and shouted 'Thatcher out'. Nor the awesome, never-to-be-denied passion for freedom at Father Popiełuszko's grave in Warsaw and before that bitter monument outside the Lenin Shipyard in Gdansk. In Eastern Europe and the Soviet Union Mrs 'Tatcha', as elsewhere, was recognized as a champion of freedom and a friend of the people.

Mr Gorbachev's personality at the Bolshoi on Sunday 29 March 1987 when he and Mrs Thatcher took an extremely relaxed view of the programme. Their supper went on and on as the patient 'Swan Lake' audience chatted in the dark waiting for the political leaders to resume their box after the interval. Nigel Wicks, the Prime Minister's principal private secretary, and I decided to investigate as the minutes headed for the quarter-hour. We found them emerging from supper extremely relaxed and in full gossip. The Prime Minister read our impatience. 'Ah,' she said to Mr Gorbachev. 'Meet Nigel Wicks, head of my private office ... And this is Bernard Ingham, who keeps the press in order.' I shake the Soviet leader by the hand as he fires back: 'But I thought you said your press were independent?' Mrs Thatcher looks at me ... 'Altogether too independent for my liking, sir,' I reply. He roars with laughter.

The fog of Prague where never, even when I smoked like a

chimney, have I seen such addiction to the weed. No wonder life expectancy is going down. I reached the conclusion that the purpose of junior staff in the British Embassy at receptions was to prevent a conflagration by touring the rooms with ashtrays.

The heart-rending, tearful and throat-aching experience of a service, among a people who will not be denied freedom, in St Bryggida's Church, Gdansk, after lunch with Solidarity in the Presbytery. Lech Walesa, the irrepressible, lets himself rip over the pheasant and expresses views which are music to Mrs Thatcher's ears. 'But how,' she asked with great intensity, 'do you get these points across to the Government?' Mr Walesa, quick as a flash, replies, 'We just talk to that [the chandelier].' Mrs Thatcher ought to have known better. She herself spent a lot of time talking to the chandeliers of this world for effect and fun. She has also shushed me a lot when my Northern forthrightness, in what I forgot was probably not the privacy of her rooms, seemed unlikely to go down well with the regime we were visiting.

Picture Jerzy Urban, 'the Polish Bernard Ingham', as someone with deliberate malice aforethought described this highly intelligent gnome of a man who was the Polish Government's spokesman, in earnest conversation with me over an official lunch in Warsaw. He gives me to understand that governing Poles is not easy. They are a proud, individualistic and independent people. I think of home and Yorkshire. 'You think you've got problems, Mr Urban,' I retort. 'You try running Yorkshire County Cricket Club.'

Economic summits were the one relative pleasure in the calendar of overseas engagements. This was because the media found it difficult to isolate Britain. We were, I am glad to say, all too often mainstream common sense and conciliation. Consequently we were relatively boring. Mrs Thatcher could, however, never be described as absolutely boring in media terms. She was too sexy.

The economic summits I attended were held in all the best places. It is difficult to improve upon the Isola San Giorgio Maggiore near the Grand Canal in Venice. In 1980 I briefed journalists on the island in a stifling barrack room with at least as many reporters looking in through the windows as there were those sweatily looking out and longing for air. There were compensations in the evening, such as dinner with Mrs Thatcher in the Gritti Palace (I stayed in the allegedly superior Cipriani). She became terribly expansive on our first evening in June 1980, and entrusted the choice of wine to the waiter. Suddenly realizing the enormity of what she had done, as head of an austere Government, she asked her Chancellor of the Exchequer (Sir Geoffrey Howe), with a touch of insouciance, whether he had brought his Barclaycard. Sir Geoffrey smiled weakly.

In 1981 Mrs Thatcher stayed in the biggest log cabin in the world at Montebello in the forests east of Ottawa in Canada. This was extremely convenient for bilateral meetings: your Prime Minister just walked down the corridor because all heads of state and government were quartered in the wheel shaped cabin with corridors running like spokes from the central hub. I used to beg a helicopter lift from the American Government into Ottawa fifty miles away to brief the British press; otherwise, if I could find no transport, I relayed the news down the line through Liz Drummond, one of the most forthright of Number 10 press officers, who used a squawk box to good effect. Versailles (1982) – to start the second cycle of summits – was fraught because it came towards the end of the Falklands campaign. Williamsburg, Virginia, (1983) came in the middle of a British general election which made for great excitement among the media. And so on through London, Bonn, Tokyo, Venice (again), Toronto, Paris and Houston.

My fifty-sixth birthday occurred during the Toronto Summit. The British contingent presented me with, among other things, a cake and a teddy bear called Bernard, all the while singing 'Happy birthday'. This rather touching – not to say moving – scene confused the overseas press who thought I had a rough and tough relationship with British journalists. Bernard, the teddy bear, occupied a distinguished place at the late-night birthday party Mrs Thatcher threw for me in her suite. She advised me to provide him with some rompers. I have yet to do so.

Economic summits attracted vast crowds – thousands – of journalists, cameramen and crews and photographers. Planning the media facilities was the most complex of all the problems presented to host nations because a bad impression could sour all the good work inside the conference hall. And, of course, impression is everything. What about the substance?

I believe that the effect of economic summitry has been beneficial. I think Mrs Thatcher would now agree with that, though she expressed the utmost scepticism about the value of all summits at whatever level in her early days. 'Why are we going to X?' she used to ask. But, looking back on oil and stock market crises, budgetary and trade deficits, inflation, unemployment followed by sustained growth, cultivation of enterprise, and protectionism (which is chronic the world over), Economic Summits have much to commend them as fora in which heads of state and government agree to be judged. It is my belief, though I have no means of proving it, that the world has handled the economic and political crises of the 1980s much better than it would otherwise have done.

I am less clear about the value of the Commonwealth, which is curious because I am an archetypal Commonwealth man. I was brought up in an era when the map was covered red. Not the red of the Red Flag of the Soviet Union but more the scarlet of the British Empire. I feel an affinity with members of the English Speaking Union whose membership was greatly extended by the growth of the Commonwealth, as the Empire became. As with the European Community, I did not go to Number 10 prejudiced against the Commonwealth. On the contrary, it had my goodwill. While its economic significance to Britain has long been overtaken by the European Community, the Commonwealth remains a potentially powerful force for good because it brings together nations of all races and conditions under one Queen.

Prejudiced though I was in favour of the Commonwealth, I found Commonwealth Conferences extremely trying. I think this was primarily because the precious journalists who have made the Commonwealth an industry instinctively regarded Mrs Thatcher as hostile. This was a gross misreading of the British Prime Minister. She was as much a Commonwealth baby as I am. Indeed, more so, since she is seven years older than me. But she was not in the business of tokenism – of going along with any old measure, regardless of its effect, simply for the sake of demonstrating her Commonwealth credentials. In any case, Britain did not need to prove her Commonwealthery; she was, and remains, its financial mainstay, contributing roughly a third of its budget.

Mrs Thatcher looked behind and beyond the issues confronting the Commonwealth, as only one among many other members of the global village, to try to identify a way forward. She was never content to settle for the *status quo*. Her driving passion was to change things for the better. For the Commonwealth, she reached some uncomfortable conclusions. They were concerned almost entirely with South Africa.

Mrs Thatcher hates apartheid. Her entire philosophy is Napoleonic: every private has a field-marshal's baton in his knapsack. 'In my kind of society,' she used to say, 'we care nothing for what your father was or did. We care only for what you are.' She believes in merit. If you had the merit and capacity for hard work then you deserved to get on and your antecedents were irrelevant, colour, race and creed included. She got a lot of pleasure out of welcoming to general receptions in Number 10 members of the coloured community who were making a contribution to the life of the nation. She wanted to see many more such examples to set before the younger generation of coloured people in Britain.

The issue between Mrs Thatcher and the Commonwealth throughout her term of office was not therefore apartheid, though she was often portrayed as the white South African's best friend. (She has had fewer more difficult people to help.) It was an argument not about substance but about tactics. Her concern was how best to bring a speedy end to apartheid. She utterly condemned black terrorism which, apart from anything else, she felt was counter-productive. She did not believe sanctions would achieve results. Nor did she believe that squeezing South Africa out of the Commonwealth in the early 1960s had been wise. It had removed the South Africans from direct Commonwealth influence. She believed profoundly in Aesop's fable which teaches that the quickest way to get a coat off a man's back is by encouragement rather than force: through the sun's rays instead of by the force of the wind which only makes him wrap his coat more tightly round him. In short, Mrs Thatcher believed in encouraging South Africa to reform rather than in trying to force them into it by punishing, browbeating or isolating the country.

Of course, Britain has very substantial interests in South Africa. It was therefore easy for anti-apartheid and pro-sanctions campaigners to claim that, in opposing sanctions – or their substantial extension – Mrs Thatcher was merely serving British industry and commerce. But Mrs Thatcher increasingly came to see British investment in South Africa as a means of developing the skills and potential of black workers and managers and so positively encouraging the dismantling of apartheid. It is also true that she recognized the strategic geopolitical significance of South Africa. But that only served to encourage her positively to promote reform to avoid the development of a Communist salient in the southern oceans.

The plain fact is, however, that Mrs Thatcher had simply no confidence in either the operation of sanctions or in their efficacy if, by some miracle, they were observed. Action against Rhodesia had shown the severe limitations of international sanctions. All too often sanctions seemed to be a sure way of guaranteeing our competitors easy pickings in our former export markets. And to the extent that sanctions proved effective against South Africa, the severest sufferers would be the blacks whom they were supposed to be helping. Research showed that ordinary black workers, as distinct from those who professed to represent their interests, were not keen on sanctions if they would cost them their jobs. There was also more than a suspicion that in the innately protectionist European Community sanctions against South African wine and produce, for example, were only too welcome.

Finally, Mrs Thatcher was not in the business of tokens. The easiest thing in the world, if you were not Mrs Thatcher, was to go along with the herd. But Alderman Roberts, her father, had dinned into her that you didn't do something just because others did. You did what you felt to be right even if it was uncomfortable to be alone. You then stuck to your guns. It was often uncomfortable in the Commonwealth to be against sanctions. Mrs Thatcher substantially stuck to her guns. She lived politically long enough to see her policies bear fruit thanks, in part, to some very plain speaking at Chequers to the former President Botha and to active encouragement for President De Klerk who seems to be counting the last days of apartheid.

As with economic and European policy, so Mrs Thatcher's will was tested and not found wanting in the Commonwealth. It did not make for an easy life for her Chief Press Secretary. In the Commonwealth Britain's favourite position among journalists was in a minority of one out of forty-six, give or take a country or two, depending on whether they were attending the conference. The Commonwealth also bred a kind of (white) journalist whose exaltation of the institution ensured that he dismissed with obvious contempt only a little short of loathing such agents of Mrs Thatcher as myself. And it ensured that I was an Aunt Sally to be knocked down, in the inconvenient absence of Aunt Margaret herself, in my familiar efforts, alongside the FCO spokesman, to inform the army of reporters of the British view and of our contribution to the debates. I never thought that such a Commonwealth chap as I would find the Commonwealth quite so trying. It was all the worse for knowing that all too many of the regimes represented in the Commonwealth could not hold a candle to British democracy and would not dare to try. That was compounded by knowing that most of them either had next to no trade with South Africa or benefited substantially from the relative buoyancy of the South African economy. My Commonwealth briefings were a triumph of restraint over provoked inclination.

Melbourne (1981) and New Delhi (1983) passed reasonably quietly on this subject. But in 1985 we had got only half-way across the Atlantic to Nassau, Bahamas, when South Africa gave me a nasty turn. Bermudan television, during a refuelling stop, did their level best to embroil me in their election on the subject of sanctions. I also got it hopelessly wrong. I completely forgot that as a colony the British Government is responsible for their foreign policy. So apparently did Mrs Thatcher. She comforted me on the next leg of the journey with the news that she had told Premier Swan to do what he thought was right over sanctions. That was more or less how I had outlined the British attitude for Bermudan television. I consoled myself with two thoughts: first, it is better to be liberal than colonial in these matters; and, second, Bermuda's trade with South Africa was not exactly a big deal – worth all of £12,000, I was told, of which two thirds were on account of communion wine.

The first five days of the Nassau Conference were tough. Mrs Thatcher's will was being tested and so – by the media – was mine. It all ended in typical fashion. The heads of state and government went off for a week-end retreat to the exclusive Bali Hai Club at Lyford Key where Kennedy and Macmillan agreed the Polaris deal. While the rest deliberated how to apply the decisive pressure on her, Mrs Thatcher spent Saturday morning working on a speech to the United Nations in New York the following week. She had a meeting with Mr Gandhi (India) and Mr Mulroney (Canada) in the afternoon and then in the evening with them and the other members of the so-called Group of Seven (Kaunda, Mugabe, Hawke, Pindling [the host] and Ramphal). There was a lively plenary on Sunday morning followed by an even livelier meeting between the Group of Seven and Mrs Thatcher in the afternoon. She shook them by saying that she would actually prefer no agreement on sanctions to returning home with the tiny concessions she had offered: banning the import of kruggerrands from South Africa and trade promotion within the country. They decided they had better take what was on offer. And that was that. The conference petered out.

London 1986 was altogether more unpleasant. This was the year of the sanction as a measure of the individual's revulsion at apartheid. The Foreign Secretary, Sir Geoffrey Howe, had made very little progress with President Botha in South Africa before Mrs Thatcher went off to the boycott-hit Commonwealth Games in Edinburgh. Predictably, the Games were all rotten eggs and boos in the press the following day, though that is not my recollection of this part of the run up to the special Commonwealth Conference at the week-end. But it was all of a piece with the BBC's coverage which, I felt throughout this period, was itself an integral part of the campaign to bend Mrs Thatcher to the Commonwealth's will. Not a bulletin passed, it seemed, without pressure mounting on Mrs Thatcher to change tack. In the end the Commonwealth agreed to differ. I am convinced that this display of political courage and resolution contributed to Mrs Thatcher's fight back from the depths of the Westland affair earlier in the year.

Vancouver, 1987, was hilarious, though Chris Meyer, the FCO

spokesman, and I approached it quietly. On arrival in this glorious city and port, however, we found the press, radio and television assiduously trying to stir it up against the UK over sanctions. We had in our possession some figures which showed significant increases in Canadian trade in 1986 (over 1985) compared with a slight fall in British commerce with South Africa. We debated whether to reveal them, bearing in mind annual fluctuations, and agreed to decide on the spot, depending on our treatment by journalists. Predictably, we came to feel it necessary to disclose them. All hell broke loose. Canadian journalists, whose skin is as thin as their sanctimony is deep, waged war with trade statistics. One of them even invented (so far as I am concerned) a British quote, 'Mulroney [the Canadian Prime Minister] is all puff and blow and without substance.' Mr Mulroney understandably took exception to this and had to be calmed down. Chris Meyer and I were in danger of becoming the conference personalities, so on the penultimate day we gave an interview to the Canadian Broadcasting Corporation on our briefing style. It all ended at the final press conference with Mrs Thatcher, far from repudiating her spokesmen as the Canadian press hoped, defending them to the hilt in a crisp thirty seconds of power play. Only one Canadian reporter, I noted, went to the microphone to ask a question of the Prime Minister. Chicken!

I very much hope that the Commonwealth Conference at Kuala Lumpur in 1989 was the death rattle of the sanctions industry and that my successors will be able to celebrate the ending of apartheid and even the return of South Africa to the Commonwealth. My final Commonwealth Conference began in low key with Mr and Mrs Thatcher sniffling with colds, the rain teeming down and Mr Gandhi absenting himself from the conference because he was in deep electoral trouble. The second day was overshadowed by the San Francisco earthquake. Benazir Bhutto cut an impressive figure in bright green on Pakistan's return to the Commonwealth. Chief Anyaoku, a long-time servant of the Commonwealth, was elected secretary-general in succession to Sonny Ramphal and gave me a chance to congratulate him in person when he introduced himself to me in the lobby of the Pan Pacific Hotel. I warmed to him. We had some ritualistic Brit-bashing in the opening speeches but I managed to keep journalists' temperatures down in what, so far, had been one of the more pleasant Conferences. This was not solely because we were quartered in the Shangri La, with its magnificent view of the racecourse. Our breakfasts with Mr and Mrs Thatcher afforded a grandstand view of strings of horses being given their morning rides.

It was all very deceptive. On the third day – 19 October – Mrs Thatcher had breakfast in her suite with Bob Hawke, the Australian Prime Minister, who omitted to mention a five-point plan for intensified financial sanctions against South Africa. Mrs Thatcher only learned of this proposal just before she contributed to the Conference debate on sanctions. She was understandably tough, contrasting the efforts of the United Kingdom to reduce poverty and hunger in South Africa while the rest apparently wanted to increase it. She refused to have anything to do with further sanctions and called for incentives to encourage reform in South Africa. It was like talking to a brick wall. The journalists were all a bit stunned by the turn of events. But they had to accept my point that, whatever Commonwealth leaders may say in public, they acknowledge in private that only Britain has any influence with South Africa.

Mrs Thatcher and Benazir Bhutto contributed a display of Malaysian traditional dancing to the familiar do-it-yourself concert at the week-end retreat at the Langkawi resort to the north. She also thoroughly enjoyed herself playing with the Bhutto baby while John Major, then Foreign Secretary, battled for fifteen hours with some success for a better rather than worse communiqué on South Africa. It did not, of course, meet all our requirements – it would be a miracle if these communiqués did – but Mrs Thatcher signed up on the Sunday, with reservations. As usual, the British were not allowed space in the communiqué to express their point of view, so Mrs Thatcher decided to place them on record in a separate statement of our own. After John Major had approved the text, I presented it to a press briefing at 6 p.m.

There is nothing quite so preposterous about the British press as when they are protesting about open government (unless it is when they come over all righteous about leaks). Reinforced by their concept of the sanctity of Commonwealth solidarity, even some of my journalistic friends scaled new heights of indignation. I made it worse by suggesting that there really must be something synthetic about their fury. Since when were they against free speech?

The following day Messrs Hawke and Mulroney lodged a protest in the conference against this unilateral British action. Mrs Thatcher, in return, lodged a protest against attempts to gag her. With the formal business over, she then concentrated on meeting people who, of course, never uttered a word of complaint about her text to her face. The conference ended with a farewell dinner and concert. I am afraid it was only too reminiscent of the false camaraderie of Trades Union Congresses in Blackpool and Brighton. Somehow, I find it difficult to be nice to people I would love to grasp warmly by the throat. I'm funny that way.

18

The Falklands Campaign

Nothing I did as a Government information officer was more difficult, more nerve-wracking and ultimately more rewarding than trying to maintain relations between the Government and the press, radio and television during the Falklands campaign. I went into the campaign believing that it would be a miracle if I came out at the other end with any credibility left. And, as I have explained, credibility as an informant is crucial to a press officer; without it he is of no use either to the Government or to journalists. In the end I think I can reasonably claim that the Falklands enhanced my reputation as a press secretary, but it was a hard, often unpleasant and exasperating road to travel; though not, of course, as hard and unpleasant as the road taken by our troops yomping to victory across the Islands.

I would like to record my gratitude at the outset to those press officers in Number 10 who shared a most extraordinary period. My deputy was Brian Mower, currently the FCO's spokesman and prior to that Director of Information at the Home Office. He went to the Home Office in 1982 after a truly magnificent supporting performance in Number 10 during the campaign. One of the three press officers was Hugh Colver who so wanted to be in the Falklands himself that I sometimes felt I would have to chain him to his desk to make sure that he did not slope off to the front. Hugh is now Chief of Public Relations at the Ministry of Defence. For me, now in the comfort of my home, writing this book, he seemed to achieve the impossible during the Gulf War: he applied the lessons learned during the Falklands with conspicuous success. An extremely loyal and robust team was completed by Ian Kydd, now the economic and commercial secretary in our High Commission in Ottawa, and for part of the time until she left on promotion Liz

Drummond, now head of public relations and publicity at West-minster City Council. Liz was succeeded in the midst of the conflict by Sheenagh Wallace, from the Department of Trade and Industry, who had a happy knack of compiling a usable brief in quick time.

Our problems stemmed from a lack of preparedness in Govern-ment, a hostility to the media on the part of the Royal Navy, concentration within Government on the issues to the virtual exclusion, for a time, of presentational consciousness, often a dearth of hard information, some rivalry and the controversial issue of the role of the press – and more especially of television – in a war. There was also an inherent conflict between the military who, understandably, wished to confuse the enemy, and the Government Information Service, including myself, among whose jobs it was to maintain public support for the Government's conduct of the war. Underlying that was my utter refusal to get involved in dis- or misinformation. I sometimes felt that there was more unarmed combat both between Government and journalists and within Whitehall than was ever seen in Port Stanley.

It all began so farcically with a group of Argentine scrap metal merchants landing on South Georgia, an administrative dependency of the Falklands, where Shackleton, the Polar explorer, performed prodigious feats of endurance. Journalists derived some amusement from these Latin Steptoes, as they were called in lobby briefings, and rather saw their illegal landing as imperialist Argentinian pin-pricks. Then suddenly the Argentine struck. It invaded on Friday 2 April 1982. Nothing was funny any more.

I can only describe as shell-shocked the atmosphere the following day in the House of Commons which sat, because of the crisis, on the Saturday. The Government was severely criticized for failing to read the signs, for a lack of military preparedness and even for encouraging the Argentine by its earlier proposal to withdraw the armed survey vessel, HMS *Endurance*, from the South Atlantic. All these issues caused me a great deal of difficulty in my contacts with journalists. Then Lord Carrington, the Foreign Secretary, indicated to me his decision to resign before he did so. He gave me the thumbs-down signal as he walked down the corridor to the Prime Minister's room in the House. He felt that was the only honourable thing to do because the judgement of intelligence information had been wrong. With him went Humphrey Atkins, Lord Privy Seal and Foreign Office spokesman in the Commons, and Richard Luce, the Minister of State who had been conducting negotiations with Argentina. The Prime Minister had to reconstruct the Government. I lost the Minister responsible for co-ordinating presentation: Francis Pym. This superb Parliamentary performer with a magnificent speaking voice became Foreign Secretary. His successor as Leader of the House with responsibility for co-ordinating Government presentation, John Biffen, did not attend the 'War Cabinet'.

Prepared or not, the vanguard of the Task Force sailed on the Monday, 5 April, in a triumph of swift organizational reaction, to confront the Argentine invader 8000 miles away. Whatever criticisms there were of the Government – and journalists did not spare me their rod – there was overwhelming support in the Commons for the Government's determination to uphold the right to self-determination of the Falkland Islanders and respond firmly to an act of aggression. But behind the scenes another war was being fought – by British press, radio and television for the right to report any campaign from the front. I could understand the reluctance of the Royal Navy to take journalists to the islands. They were embarking upon a long voyage and a most hazardous mission, with almost impossibly extended supply lines. The last thing they needed on board was the potential disruption threatened by landlubbers with weeks in which to dream up stories. Yet however desirable it may have seemed to the Royal Navy to sail alone, I took the view that it was politically impossible to exclude journalists from the enterprise. The last thing the Government – nay, Britain – needed at that time was a thundering great row with Fleet Street, the BBC, ITN and IRN, not to mention the grossly underrated provincial press. The Government – and not least our boys, as Mrs Thatcher called them to the distaste of some – needed the support, not the antagonism of the communications industry.

I was left in no doubt that trouble was brewing in a big way by editors who besieged me over the telephone at home throughout the first four days of the crisis. They were exasperated with the idea that they would be excluded from covering the campaign, especially when it seemed likely that there would be unlimited pictures from Buenos Aires. It was unheard-of; an outrage; bloody silly; incompetence of a high order; somebody's backside had to be kicked and Ingham, you're the man to kick it – you'd better. I could hear a graveyard of tabloid leaders being chiselled in stone. Others pleaded, even prayed, for my intervention. Max Hastings, then on the *Evening Standard*, seemed near to tears at the thought of being prevented from covering a war. He showed his gratitude after securing a place on the expedition by sending me an autographed copy of his book *Bomber Command*.

Editors could, of course, have protested until they were blue in the face had I felt there was a good case for advising the Prime Minister to exclude them. No Government should get itself into the position of being ruled by the media. But there was only one good case. That dictated that, in the national and Government interest, the war should be reported from the front. Without consulting the Prime Minister – though I reported what I had done to Clive Whitmore, her principal private secretary – I made it clear to the Ministry of Defence (MoD) that we must have journalists on board. Having got the principle accepted, I then negotiated up the numbers, recognizing that there would be hell to pay if one newspaper group was put at a disadvantage, even though the Press Association and Reuters news agencies were accredited. In the end, only the *Financial Times*, among national newspapers, was not represented, though a number of Sunday newspapers had to rely on a reporter from elsewhere in their company. With hindsight, it might have been better to have had a foreign journalist in the party, though Reuters is an international news agency. But I had had so much trouble getting a modest number of British journalists on board that I felt I simply could not push it further. I subsequently made the point, with some feeling, that I could see little force in the argument about the need for a foreign journalist when some sections of the British media duly accredited to the Task Force could be relied upon to take, if not always an anti-British line, most certainly a critical anti-Thatcher line.

I have very little time for the claim afterwards that a total of twenty-nine pressmen, including cameramen, engineers and still photographers, was excessive. It is true that, after the event, a 1977 MoD media contingency plan, providing for twelve media places, was recalled, though I am told that a copy was never found. But a media contingent of twenty-nine represented little more than 0.001 per cent of the total task force. If the MoD could not cope with that tiny fraction of journalists, I felt they should wrap up. For twenty years they have been handling proportionately many more reporters, photographers and camera crews in admittedly the different circumstances of Northern Ireland, and they did so again – with considerable success – in the Gulf War this year.

When I was called upon to give evidence to the Defence Select Committee which examined the 'handling of press and public information during the Falklands conflict' I took them through the problems of fitting the gallonage of media demands into a pint pot of twelve places. This is what I said:

'. . . how you select the twelve is a fascinating exercise. First of all, if you are to take BBC and ITN you need three: a reporter, a cameraman and a soundman. I am sure the television people would say there is no editor and they will need some engineers, but let us say you keep it down to three. Then the plan says we ought to have a radio reporter. We hope that the BBC and IRN will agree on who should go. Then we have to have the PA and a still photographer. We have reached six and we have not started on the national press, let alone the English provincial press or newspapers serving the garrison towns of Plymouth, Portsmouth, Aldershot and Catterick ... nor the Scottish, Welsh and Northern Ireland press. We have not got to the very important foreign journalists. How on earth we sort out the national newspapers, dailies and Sundays is very interesting. I have done it on the basis of companies – and the companies showed no inclination to pool [that is, to share] even across a company early in April. I am being mischievous now in making the point that I look forward to the day when *The Times*, the *Sunday Times*, the *Sun* and the *News of the World* [Murdoch newspapers] agree on one reporter. The *Express*, *Daily Star*, *New Standard* and *Sunday Express* [that is, United Newspapers] are perhaps a bit easier. The *Mirror*, the *Sunday People*, *Sunday Mirror* and *Daily Record* [the Maxwell stable] might agree, but there would be an enormous outcry if we took the *Mail* and the *Mail on Sunday* and the *Telegraph* and *Sunday Telegraph* separately because the other groups would say the latter groups were getting an unfair advantage. And God knows what my former newspaper, the *Guardian*, would say if it had to sit down with the *Observer* and the *FT*. And we have not yet started with the provincials. I think twelve would give rise to an extremely difficult problem.'

I got the impression that the Select Committee felt I had a point.

From all I heard at the time, I cannot say that my assistance was rewarded with an impeccable performance on the part of some journalists in the party. The journalists failed to get on with each other and some of them treated the Ministry's civilian press officers disgracefully. The admirals were no doubt right that having journalists on board did not make for a happy ship. But there comes a time in free societies when some media crosses have to be borne. This was one of them. I was pleased that the Select Committee, in their report, deplored 'some of the hysterical and often personal abuse' which the civilian press officers in the Falklands attracted. They apparently accepted my view that it was unfair to castigate officers who were too junior for the job. The prize for the best quote to come out of the Select Committee's inquest into the handling of the media goes to Ian Bruce, of the *Glasgow Herald*. In a memorandum to the Defence Select Committee he said: 'I, for one, would not contemplate covering another British confrontation unless proper facilities were available.' The poor chap seems doomed to lead a sheltered and disappointed life.

The initial problem of securing places for press, radio and television in the Task Force should not be laid at the door of Ian McDonald, the deputy director of public relations at the MoD. He was in an impossible position as a career civil servant, dependent upon the Departmental hierarchy for his progress and with no professional media background to give him some standing with, for example, Permanent Secretaries and the top military brass who deceive themselves when they think they know how to handle the press. He was thus landed, without any consultation with me whose job it was supposed to be to advise the Prime Minister and

Government on presentation, with the task of being the Ministry's front man in communicating with journalists and, through them, the public. His Dalek-type delivery (which would have been necessary had journalists of a younger generation than Michael Jones (*Sunday Times*), Chris Moncrieff (Press Association) and myself had no tape-recorders to compensate for their lack of shorthand) made him a figure of fun. He should never have been put in this position. In our kind of democracy the only acceptable spokesman (outside the theatre of war, where clearly the military have to give expert appreciations) is a Minister. Ian McDonald's up-front job was for a Minister of the Crown and no one else.

The next problem left me convinced that the Ministry of Defence had gone barmy. For months I had been trying to persuade them to fill the vacant post of Chief of Public Relations. Neville Taylor had been given the job in November 1981. He had been chosen after an interview – and not by me – but he had my support as a friend and as a former MoD Chief Press Officer and deputy director of PR for the Royal Navy. If he had been in post when the Falklands invasion occurred the British Government would have had an experienced professional at the helm. This would have given me – and, through me, the Prime Minister – confidence in the MoD's handling of the entire media dimension. It was not, however, the MoD's fault that Neville Taylor was not their Director of Public Relations when the Falklands crisis broke. Norman Fowler, Secretary of State for Social Services, had been understandably keen to hang on to Neville as his Director of Information for as long as possible. I prevailed upon the system to move Neville to the MoD when the Falklands crisis broke only to find that, when he arrived in the Ministry, a letter awaited him saying that he was in charge of everything but the Falklands. Some accounts suggest that the reason for this was that Sir Frank Cooper, Permanent Secretary at the Ministry of Defence, was determined that I should not co-ordinate the information effort from Number 10 and viewed with suspicion my good relationship with Neville Taylor. There is certainly a great deal of evidence to suggest that Sir Frank was hostile to me -- apparently because of an unhealthy respect for my alleged capabilities – but I do not believe this was the reason for Neville being excluded. I think there was a much more simple explanation.

John Nott, the Secretary of State for Defence, had got used to working with Ian McDonald and wanted to preserve that arrangement for the duration of the crisis.

It is interesting to note the conclusion reached by the Defence Select Committee. It said: 'The evidence which we received indicates overwhelmingly that the lack of an experienced professional public relations officer at the head of the Ministry of Defence PR organization was widely felt in the Ministry's response to the need to make arrangements for media coverage of the Falklands campaign.'

Having sorted out the problem of media representation in the Task Force I tried to get on with my job. Perhaps it might be useful at this juncture to remind readers that my job was to speak for the Prime Minister and Government as a whole and similarly to advise them on, and co-ordinate at official level, the presentation of their policies and measures. Not unnaturally – since my predecessors as Chief Press Secretary had done it as the occasion demanded – I called a meeting each morning at ten o'clock of the Departments principally involved. I did not care whether they sent their Permanent Secretary (which was unlikely) or an office junior, provided they knew what was going on. It was clear that all too often the unfortunate MoD representative had been denied briefing. This called for exceptional measures. Once the initial diplomatic phase of the crisis was over, Cecil Parkinson, Chancellor of the Duchy of Lancaster and a member of the 'War Cabinet', was appointed to oversee presentation. This was a substantial step forward.

I was next confronted with a decision by the MoD to suspend background briefings for reasons which I – and, I was told, professional PR officers in the MoD – never pretended to understand. The suspension lasted for most of the conflict and was, in my strong view, misguided. If Sir Frank's objective had been to neutralize me, this move served only to increase my importance to journalists since I was at least functioning. I told the Select Committee that 'the last thing you do in a crisis is withdraw your service to the media'. In its report the Select Committee observed that the Ministry's decision was 'probably the wrong one and the media's criticism in this instance is substantially vindicated. In a time of difficulty, except in the most special circumstances, briefings at all levels should be maintained'. My life would have been a lot easier had they been.

Throughout all this, Mrs Thatcher showed little interest in presentation outside her appearances at Question Time in the House. Her every nerve and sinew were devoted to the prosecution of first, the diplomatic operation through the UN, the Americans and elsewhere and second, the preparation for war which I must say I always felt inevitable. I was left to represent her interests with journalists, often feeling extremely exposed and ill-equipped and fearful, during the actual fighting, lest I put a foot wrong and compromise lives. It was nerve-racking and I never wish to experience it again. I began to feel so exposed that I had to take Clive Whitmore on one side and make arrangements to safeguard my position by improving the flow of information. He sorted it out.

Then on Sunday 25 April a helicopter-borne detachment of Royal Marines liberated South Georgia. This was wonderful news for Mrs Thatcher – and it came with considerable relief because there had been earlier fears that the operation had been a horrible disaster when the weather turned violent. She immediately saw the presentational value of an announcement outside Number 10 where the press, radio and television were massed in a pen. While they endlessly clamoured for theatre and pictures, they were also the first to criticize what Ministers said or did in satisfying their appetite. And so it was with the first success of the campaign. Mrs Thatcher called John Nott over to Number 10 and, amid the Sunday untidiness of the Press Office, she arranged to join him outside while he made the announcement. In the course of briefing the Prime Minister what to expect on the doorstep, I told her that the very first question reporters would ask would be: 'And are you now going to declare war?' They had been asking me the same question all day. I am not sure whether I registered this with her, such was her relief and elation at the news. But, sure enough, came the question. Somewhat *sotto voce*, Mrs Thatcher said to me, 'Fancy asking a question like that at this time.' And then she called upon the media to 'Rejoice.'

I can only conclude that, under the influence of Mrs Thatcher, Britain has grown up a bit since the Falklands. At the victorious end of the Gulf War the British commander, Lieut-General Sir Peter de la Billière, urged people to go out and ring the church bells. Mrs Thatcher simply called upon journalists, who apparently found little significance in the recapture of South Georgia, to rejoice. The general's was regarded as a good quote. Hers was ridiculed. Well, we rejoiced inside Number 10 even if others sneered. Dammit, what else did they expect Mrs Thatcher to advise? Moan?

At risk of further provocation, I must report that, while I did not rejoice over the sinking of the Argentine cruiser, *Belgrano*, in the South Atlantic, I took a grim satisfaction in the news. This confession will no doubt launch another 1000 Parliamentary questions from Tam Dalyell MP who, to do him justice, has been consistently outraged by the demise of this Argentinian warship. I was brought up in wartime. Our aim was to win. We did not flinch at the sinking of German, Italian or Japanese vessels. They sent altogether too many of ours to the bottom of the Atlantic, the Pacific, the Mediterranean or wherever they unfortunately found them. The *Belgrano* was not a benign influence in the South Atlantic. It would have sent our ships to the bottom if it had had the opportunity to do so. I rejoiced at the removal of this threat to our forces. I did not rejoice at the loss of life.

On Tuesday 11 May we sank an Argentinian supply ship in the Falklands Channel. On that day I was having lunch in the small dining-room in Number 10 on stand-by for Mrs Thatcher's briefing for her questions in the House that afternoon. Towards the end of the meal I received a telephone call from Mayday Hospital in Croydon to say that my wife had been admitted with serious injuries after a road accident but was not in danger. Clive Whitmore dispatched me in an office car to the hospital. I discovered that Nancy had fractures on either side of the pelvis near the hip joints. She had been pulled under a lorry which had run away down the Surrey Street open-air market in Croydon and was among the most seriously injured of seven victims. She was immobile in hospital for ten weeks – well beyond the duration of the Falklands campaign which ended with the white flag being hoisted in Port Stanley on 14 June.

After news of the accident, Mrs Thatcher promptly called me into her study and told me that, notwithstanding the war, she would now expect to see a lot less of me around Number 10. I said that I doubted whether I would take time off because what I needed to do now was to work, subject to visiting the hospital every day. I then settled into a pattern of driving from Number 10 each evening about 6 to 6.30 p.m. to the hospital some twelve miles away and returning to the office as required. I ate out and cleaned the house, war permitting, on Saturday mornings. This lifestyle meant that I was in Croydon when great popular rejoicing – note the word – broke out in Downing Street with the fall of Port Stanley and victory.

From 11 May to 14 June, while my wife was healing without any residual disability, my efforts were concentrated on keeping Government presentation on as even a keel as was possible in all the difficult circumstances and protecting Mrs Thatcher from media distractions while she got on with winning the war. There were many traumas to deal with: the sinking by air attack or Exocets of HMSs *Sheffield*, *Ardent*, *Antelope* and *Sir Galahad* and the supply ship, *Atlantic Conveyor* and the severe damaging of HMSs *Coventry*, *Plymouth* and *Sir Tristram*, for instance. The San Carlos landing, the epic battle of Goose Green and the tragedy of Bluff Cove where the troops were attacked from the air before they had set up anti-aircraft defences or had even disembarked were other landmarks of the campaign.

I will mention only four issues which are indicative of a Chief Press Secretary's problems in wartime. The first was the loss of two Harrier aircraft in fog in the South Atlantic. The military apparently were horrified at the idea that we should let the Argentinians know we had lost 10 per cent of our Harrier capability. That was perfectly understandable, though it would have helped if the MoD had been candid about it with me. But they had journalists on board and such losses leak out. And leak out the news did on the very day – 6 May – that local elections were being held in Britain. When I went over to the House in the evening I was confronted in the Press Gallery by a perturbed Noel Lewis, then of the BBC, who said that the Government was being accused of cynically delaying the release of the information until after the polls closed. Noel offered me a sound-proof broadcasting kiosk in which to argue the toss with the MoD over the telephone. The news was released. I was adamant that the Prime Minister was not going to be accused of playing local politics in the South Atlantic. That would have been very damaging. This is a simple illustration of where perfectly reasonable military considerations conflict with the wider need to keep public opinion behind the operation.

The Chief Press Secretary is also a convenient repository for blame in the heat of battle. It was alleged that I released news of victory at Goose Green before the battle had been fought. This surprised me, as did the allegation that Sir Frank Cooper telephoned me to tell me that if I did that again he would have my 'bloody head off'. Had he done so, he would certainly have been very wise to hang up, as the story has it, before I could reply. Unfortunately, I have no recollection of this, though it may be that once again in life I was, as Denis Healey put it, savaged by a dead sheep, and my memory consequently bears no marks. The Select Committee did not pursue this issue with me. Their report records: 'The Ministry of Defence now admit that in the evening of 28 May they announced the fall of Goose Green before it had actually been captured . . .' The Select Committee did, however, raise with me the allegation in a BBC TV 'Panorama' programme that I briefed political correspondents on Sunday 23 May, a few days before Goose Green, to the effect that the War Cabinet had told the assault force to move as fast as possible. I told the Select Committee:

'I think I am right in saying that the Admiral of the Fleet said in the *Observer* on May 23 "We are going to move and move fast. You can expect a great deal of activity within the next few days." The Chancellor of the Duchy of Lancaster [Cecil Parkinson] . . . in a broadcast the same day said: "Having established a secure base we are planning to move and to move fast. It is not our intention to be lured into a long and bloody war." That day, 23 May, the *Sunday Times* had a headline, "We are moving fast"; the *Sunday Express* said: "Our troops go sweeping on", and the *News of the World* said "Troops set for a quick victory". I appeared before the lobby that afternoon against that background. I did not volunteer anything about moving fast or slow. I was put up against the wall and they said "Is it going to be days or weeks?" and I thought if I said weeks then we would get a splendid story tomorrow about delay and, therefore, I said "I would guess it is days not weeks but . . ." . . . What I said additionally was: "but it is for the

Commander on the ground to decide how quickly he will
go" . . .'

One example of where closer liaison between Number 10 Press
Office and the MoD would have assisted the military was over the
level of casualties at Bluff Cove. The military, for their own good
reasons, were content for exaggerated reports of the level of casualties to remain uncorrected. That message did not reach me. Had it
done so I might not have discussed numbers of casualties with
journalists. To preserve my credibility I would have said that I was
not in a position to help. However, I knew that the figure of seventy
was exaggerated and told the lobby that I hoped it would prove to
be an exaggeration. I mentioned no figures, but the press took the
hint and speculated about a lower figure. I told the Select Committee frankly: 'This was the one occasion that I can recall when I did
not get the message early enough.'

I find Sir Frank Cooper's reported attitude towards me inexplic-
able except in one sense. When war breaks out the Permanent
Secretary of the MoD finds himself somewhat out of it. The military
take over and become closely involved with the Prime Minister. Sir
Frank clearly decided to devote some of his energies to presentation. Some of the consequences bore the hallmark of the amateur.
It would have been better for all concerned had he recognized that,
as Chief Press Secretary, I had a number of standing engagements
each day with lobby journalists and foreign correspondents and was
in a position to help him. I would have done so more effectively
had I not apparently been regarded as a competitor. Because the
MoD ended general background briefings, as distinct from some
memorably fierce encounters with editors who told Sir Frank what
they thought of him, my gatherings attracted larger numbers of
correspondents than would otherwise have attended. Sometimes
there was scarcely room to breathe in my room in Number 10. The
problems over presentation between Number 10 and the MoD
during the campaign were one of the sadder aspects of an outstanding feat of arms. I wish it had been otherwise.

Leaving aside the strained relationships between journalists and
military and civilian press officers in the South Atlantic, the
campaign brought its inevitable crop of complaints from the

Government against the media and, more especially, the broadcasters. I saw my job as being to try to keep the lid on it and, on the whole, I think I succeeded.

It was, however, rather trying when notably the BBC gave an impression of neutrality as between Britain and the Argentine. This caused some outrage among MPs and the Prime Minister herself was not best pleased. I discuss this attitude on the part of some journalists – their separatitis, as I describe it – in Chapter 22. I found the criticism of the BBC by MPs a valuable safety valve. It put the issue before the public and thereby helped the Government to avoid becoming more deeply embroiled in such essentially ephemeral matters when it had bigger issues on its plate. I noted with some wry amusement during the Gulf War that the broadcasters were again sometimes in hot water with the Government for their coverage.

There were two other problems, both affecting television coverage, during the crisis. One was the plenitude of pictures from the Argentine for much of the period and the other was that posed by British television coverage of the war itself. Television has changed the rules of war. Now it seems that no conflict is complete without the presence of television crews in the enemy camp. They would not remain there if the host Government did not think that on balance their presence was helpful. But the nature of arrangements between television organizations across the world means that sooner or later they have access to whatever pictures and reports are going. In these circumstances, I would prefer to have our own nationals, subject to British editorial control, reporting from the enemy's capital than rely on others. No one can deny that this places a heavy responsibility on both the reporter and his editor to ensure that they are not being used to undermine their own country's war effort. On the whole I think news reporters, as distinct from current affairs programmes which are in the business of making a point, have served Britain pretty well. I am also clear from the Falklands experience that propaganda counter-productively shines through. For this reason I was relatively relaxed about the use made by British television of a great deal of footage that came out of Buenos Aires.

I was much less relaxed about British still photographs and television pictures from the Task Force for two reasons: the difficulties in securing transmission of TV film and of establishing a good service of still pictures; and the possible effect on the public, bearing in mind the Vietnam experience in the United States, of television pictures from the battlefield. In the event, the latter issue scarcely arose because the technical problems of transmitting television pictures from the South Atlantic were never resolved. Film shot in the South Atlantic and on the Falklands had to be shipped to Ascension Island and then sent by satellite to London. ITN evidence to the Select Committee showed a variation of from nine to twenty-three days from filming to transmission. I tried to help editors, and not least television editors, but they remained convinced that the problems could have been overcome with a bit more effort and greater goodwill on the part of the MoD. The Defence Select Committee left the impression that there was more justice in complaints about the still picture service than about television transmission, though experiments suggested that a television signal, as distinct from commercial quality pictures, could have been transmitted direct from the South Atlantic if an American satellite had been tilted for the purpose. Informal approaches to the Americans offered no encouragement because of the load already being carried by the satellite and the matter was not pursued further.

So far as censorship is concerned, I remain as unsqueamish about it today as I was in 1982. Journalists who are affronted by this can put it down to my age. I have an old-fashioned view that wars, if they must be fought, are there to be won. The problem in these days of instant satellite communication is how to operate a formal, effective and reasonably even-handed system. Assuming that such a system could be devised, I think it would perform a service for editors in the intensely competitive news business. Fortunately, I did not become deeply involved in matters of censorship, except in one respect: the extensive use by television of retired military officers to offer their two-pennyworth on strategy, tactics and, most important, what should happen next. This was a matter of continuing concern throughout the campaign. The argument that the Argentine military could reason just as well as those retired British officers appearing on screen did not impress Ministers. It is one thing for television pundits to express their views on military options; it is entirely another for recently retired senior members of the British armed forces to do so. Towards the end of the conflict the MoD organized a specially briefed panel of officers to respond to television requests for experts. I can only reflect on how life has changed. As a boy I was taught that 'Careless talk costs lives.'

After the conflict – and a splendid dinner in Number 10 to celebrate the recovery of the Falklands – I was presented with arguably my greatest single challenge in Downing Street. My job in January 1983 was to get the Prime Minister from Number 10 to Port Stanley without anybody knowing she was on her way and finding out until she was safely there. We did not wish to put any temptation in the way of the Argentine. Mrs Thatcher did not lead a sheltered life. Her daily routine was the subject of intense interest. Her week-ends were monitored. Her failure to go to Chequers at week-ends needed to be explained if idle speculation as to the reasons was to be avoided. There would also be an awful rumpus if we failed to have a reporter and television cameraman conveniently on hand to film her arrival in Port Stanley. (I would also just as surely be criticized for, among other things, trying to win the next general election for Mrs Thatcher by laying on cameras.) I asked the MoD to detain Nicholas Witchell and his BBC camera team on the Falklands for an additional few days on as convincing a pretext as they could assemble. The programme they laid on for the BBC team worked like a charm, though Nicholas Witchell told me on arrival that he had suspected what was in the offing. If so, I am indebted to him for his restraint.

The British press presented much more difficulty. There was, I fear, no way of achieving my objective without being evasive. I was greatly helped by the Sunday lobby whom I saw at 4 p.m. on Friday 7 January. They asked me where Mrs Thatcher was due to go that week-end. I told them that her programme said 'Chequers', as indeed it did. But before I left I arranged for Romola Christopherson, my deputy, to log every journalist who might reasonably complain that we had misled him and give him an explanatory – and apologetic – call after Mrs Thatcher had arrived in the Falklands. It is perhaps an indication of the strength of our relationship with the lobby that I cannot recall a single recrimination, galling though reporters must have found it to miss breaking the news of the Prime Minister's visit.

After a farewell drink with my staff, I sauntered out of Downing Street at 6.40 p.m., to divert any watching pressmen, to a car, containing my luggage, outside the Cabinet Office in Whitehall. Mr and Mrs Thatcher set off for 'Chequers' and we met at RAF Brize Norton in Oxfordshire at 8.30 p.m. The party – Mr and Mrs Thatcher, Admiral Sir John Fieldhouse, the Falklands Task-Force commander, Robin Butler, Mrs Thatcher's principal private secretary, John Coles, her foreign affairs private secretary, Alan Logie and myself – flew overnight by VC10 to Ascension. We had a lively dinner with Mr and Mrs Thatcher on board and then the rest of the party retired to the barn of the stripped-out aircraft to sleep on our mattresses. I discovered that Admiral Fieldhouse came from Leeds and we talked into the night about Armley and Bramley, where I had lived and which he knew well.

We transferred to a Hercules aircraft with dawn breaking over Wideawake airfield on Ascension around 6 a.m. Inside was a Porta-kabin for the Prime Minister which would have been fine but for the fact that it quickly became stuffy if any number sat in it. The thirteen-hour flight to the Falklands was memorable for the two refuellings. The first occurred 1200 miles out. We all stood on the ample flight deck watching the shuttlecock fan at the end of the pipeline from the Hercules tanker slapping around in front of our cockpit. I recall saying to Admiral Fieldhouse: 'I've not lost a Prime Minister yet but I reckon this is a bit dodgy.' The second, a long way off Montevideo, was even dodgier. It was accomplished in driving rain. We could not see the Hercules tanker in front of us as we dived through 7000 feet as part of the topping-up process.

The Falklands reminded me of the Shetlands. My memory of them is a tapestry composed of Mrs Thatcher's bone-crunching drive over rutted roads from the airport to Port Stanley in Governor Rex Hunt's red London taxi; the emotional scenes among these simple, direct people when they first encounter Mrs Thatcher in Port Stanley; the magnificent mutton at Rex Hunt's welcoming dinner in Government House; the phenomenal pace of changes in the weather; the arrival at Fitzroy some thirty-six hours after Mrs Thatcher of Messrs Jack Warden (chairman of the lobby), Chris

Moncrieff (PA) and David Walter (ITN) – who had been flown out by special aircraft as the accredited London 'pool' – as Mrs Thatcher was preparing to bang away on field guns; Goose Green community centre where 100 inhabitants were incarcerated for a month by the Argentinians; Rupert Brooke's '. . . some corner of a foreign field' at the British San Carlos military cemetery – except that the Falklands are manifestly, texturally as British as the Scottish piper's heart-rending lament at the gravesides; Mrs Thatcher's speech of acceptance of the first Freedom of the Falklands – how did she keep control when all around her were losing theirs?; on HMS *Antrim* in San Carlos Sound imagining what it must have been like six months earlier during the landing; Mrs Thatcher's interview with a terrified reporter for *Penguin News* whom I did my best to fortify with questions; and the final dinner with the British forces and Merchant Navy where, in a deeply emotional experience, we all sang 'Rule Britannia'.

The next problem was getting off the Islands as secretly as we had arrived. Jack Warden telephoned me to ask, with enormous emphasis, whether I could honestly say that the Prime Minister would be seeing penguins and seals tomorrow (as arranged) since the pound sterling was falling in the markets. I assured him, with a certainty borne of telecommunications across 8000 miles, that we would. And we did. Mrs Thatcher's party got up at 5 a.m. to fly by helicopter to Mount Tumbledown to inspect the Argentine positions with General Thorne, the Falklands force commander. Then we hunted the penguins and seals at Seal Point. I was profoundly relieved that none of us had trodden on a mine. We breakfasted at Government House and then, to confuse the press, we flew west before turning east to the airport. I comforted myself with the letter I had written to the press contingent apologizing yet again for not coming clean about our departure. It all seemed very academic when our Hercules aborted its take-off, with great straining and braking half way down the runway, because Number 2 engine was out of order. I envisaged Jack Warden opening my letter and telephoning London with the news while the Prime Minister was still sitting around awaiting the preparation of a replacement Hercules. We took off an hour late but with the story of her return home as yet unbroken.

Before leaving the Falklands behind I must set out the facts of my great row with the BBC which was subsequently broadcast by Channel 4. My telephone calls from Port Stanley were broadcast, I imagine, in contravention of the law. This proved conclusively to me that the media are against telephone tapping – or interception of the air waves – unless the telephone happens to be the one I am using. What a bunch of hypocrites I had to put up with! Given the secrecy of Mrs Thatcher's mission to the Falklands, I found it impossible to stipulate in advance that Nicholas Witchell's reports and pictures should be pooled – i.e. made freely available across the world. I told Mr Witchell on arrival that that was my requirement. He very fairly said that it was not a matter for him but for his superiors in London. I found his superiors in London had turned awkward: they were denying ITN their film coverage. With a disingenuousness worthy of a British Academy of Film and Television Arts (BAFTA) award, Alan Protheroe found it very difficult to accept that I could declare a pool – i.e. a shared facility – as and when I thought fit. There would have been some force in his argument had I been in a position to set the rules in advance. But I had not. I detonated:

'ME: It is childish behaviour that when indeed we have done you a signal service – a signal service – by keeping your people in the islands, as I say and to repeat, at considerable risks to ourselves, I frankly don't believe that the British public, when it is explained to them, will understand this childishness. I do expect more actually from the BBC and I am deeply hurt.

'ALAN PROTHEROE: It would have been a lot easier if somebody in your office had asked us or told us twenty-four hours beforehand.

'ME: I am sorry, there is absolutely no question of us doing that. You have got to get it into your mind, and the media have got to get it into its mind, that we don't operate for your convenience, we operate for the security of the Prime Minister. I'm fed up with this. I had it in Northern Ireland.'

I then turned nasty. Once again I found the top brass of journalism singularly deficient in their economic education. The BBC had failed to appreciate that the British Government had a monopoly in air services out of the Falklands just as the *Guardian*, the *Independent* and the *Scotsman* later overlooked my monopoly in Number 10 briefings in departing from the lobby. Some editors seem to be as ineducable as the Bourbons. I told Mr Protheroe: 'No film is coming out [of the Falklands] tonight unless I have your absolute assurance that it will be freely available to ITN and Independent Radio News.' I added that I was sure that the Prime Minister 'if I had to tell her what is going on ... would scarcely credit it'.

The telephone tappers club – or Interceptors Inc. – even taped my subsequent call to Romola Christopherson reporting the outcome of this entirely unnecessary row:

'ME: I've won.

'ROMOLA: You've won?

'ME: Yes.

'ROMOLA: What happened?

'ME: I rang Protheroe and I told him in no uncertain terms that he wouldn't get it [the film] back tonight unless it was freely available ...'

Walter Terry, the great political editor of the *Daily Mail* whom I last saw just before his death at the lobby's retirement dinner for my wife and me on 16 January 1991, once told me that my signal contribution to Mrs Thatcher's premiership was to save her endless amounts of trouble with the press (by which he also meant radio and television). The telephone tapper or interceptor of Port Stanley, or somewhere, provides a unique insight into how, in one instance, I did so. There is no doubt that, had I not stamped on the BBC's remarkable behaviour, Mrs Thatcher's visit would have become the subject of great controversy. He or she also explains how I became known as the 'Rottweiler of Number 10'. It was regrettably necessary to bare my fangs on occasions.

I have never had a more extraordinary flight than that on the replacement Hercules from Port Stanley to Ascension. There was no Portakabin this time. It took three hours to warm up the aircraft. All of us – Prime Minister and Mr Thatcher included – wrapped ourselves in blankets to keep warm in the hangar of the hull as we ploughed northwards. I read the report of the Franks Inquiry into the Falklands affair and generally prepared myself for its publication six days hence – on 18 January. There is nothing like a long flight for getting essential work done. I mention Franks only to round off this unforgettable Falklands period in my life.

Mrs Thatcher was adamant that the report would be published without advance copies to the lobby or any other journalists. She – like me – was fed up with the way journalists leaked advance copies of reports to anyone who might usefully express a destructively newsworthy view on them. I was in no mood to argue with the Prime Minister about this, even though I knew the interests of responsible members of the lobby would suffer for the sins of the irresponsible. After requests from lobby correspondents for help, I agreed that at 2.45 p.m. – forty-five minutes before publication – I would identify the important paragraph numbers in the report which lobby members would get at 3.30 p.m. so that when they received their copies reporters could quickly transmit the key news passages to their offices. The destructive tendency in the lobby leaked that plan to the Opposition who made a fuss on the floor of the House. The Prime Minister decided, after discussing the matter with me, to deny the lobby all briefing before publication. Jack Warden, chairman of the lobby, was exasperated and read his members a lecture about lobby rules. The outcome of all these shenanigans was that at 3.30 p.m., when the report was published, members of the lobby fell upon me like wolves for a quick rundown of the key passages of the report. The machinations of the malevolent minority had simply lost their colleagues forty-five minutes. And to what purpose?

The Franks Report found no justification for criticizing or blaming the Government for the Argentine invasion on 2 April.

19

Terrorism and Tragedy

If Mrs Thatcher's Iron Lady image was ultimately forged in 1981 through her perseverance with her economic policies, her reputation as an outstanding national leader was confirmed by the Falklands campaign. Wherever she went she was recognized and applauded, though of course there was a militant minority who abused and occasionally pelted her with the odd egg whenever a television camera was in sight. Eventually even they got bored. Far more seriously she was hunted as a prime target by terrorists and very nearly blown up by the IRA in the Grand Hotel in Brighton in October 1984. I would like to salute that gallant group of officers who for eleven and a half years protected her – and myself and my official colleagues – and continue to do so.

During her careers as Leader of the Opposition and as Prime Minister she lost two close political friends – Airey Neave and Ian Gow – to car bombs. Five others died and thirty-two were injured in the Grand Hotel, Brighton. Some of those injured were crippled or marked for life such as Mr and Mrs Norman Tebbit and my close friend and confidant, John Wakeham, whose wife was killed in the conference hotel explosion. I felt so angry after visiting John Wakeham in his Brighton hospital that I was not fit to drive myself back home. None of this is to forget the hundreds of other victims who lost their lives or were maimed by the evil hands of terrorists. Mrs Thatcher bore the losses of those close to her with great stoicism in public. She kept herself under tight control when the news was brought to her. However shocked and shaken she was by it, she exhibited a remarkable calm in such crises and probably sublimated her true feelings in an active concern for the families. In the course of our daily lives we in Number 10 made light of the personal risk from terrorism but the threat was always there at the back of our minds and it increasingly affected our routine. The important thing, however, was to demonstrate an utter and absolute determination not to be beaten by the psychopaths who carry out acts of terrorism. Mrs Thatcher's resolution never shone through more inspiringly than in her speech on the last day of the 1984 party conference – the day, she later recognized, she was not intended to see.

If all national leaders had shown the same resolution against terrorists as Mrs Thatcher the world would be a safer place. No one ever had any doubt where she stood when the issue arose, as it all too often did, in Economic and European Summits. Nor did she flinch on 14 April 1986 from assisting President Reagan when he determined to teach Gaddafi, that well-known supplier of arms to the IRA, a lesson about his support for international terrorism. The French refused to allow American F-111 bombers from British bases to fly over their territory. Consequently, the aircraft had to go the long way round the Iberian peninsula, via Gibraltar, to Libya. Mrs Thatcher never pretended that this was an easy issue. She needed to be satisfied by President Reagan that the raid could be justified under international law and that the targets were strictly military. There was a great deal of trans-Atlantic consultation during the previous evening after which British support was confirmed. Ministers met for two hours or so in the Cabinet Room on the evening of the raid after Mrs Thatcher had returned from *The Economist* where she launched Norman St John Stevas's Bagehot tomes. The wit of the occasion belied the serious business on the Prime Minister's mind.

The meeting in the Cabinet Room was preoccupied with drafting the Prime Minister's Parliamentary statement on the raid which she eventually delivered the following day. She had, however, to be ready with a statement that night should news of the attack break while Parliament was sitting. There was a distinct possibility of this because that evening the House was debating the Shops Bill – that is, the controversial issue of Sunday opening. I was in the House that evening, ostensibly awaiting the outcome of the Second Reading debate on the Shops Bill which the Government lost to great excitement at around 12.30 a.m. I got home for around 1.30 to receive a telephone call from Charles Powell that the raid was taking place. I had spent most of the late evening in the House with Murdo Maclean, principal private secretary to the Chief Whip. Subsequently, our presence together in the precincts of the House rang alarm bells for some MPs and journalists. They wondered what was happening when we two appeared. Mark Hughes, former Labour MP for Durham, saw us in the Strangers' Bar about three weeks after the attack on Tripoli. He stepped back in mock alarm, 'And what,' he demanded, 'are we bombing tonight?' When he was feeling mischievous, Murdo used to invite me over to the House to go on walkabout together just to get people jumpy!

Hi-jackers knew there was not much point in landing in Britain. They would never get away with their demands. It was tried only once – at the end of February 1982, when the passengers and crew were released unharmed from a hijacked Tanzanian aircraft at Stansted airport. This event was notable for me because of the way in which news of the hijack, received by the Prime Minister around 2.20 p.m. on a Saturday, terminated a lunch she was giving in Number 10 for the *Economist* editorial team. I have never seen a lunch break up so quickly or the Government's emergency arrangements be instituted so swiftly – by the Prime Minister herself. She also organized the catering, bringing two Christmas cakes from her flat to provide afternoon tea for the staff manning the nerve-centre in Cabinet Office.

If there is one thing a Chief Press Secretary should not talk about it is anti-terrorist arrangements. I do not intend to start now that I have retired for the threat remains. Terrorism was, however, part of my life for the whole of the 1980s and in a variety of ways it is sharply etched upon my memory. Robert Carr, as Secretary of State for Employment, introduced me to the feeling of helplessness it can induce in press secretaries who are separated by miles from their principal when the attack takes place. Early in 1971, he and his family narrowly escaped being blown up late at night by a bomb at their front door. It occurred on the same day that nationwide demonstrations had been held against the Industrial Relations Bill, but the two were not connected. Mr Carr and his family were the targets of the so-called Angry Brigade, a tiny group of revolutionaries. The explosion left me besieged by reporters on the telephone to my home on the southern outskirts of London and the Secretary of State on the northern outskirts of the capital. There was only one thing to be done: stay put and try to reach Mr Carr in his damaged home. Eventually, I succeeded in confirming with him personally that he and his family were uninjured and getting from him a résumé of the incident so that I could cope with reporters' inquiries. From then on Mr Carr was accompanied by protection officers who, sadly, have become such a feature of Ministerial life.

As a civil servant I never knowingly set foot in Mrs Thatcher's constituency of Finchley in north London. Nor did I visit a Conservative Party conference – not even as a journalist. Consequently, I was nowhere near Brighton when the Grand Hotel was blown up in 1984. I used to take a holiday during party conference weeks. In 1984 I spent the first five days in Hebden Bridge. On the Thursday we drove down to Thornbury Castle, near Bristol, where I was to give a talk the following day. I was awakened by a telephone call early on the Friday from Sheenagh Wallace, from Number 10 Press Office, to inform me of what had happened on the eve of Mrs Thatcher's fifty-ninth birthday. Once again after a terrorist attack I felt professionally helpless and useless, reduced to watching the harrowing scenes of Norman Tebbit's rescue on television. I dispatched my deputy, Jean Caines, from London to Brighton to represent the Prime Minister's interests. The group assembled for my talk by the Shepherd building group in Bristol were shocked and bewildered and so much wanted to support the Government. I concluded – not for the first time – that terrorism has entirely the opposite effect in the UK to that intended.

I was similarly not much good to anyone when terrorism came to my home in Purley immediately before Easter 1987. I had been invited to lunch by the British Columbia Government who were to co-host the Commonwealth Conference in Vancouver in October. No sooner had I sat down with their representative, Bob Lillicoe, at the Ecu de France restaurant than Nigel Wicks, principal private secretary at Number 10, rang to say my wife had received a letter bomb which had been defused. I could not raise Nancy on the telephone because, it turned out, she was still sitting outside our home in a police car while the bomb squad completed defusing the device. When I did get through to her I warned her that reporters would soon be swarming all around the bungalow. She told me that the postman had given her the mail while she was in the front garden. She was immediately suspicious of a torn, cheap brown paper envelope marked from the University of Ulster. There were no wires protruding from it so she opened it and found the *Observer's Book of Fossils* with tape around it. She suspected it was a bomb, left it in the garden and telephoned the police. It was one of a batch sent to civil servants and others associated with Mrs Thatcher. All were defused. I thanked God for Nancy's vigilance and did not feel like helping the last remnants of the press and radio when I got home, especially as Nancy had already given them an interview. I am told that a radio channel broadcast a conversation between me and reporters through the front door which went something like this:

'JOURNALISTS: Oh come on, Mr Ingham, you're a press officer, you can talk to us.

'ME: It is precisely because I am a press officer that I don't want to talk to you.'

And I didn't. There are times when, quite simply, you have had enough.

I must confess that, for me, Northern Ireland and despair are as inseparable as are Wales and rugby. I find it unutterably depressing that too many in Northern Ireland seem to have two occupations: preaching the Christian faith and denying its tenets at every opportunity. This made visits by Mrs Thatcher to the province all the more frustrating for she obviously met representatives of the peace-loving, constructive and socially responsible who form the vast majority of Ulster people. Her walkabouts to meet those people – a most dangerous form of political activity, even on the mainland of Britain when the crowds are controlled by steel barriers – underlined her courage, though her trips were planned in great secrecy. Number 10 and the Northern Ireland Office never confirmed them until they were underway. Nonetheless, reporters and cameramen always managed to follow her around in flocks.

I found press, radio and television in Northern Ireland just about the most difficult to deal with in the whole of the United Kingdom, even with the highly professional help of first, David Gilliland, and then Andy Wood, and their staff in the Northern Ireland Office.

This was partly because, against a background of continuing violence, the journalists' objectives and the Prime Minister's were diametrically opposed to each other. They wanted to accentuate the negative, the difficulties and the conflict, whereas Mrs Thatcher – and I must say myself – wanted to underline the positive achievements in Northern Ireland, to highlight the peaceful normality of life over most of the province and to encourage the public in their fight against terrorism. Once I raised with both the BBC and ITN the frustration felt in Belfast that a festival and parades there attended by the Mayors of Dublin and Belfast had passed off peacefully – and without any coverage whatsoever. In some respects reporters working in Northern Ireland are no different from those anywhere else. Bad news is the only good news. Mrs Thatcher once told journalists on Tyneside to stop being 'moaning minnies'. Nor are the media in Northern Ireland unique in transferring the province's own responsibilities on to central Government. On a quiet day, when there was no obviously topical issue to raise with her, Mrs Thatcher could normally rely on the same first question wherever she went in the United Kingdom: 'And what have you brought to this region, today?' I used to growl under my breath the answer I hoped she would – just once – give: 'And what, may I ask, are you doing for yourselves?'

The behaviour of the journalistic profession in Northern Ireland was therefore only a question of degree. But I sometimes thought that the circus was getting out of hand. They seemed to assume they could claim anybody and everyone as their own. They had no compunction about forming a scrum around Mrs Thatcher, seething with indignation at the thought that she might have something better on her mind than talking to them. I could absolutely rely on interviewers to go on and on, to coin a phrase, in the hope of tripping her up. I could be more certain than anywhere else that television cameramen and soundmen would entangle you in their umbilical cords and bring you crashing to the ground if you did not watch out. It was inevitable you would be knocked about. And sure enough when I fought what became known as the War of Ingham's Buttock, by simply bouncing one or two marauders off my backside as they piled in with their microphones, complaints were registered. There is one thing I hope never to see again: cameramen walking the length of display counters in the Marks and Spencer store in Belfast, trampling knitwear and other soft goods under foot in order to get an elevated shot. Who the hell do these people think they are?

On most visits Mrs Thatcher went to support the Royal Ulster Constabulary and the British Army, including the UDR, in the more fraught areas of Northern Ireland and on several occasions she flew by helicopter to border posts which come under attack – for example, Forkhill, Aughnacloy and, on the last occasion just before she resigned, Kinawley, not far from Enniskillen. She always joined the police and troops in their look-out posts. She also invariably met widows of those who had died at the hands of terrorists or wives of men who were continuing to represent law and order. In all these meetings she showed her outstanding quality as a national leader: her ability to talk to ordinary people – if anyone in the police or Armed Forces in Northern Ireland, or their wives, can be called ordinary – and to set them at their ease. I never felt apprehensive on these visits, except on the last at Kinawley, five days before Mrs Thatcher resigned. I must confess that on this occasion I wondered whether the IRA would make a desperate attempt lest she lose the impending leadership election.

Mrs Thatcher spent a lot of time in helicopters. They are a superb form of transport for a Prime Minister. She went up the Khyber Pass in one. She has flown offshore in them to land on oil rigs and warships. They are the accepted form of travel for visits to Camp David. She was required to fly into Dublin Castle in one for European Councils – a manoeuvre which, in the confined space, seemed to me to be a greater temptation of fate than driving in from the airport. Helicopters also carried her around Northern Ireland on her ten visits to the province. These – in fact, virtually all the helicopters Mrs Thatcher used in Britain – revealed the Spartan nature of public life in this country as compared with abroad. She flew out of Wellington or Chelsea barracks in central London or Aldergrove in Northern Ireland in ordinary Service helicopters which conceded nothing to their Prime Ministerial passenger unless it was the white covers on the ear muffs. Mrs Thatcher used to wear the ear muffs upside down, with the head rest under her chin, to avoid spoiling her hair. Often we were showered or dampened by condensation and sometimes the helicopters even dripped oil on us. And on long flights across Northern Ireland to Londonderry or Enniskillen, or down to border posts, she wore blankets or overcoats around her legs to keep warm. But we always felt safe with the RAF, even when, to quote Charles Powell, we 'flew underground' for the first time on 16 November 1990 as we scattered cattle and sheep with the clouds down low over the hills east of Enniskillen. Mrs Thatcher found her luxury in helicopters abroad.

I played little part in the build-up to the signing of the Anglo-Irish Agreement on 15 November 1985, except to try to keep reportage on an even keel. I also conducted for Mrs Thatcher and Garret Fitzgerald, the Irish Prime Minister, their subsequent joint press conference in Hillsborough Castle. The Agreement represented yet another attempt to encourage political movement in Northern Ireland and it cost Mrs Thatcher a member of her Government. Ian Gow resigned on her return that day from Northern Ireland. In spite of its often being written off, the Agreement remains in force and a framework for political development. Knowing the propensities of journalists operating in Northern Ireland, I ran the Hillsborough press conference to launch it with a rod of iron. It worked a treat. As press conferences go, it was an excellent one. Mrs Thatcher thanked me immediately it was over for conducting it effectively. I very much liked Garret Fitzgerald, with whom I sat from Bahrain to the Alps when Mrs Thatcher gave him a lift back from Mrs Gandhi's funeral in November 1984. He is a wonderful conversationalist and an expert in devising the cheapest – if not the shortest – air route from A to B.

The continuing tragedy of Northern Ireland too often took Mrs Thatcher to the scene of terrorist outrages and the hospitals coping with the casualties, or to subsequent memorial services – for example, Warrenpoint, Harrods, Hyde Park, Regent's Park, Enniskillen and Deal. She did this as an act of leadership, as a demonstration of resolve against terrorism and out of sympathy and support for the injured and bereaved. A spate of appalling civil disasters and outrages before and after Lockerbie – the Hungerford massacre, Zeebrugge, the Clapham rail crash, the Kegworth air crash, the *Marchioness* disaster on the Thames and the Hillsborough soccer tragedy – brought whisperings that Mrs Thatcher was 'ambulance chasing'. Of all the allegations made against her – and they were numerous – I thought this the most objectionable. Members of the lobby were forced to admit that her failure to go and view the scene for herself or demonstrate her concern in this way would serve only to prompt stories that she was 'uncaring'. The Towyn flood disaster, in which no one died, proved the point. There were complaints about her failure to visit the area.

The deaths of ten hunger strikers in Mrs Thatcher's first administration changed the background music to my working day. Until they starved themselves to death in prison I had done my job in my bow-fronted office, looking out on to Downing Street and commanding a view both up and down it to the door of Number 10, to the constant twitter of tourists. The public could come and go reasonably freely through Downing Street. Parties of excited schoolchildren (hence the twittering) poured through and demonstrated all the cruel innocence of youth: whenever people like me walked out of the door of Number 10 they groaned *fortissimo* in such a devastatingly deflating way that the only thing to do was smile and wave. It was much worse for Cabinet Ministers, for only Mrs Thatcher could win a big cheer. For the rest of the 1980s (after 1981) entry to Downing Street was controlled. A plastic carrier bag left in the street could set off a major security alert.

None the less, parties of children continued to be allowed up the street by arrangement to be photographed by their friends or relatives, as the boy Harold Wilson did, in front of the famous door. Around 2 o'clock on Tuesday and Thursday afternoons was an exceptionally popular time for school visits. This was because the parties could be sure of seeing the Prime Minister if they hung around for her departure for the House of Commons. Mrs Thatcher often used to go over to talk to the children before going to do battle on the floor of the House. Eric Marney, a headmaster who was at HBGS with me, once brought a group of prize-winning children down from Sedbergh. They not only interviewed Mrs Thatcher on the doorstep but also gave me a grilling in my room. The lobby could learn a thing or two about awkward questions from schoolchildren. As Mrs Thatcher often said, the curiosity of a child is quite uninhibited. It is the simple questions that can give most trouble because you often lose your young audience in the long answers they require: such as, for example, 'Why don't we see you much on telly, Mr Ingham?' Please see Chapter 12 of this book.

For much of the 1980s Downing Street was controlled by means of a flimsy metal barrier at the Whitehall end of the street, as compared with the substantial, solid metal railings at the St James's Park end leading to the Foreign Office and Horse Guards Parade. The Whitehall barrier was tatty, insubstantial and ultimately useless. It is astonishing that no one – not even the innocently loopy as distinct from the criminally mad IRA – ever tried to breach this rudimentary defence. When Nigel Wicks told me of the intention to defend the Prime Minister more effectively, I knew exactly what would happen: the media would write about the 'bunker mentality'. I took the view that the security improvements, including new, specially designed high gates, a road blocker and a new garden wall to replace one that was falling down, were entirely defensible. It was, however, very hard work to persuade most journalists that this was not a public relations mistake. Mr Kinnock was even reported as saying that he would remove the gates if he ever reached Number 10. The Prime Minister's security cannot be left only to what is presentationally acceptable. I did not hear many reporters recanting about the gates after the Trafalgar Square/Whitehall poll tax riot or after the mortar bombing of Mr Major's 'War Cabinet'. However much I regret that our democracy no longer allows the public free passage through Downing Street, I consider that the new gates are a substantial aesthetic improvement. Visiting heads of government would have been amazed to learn that their installation had provoked controversy. Alternatively, knowing the British well, they might have said that such a move could only generate a row in London.

Mrs Thatcher was also tried and tested by civil riot, commotions and crowd violence whether in Toxteth, Brixton or Manchester's Moss Side; on the picket lines in the Yorkshire coalfield and at Eddie Shah's *Stockport Messenger* and Rupert Murdoch's Wapping; or on football terraces culminating in that appalling tragedy at Hillsborough, Sheffield, on 15 April 1989 when ninety-five football fans lost their lives. Mrs Thatcher was determined to see law and order upheld and to support the police. She was also determined to make soccer safe for fathers to take their sons to watch. She got very little help from soccer itself. I sat through all her meetings with the Football Association and the Football League with mounting despair. Their standard response was that hooliganism was not their problem but society's. They presented such a picture of helplessness and inertia that I was forced to wonder whether they really cared for their game. And, unlike Mrs Thatcher, who did not make a habit of going to football matches, they could not dismiss people like me as knowing nothing about soccer. The Grant, Dodd and Ingham families had had a standing arrangement since our sons were about seven to meet behind the goal at the Whitehorse Road end of Crystal Palace's Selhurst ground near Croydon. Subsequently, my son, John, and I graduated to seats in the stand.

I stopped going to matches from the mid 1970s – except to watch in the comparative safety of Halifax Town's empty terraces while on holiday in Yorkshire – because of widespread hooliganism and the atmosphere of barely suppressed violence, even in the stands. Not that Halifax Town's best stand was free of menace. Once, in the company of my son and his wife, I suffered a big let-down when my seat collapsed under me to the amusement of the other spectators. I can assure you that it was the funniest thing that happened at The Shay ground that afternoon. For years there had been nothing funny about soccer; just tragedy. And the atmosphere as Mrs Thatcher boarded her helicopter for Sheffield on the morning of Sunday 16 April 1989 was one of despair at the ever lengthening list of deaths associated with the game. I never again wish to see rows of youngsters on life support machines as I did in the hospitals Mrs Thatcher visited, their parents at their bedside not knowing whether they would survive nor, if they did, whether their brains would have been damaged.

I hope Hillsborough has brought soccer to its senses. The tragedy did not make a membership card scheme proposed by the Government any more attractive to the sport. I shared the view of Colin Moynihan, the courageous Minister for Sport, that such a national scheme, properly organized to cater for the casual spectator and with reliable technology, could have been a valuable asset to the game. The scheme fell with Lord Justice Taylor's report into Hillsborough. The report came as something of a surprise to me in view of all that I had heard in Sheffield, on 16 April 1989, about the nature of the late-arriving crowds. I find it interesting that since the report killed off a national membership card scheme there appear to have been more all-ticket matches.

In all my eleven years with Mrs Thatcher I cannot think of a more depressing aspect of our national life than that presented to her by the management of our national game. I do not overlook the calculated, boorish disrespect and insolent contempt exhibited by Derek Hatton, the former Liverpool councillor, when he met Mrs Thatcher across the table on Merseyside. The egregious Mr Hatton will no doubt be pleased that he wins my Moron of the Eighties Award. However, unlike soccer's ruling bodies, no one expected anything of Mr Hatton. Only the much more constructive attitude in Mrs Thatcher's meetings of the Football Ground Improvement Trust, which channels pools money to the game, saved the entire episode from utter disaster.

Crime and punishment were never calculated to lighten Mrs Thatcher's heart. She ensured that the police were well paid, strengthened and well equipped. Crime prevention programmes and the criminal law and its processes were strengthened. But reported crime continued to rise for most of the 1980s. This raised serious questions about the nature of family life and parental discipline since young teenagers are the major offenders. Crime was much less of a political issue than I expected it to be during the Thatcher years. Perhaps this was because the public recognized the limits of what the Government could do. But by the end of Mrs Thatcher's period in office two issues were coming more into focus: the efficiency of police forces and the disciplines under which prison officers should work. I cannot pretend that journalists frequently or systematically pursued either topic with me, but I thought I could see in them matters of growing future concern.

Concern over police efficiency manifested itself to me in the form of reports that Mrs Thatcher wanted Army officers to run police forces. This understandably created difficulties. It also illustrated the problems a Chief Press Secretary faces because of ill-informed or exaggerated gossip. I have no evidence that Mrs Thatcher ever contemplated the wholesale import of Army officers to improve leadership and management in our police forces. But she was certainly concerned to raise the quality of police leadership and she saw an opportunity to do so in the 'peace dividend' arising from arms control agreements. She recognized a real chance to reinforce police management over time by redeploying good Army officer material, provided agreement could be reached that they need not start at the bottom on the beat. The issue remains on the table.

So does the problem of public sector unions as presented by the Prison Officers' Association. The sight of prison officers serving as unofficial briefers of the media while simultaneously negotiating in their own cause through television during the Strangeways prison riot raised fundamental issues about both the management of the prison service and presentation. For myself, I can see no reason why prison officers should retain the right to strike, but that is a wider question. Strangeways, as presented by television, provided the nation with a curious kind of anarchist theatre for the better part of a month. It illustrated yet again how television becomes an integral part of an emergency and the lengths to which it will go to secure a grandstand view to bring any pictorial event to our firesides. It begged questions about television's role in, and responsibilities to, the society of which it is a part. The Government Information Service, which I led for nearly two years, has long been acutely aware of these problems in serving the Government, media and public in an emergency. Those problems, which in this case are inseparable from the management of the prison service, form part of the law and order agenda for the future and illustrate the need for an acceptable – and accepted – definition of the pictorial media's responsibilities to the nation.

A subject of inexhaustible fascination to journalists is the activities of the security and intelligence services. That is precisely because these activities must remain secret in the national interest. Careless talk about counter-terrorism, for example, could literally be a matter of life and death so I neither briefed the press nor sought to brief myself on their work during my eleven years as Chief Press Secretary. I sometimes felt it a pity others were not as uncommunicative as I was. A feature of the 1980s was the emergence of a small group of journalists who specialized in embroidering whatever snippets of material they could find about the security and intelligence services. It is presumably a rewarding job in its own way; if you are irresponsible enough you can write almost anything in the safe knowledge that it will neither be confirmed nor denied. I had no means of telling whether much of what I read was just a load of old baloney, gossip or grained with truth. Everyone would be guessing, as I was. I am still guessing. I know that this is disappointing to those journalists who always believed that I had an inside track on everything. But that is how it was. And how it should be.

Mrs Thatcher was able to take some romance out of the business through her relative openness on various security issues such as her revelation that Professor Sir Anthony Blunt, the former Surveyor of the Queen's pictures, was a self-confessed spy and the fourth man in the Burgess, Maclean and Philby spy ring. She earned some praise for this, but it won her no lasting credit from some sections of the press, which wrote on these issues with all the authority that comes of ignorance, arrogance and probably disinformation.

They were later to be in full cry in support of Peter Wright, a former member of the Security Service who insisted on publishing his memoirs from Australia even though, as a former member of the Security Service, he owed a lifelong duty of confidentiality to the Crown. I had great difficulty with journalists over this case. This was because they took the view that once something – that is, Wright's book – had been published anywhere in the world that was it; there could be no justification in their eyes for trying to stop the book's publication in the United Kingdom or elsewhere. This entirely self-serving argument cut no ice with Mrs Thatcher. Nor did it, in my experience, with ordinary members of the public, who grasped two essentials: members of the Secret Service need to remain secret and silent if their operations are to be effective; and the concept that the Government should capitulate to a renegade simply because his book had been published abroad was an open invitation to irresponsible elements to do their worst, if only initially in Swahili or double Dutch.

The media profess to be wholeheartedly in favour of the security of the realm and kick up an enormous fuss whenever a spy scandal breaks. They then ritually call for heads to roll within Government. Yet their commercial interest is anything but the security of the state; it lies in full disclosure, for their fundamental interest is in circulation and ratings. Once we had identified the fourth man

(Blunt) the media were hot on the trail of the fifth man. And when it becomes fashionable again to go spy hunting the hunt will be on for the sixth, seventh and even eighth man. There is no end to such things. Beware the commentator who professes to be able to identify what it is in the national interest to disclose and what (if anything) to keep secret. He is a charlatan. He simply does not know. And even if he did, he would probably still say 'Disclose', because that is how he is made.

Having said all that, I must record my gratitude to Mrs Thatcher for her statement on Sir Anthony Blunt. If anything got me off to a good start with the lobby, within a fortnight of becoming Chief Press Secretary, it was playing the Blunt game with them. Come to think of it, I could not have had a more symbolic start either.

20

Rubbishing and Leaking

Mrs Thatcher never once asked – let alone instructed – me to criticize a Ministerial colleague in my dealings with journalists. Nor did she ever imply that I should do so. She was not in the 'rubbishing' business, though she could be very direct, not to say tactless, with Ministers to their faces. Nor did she ever ask or imply that I should 'leak' any document or piece of information. She was not into leaking, either. She was far too straight for such things. That was what exasperated so many of her political enemies. It was why they spent so much time laying siege to her reputation and that of her family. It also partly explains why I secured an unenviable reputation as a rubbisher of her Ministers and as a leaker of documents. If they could not impugn her, then I was better than nothing, however flimsy the evidence. If they could nail me to their satisfaction they could then attack her integrity by suggesting that I was operating as her agent.

Rubbishing and leaking were not my style either but they have become my hallmarks. How I came by them is an interesting commentary on the conduct of politics and journalism in Britain. It is also an interesting reflection on the libel laws. If I were a rich man, I should be far richer by now because of the libels committed against me over the last eleven years. That would not, however, have staunched the flow of libel. It would merely have driven it deeper into the House of Commons where the greatest rubbishers of them all, a low class of journalist, seek to persuade MPs to operate on their behalf behind the protective wall of Parliamentary privilege. They can blacken anyone if they can persuade an MP to make allegations or insinuations against an individual whether through a Parliamentary Question or an Early Day Motion, tabled on the Order Paper, or through an intervention on the floor of the House.

My reputation has to be examined, first, in relation to my exposure as the Prime Minister's spokesman. As I have already indicated, I gave some 5000 lobby briefings in my time at Number 10 and about 30,000 other individual briefings. These figures include lunches and dinners with journalists, a substantial proportion of which were with groups rather than individual reporters. If these averaged only two a week over eleven years, I chomped my way through at least 1000 meals with the Fourth Estate. (This makes me sound like the best fed Chief Press Secretary in the annals of Government. I certainly ate well, whenever I was given a choice in London, at Beotys in St Martin's Lane or the Howard Hotel on the Embankment.) Not even the most malicious commentator has yet been able to come up with more than half a dozen allegations against me of briefing against Ministers. Yet if I had been doing so, no one need have any doubt that I should have been quoted in the press. This means that, on my calculations, the most my critics feel able to allege – and they were never known to understate my failings – is a 'rubbishing rate' of little more than one per 6000 briefings. On such insubstantial bases are reputations constructed.

My reputation also needs to be examined against my position as an informant within Government. Let us leave aside the majority of Ian Aitken's 650 MPs who are dying to talk to him before he sets foot outside the Palace of Westminster. They, by definition, know so much less than members of the Government. There are always 100 or so members of the Government – Mrs Thatcher mostly excluded – chattering away to journalists and heaven only knows how many Government officials, all of whom brought their gossip (as distinct from information) and prejudices to their contacts with the media. And within Number 10 my monopoly was confined to formal meetings at 11 a.m. and 4 p.m. with the lobby. For the rest, journalists talked freely to whomsoever would answer their telephone calls or go out for a meal with them. When all that lot had finished yacketing away to each other, sometimes the more fastidious journalist would check a point with me.

This is where we need to examine my reputation against my need to retain my credibility as an informant. If the point raised by a journalist concerned the standing of a Minister, the caller might well read all kinds of unjustifiable implications into my refusal to

discuss the matter with him or my equivocation. The same considerations apply to my briefings of the lobby. I had to perform an
exceptionally difficult balancing act. I needed to be careful not to
damage my credibility while at the same time avoiding the charge
of undermining Government Ministers. This was not easy when
news reporters were not simply concerned with reporting what
people said or did but with drawing conclusions from what they
did not say or did not do, or how they said or did it, or from the
tone of their remarks. My reputation could consequently be at the
mercy of the quirk of the least well-informed, naive or the most
prejudiced of contacts with journalists. In these circumstances, my
exposure rate extended almost infinitesimally. By the same token,
my alleged 'rubbishing rate' declined steeply. You could get an
airworthiness certificate on the basis of this measurement of my
performance.

My reputation must also be examined against my recognizable
and readily acceptable interests. How, it may be asked, did I stand
to profit from doing down a Minister? What conceivable advantage
could have accrued to me from lambasting a member of the Government? The cynical might argue that I stood to gain every advantage
if I were acting at the behest of the Prime Minister and thought I
could get away with it. However, as I have explained, the Prime
Minister was not in this business. I recognize that this is an assertion
which I have no means of proving. But if Mrs Thatcher had been
keen for me to play it by the Queensberry rules of politics – as
distinct from her own far higher and more decent standards – I
would have been bound to advise her that she would not get away
with it. I would have had to be extraordinarily naive – indeed, naive
to the point of being dangerous – if I thought I could get away with
anything that the malevolent among lobby members could identify
as a rod with which to belabour me and, more important, through
me, the Prime Minister. I knew that anything I said at lobby meetings would, notwithstanding lobby rules about the unattributable
nature of the proceedings, be rapidly traced back to me, even if I
were not immediately identified as the source. I could guarantee
that the vicious tendency among the lobby would work hand in
glove with MPs to cause trouble on the floor of the House out of
anything I might – or might not – say, if only for the sake of a story

as distinct from the pleasure of supposedly causing me pain. I was also sufficiently experienced to know that even private conversations with individual journalists were by no means secure. As I have explained, too many members of the lobby were only too ready to reveal their sources to me and, therefore, presumably my remarks to others.

My reputation has also to be examined in the light of my being a team player – in fact, as the team leader in terms of the co-ordination of the presentation of Government policies. What conceivable gain could I have secured from undermining Ministers when my every working hour was spent – admittedly, mostly through my staff – in contact with Departmental press offices and heads of information? A life spent bad mouthing, as the phrase has it, their Ministers, to whom Departmental press officers owed their first loyalty, could only be calculated to cause disaffection and dissension within the ranks of the Government Information Service.

To summarize: I most certainly had the opportunity to criticize and undermine Ministers in my contacts with journalists. But my motives pointed conclusively the other way: it was much more in my interests to talk up rather than talk down individual Ministers. I had absolutely nothing to gain from criticizing them. On the contrary, I had everything to lose.

That does not, however, entirely dispose of the question of motives. It might be argued that, such was my relationship with the Prime Minister, it served her purpose admirably to keep Ministers on their toes. As sea captains go, she ran a hard ship. She did not spare her officers her tongue when she was on the quarter-deck with them. Two years before the Thatcher mast and you were either made or marred. So why should she baulk at some public 'withdrawal of affection', as it was described? This might be a good question but for two factors. The first is the malicious and gossipy nature of politicians themselves. They are almost paranoid about who is 'in and out' and 'up and down' in the Prime Minister's estimation. The second is the lack of evidence of a systematic operation by Number 10 against members of the Government. My worst-case 'rubbishing rate' of 1 in 6000 is not exactly systematic.

Unfortunately, it remains the case that I acquired the reputation as a scourge of Ministers. There is no point in evading the issue. Time and again my friends among journalists ruefully reported to me that Ministers were obsessed with my activities, dreading lest I would give them the black spot. My journalist friends were rueful, they said, because life would be so much more fun for them if only I would let myself go. Yet whatever the evidence, or lack of it – and not even a former Prime Minister, Mr Heath, or a former Lord Chancellor, Lord Hailsham, allowed that to get in the way – the perception was that I was never up to any good when I was commenting on Government Ministers. The thought that I might conceivably have a good word to say for any of them never seemed to enter the heads of most politicians, and least of all the heads of a lot of Ministers, to judge from what my journalist friends told me. How, then, did I acquire this remarkable reputation?

Before attempting to answer that question, I should make one obvious point. It is just possible that, Chief Press Secretaries being human, they can make mistakes. Unhappily, this is an unfashionable idea. Chief Press Secretaries seldom, if ever, make mistakes if the story dictates otherwise. They invariably have an ulterior motive. They are victims of the conspiracy theory of Government. I have been telling journalists for years that if only they would go for the cock-up theory they would be so much more accurate in their interpretation of events. It is a tip which I commend to all who would judge my reputation.

This rests on two statements which I made to the lobby. In relation to Francis Pym, then Lord President and Leader of the House of Commons, I said in 1982 that, like Tommy Handley's war-time 'ITMA' radio character, Mona Lott: 'it's being so cheerful as keeps him going'. (Unfortunately, I got it wrong and attributed the remark to Mrs Mopp. This hardly supports the theory of pre-meditated crime.) Four years later, in relation to John Biffen, Lord Privy Seal and also Leader of the House, I described him as 'that well-known semi-detached member of the Cabinet'.

Some people with whom I have discussed these remarks over the years feel that, as political currency goes, they were neither particularly cutting nor unkind. Indeed, John Biffen is reported to have found my remark about him rather witty. However, I make no bones about it: I should not have made such remarks and I wish

I never had. But I did. I have never tried to deny doing so. The offence lay in two essentials: first, that I was a civil servant – and civil servants, however much they may swear about their Ministers under their breath, do not make their criticisms to journalists. Second, each of the remarks was all the more offensive for being accurate. Their accuracy was not surprising since Mr Pym and Mr Biffen were at the material times the Ministers responsible for co-ordinating the presentation of Government policy. I worked with them. I reported to them. I knew them well. I also had to face them after my remarks.

But how did I come to make them? The answer to this question puts the issue in perspective. It also shows the profession of journalism in a less than adequate light. I most certainly did not volunteer the remarks. Each arose from speeches made by Mr Pym and Mr Biffen.

First, Mr Pym. On 1 February 1982 he addressed the Allied Brewery Trades Association annual dinner. Reading again reports of his speech, I can only say how much sound, solid stuff there was in it. But I can also see why it was interpreted as a gloomy speech and why it raised critical questions in the minds of lobby journalists. The particular passages that were seized upon, according to the *Financial Times*, read:

'The Government is completely committed to a long-term economic recovery that can be sustained, and a restoration of our ability to compete with, and beat our overseas rivals; but this cannot lead to an early return to full or nearly full employment, or an early improvement in living standards generally. New businesses are growing up all the time ... but it will be a long time – and no one can say when it will be – before the new industries can hope to replace all the jobs lost by the demise of the old ones ... this is a very painful period of transition and I think it would be dishonest to pretend that there is going to be a quick transition towards higher living standards. In the short run, living standards generally can only fall – which is part of the price we are paying for being too complacent.'

324

Four years later, on 11 May 1986 Mr Biffen, speaking on London Weekend Television's 'Weekend World' programme in the wake of heavy Conservative losses in the local elections and the loss of the Ryedale constituency in Yorkshire in a by-election, called for a 'balanced ticket' at the next general election. This, according to *The Times*, was to 'offset Mrs Margaret Thatcher's growing electoral liabilities'. Mr Biffen said:

> '. . . there is nothing extraordinary about the balanced ticket of the Prime Minister and some of the most powerful in the Conservative Party, one of whom probably would become Prime Minister in due course, being represented as a team. There is nothing extraordinary about presenting a team based upon experience and based upon a spread of views as being something which will be appealing to the public and which will secure their trust.'

Mr Biffen added that, to assume because one party had a dominant figure, it thereby benefited at general elections 'is not necessarily true at all'. Without a team approach it would be much easier for political opponents to represent the Prime Minister as uncaring or trigger-happy, and take advantage of her supposed failings. 'I have no intention,' he said, 'we should fall for these kind of accusations. One very sensible way of offsetting it is to represent the Conservative Party along the lines I have indicated.'

I cannot pretend that Mrs Thatcher was best pleased with either of these public contributions from members of her Cabinet, though Francis Pym's was more a problem of tone than content. It reflected his deep concern, as a thoroughly decent man, about the level of unemployment and the need to avoid exciting expectations of an early improvement. He was by nature a little gloomy and events proved him to be unduly so. But it said nothing for the co-ordination of Government presentation, for which Mr Pym was responsible, since only a few days earlier, Sir Geoffrey Howe, the Chancellor of the Exchequer, had detected signs of recovery in the economy. Nor had Mrs Thatcher had prior notice of the speech. Mr Biffen's offence was much the greater. Leaving aside his responsibility for co-ordinating presentation of policy, which he left to me, he had publicly criticized the Prime Minister of the

Government in which he served in terms which suggested she was an electoral liability. As the leader of the presentational team, he had justified doing so in team terms. A team player would have consulted the captain first. Neither of these contributions was calculated to make Mrs Thatcher's life easy on the floor of the House at her regular bi-weekly question times.

Her response to both incidents on the floor of the House has been cited by the conspiracy theorists as evidence of duplicity. A contrast is drawn between her identification of what was good in each contribution and my alleged undermining of each Minister in the lobby room in the loft above. When the circumstances are stripped of journalistic cant, the picture that emerges is that Mrs Thatcher had not much option and that I tried to play down each incident. This is so far from the accepted conspiratorial account as to require some explanation.

First, what was Mrs Thatcher bound to do on the floor of the House, given that the Opposition (not to mention the press) were baying for blood and that she had not sacked Messrs Pym and Biffen? She most certainly was not going to give the Opposition the satisfaction of hearing her criticize her Ministers on the floor of the House. In these circumstances, it does not take a genius to identify the solution. She would seize upon those many aspects of Mr Pym's speech and those (much fewer) of Mr Biffen's broadcast which served her purpose. If she had not sacked them, then she had to support them, even through clenched teeth. I did not have to do anything except support the Prime Minister and the Government – that is, the team. And that was not easy since they were not playing as a team.

Let me conflate the two incidents, four years apart. Picture the lobby, all foregathered, in its afternoon eyrie all scenting trouble. It is not a pretty sight. The lobby in full tally-ho cry after a Minister – which happened roughly once every full moon – never was, though sometimes they could be painfully funny when they almost parodied themselves. Messrs Naughtie and Bevins are both fuming with synthetic indignation. How, they complain, can the Prime Minister put up with Messrs Pym and Biffen when they are so unhappy either with Government policy or the Prime Minister? When Mr Pym, as the Minister responsible for the presentation of Government policy, has set such a pessimistic tone? When Mr

Biffen has been insubordinate? The very authority of Government requires instant explanation and action – that is, sacking. How can you (you being the pronoun for Government) allow this to go on? How can these people be allowed to remain in the Cabinet?

I could, of course, have smiled blandly – always assuming that was within my capabilities – and told them not to be so preposterous. They knew the score. They were not born yesterday. I did all that, without the bland smile. I also tried to play down both incidents as hard as I could. Unfortunately, I did not make much headway through the rough water as the lobby came at me in waves. While they were just about ready to recognize that Mr Pym had expressed some admirable sentiments, his pessimism gave me difficulty. Mr Biffen, while recognized as 'the nearest thing to a Government guru' (The Times), was felt to have gone a bit far, even for him. What was Mrs Thatcher going to do to re-establish her authority? No need to do so, I assured them. The matter was under control. They looked at me as if to say 'Pull the other leg, it's got bells on it.' After repeated – four or five at least – attempts to get me to give ground and to acknowledge that the Prime Minister was considering the future careers of Mr Pym and Mr Biffen (which would have produced the story the lobby wanted: 'Maggie threatens sack'), I became exasperated with this play-acting. I tried to bring some reality to the proceedings by referring to the well-known propensities of Mr Pym as a somewhat gloomy chap and Mr Biffen as a well-known and, often entertaining, commentator upon the political scene from within the Cabinet. Had I left it at that I might have escaped the reputation that was to come. Instead, I expressed myself somewhat colourfully in each case. In the case of Mr Pym I said something like: 'Oh for God's sake come off it, you know as well as I do it's being so cheerful as keeps him going.' And in the case of Mr Biffen I said: 'I really am surprised at you lot. You all know as well as I do that John Biffen is that well-known semi-detached member of the Cabinet.'

Those remarks were interpreted as a fierce attack by Number 10 upon the respective Ministers, whereas they were not intended unkindly and represented an attempt on my part to pass off Ministerial remarks in the most convincing terms. The circumstances in which they came to be made were never reported by journalists.

Members of the public might have imagined that I had deliberately set out to denigrate the Ministers. In fact, my comments were not volunteered. They were dragged out of me. They were neither premeditated nor authorized. They came off the top of my head. Those directed at Mr Pym caused a terrible fuss within Government. A number of senior people, including members of the Government, called for my head. I had fewer problems over Mr Biffen, even though it might be described as my second offence. On each occasion I immediately reported my remarks, and the circumstances in which they had been made, to Mrs Thatcher and expressed my concern about the use that was likely to be made of them by journalists. She recognized that I had been put in a difficult position and made it clear that she would stand by me. Like Lord Whitelaw, she recognized that I occupied just about the most exposed post of any official in the Government service. But the notion that she either explicitly or implicitly licensed me to rubbish Ministers is just that: rubbish.

So, too, is the conspiracy theory that I was hounding each of these Ministers out of Government or heralding their demise. I was doing no such thing. Francis Pym went on to become Foreign Secretary during the Falklands campaign before he left the Government more than a year later after the 1983 general election. Similarly, John Biffen remained in office for a further twelve months before he was dropped after the 1987 general election. It is a profound relief to me as a law-abiding citizen that the sleuths of the communications industry are relatively harmlessly employed in journalism instead of applying their concepts of evidence and logic within Scotland Yard.

Another charge against me is that I gratuitously attacked Norman St John Stevas when he was sacked as Leader of the House in 1981. This came as a considerable surprise to me for two reasons. First, I am not usually accused of attacking Ministers after they have ceased to be a member of the Government because I cannot then be charged with undermining them. Second, it is not among my strongest recollections of Mr Stevas's Ministerial career. I recall much more his leading role in establishing Departmental select committees, his attachment to shocking pink as an office decoration and his coining of a number of witty phrases about the Prime

Minister. I believe he is entitled to claim parentage of 'The blessed Margaret' and 'The Leaderene'. But my strongest memory is of the extent to which I – and, more especially, my deputy, Neville Gaffin – tried to help him in those early years. As Leader of the House, Mr Stevas used to take the Thursday afternoon lobby to discuss first, the progress of Government business and then the Government scene and its policies. He never used a short word where a long one would do, and I recall one member of the lobby asking him what 'exegesis' meant. Mr Stevas effortlessly and elegantly obliged. The problem for Number 10 Press Office was that Mr Stevas often enjoyed himself too much. His problem was not, as some alleged, that he leaked. It was that he sometimes did not get it quite right. Neville Gaffin, who used to attend Mr Stevas's Thursday lobbies, and I found ourselves a little too often having to clear up, as best we could without making too much of an issue of it, after the Lord Mayor's Show.

The lobby loved all this. But they also knew first-hand what my problems were with Mr Stevas. Inevitably those problems were recalled when Mr Stevas left the Cabinet. In the circumstances, the suggestion in the *Daily Telegraph* the following day that 'sources close to her [Mrs Thatcher] were suggesting that he [Mr Stevas] had borne the brunt of concern about open and at times inaccurate portrayals in the press of what had been going on in the Government' were scarcely avoidable. I could not suddenly start denying to Jim Wightman, then the *Daily Telegraph*'s well-informed and dead straight political editor, what from close observation he had long known to be the case. Nor was I going to do so. But there is one thing no one can allege against me in respect of Mr Stevas: that I sought to undermine him in office. On the contrary, both Neville Gaffin and I tried to help him. For performing this task St John christened Neville Gaffin St Neville.

I was relieved after I had retired from the Civil Service to read Robin Oakley, in *The Times*, write that I was 'more sinned against than sinning' in respect of another charge against me. This was that I cruelly left Patrick Jenkin, Secretary of State for the Environment, and Peter Rees, Chief Secretary to the Treasury, 'twisting in the wind' for the whole of the summer of 1985 before they were sacked from the Cabinet in September. Of all the allegations made against me, the claim that I briefed journalists months before the reshuffle that Messrs Jenkin and Rees were to be dropped caused me greatest distress. There is no doubt that both were treated disgracefully if someone actually knew, months ahead of the reshuffle, that they would be asked to go. But the person responsible was neither me nor any of my agents. We neither knew when the reshuffle would be nor who would be involved, even weeks ahead. Had we done so, we would have been mad to speculate, for – apart from anything else – a week is indeed a long time in politics.

I knew little of Mr Rees but I had the highest regard for Patrick Jenkin as a man, having served him as a Minister. I would have done nothing to hurt him and everything to protect him. It was therefore a bruising episode for me. It illustrates one of the problems of a press secretary operating in the highly gossipy and catty political environment who is determined to preserve his credibility. For whatever reason, anyone can start the hare of a Ministerial sacking. A press secretary, by definition, cannot stop it running when he neither knows when the reshuffle will be nor who will be involved. The best he can do is to discourage speculation well ahead of his best estimate of when the Prime Minister will make changes. That is what I did.

For the rest – apart from the charges against me in respect of Michael Heseltine and Sir Geoffrey Howe, which I deal with separately – I spent my time defending Ministers against their own kind. None the less others blamed me. My remarks about Francis Pym and John Biffen lent their blame credibility. Give a dog a bad name . . .

Before I discuss the unfortunate Sir Geoffrey Howe, I must record my surprise that the case of Michael Howard, as Minister of State at the Department of the Environment prior to water privatization, has not been entered upon my charge sheet. To be charitable, this is probably because not even the conspiratorial tendency among the lobby have the gall to list it. The background is that on 15 March 1989 Martin Dowle and a BBC colleague took me to lunch at Beotys. They were particularly interested in water privatization against the background of Mrs Thatcher's having said that the issue had not been well handled. Who, they wanted to know, had she intended to criticize? I could see trouble a mile off. They were not going to get me to criticize Ministers in the Department of the Environment. I told them that Mrs Thatcher was criticizing the Government collectively. No Government could leave the presentation of such an issue to a single Department – as was generally Mrs Thatcher's point in relation to all Government policies. Everyone had to be involved and supportive. Whatever they (repeat they, the BBC's two reporters, for they were trying it on) might feel about Michael Howard's presentational skills, I told them that he was doing a remarkable job (brilliant might have been a better word) in processing the legislation through the Commons.

Three hours later the BBC news was running a story, which had no foundation whatsoever in fact, that the Prime Minister was to take charge of presenting water privatization and was critical of Mr Howard. They even attributed all this to sources close to Number 10 and flashed up some film of me for good measure, just to make sure that no one was in any doubt who the culprit was. Journalist friends rang me to say that I had been 'stitched up'. Not surprisingly, Nicholas Ridley and Michael Howard were very concerned. I had a number of conversations with them that evening. I also had a brisk discussion with Martin Dowle who had told the tale on the BBC's news bulletins. By the time I had finished with him, I think he clearly understood that never again would he have the benefit of my personal briefing. He had blown it with me. Nor did he or his colleague ever have a personal briefing from me subsequently. So far as I was concerned, that kind of journalism left them dead in the water. Those who seek to impugn my integrity have to pay a price, and the more inconvenient that price for them the better. Just before I retired, Mr Dowle tried to get a private word with me in the Commons Press Gallery. I simply waved him away. I operated on the basis that those who thought they could treat me in this disgraceful way would have to whistle for it in the future.

And now to Sir Geoffrey Howe, against whom I am alleged to have done irreparable harm on his assumption of the role of deputy Prime Minister. That is inevitably a matter for dispute after his resignation speech in 1990 which prompted Michael Heseltine's fateful challenge to Mrs Thatcher. It might be argued that all else pales into insignificance. However, let me face the charge. On 24 July 1989 John Major emerged from Mrs Thatcher's study positively dazed. In the corridor I warmly congratulated him on his elevation from Chief Secretary to the Treasury to become Foreign Secretary. His elevation had been somewhat delayed. Sir Geoffrey Howe, the former Foreign Secretary, had had protracted discussions with the Prime Minister and had eventually been given the courtesy title of deputy Prime Minister which had previously been personal to Lord Whitelaw. I congratulated myself the following day on the good reception in the press for the reshuffle. But by 11.15 a.m. all my alarm bells were ringing. At that morning's lobby I had been confronted, mostly by John Cole, BBC, with the most remarkably upbeat account of what Sir Geoffrey Howe's role as deputy Prime Minister would entail. It somewhat enlarged that played by Lord Whitelaw. And no one would ever play a bigger role than Lord Whitelaw did in any Government led by Mrs Thatcher. Sir Geoffrey, I learned from the lobby, was to chair numerous committees. He would also deputize for the Prime Minister when she was abroad. Indeed, to hear the lobby talk, Mrs Thatcher was going out of business.

In spite of this, I did not seek to diminish Sir Geoffrey's role. I sought to explain the job as Lord Whitelaw had done it. (And subsequently, over lunch, I checked with Lord Whitelaw that I had got it right. I had.) I was unable to say which Cabinet committees Sir Geoffrey would chair because the issue had not been decided. I assured the lobby that he would no more deputize for Mrs Thatcher when she was abroad than Lord Whitelaw had done. In these days of modern communications, with Mrs Thatcher in constant touch with Number 10, there was no need for that. I thought it reasonable to assume that if Mrs Thatcher were to undergo an anaesthetic then Sir Geoffrey would assume responsibility for the period that she was incapacitated. But I had to remind the lobby, when it was clear they were investing the post with a grandeur it did not possess, that it had no statutory foundation. It was a courtesy title bestowed at the whim of the Prime Minister herself.

This was not the only problem I had to face that day. When I met the lobby at 4 p.m. I was completely flummoxed by the suggestion that Mrs Thatcher, the previous day, had offered Sir Geoffrey the position of Home Secretary at the possible expense of Douglas

Hurd, who occupied that post. I had no knowledge of this and discounted the idea, only to discover when checking with Number 10 that it might have been so, though no one could be certain because they did not know what had passed in private between Mrs Thatcher and Sir Geoffrey. This disclosure could only have been made by those wishing to damage the Prime Minister, regardless of the wider interests of the Government. It had not been made by Number 10. The effect of this was to leave the reshuffle a wreck. The Prime Minister – and I, it was implied – had botched it. Meanwhile, of course, friends of Geoffrey Howe – to wit, David Howell MP, Patrick Cormack MP and the Fleet Street coterie led by Peter Jenkins (*Independent*) – spent their time on radio and television or in the newspapers attacking the wrong target. Instead of rubbishing me they should have turned on those who had so ridiculously talked up the role of deputy Prime Minister and revealed a private conversation between the Prime Minister and Sir Geoffrey about what post he might fill in the Government.

I used to have a certain fascination with Michael Heseltine as a Minister. This was in no way diminished when I worked fairly closely with him, alongside Neville Taylor, in the Ministry of Defence in 1983 trying – successfully – to win the argument over nuclear defence prior to the deployment of cruise missiles in this country at the end of that year. I decided that, as a Minister with an eye for presentation and for conducting a campaign, he would be a joy to work with. We were on the same wavelength. He was informal, unstuffy and resourceful and he had a built-in – or had probably built in a – corrective to his flamboyance and tendency to go over the top.

The Westland crisis in Government built up slowly. As it did so, it caused incredulity in Government that the fortunes of a company of such modest size could wreak such political devastation. The Government had a clear policy: it was for the company to take decisions about its future in the interests of its shareholders and employees. But, given that the Government was a major customer, its policies and intentions were very relevant to those decisions. It was therefore very important that the company should be in no doubt about the Government's position. Mr Heseltine was determined that Westland should become part of some European consortium. The rest of the Cabinet, in the absence of any viable European consortium, wanted to keep Westland's options open, so allowing the company to link up with the United Technologies Corporation (the American Sikorsky company) and Fiat, if it so chose. That is what eventually occurred.

Consequently, the story of Westlandgate, as the Watergate generation of journalists inevitably described it, is the story of one man's difference with his colleagues. I spent a lot of time in my relations with political correspondents trying to keep the lid on Westland, and as it developed I learned in detail and in depth the pressures that can be exerted on a Chief Press Secretary when Cabinet collective responsibility has broken down and Ministers are at war with each other. I was even involved on Sunday 22 December in trying over the telephone from home to persuade at long distance Leon Brittan, the Minister responsible for the Westland company, at his home in North Yorkshire, and Michael Heseltine in Oxford not to broadcast. My objective, on behalf of the Prime Minister, was to try to persuade both Ministers not to go on air, as arranged. I failed because Mr Brittan had by then recorded his interview and the BBC, having got him on tape, were not surprisingly disposed to use it. And Mr Heseltine was not prepared to remain silent if Mr Brittan was to broadcast.

My first day back from a much interrupted New Year break on 6 January 1986 was a fateful one. Over the previous week-end I had read of yet another initiative by Michael Heseltine in his pursuit of a viable European consortium. This was his letter, which found its way into The Times on the Saturday, to the managing director of Lloyds Merchant Bank. It suggested that Westland might lose work in Europe if it linked up with Sikorsky/Fiat. I learned from Charles Powell during the week-end that Mrs Thatcher was concerned about its accuracy in suggesting that all European governments and all European companies involved in a couple of projects had indicated that Westland's participation in them might be incompatible with a Sikorsky link. Charles told me that the Solicitor-General (Sir Patrick Mayhew) had been asked to look at the text and that he had reservations about its accuracy. The law officer had been called in after the Prime Minister had discovered that Michael Heseltine had not cleared his letter with the DTI and the Solicitor-

General as she had cleared an earlier letter of her own on the subject. After all this, I found a strong feeling in Number 10 and elsewhere in the Government on the Monday morning that we would have to be more robust in defending the Government's line on the need to keep Westland's options open. I conveyed that feeling that morning to Colette Bowe, an administrator without a background in information work who was doing a spell as the head of information at the DTI.

Had I not just been back from holiday and clearing a backlog of work over a salad in my office, Colette Bowe might have had some difficulty in getting in touch with me at around 1.30 p.m. Normally, I would have been lunching with journalists. To my surprise – indeed, my eyebrows shot up – she told me that she had been given Ministerial permission to 'leak' the Solicitor-General's letter to Mr Heseltine claiming that there were 'material inaccuracies' in Mr Heseltine's letter published on the Saturday. Leaving aside Ministerial approval, I expressed grave reservations about the plan to give this information to Chris Moncrieff (PA) and wondered whether the point could not be made public in another way. I was told that the news needed to be in the public domain before a Westland press conference at 4 p.m. And Colette Bowe made it clear to me that the DTI hoped that Number 10 – namely myself – would do the leaking. I refused to do so point blank. I had no authority to disclose the Solicitor-General's letter. I told Colette Bowe that I had to keep the Prime Minister above that sort of thing. At no time was I asked to approve of the disclosure. I could not have done so without seeking Mrs Thatcher's specific permission, and I would not have been prepared to put such an idea to her.

What I ought to have done – and regret to this day that I did not – was advise Colette Bowe, regardless of her Minister's permission, to have nothing to do with the ploy herself. It is on the basis of this failure that the DTI felt able to claim that I – and, indeed, Charles Powell – had accepted that the letter should be disclosed. It was at best tacit acceptance in the sense that I did not actively object to a Ministerial decision to disclose it. Looking back on the entire incident, I can only put my failure to do so down to the extraordinary circumstances created by the breakdown of collective Cabinet responsibility. Although Colette Bowe said that

335

her Minister had cleared the disclosure, unilateral action of this kind was unorthodox, to say the least. It was, however, no more unorthodox than the entirely independent and minority line being vigorously pursued by Mr Heseltine. In the event, the DTI telephoned Chris Moncrieff, disclosing the Solicitor-General's opinion, though it did not release the text of his letter. I did not dissemble when journalists telephoned me when news of the letter broke. I confirmed that I knew of its existence and that it referred to 'material inaccuracies' in Mr Heseltines letter.

Much was subsequently made of my failure to inform Mrs Thatcher about the circumstances. I was in a position to reassure her that she had not been implicated and I did not see it as my responsibility to tell her that one of her Ministers had given permission for the information to be disclosed. Moreover, I began to get early warnings of an inquiry. The more the idea of an inquiry was canvassed, the more Charles Powell and I wanted one. And the more determined we were to say what we had to say to an investigation – and to the investigation alone. Indeed, speaking for myself, the more blackened my character has been by my alleged involvement in this affair the more I wish there had been the police inquiry with which the Attorney-General (Sir Michael Havers) threatened Number 10. Eventually, Sir Robert Armstrong, the Cabinet Secretary, took evidence from me and others. Mrs Thatcher told the Commons on 23 January that Sir Robert, with the full agreement of the Director of Public Prosecutions and senior Treasury counsel, had decided that there was no justification for the institution of proceedings under the Official Secrets Act 'in respect of any of the persons concerned in this matter'. I was never reprimanded. Indeed, throughout I – and Charles Powell – had the strongest support from Mrs Thatcher and Sir Robert who later gave evidence to the Defence Select Committee's inquiry. I and the other official players in this drama did not give evidence. That was because Ministers decided otherwise.

Ten months after these events Adam Raphael, then the *Observer*'s political editor, wrote: ' "You will . . . do as you are . . . well told." With these blunt expletives the Prime Minister's press secretary, Bernard Ingham, touched off the Westland affair. The instructions were directed at his subordinate, the chief information officer at the Department of Trade and Industry, Colette Bowe, whose reluctance to leak the Solicitor-General's letter was the first stumbling block in Mrs Thatcher's campaign to discredit her then Defence Secretary, Michael Heseltine, without leaving any fingerprints.'

I confronted Mr Raphael over this. I told him, as bluntly as I could, that I took the greatest possible exception to his retailing this entirely fabricated tittle-tattle without so much as a reference to me. I said that no doubt the reason he had not checked with me was that he knew I would deny it absolutely, thereby robbing him of a front-page lead. I also read him a lesson on the implications of a Cabinet system of Government. Unfortunately, I said, I was not in a position to order anyone around. If I were, things might be different. I could merely persuade and advise. Hence his suggestion that I spoke to Colette Bowe in those terms was a plain, straightforward lie.

Another sentence in Mr Raphael's story stated: 'Few of the Prime Minister's colleagues are now in any doubt that she inspired the leak of the Solicitor-General's letter in an attempt to bring her errant Defence Secretary to heel.' Well, I hope that they are now in doubt on the basis of my testimony. If there was a conspiracy to leak the Solicitor-General's letter then the conspirators forgot to include me in it. There was no conspiracy. There was no Westlandgate. My brother, speaking from his upland Pennine farm at the height of it all, got it right: 'All you silly bloody lot down there have gone daft.'

Mr Heseltine resigned over the affair. He walked out of Cabinet on Thursday 9 January 1986. I had to dispatch every press officer into Whitehall to try to establish what he had said from reporters telephoning their copy from kiosks. His resignation took us by surprise. Eventually Christine Wall located Chris Moncrieff and got a verbatim account. Mr Brittan was forced out of office as a result of it. I am afraid, however, that the skids were under him long before this. The Parliamentary Conservative party wanted him out for a variety of reasons, most of which were presentational. Mr Kinnock acquired a reputation for failing on the great occasion – the debate on the affair on Monday 27 January. Mrs Thatcher, after jokingly saying, while she was writing her speech, that she might be out of office by 6 p.m. that evening, went on to win her third general election. And I added a reputation for leaking to my many alleged failings. It's a funny old world, as someone once said. On Sunday 26 January 1986, while we were heavily engaged with the Prime Minister in drafting her speech for the Parliamentary debate the following day, Jim Wightman, my friend and political correspondent of the *Daily Telegraph*, asked to see me in Number 10. What on earth, he asked, was going on? Here was I being accused of leaking when in the whole of the five years he had known me he had never had a single leaked document from me. He had never known me to leak anything. Could I please explain? I was a bit inhibited then. Now, Jim has the answer.

In my time I have also been accused of being careless with the currency. This is a rich thing to say of one of a large band of Yorkshiremen who are Scots shorn of all charity. We look after our brass. Moreover, I have spent most of my time in the Government's service trying to safeguard the value of the currency, with a conspicuous lack of success. It was not until Mrs Thatcher came along that someone really meant to do so. Yet it was under Mrs Thatcher that I acquired my reputation for being expensive with the reserves. I assume most commentators – Nigel Lawson's teenage scribblers – are too young to recall November 1967. Very soon after the Government had devalued, Aubrey Jones, chairman of the Prices and Incomes Board, made a lunchtime speech in which he spoke theoretically about a second devaluation. (So late had the text of the speech arrived in the press office that I read it properly for the first time travelling to the event in the back of a car with Mr Jones.) Talking of a further devaluation was an absolutely shocking thing to do – careless talk about the currency was as bad as careless talk about Britain's defences in wartime – and it temporarily knocked the pound for forty points. Some of us later suspected that Mr Jones was in league with Mr Jenkins, the Chancellor, to knock the pound off its parity because it was costing too much of our reserves to keep it on $2.40. However, I learned at a relatively early age that the pound was sensitive to what I did – or did not do in the case of Mr Jones, which would have been to tell him to scrap part of his speech. I was therefore programmed to be careful with the currency. I knew from experience the consequences of a wrong word in this area.

This leads me to my encounter with the Sunday lobby on Friday 11 January 1985. After a rather indecisive increase in interest rates that day, the pound was threatening to fall to parity with the dollar: £1 = $1 (compared with around $1.80 at the time of writing). Seldom outside the European Community or the Commonwealth have I encountered such an hysterical lot of journalists. What, they asked, was the Government going to do about the pound? Soon it was going to be worth no more than $1. Was the Government happy to see it continue to plummet? To find its own level? Or was it going to support it? This was not one of my happiest moments in life. I found this lobby extremely difficult just as Chancellor Nigel Lawson found exasperating another (later) Sunday lobby over social security when his staff tried but failed to make a tape recording of the proceedings. No recording was made of mine, but there is no dispute about the facts.

I vehemently stated that the Government was not going to waste its reserves on supporting the pound. This was true since the Prime Minister had long concluded that trying to fight the markets with reserves was a waste of money and in the end ineffective, though there was always room for some short-term 'smoothing' of currency movements. Whether it was wise to say so was entirely another matter. Denis Healey, in the Committee corridor of the Commons, later rebuked me. Never ever, he said, give the speculators a one-way bet. As a matter of fact, I had not done so. I had confused the issue. Alone that Sunday, the *Observer* had forecast a further increase in interest rates which my briefing could have implied.

Mrs Thatcher was deeply concerned to awake to the BBC news on Sunday morning that the Government did not care about the level of the pound. My briefing had come out very badly. We began to turn it round. But it was not until next day – the Monday – that the Government raised interest rates by another 1.5 per cent.

Of course, I was pilloried in the press by experts such as Sam Brittan, *Financial Times*, who never once approached me for a view. I often marvelled at the ease with which journalists who claimed a certain objectivity and uprightness for their journalism never practised it with me. Mr Brittan was all condescension and intellectual snobbery which are his stock-in-trade. I took it on the chin. I accepted responsibility. I did not blame the media for misreporting. I told the lobby that sooner or later a Chief Press Secretary was going to make a mistake and all I could ask of them was to look at my record of reasonably accurate guidance over the last five years. This went down very well with the lobby. Michael Jones (*Sunday Times*) whom I could have been accused of misleading the previous Friday, and Jim Wightman (*Daily Telegraph*) were particularly supportive. So were Lord Whitelaw and Mrs Thatcher. Indeed, at a lobby party at the House of Commons on Tuesday 15 January, when criticism of me was at its height, she went out of her way to praise me to groups of journalists: 'Bernard's marvellous. Isn't he marvellous? He's great. He's the greatest.' It was very kind of her. I would not exactly have described myself as marvellous or great at that time.

Throughout her years as Prime Minister Mrs Thatcher was dogged by reports that she did not get on with the Queen. These were easy to deal with. I refused, as a matter of principle, to discuss relations between the two of them. Nor was I in any position to do so. Mrs Thatcher disclosed nothing of her relationship with the sovereign. She regarded it as entirely confidential. It was a closed book. Consequently, when the *Sunday Times* on 20 July 1986 threw the book at the Prime Minister over her relations with the Queen I steadfastly refused to say a word. I was tipped off on Saturday lunchtime that the *Sunday Times* would report that the Queen was fed up with Mrs Thatcher's South Africa policy, her uncaring nature, her allowing the Americans to use British bases to bomb Libya a few months earlier, her approach to inner cities; and with an alleged breakdown in consensus within the realm. Andrew Neil, the editor of the *Sunday Times*, was never known to do things by halves on this subject. I tipped off the Prime Minister and the Palace. And only silence emanated from Number 10.

Two years later, however, the Sunday lobby asked me when the Queen would be making a State visit to the Soviet Union. I knew there were no immediate plans but I assumed that it could not be ruled out eventually, provided that reform in the Soviet Union proceeded satisfactorily. Mr Gorbachev had pulled out of Afghanistan. Consequently, I did not reject the idea of a State visit. Nor could I when it was perfectly clear to anyone that under Mr Gorbachev's leadership our relationship with Moscow was warming. (The Princess Royal went there officially in 1990.) Instead, however, of simply saying: 'Not yet a bit', I talked around the subject, pointing up some of the considerations which might have to be weighed – the 'butchering' of the Tsar and his family, admittedly seventy years ago, and the progress of reform and the improvement of human rights. I had no idea what advice the Government might eventually tender to the Queen because I did not know how the circumstances might develop. I could therefore scarcely be accused – as I was by a notably pompous *Daily Telegraph* – of doing so. I also told the Sunday lobby, when I realized from their further questions that they were likely to present my background briefing in that light, that I would regard it as an extremely unfriendly act if they were to do so. They did. There followed one of those brief storms in the life of a Chief Press Secretary in which he is accused of behaving unconstitutionally, revealing the nature of the Prime Minister's advice to the sovereign and generally being disgraceful. And the Sunday lobby went on short rations for a few weeks.

21

Playing It Straight

My relationship with journalists over my years with Mrs Thatcher at Number 10 – and before – rested fundamentally on fair dealing. I tried to treat them as I would have expected to be treated as a journalist. And as a journalist I would not have expected much co-operation or help from someone whom I had not treated fairly. There are many facets to fair dealing in Government-journalism relations. The first absolute requirement on the part of a Chief Press Secretary is to give everyone the same basic service. I believe that I achieved that at Number 10 through the much maligned lobby system. All members of the lobby who wished to attend were given exactly the same raw material on which to work. This included the Communist *Morning Star* whose representative, Mike Ambrose, spoke to me appreciatively of my service after I had retired. Hugh Macpherson, of the Left-wing *Tribune*, also acknowledged this from time to time in his support for the lobby system. Neither Mr Ambrose nor Mr Macpherson was ever likely to have much good to say about Mrs Thatcher's works any more than Alastair Campbell (*Daily Mirror*), with whom I always had a friendly relationship, not solely because we are both fans of Burnley AFC, was programmed to pay her compliments. That is not the point. In a free society journalists are not to be judged when providing a basic service to them by whether they are congenial in print or on the air.

Fairness also extends far beyond looking after national news outlets. It requires the Chief Press Secretary to respect the interests of the huge provincial press which is represented in the lobby. I would also argue that self-interest requires him to look after this substantial and important part of the communications industry. It reaches deep down into the community and is read more exhaustively than the national press. While provincial newspapers lack the resources of what used to be called Fleet Street, they are likely to be more objective – or perhaps less tendentious – in their reporting. I made it my business to see that Number 10 took due account of provincial newspapers. From time to time Mrs Thatcher invited their editors to Number 10 for briefings and drinks.

One way of ensuring fairness in dealing with all concerned – including, I may say, those like the *Guardian*, the *Independent* and the *Scotsman* who wanted to deal with Number 10 on their own terms – was to release information through the news agencies – and notably the Press Association or, usually when abroad, Reuters and Associated Press. In this way everyone receives the news simultaneously. It is, however, necessary to be careful in using this news agency facility not to embarrass journalists, for example, travelling with the Prime Minister. They would not appreciate being chased by their offices in London about information, of which they should have been aware, already running on agency tapes.

Having offered the same basic service, fairness also requires a Chief Press Secretary to help journalists pursuing their own inquiries, perhaps based on an earlier lobby briefing, as impartially as he can. Given the calls upon his time during the day – and night – this in turn requires him to ensure that his staff are properly briefed. And this, from bitter experience, is one of the most difficult things to achieve. Nothing is more calculated to send a press officer screaming up the wall than to discover that his boss has been systematically deploying a line which he would have found invaluable an hour earlier. Similarly, a Chief Press Secretary needs to be kept informed by his staff if he is to be prevented from emitting steam at the ears. Fairness does not, however, run to helping reporters on a subject when it is policy not to do so or to helping those who are either trying to take the mickey out of Number 10 or just being gratuitously awkward. I am not aware that the rules of a free society require Number 10 to connive at its own ridicule. Number 10 Press Office is entitled to make judgements about what best serves the Prime Minister and his or her office. That, in fact, is part of its job.

Playing fair with journalists also means trying to provide accurate information as quickly as is possible in all the circumstances. It does not preclude number 10 Press Office from trying to present that

343

information in the light most favourable to the Government, consistent with its credibility. Again that is what it is there for. It is for journalists to reach their own conclusions on the basis of the totality of their information.

So far as I was concerned, fairness also required me to try to maintain a reasonable balance in allocating interviews with Mrs Thatcher between press, radio and television and, within those headings, between the national, provincial, local and magazine press and between the BBC and commercial broadcasting. It was much more difficult to achieve such a balance in handling the foreign media. But one example of how Mrs Thatcher tried to work it through was her practice when in Washington or New York of giving four interviews on the trot between 7 and 8 a.m. to the four American breakfast television channels – to CBS, ABC, NBC and CNN. These four channels used to convert the elegance of the British Embassy in Washington into a four-cornered studio – a near lethal clutter of lights, mikes, monitors, metal chests and wires. I always breathed a sigh of relief after I had safely conducted Mrs Thatcher, without her tripping up, to each of the four corner stations to spend six minutes on air with each of her dishy interviewers.

Similarly, I tried to play fair with radio and television after the Prime Minister's press conference which she invariably gave at the end of a European, Economic or NATO summit. But the proliferation of broadcasting over the Thatcher years made for indigestion. If I had accepted on Mrs Thatcher's behalf all the requests for interviews on these occasions at least another hour would have been added to her working day. Ideally, I would have liked Mrs Thatcher to give interviews only to BBC radio and television, IRN and ITN. Saying the same thing in slightly different ways four times over is enough for any Prime Minister, even if it might be to her advantage. But the BBC World Service could not always be ignored. Nor could TV-am or Sky Television, both of which Mrs Thatcher wanted to help and encourage as further competition for the BBC and as examples of entrepreneurial developments during her time in office. There was also usually a good case for giving Channel 4 an interview because of the quality of this news programme. And BBC TV 'Newsnight' would always have liked to have had more of her. This catalogue of interest does not take account of foreign broadcasters who often tried their luck with a bid. I attempted to hold down the number of interviews on these occasions to six. Fortunately, Mrs Thatcher regarded them as a challenge to be overcome rather than a chore – except when cameras or microphones did not work or the lights went pop.

One of my worst television moments was during the Prime Minister's visit to Moscow in 1987 when she took on – and vanquished – three Soviet interviewers to the delight of the Russian people. We had successfully negotiated with the Soviet Government that Mrs Thatcher's interview would go out as recorded without any editing. For the British journalists this was a point of honour and the Russians' failure to broadcast it in full would have marred the visit. Unfortunately, we had not agreed on the length of the interview. When I arrived at the studio I was unable to establish when it would be broadcast, except that it would be that night, or which slot in the programme it would fill. The Soviet television authorities were extremely relaxed about the length and, with much shrugging of shoulders, as if it did not really matter, agreed with me on a forty-minute interview. I accordingly informed Mrs Thatcher what to expect. She made herself up – no make-up girls here – and then entered a studio full of not very comfortable utility furniture. The floor manager, as a concession to her, suddenly produced a huge bouquet of red roses and stuffed them unceremoniously into a large vase which someone then knocked over.

As water from the vase steadily spread over the floor and wires, threatening everyone, I feared, with electrocution, the interview got underway. The old pro had a wonderful time, but with a good thirty-five minutes gone her interviewers had got nowhere near the personal stuff, about how a wife and mother copes with being a Prime Minister etc, which I had been assured every Russian woman wanted to know. They were still stuck on arms control and SDI and Soviet star wars systems of which the Soviet people had probably been blissfully ignorant until then, and as they would remain if the programme were not broadcast. But would it make the air? I asked myself, as forty and then forty-five minutes went by, with everyone chattering away merrily, especially Mrs Thatcher. I began to make circular motions to the floor manager with my hand, hoping that this was the international television wind-up sign and that he would heed it. With the clock ticking away, I enlisted the aid of the British Embassy's Russian-speaking information officer, Donald MacLaren, The MacLaren of MacLaren, who ducked and weaved his way under cameras to get the message home. The interview was brought to a close after nearly fifty-five minutes. It was broadcast that evening uncut. The audience loved it, I was told. I had wrongly assumed that Russian television was burdened with unbreakable schedules. I concluded that I was excessively modest about my Prime Minister.

Another token of my fair-play approach was to arrange interviews for Mrs Thatcher well in advance of the event. There was not much last-minute wheeling in of the broadcasters or the lobby for hastily arranged interviews under Mrs Thatcher's premiership. Nor was there much cancellation of previously arranged interviews. Only one stands out in my mind: the cancellation, just before Mrs Thatcher made her first visit to Hungary in February 1984, of an interview with John Cole, BBC. This was because she was up to her neck in work and briefing and she was worried sick for her son, Mark, who was under attack again by a Sunday newspaper: this time, the *Observer*. I called it off because her mind was just not on it.

Serving journalists unknown either to myself or my colleagues presented more difficult problems. By and large, journalism is not a profession which invites trust. The journalist regularly comes bottom with the politician in the league table of public esteem in which occupations are held. With the best will in the world, press officers, being human, are unlikely to take too many risks with unknown quantities. It is bad enough taking risks to try to help friends or acquaintances, as I once did for Paul Barker, a former pupil of Hebden Bridge Grammar School, who wanted Mark Lawson, their television critic, to write a profile of me for *The Independent* magazine. First Mr Barker, husband of my first editor's granddaughter, sent a teenage photographer whose sole purpose so far as I could see was to twist me into the most unnatural and painful pose so that he could return to base with a leering Ingham playing Richard III. Then the bearded hulk who answered to the name Lawson arrived at the door of Number 10 dressed as if reporting for an expedition to the Pamirs. He wore an anorak and boots and carried a rucksack and his shirt was open virtually to the navel, exhibiting his beary chest. I do not know whom this statement was intended to impress but it can't have been me.

Three other aspects of fairness need to be discussed: leaks, embargoes and 'pooling' arrangements. A Chief Press Secretary would not last eleven years if he made a habit of leaking – that is indulging in 'unauthorized disclosures of information'. Neither politicians nor Civil Service would permit it. In my time he would either have been sacked or charged before the courts. Leaking is, almost by definition, the selective use of individuals for the leaker's own purposes. In other words, as I used to put it to the lobby: 'Someone is using you'. Many journalists are, of course, happy to be used. They are in the business of stories. Editors love leaks, especially when they think they can pillory the Government with them, and give inordinate space to them. It is a well-worn joke within Government that the quickest route to the most publicity on the most boring issue of the day is to leave a document about it marked 'Secret' in a Commons photocopying machine. It follows that leaking involves a degree of favouritism and, on that account alone, a Chief Press Secretary who made a habit of it would soon rouse the ire of the lobby. That was exactly the reaction of the lobby when, in the early days, I conceived the idea of Mrs Thatcher briefing small pre-arranged groups of political editors so that they could have a fuller discussion with her than was possible with the lobby as a whole. This was immediately seen as a revival of the 'white Commonwealth' – a privileged group which existed in Harold Wilson's day. This horse fell at the first hurdle and I never tried to run it again.

Chief Press Secretaries are, however, perceived to be in the business of leaks if only because they spend their time talking to journalists. Even some civil servants believe that no sooner has a press officer been given some information than he picks up a telephone and rings a journalist. In my experience press officers are infinitely more secure than many Ministers and senior civil servants. None the less, members of the Government Information Service (GIS), at the sharp end of relations with journalists, have to meet the charge that they are 'licensed to leak', as I ironically put it in lectures. (I also added, for the sake of the completeness – and to demonstrate that I was poking fun at critics – that leaking 'can be a comfort at times'.)

At an Independent Broadcasting Authority consultation with the GIS on 28 October 1981, I commented:

> '. . . I must tell you that I – and I am sure my colleagues – have never regarded the Official Secrets Act as a constraint on my operations. Indeed, I regard myself as licensed to break the law as and when I judge necessary; and I suppose it is necessary to break it every other minute of every working day, though I confess the issue is so academic that I have not bothered to seek counsel's advice.'

This was an attempt to bring out the difference between briefing on the options and choices facing Ministers and the background to policies and 'leaking' classified documents or briefing orally on information which the Government intended should remain confidential. It also sought to underline the fact that all Departmental heads of information have to decide on the spot how far they can go in briefing, recognizing they will be judged by their Minister and Permanent Secretary after the event. And if it was technically an offence under the old Official Secrets Act even to disclose, without prior authorization, what the Prime Minister had had for lunch or the level of paper clip stocks in the Department then heads of information had perforce to be licensed to 'leak' if they were to do their job. But we had a pretty clear idea of what would and would not be authorized. And we were not in the business of leaks – 'unauthorized disclosures'. We played fair.

Embargoes are a system by which Government Departments allow members of the lobby and some other groups of journalists copies of documents – reports, White or Green Papers or whatever colour of book served the Government's purpose – in advance of the time of official publication so that they can prepare their reports for immediate release. The system is intended primarily to help journalists to prepare more considered reports and comment. The balance of advantage for the Government is much finer, especially if journalists abuse the embargo by showing copies in advance of publication to interested parties and make their destructive re-action, and not the point of the report, their main story. Any value to the Government virtually disappears overnight when the BBC 'Today' programme, for example, wheels in members of the Opposition to comment on a report, allegedly on the basis of speculation but presumably on the basis of information derived from the embargoed copies in its possession. The abuse got so bad in my time that I was once handed an extreme example: a firm in the City circulating to its clients photocopies of the weighty advance lobby briefing on the Queen's Speech – the Government's legislative programme – drawing attention to the Government's own embargo on the material! As a result journalists ensured that embargoes, which were intended to help them, were severely curtailed during the 1980s.

'Pooling' – agreement on a small group of press, radio and television reporters, television cameramen and still photographers, with privileged access or location, who will make all their material generally available – is another example of where the Government seeks to help journalists, and especially photographers, on a fair basis. With the proliferation of news outlets and the attendance at events these days of armies of cameramen, soundmen with their curious little furry creatures at the end of long poles, photographers and radio reporters with their indelicately intrusive sticks of microphones, pooling is essential. Without a pool – or a central microphone – no one would properly hear Mrs Thatcher say anything. She would be prevented by cameramen from meeting members of the public and cameramen would prevent each other from getting a decent picture. Chaos would ensue – as indeed it did in the military cemetery at Scutari where, it was rumoured, the purpose of gross overmanning by Turkish newspapers was to prevent the opposition from getting a good photograph! Yes, while pooling is essential in the media's own interests, pools satisfy only those chosen to join them. Understandably, every outlet wishes to have its own staffman in the most advantageous position. But the numbers turning up for events are now completely out of hand. Number 10 placed the onus for nominating pools on the various representative media organizations, on the understanding that if agreement were not reached a pool would be imposed. What could be fairer in the most difficult circumstances than an equitable sharing of the pool's reportage and pictures? Who would be a Chief Press Secretary?

In spite of all these trials my relationship with journalists was continuing and mostly lasting. But I did sometimes reach meltdown. What on earth can you do when even such an experienced foreign correspondent as Ian Murray (*The Times*) fails – if that was what he did – to recognize irony at five yards? The occasion was a most fractious European Council in Milan in 1985. Relationships were getting very frayed among statesmen – and stateswomen – and there was a popular impression abroad in the press tent that someone was for an early handbagging. Reporters asked me what Mrs Thatcher felt about it all. With masterly understatement, I said that she was not best pleased. A smile of satisfaction suffused the collective face of the assembled corps who allowed Mrs Thatcher only one emotion: fury. And it was at this point that I lapsed into irony, which is clearly a most dangerous game. 'Ah ha,' I cried. 'I know what you lot will be writing tomorrow. This time Mrs Thatcher won't just be furious. Nor livid. Nor incandescent. Nor even volcanic with rage. This time she'll be positively erupting. Krakatoan on the Richter scale.' And that was how the aforesaid Mr Murray, quoting sources close to the Prime Minister, portrayed Mrs Thatcher's humour. Mr Heath promptly went on the air and called for my dismissal. And soon afterwards an indignant seismologist wrote to me. 'Ingham,' he said, 'a man in your position should know better. Volcanic eruptions do not register on the Richter Scale.'

Both before and after this, my relationship with journalists did not rest upon a false amity, an anything-for-a-quiet-life philosophy, a chronic inclination to turn the other cheek, an ability to soak up punishment quietly or a willingness to put up with taunting and other provocations. I operated on the basis of mutual respect. If it were not forthcoming the consequences could be explosive, especially when members of my staff had been subjected to abuse from journalists. If my guiding philosophy was fair dealing, I was determined that I was going to have a measure of it in return. This earned me the reputation for being a thug – an accolade bestowed upon me by no less an authority than Lord Bill Deedes, ex-editor of the *Daily Telegraph* and formerly a Minister with responsibilities for co-ordinating the presentation of Government policy. Lord Deedes has never to my knowledge attended any briefing I have given. Had he made a habit of doing so, he might have discovered the kind of thuggery practised by his own kind. I can, however, assure him that the British lobby has a long way to go before it subjects the Chief Press Secretary to the mindless disrespect and abuse handed out by the White House Press Corps on the two occasions I have sat in on press secretary briefings in Washington. One reason for this is probably the excellent British practice by which the lobby invites the Chief Press Secretary to brief them, with its chairman technically, if not actually, presiding.

I find it curious that no one has suggested over the last eleven years that I was temperamentally unsuited to the job of Chief Press Secretary. Not even my severest critics – those who would kill the messenger on sight if they thought they could get away with it – have advanced that theory. Yet there is at least a case to be made that no one with my temper (which is as quick down as it is up) and robust approach to the would-be bullies of this world should never be allowed within a mile of Number 10 – except, perhaps, to represent that similarly straightforward person, Mrs Thatcher. On the other hand, one advantage flows from having my sort there: those with red blood in their veins, as distinct from pale diplomatic wetness, know where they stand.

Contrary to rumour I did not devote my time to having rows with journalists or to complaining to editors or to the BBC, ITN or IRN. That would have been far too wearing because when I had a row – a real row – I meant to have one. I also meant it to be felt. Nor did I waste my credibility on artificial eruptions or complaints for the sake of appearing to be virile. I did not argue over matters of opinion – unless those opinions were formulated on the basis of wrong information. I dealt in fact. If the facts were wrong, I – or others at my prompting – tried to get them corrected. I did not rush to a telephone or to write a letter just because the Prime Minister happened to blow a fuse over something she had read or heard. I called for a text or a transcript. Sometimes, I must confess, I did absolutely nothing if I thought she was wrong. If she pressed me for action in these circumstances, I used to tell her there was no case and backed up my point with evidence.

It is, of course, conceivable that Mrs Thatcher's political friends took up complaints on her behalf. Norman Tebbit, as chairman of the Conservative Party, complained to the BBC about Kate Adie's reporting from an F-111-damaged Libya in 1986. I distanced the Government from that and personally believed that a stronger case could have been made against the BBC over its treatment of sanctions against South Africa in the run-up to the special Commonwealth Conference a few months later. I have very little impression of the extent, and still less the effect, of interventions with editors, whether sanctioned or otherwise, by Tim Bell and Gordon Reece, both her political friends. Apart from their apparent advocacy from time to time of American presidential-style press conferences during Parliamentary recesses, which I considered would appear transplanted and artificial, I recall only one occasion when, against my better judgement, one or other of them persuaded Mrs Thatcher to go on the Michael Aspel chat show – with Barry Manilow, as it turned out. Too many chat show appearances, I feared, could cheapen the office of Prime Minister. There was, however, more substance than I had expected to the show and Mrs Thatcher gave a sparkling performance. I think there was inevitably a latent tension between Messrs Bell and Reece and myself because they are much deeper into show biz than I will ever be, appearing in the gossip columns, with the inevitable references to their 'close relationship' with the greatest living English stateswoman.

I started from the proposition that political editors – the most senior lobby correspondents – would hold it against me if I spent my time talking to their editors behind their backs. Consequently, I channelled virtually all my dealings with press, radio and television through political editors, apart from my exchanges over lunches or dinners with their editors whom I did not burden with minor complaints. I believe that the BBC, ITN and IRN would agree that Mrs Thatcher's eleven years were among the quietest they have known for complaints, carping and general aggravation. This is an inconvenient fact for that element in the communications industry which believes that she sought to manipulate, damage or even destroy the free expression of opinion. The truth is that she was not much interested in what they said, except when she happened to hear it early in the morning listening to the BBC World Service and the BBC's 'Today' programme. For the rest her viewing and listening were random. I am pleased to report that the Thatcher Government did not make a profession out of complaining to editors. It seldom does much good unless the case is firmly rooted in facts, as distinct from opinions or emotions.

My relationship with the broadcasters is a repudiation of the conspiracy theorists. I did not, as Tam Dalyell MP claimed, put the Special Branch of the police into the BBC's headquarters in Glasgow over the Zircon affair – a BBC programme about a secret Government satellite communications project. I suspect that I have a singular lack of influence over Her Majesty's Constabulary. I have never put it to the test. I am just grateful that they have got me safely through life this far. If ever I have been fortunate in an enemy it is in Mr Dalyell whose capacity for believing anything bad about me is exceeded only by his readiness to suspend his critical judgement about any information supplied to him about me if it serves his purpose. In short, Mr Dalyell will believe anything if it accords with his prejudices. Is this, I wonder, the definition of a dangerously happy man?

So far as the BBC is concerned, I faced the fact that they were the most awkward organization I was ever likely to deal with. This was because they relied on Government for their income – or for increases in that income through the licence fee. Mrs Thatcher described the fee as a compulsory levy on the individual, enforced by criminal sanction. It is not the best foundation for Government–BBC relations. It is guaranteed to cause difficulty of the kind I encountered in the Department of Energy when the Government had a majority shareholding in British Petroleum. Both organizations – the BBC and BP – were determined to demonstrate their independence of Government. There was a built-in tension between the Government and the BBC which could only be dissolved by a new method of financing – and the BBC were very attached to their licence fee. They were also an extremely arrogant organization until Duke Hussey (chairman of the board of governors) and John Birt (deputy director general) came along. The BBC was encouraged in that arrogance, in a sense, because politicians expected a great deal of it, probably more than it was capable of delivering. In turn, I feared that every suggestion by the likes of me to the BBC would become a criticism or interference, every criticism a provocation and every complaint an incident. It came as no surprise to me to discover that my piece of banter at a BBC

353

lunch with Alasdair Milne, former Director-General, was taken at face value. When the assembled BBC company moaned about the inadequate financing – as if they were entitled to unlimited amounts of public money – I stirringly told them to take advertising on Radios 1 and 2, and not to argue. Anyone but the blindly prejudiced or hypersensitive at the lunch could see that I was just stoking them up.

I observed relations with the BBC under both Labour and Conservative Governments. I never knew either party in office to be entirely happy with what it saw and heard on BBC programmes. That, however, is not necessarily a justification of the BBC, as it claims. It could just as easily mean that both complexions of Government were entitled to complain. For my part I believe that the BBC is not so much Left or Right-Wing as anti-government. It feels that it has to challenge authority of whatever political colour. Under the Conservatives, where my observations were closest, two elements of the BBC's output gave most offence. One was the 'Today' programme, which arguably commanded the largest Governmental audience of any BBC programme. Most damage to Government–BBC relations was done between 6.30 and 9 a.m. by my former *Guardian* colleague, Brian Redhead. I have no idea who he voted for in general elections. Nor do I care. To me his politics are neither here nor there. What matters, in this context, is what he says. For example, he once called me 'a conspiracy'. From then on I was. His failure to apologize meant that he never got another interview with Mrs Thatcher as Prime Minister. The 'Today' programme also caused problems by its ill-considered output. It ran a 'mini-saga' competition in 1987–8 and on Thursday 14 January 1988 – immediately before Mrs Thatcher's question time in the House – it broadcast the following offering entitled 'Thatcherism, the final solution' by a London listener:

'Ingenious. Individual choice must be paramount. With growing confidence she legalized hard drugs. Prices fell sharply. Legitimate outlets replaced bankrupt drug syndicates. Crime figures plunged. Crematorium shares surged. City populations thinned as the weak-spirited succumbed. Unemployment vanished. Only the worthiest survived. Nobody could complain. The unfit died of freedom.'

354

Only a sick mind could sanction such a broadcast. No one needed to be a Tory to be revolted by it. Yet the 'Today' programme broadcast it. No wonder some politicians take a dim view of the BBC. However, the main irritant in relations between Governments and television – and not merely BBC television – has for long been current affairs programmes, whether, for example, Granada's 'World in Action', Thames's 'This Week' or the BBC's 'Panorama' programmes. With their record, one might assume that they have a more tender mercy for the sinner than the sinned against; for the criminal rather than the victim; and for the terrorist rather than the dead and bereaved. They seldom appear to be on the side of the forces of law and order. The courts, one fears, are unlikely ever to carry, only to miscarry, justice. One feels that no sooner has someone else gone down for a most heinous offence than someone in television will be trying to get him out of gaol. One might even assume that Governments and individual politicians are crooked – and certainly never capable of getting it right. This was inevitably the genre which produced 'Death on the Rock', a classic television account of how three IRA terrorists who were plotting carnage in Gibraltar might have come by their deaths there at the hands of the security forces. Current affairs television is calculated to encourage the viewer to believe that there is something rotten in the state of Denmark. Why?

There are two reasons. One was best illustrated by my conversation at a lunch with the programme makers rather than the management of Thames TV. David Elstein, Jonathan Dimbleby, Margaret Jay and Roger Bolton (the last – later – of 'Death on the Rock' fame) were gathered with others. They went on a lot about their responsibilities to society, the nation, their viewers, the truth. I found it nauseating. In the end I had had enough before the soup. I told them to stop being so bloody pretentious and precious and admit they were in television for only one thing: ratings, their audience pulling power, their entertainment value. (Displaying more tact than I am given credit for, I did not add their fat salaries to the list.) To their credit, I was able to eat a hearty lunch. And Thames TV, like the rest, continued to produce programmes which challenged authority because agreeing with it makes for boring television. And yet these saintly people, living off the fat of the land, try to kid you they are guardians of the common weal! They would not recognize anything common at five yards.

The second reason is that current affairs television and a certain sector of 'quality' newspaper journalism attract the kind of journalist who is never content to report what he finds going on around him; only those who have a highly developed suspicion, if not conviction, that what must be going on around them is bad and must be exposed. As Brian Walden wrote in the *Sunday Times*: 'I can tell of a generation of journalists who have Watergate on their brain, and think they could be the next Carl Bernstein, if only they were encouraged to betray every confidence, violate everybody's privacy and read every top-secret document.' They want to change the world and for them the means justify the end. As a result, they will cheerfully falsify the account by the selective use of facts while, at the same time, accusing the Government of sundry malpractices.

When I retired from the Civil Service, I knew of no Departmental head of information in Her Majesty's Government who would trust current affairs television producers any further than he or she could throw them. It was impossible to have confidence in any agreement reached with them. It was expected that when they broke such agreements they would try to finesse their way out of it. Current affairs television in Britain is in a most unhealthy state. But so is that similar and inter-active clique in newspaper journalism. Each scratches the other's back and confirms the other in its effortless superiority of intelligence and morality. This is the real corruption which Peter Jenkins has diagnosed in the British press. Never look for merit in British media awards: only look for the official-back-side-booting which the nominees have indulged in. There is only one qualification for a media award these days: the undermining of elected authority. Never was there a greater give-away than the front page of the *Independent* on 22 February 1991. 'Anthony Bevins', it recorded, 'political editor of the *Independent*, yesterday won the Political Reporter of the Year award presented by Granada Television's "What the Papers Say". His output of "intelligent and informed speculation" (sic) during last autumn's Conservative leadership race stood out, the judges said.' No wonder Granada tried – and failed – to get me to present these awards. They are in the business of entertainment. I am not a prostitute.

My relations with ITN (and, though with much less frequency, IRN) were much easier. I got on extremely well with Sir David Nicholas (and before him as chairman Lord Buxton and George Russell), Sir Alastair Burnet and Sue Tinson. The reason for this easier relationship was primarily that they financed themselves either directly or indirectly through advertising. This is not to suggest that they were never looking for an easier financial regime or that their reporters and programmes were a model of journalistic perfection in the eyes of the Government. I could retail some extremely lively exchanges with commercial radio and television. But the fact is that, until Sky TV brought its potential – yet to be realized in terms of homes taking it – to the television screen, ITN and IRN represented the only national competition to the BBC as a news organization. I became extremely concerned, after consultation with David Nicholas and Alastair Burnet, that the effect of the review of broadcasting during the late 1980s would be to ensure the BBC's future on the basis of the licence fee but to generate great uncertainty about ITN's prospects. Accordingly, I moved heaven and earth to safeguard for a period the position of ITN as the alternative national and international television news channel in the United Kingdom. I believe that I succeeded.

By comparison with television current affairs programmes, my relations with newspaper political reporters and others were sweetness and light. They were also remarkable in the sense that my journalistic career had been spent at the 'quality' end of journalism. Yet I formed at least as many good friends among the lobby correspondents representing 'popular' tabloid newspapers as I did among the qualities. The cynics would say that this was because all the tabloids apart from the *Daily Mirror* – the *Daily Star, Sun, Express, Mail* and, uncertainly, *Today* – supported Mrs Thatcher. In the end what mattered was not whether a newspaper backed the Government but the personality of its correspondents. When I retired I had a long list (approaching twenty) of journalists who were still trying to take me to lunch, and many were from 'popular' newspapers. My friends among these newspapers were refreshingly free of pretence. They exhibited an enthusiasm for life and stories. They had no ambition to change the face of the earth; just a healthy earthiness and a needle-sharp appreciation of the story possibilities in a particular situation. And they did not spend their time trying to impress me. They were journalists without need to justify themselves and not campaigners in league with all kinds of pressure groups. I could do business with them.

I find the list of lobby chairmen during my eleven years in Number 10 provides one of the more fascinating insights into relations between political correspondents and Number 10. They were:

1978–9: George Clark (*The Times*)
1979–80: Richard Evans (*Financial Times*)
1980–1: Gordon Jackson (Thomson Regional Newspapers)
1981–2: David Rose (*Liverpool Daily Post*)
1982–3: Jack Warden (*Daily Express*)
1983–4: John Desborough (*Daily Mirror*)
1984–5: Glyn Mathias (ITN)
1985–6: Chris Moncrieff (Press Association)
1986–7: Julia Langdon (*Daily Mirror*)
1987–8: George Jones (*Daily Telegraph*)
1988–9: Geoffrey Parkhouse (*Glasgow Herald*)
1989–90: Robin Oakley (*The Times*)
1990–1: Trevor Kavanagh (*Sun*).

I had a proper, sensible and constructive relationship with all of them. Having been elected, they also had the confidence of their membership. When Mrs Thatcher resigned, and I retired, Trevor Kavanagh, as the lobby chairman who went off to cover the Gulf War, wrote this unsolicited testimonial to *The Times*:

'The vast majority of the 226 accredited lobby journalists at Westminster will agree with the warm sentiments expressed by Robin Oakley towards Bernard Ingham (article, December 3).

'Very few of us recognise the image of Mrs Thatcher's former Chief Press Secretary as the manipulative character portrayed by Robert Harris in his book *Good and Faithful Servant*.

'Sadly, there is a danger that this version will enter the record as the definitive account of Mr Ingham's 11 years as "sources close to the Prime Minister".

'I believe it is important to understand that Mr Ingham's

first duty was towards the Prime Minister and not the media. That was certainly the basis on which we treated his briefings. There were times when he could not in all conscience tell us the whole truth. But I believe I speak for my colleagues when I say that he was unfailingly straight, honest and fair. More senior members of the lobby with experience of earlier Downing Street press secretaries rate him as the best.'

I much appreciated Trevor Kavanagh's letter at a difficult time. It kills, I hope, any idea that Mrs Thatcher's Chief Press Secretary's performance was out of character with her conduct as Prime Minister. Straightforward and fair were the principles which guided her, often to the exclusion of her reputation and advantage. I sought to reflect them, not necessarily to my advantage either, in my dealings with reporters. There were relatively few complaints on that score – either at home or abroad. The United Kingdom could always command a press briefing audience at international summits.

22

'Separatitis'

The longer I continued as the Prime Minister's Chief Press Secretary the more I was invited to broadcast and asked to speak or perform .on various platforms. I was highly selective and turned down virtually all invitations from broadcasters. I had no intention of becoming a media plaything. Unfortunately, in the eyes of programme makers I had become a hot property – controversial, menacing, dissolute, unconstitutional and criminal, to hear some people talk. This was entirely understandable because I was rich in the right kind of enemies, who sang like canaries about my alleged failings. As a Yorkshireman who knows how to weigh the value of notoriety in sterling, I would formally like to thank all those who have contributed to my commercial potential in retirement.

The following is an inadequate and incomplete record of those who have created a bull market in Ingham futures:

'The eyebrows could win Crufts and his hair, the colour of an orange left too long in the bowl, is as thick as the jowls which give him the appearance of disapproval even ... when he doesn't feel it' (*Daily Telegraph*, 9 February 1990).

'He is large and craggy and rather loopy-looking, like one of the background soldiers who used to be employed on Dad's Army ... such a colourful cove – his hair is a peculiar red, like a carrot with anaemia' (Craig Brown, *The Times*, 10 May 1988).

'An omnipotent ogre ruling over us all with a malignant eye' (*Scotsman*, 23 November 1990).

'... Mrs Thatcher's personal Rottweiler' (Tom Condon, *Scotland on Sunday*, 25 November 1990).

'Purveyor of half truths' (*Daily Telegraph*, 9 February 1990).

'. . . her vicar on earth' (Colin Welch, *Daily Mail*).

'Labour MPs call him "the real deputy Prime Minister"'
(*Daily Telegraph*, 9 February 1990).

'. . . in the Burke and Hare mould, a man not averse to drum-
ming up trade and running a small sideline in assassination to
help him through liquidity problems in his basement establishment in Downing Street' (Edward Pearce, *Daily Express*, 25
October 1989).

'The Iago of Downing Street . . .' (Martin Linton and Paul
Nettleton, *Guardian*, 1989).

'A political ruffian' (Tam Dalyell MP, 17 April 1985).

'One would begin to imagine that we have in Mr Bernard
Ingham some sort of rough-spoken Yorkshire Rasputin who
is manipulating Government and corroding the standards of
public morality' (John Biffen, House of Commons, 8 February
1983).

'He is not the sewage, only the sewer' (John Biffen, January/
February 1989).

These – and many other testimonials to my extraordinary character
– tell the reader more about journalists and politicians than they
do about me. They also demonstrate why, like pianists and never
composers, messengers get shot. They are so much easier to get at.
As a result of the natural human tendency to kill the messenger if
they do not like the message, I have been shot so many times that
John Biffen's sewer is now lead lined.

One of the problems, as Paul Johnson, the author and writer, has
observed, is that journalists are extraordinarily sensitive to criticism.
They are notoriously good at dishing it out and outstandingly bad
at taking it. The same might be said of some politicians. I fought
shy of recording my views about journalism for three and a half
years after becoming Chief Press Secretary until I felt I was running
out of excuses. I also felt that I might be running out of time as an
election was looming. And when Mrs Thatcher entered the 1983
election I told her that she should not hesitate to recruit someone
else if she thought it would serve her purpose. (I did exactly the
same again before the 1987 election and, again, Mrs Thatcher asked

me to stay on. Each time I had no excuse for leaving, assuming that I had wanted to do so: I had had a Civil Service medical and been pronounced fit.)

Early in May 1983, I was invited, along with Michael Shea, the Queen's Press Secretary, to address the bi-annual meeting in Cardiff of the Guild of British Newspaper Editors, which is dominated by provincial rather than national editors. In Cardiff I set the pattern of my relatively mild, constructive and good-humoured criticism of British journalism which continues to this day, subject to variations on the overall theme. I developed these criticisms through half a dozen public – and published – speeches over the next seven years, which is not exactly to demonstrate a fondness for lecturing. For me, the most important point I made in Cardiff was that journalists should have regard to their responsibilities to society rather than constantly harp upon their rights. I followed this up with a talk to the International Press Institute (IPI) at the Caledonian Club on 14 March 1985 in which I felt it necessary, in view of journalism's well-developed sensitivities, to declare my 'interest in journalism as an honourable, necessary, and useful profession'. My concern to have a better rather than worse journalism shone through the entire argument. I will quote but one passage from this talk:

> 'It has often been a source of wonder to me that the Consumers' Association has not done a "Best Buy" on Fleet Street, the provincial press and, indeed, the local press. I wish it would. It would be nice to have a check of some kind on the accuracy of prediction and advice which the press serves up daily. Perhaps not the least of the beneficial effects of a *Which?* survey would be the end of those useless, poverty-stricken intros which say such and such may or could happen. Rather as pigs might fly. Why do editors tolerate them?'

I was working up to a talk to the Media Society in the Café Royal in November 1985 in which I identified five journalists' diseases. These so took the eye of Russell Twisk, then editor of *The Listener*, that he printed the main passage the following week. It read:

> 'First, the conviction that government is inevitably, irrevocably and chronically up to no good, not to be trusted and

conspiratorial. This is known as the "le Carré syndrome" and so sours and contaminates the judgement of otherwise competent journalists as to render them pathetically negative, inaccurate and unreliable. In this context, Watergate has a lot to answer for here – and across the world.

'Second, we have the condition known as "le Carré's Conan Doyle complication". This carries deduction to such excess that two and two become twenty-two because there must be a catch in four. Never go for the simple explanation when an elaborate theory can be constructed. After all, it reads better . . .

'Third, we have "columnar pox", a social contagion particularly affecting diarists, which arises from intercourse with what Alan Watkins, of *The Observer*, would call "the chattering classes". In its mild form it is seen as a wilful refusal to check any fact lest a paragraph is lost to truth. In its more degenerative, tertiary stage, it leads on to writs whose curative effects are somewhat reduced either by the sheer cost of pursuing them to court or the supposed value to the newspaper's circulation of the offending material.

'Fourth, there is the "Coleman or Carpenter phenomenon", with my profound apologies to these blameless sports commentators. This is the condition which produces in reporters an inability to report just the facts: only their own commentary on those facts will do. This interpretation usually makes for a better story when the le Carré, Conan Doyle and columnar viruses are already at work in the journalistic bloodstream . . .

'I could go on drawing from *Black's Compendium of Journalists' Diseases*. Time – and a soft, sad heart – prevent me. Except to add one which grieves me more than most, brought up as I was on a local weekly paper – an organic, responsive and responsible part of a small West Riding town. It is what I call "separatitis". This has nothing to do with Greta Garbo's wanting to be alone. After all, journalists are as gregarious as deer. It has everything to do with the belief of far too many journalists that they somehow lead, and should develop, a separate existence from the society in which they live. It is an illness of democracy – a kind of professional apartheid – which persuades journalists that they only have rights, not responsibilities; that whatever they do is sanctified by the blessed state of freedom which they enjoy, untrammelled by any thought for the consequences of their actions for their fellow men; that they can – and should – pursue their craft on a separate privileged plane.

'John Donne wrote: "No man is an island, entire of itself". He also wrote: "Any man's death diminishes me, because I am involved in mankind. And therefore never send to know for whom the bell tolls; it tolls for thee".

'If only British journalism', I concluded, 'would catch Donne's disease. How much healthier it would be.'

Donald Trelford, editor of the *Observer*, expressed a particularly warm and gracious vote of thanks to me after this speech. Journalist friends told me they thought there was a lot in the criticism. Former journalists such as Harold Bolter, former *Financial Times* industrial editor, who is now secretary and director of corporate affairs at British Nuclear Fuels, said that, listening to my medical checklist, he found himself identifying individual journalists who were suffering from one or other of the diseases. But those suffering from separatitis clearly did not like it. It did me no good with that small but effortlessly superior and self-regarding clique of television and newspaper journalists who have got above themselves. Elie Kadourie, Professor of Politics at the London School of Economics, wrote in the *Independent* in July 1988 about 'the overweening pride of the self-appointed priesthood'.

I developed my analysis of the symptons of 'separatitis' in the last public speech I delivered on the day of Mrs Thatcher's resignation – 22 November 1990. As I could not get to Leeds to give the paper myself, I recorded my speech on video the evening before. The material passage, highlighting the problems caused by 'separatitis' reads:

'One way in which this works out in practice is the reluctance of the media to supply the police with evidence to bring wrongdoers and criminals to justice. In my days of journalism we considered ourselves part of society – and no worse journalists for that.

'Now apparently what matters most is the reporting of news even if the very presence of cameras at events could, and perhaps does, provoke the lawlessness and criminality captured on film. Hand over the film, it is argued by editors, and you put your cameramen at risk. The Government safeguarded them by requiring a judge, not a magistrate, but a circuit judge, to satisfy himself that the film will be of substantial value in investigating a serious arrestable offence and that producing this material is in the public interest. So the media now have to be taken protesting loudly to court to secure evidence of criminality. What they should be asking themselves is how they would feel if their child or relative had been seriously injured in a riot and the chance of convicting their attacker was spoiled by a refusal to release the film. There would be cries of outrage.

' "I cannot easily accept that any duty is higher than that of the citizen" says the Commissioner of the Metropolitan Police. "And in a society policed by consent every citizen has a duty to see the law maintained."

'Unless,' I added, 'you happen to be a citizen and a journalist.

'This may be what Lord Bill Deedes, former editor of the *Daily Telegraph*, had in mind when, at a retirement dinner [given by Mrs Thatcher in No. 10], he said – and I recall his words so well – "I hope my peers will say that I was a citizen first and a journalist second".'

I cannot think of any sentence which so accurately summarizes my views about the role of a journalist in society.

I made one further contribution to the debate about standards of journalism in delivering the Livery lecture to the Worshipful Company of Stationers and Newspaper Makers in the Stationers' Hall on 5 February 1986 under the chairmanship of Ray Tindle, the Master of the Company and local weekly newspaperman extraordinary. This was while the Westland affair was still a live issue. Consequently, the hall was packed by an audience which presumably hoped but surely never expected me to say a word about Westland. Anyone who expected any such reference must have been naive in the extreme. There were, however, apparently a lot of naive people around because I tended to be hounded by television cameras and the lowest form of newspaper life – the investigative journalist. I objected to their attentions – I had not gone there for this – so I went for a walk outside after the lecture and before dinner. Somehow this was regarded as bad behaviour. Apparently no one these days is allowed to exercise free choice if journalists don't like it. Well, I exercised mine. And I will continue to do so. I do not believe that journalists rule the world – yet. As Mrs Thatcher said after her resignation: 'I have no more intention of being hassled by the press now when I am not Prime Minister, than when I was.'

In the course of the Livery lecture I sought to elevate the reporter in the newspaper hierarchy. I felt for him, I said. After all, I was one for the whole of my eighteen years in journalism. 'I have shared with him,' I said, 'his perishing funerals, his sodden agricultural shows, his grisly murders, his eerie ghost hunts, his endless doorsteps, his high living at trade union conferences (and his subsequent rows over expenses) and the singular privations of facility trips, for example to the Alsace wine fair. But I cannot help noticing that no one these days seems to want to be a hard news reporter. In the words of the fashion journalist, reporters are out; commentators, interpreters and analysts are in. The facts appear to matter less these days than what so-called experts think of them . . . Time and again we need the still, small voice of the reporter to tell us precisely where we started. But where do we start if fact attracts no premium over fiction; fairness none over malice; and objectivity none over prejudice? Our democracy needs lively, determined and scrupulous reporters.'

My accent was on the scrupulous. It was a word lost on many in the Stationers' Hall.

It is of course a perfectly reasonable argument that, whatever his views, the Prime Minister's Chief Press Secretary should, as a civil servant, keep them to himself. This is a little difficult since he spends most of his day talking to journalists and inevitably, in the normal course of relationships, reveals his thinking. He also develops the habit – or at least I did – of identifying aloud as a briefing goes on how reporters are likely to treat the available facts and sometimes to make fun of their likely angle. Whether the Chief Press Secretary should set out his thoughts in formal speeches is another matter. But, after a great deal of pressure from media organizations to address their conferences, it was felt in Number 10 that it was reasonable for me to express my views on journalism from time to time, if journalists invited me to do so. They would hardly expect me to be bland. Nor could they expect anything for their comfort when even their own kind were worried about the state of British journalism. I hope I left my audiences with two predominant thoughts. First, that I do have a genuine regard for journalism and want it to improve in quality and stature. I think this was underlined by the way I expressed my belief that, overall, warts and all, the British press, radio and television convey to the public a reasonably accurate account of what is going on in the world. After likening the media to a filter or distorting mirror, I concluded a number of lectures by saying:

'One of my tasks in view of this distortion is to persuade Ministers to take a longer – rather than shorter – term view of media coverage. In doing so, I liken the media to an oil painting: close up it looks like nothing on earth; stand back and you get the drift. I believe the British public get the drift.'

The second thought I hope the audiences picked up was my concern with the developing abuse of power in journalism. That is the problem journalism has to face and is now facing with the demise of the Press Council and the introduction of a new panoply of complaints procedures which may not remain on a voluntary basis if matters do not improve. That is the clear message of the Government's response to the Calcutt report. If journalism does not respond positively, then sooner or later a Government will feel obliged to face up to journalism's problems on behalf of the public. I hope it never comes to that. As with the trade unions, I would prefer journalism to sort itself out. And so, I suspect, say a lot of sensible journalists I used to work with.

Over the last two years of my Civil Service career I did two jobs – that of Chief Press Secretary and also that of head of the Government Information Service (GIS), to which I was appointed on 9 February 1989. This Civil Service appointment was as controversial as were my occasional forays on to the communications industry's conference or lecture platforms. Some of my friends told me that it was a presentational mistake to have accepted the post of head of the GIS. Their argument was that after very nearly ten years in Number 10 I was far too closely identified with a particular Prime Minister to lead the strictly non-political GIS. They did not put it that way, but that is what they meant. In other words, they felt that I was politically compromised – not, they assured me, by the way I had done the job of Chief Press Secretary but by my long service with Mrs Thatcher. It was vital, they argued, to ensure that the GIS was not only politically neutral but was seen to be so. This was a valid argument and could not be ignored. I had not overlooked it in accepting the appointment. Neither had the Head of the Home Civil Service, Sir Robin Butler, whose appointment it was (and who had been principal private secretary to Mrs Thatcher from 1982–5), nor had Mrs Thatcher, who had formally to approve it. As will be apparent from these pages, Mrs Thatcher always had a proper sense of the division between Government and the party in office.

For my part, I thought much the most serious question was not whether I was a fit person to take the job but whether I had time to do it. I saw no reason why I should be prevented from doing my bit for the Government information officer simply on account of the unprecedented amount of Parliamentary criticism – and abuse – that I had had to suffer over the years. Nor, in my stubborn way, did I think I should be blocked by false perceptions. I had invested a lot of time over the previous twenty-one years trying to ensure that the conventions governing Government publicity were observed. These state that the publicity:

– should be relevant to Government responsibilities.

– should be objective and explanatory, not tendentious or polemical; there should be no 'knocking' copy aimed at the opposition parties.

– should not be, or be liable to misrepresentation as being, party political.

– should be produced and distributed in an economic and relevant way, bearing in mind the need to justify to Parliament the cost as expenditure of public funds.

Moreover, heads of information who had quite properly sought my good offices in preventing breaches of these conventions were well aware of Mrs Thatcher's rock-solid support for observing the rules governing Government publicity. My position was much more difficult in face-to-face contacts with journalists who persisted in asking party political questions of me – some of them, I suspect, to try to trip me up. I tried to find a way of dealing with the issues raised in an acceptable way but I did not always succeed to everyone's satisfaction – or my own. I regret, for example, snapping in a moment of heavy pressure just before the summer recess in 1983 that Peter Shore was talking 'bunkum and balderdash'. I could scarcely have got away unidentified using such a phrase. It had become my trade mark.

There is, as always, a history to this appointment. For much of the 1980s I was dogged by allegations, again mostly in the 'quality' press, that I was 'power mad'. This manifested itself in a variety of ways. As a result of a leak – and this time not necessarily from the weekly meeting of heads of information (MIO) – I was accused of trying to introduce a central computerized system of information exchange between Government Departments in order to control the presentation of Government policy. I plead guilty to the charge that I was interested in securing a single, compatible computerized system of information exchange between Government Departments. I reckoned that, in this age of information technology, I would be culpable before a Select Committee if I did not try to secure a system by which individual Government Departments (including Number 10) could call up the data bases of other Departments to check points which crossed Departmental boundaries and, separately, had access to the briefing lines being deployed within Government. Dr John Gilbert MP clearly did not think much of inter-Departmental co-ordination during his cross-examination of me during the Select Committee inquiry into the handling of the media during the Falklands conflict. Among other things, a computerized system would have been of great assistance to journalists who always complain about being passed from one Department to another in the endless search for information. It would also have been a great time-saver within Government provided the facility was handled responsibly. No Department can brief effectively in detail on another's patch, and I never tried to do so when I was at Number 10. My briefings of the lobby are littered with requests for its members to approach the appropriate Department for more detailed information. An inter-Departmental data base, however, would not necessarily have been entirely in my interests. If I had made a mistake – and it could be proved that adequate briefing had been available on screen – the press (not to mention Government Departments) would have made me a candidate for the high jump.

I also would have liked to develop a computer system which would differentiate between classified and unclassified material and make unclassified material generally available, on line, to the public. To my utter shame, there is no such computerized system in Government to this day. This is not, I may say, because of the malevolent interest on the part of the press or, so far as I was aware, blocking tactics by Departments, but because of the sheer difficulty, bearing in mind all that faces a Chief Press Secretary in the course of a normal working day, of pursuing the issue with twenty-five or so Government Departments. Chief Press Secretary power, whatever that may mean, did not enter the argument. A Chief Press Secretary has very little power at his disposal. He has, however, a great – and continuing – need for reliable background briefing if he is to perform his function of bringing Government policies and actions together in a coherent whole.

I was also accused of packing Government Departments with my placemen or, more often, placewomen to extend my tentacles across the GIS and tighten my grip on its operations. It is true that I deliberately set out to open up Number 10 Press Office to members of the GIS in three ways. After Neville Gaffin, my first deputy, who had already had substantial experience as a Departmental head of information, had left for the DES I resolved to make my deputy's post a finishing school for future heads of information. As a consequence I had six deputies in eleven years. Each of them went on to their own command, demonstrating the benefit of the scheme to the GIS as distinct from myself, whose personal interests would have been better served by less turnover. Once they had left Number 10 they were their own men and women, with their own ministerial and departmental loyalties. Each of them will, I am sure, confirm that I seldom telephoned them and that I generally behaved in such a way as to emphasize their own independence. I also made the press officer posts in Number 10 a finishing school for promising younger material. All those who served in my time either left on promotion or secured it soon afterwards. Some are now heads of information themselves. With only three press officer posts in Number 10 and on average a two-year term of service, the extent to which individual press officers could have experience of working at the centre would have been limited but for a third scheme which Neville Gaffin devised for reinforcing Number 10's often overworked press officers. This was a system of six-week training and experience secondments from departments to Number 10 from which more than eighty press officers benefited. Again, several of these secondees are now departmental heads of information.

This background reveals the utter dedication to conspiracy theory – and grave lack of understanding of how the Government machine works – of Peter Hennessy (the Lord High Butterer-up of Top Civil Servants) and his Sancho Panza (David Walker) who reported in *The Times* (7 September 1983) that I 'had secretly proposed that [I] be made head of the entire government information machine to give Number Ten a better grip on the presentation of the Thatcher message.' This, they said, was to be the 'culmination of the public relations career of Mr Ingham, whose enthusiasm as Mrs Thatcher's senior press aide has caused both MPs and civil servants to wonder if he has not become too "political". In the new role he would be "minister of information" in all but name.'

Peregrine Worsthorne (*Sunday Telegraph*) went on to demonstrate how this kind of fanciful reporting enters the world as fact. He wrote that Mrs Thatcher lacked close colleagues to 'explode her Walter Mitty fantasies'. He added: '. . . husbands are no substitute for the candid friend. Nor are Downing Street Press Officers, particularly when trying to expand their empires, as seems [why not ring me? – columnar pox?] to be the case with the power-hungry Mr Bernard Ingham, whose leaked plan to centralize all information services under his control suggests that if her delusion of grandeur takes the form of emulating Churchill, his takes the form of emulating, if not Dr Goebells [the "not" a concession to libel lawyers], then at least some wartime Minister of Information like Brendan Bracken.'

There are two morals to this tale. Chief Press Secretaries should never have any ideas which might be misinterpreted. To which Mrs Thatcher replied time and again to me when I was attracting flak: 'Don't worry. Only people who never try to achieve anything get away without criticism.' The other moral is that journalists should not assume – as they invariably do – that what another journalist has written is inevitably the gospel truth. Mrs Thatcher wrote to David Owen on 24 September 1983: 'I presume . . . you are referring to recent press stories that there was a plan to create some sort of "information overlord" and give those duties to Mr Ingham. I can assure you that those stories were misconceived and mischievous. I do not have and never have had any intention or plan to centralize control of Government information in 10 Downing Street, and I have no plans to extend the responsibilities of my Chief Press Secretary.'

It might be useful at this point to inject some background into the story. Throughout my time as Chief Press Secretary I was concerned about the calibre of Departmental heads of information and their potential successors. I had to be, for two reasons. First, Cabinet Ministers took a very close interest in their press officers, and especially their chief information officer. They have always done so, as is clear from the preceding chapters. They also tend to talk to the Chief Press Secretary about them, as Mr Benn's diaries reveal. Second, the Chief Press Secretary has to work closely with Departmental heads of information. They are his strength and shield – or not, as the case may be. The more confidence a Chief Press Secretary reposes in Departmental heads of information the more relaxed he is. (I was pretty relaxed on this score.) Consequently, there is some discussion over senior appointments between the head of the GIS – traditionally the Director-General, or as he is now described the Chief Executive, of the Central Office of Information (COI). But – and this is very important – the Chief Press Secretary knows little of the vast bulk of the GIS membership which labours outside Departmental press offices on many different aspects of communications – advertising, leaflets, booklets, films, radio tapes, posters, overseas visitors, etc. Only about one third of the GIS are press officers, contrary to the assertions of people such as Joe Haines who writes disparagingly about 1200 'public relations officers' in Government when he ought, from experience, to know better.

Chief Press Secretaries therefore know less about the quality of the GIS as a whole than does the top man of the COI, who is himself directly responsible for about a quarter of the GIS. The COI, as the Government's common service agency in publicity services to Departments, is the largest single employer of staff in the GIS. None the less, the effective management of the GIS depends upon a good rapport between its head and the Chief Press Secretary whose prime concern is the effectiveness of Departmental press officers. These are, if you like, the fast lane of the GIS because of their proximity to Ministers.

One of Henry James's great – and justifiable – prides was that he resurrected before he left Number 10 the title of head of the GIS. He did not confer it upon himself since he had long since retired as Director-General of the COI. Instead it went to John Groves who re-assumed the mantle which had fallen into abeyance. I wholeheartedly welcomed the idea when Henry let me know in 1979 what was planned. Thus, over the 1980s, I worked reasonably well, and without incident, with John Groves, Donald Grant and Neville Taylor as successive heads of the GIS. I would never have become head of the GIS had Neville not fallen seriously ill with heart trouble, requiring a by-pass operation. His illness meant that for the better part of two years before I became head of the GIS I performed his duties as a *locum tenens*. These duties were not arduous, but Neville's absence meant that the GIS marked time.

That still does not explain why, six years after Messrs Hennessy and Walker had, in the most curious terms, canvassed my GIS take-over, I became head of the GIS. The explanation is simple: the changed circumstances of the COI and my seniority. The circumstances of the COI arose because of Mrs Thatcher's revolution in Whitehall. She set in train the systematic devolution of Civil Service responsibilities to separately managed executive agencies. It was a pound to a penny that the COI would become such an executive agency. Before that decision was taken another factor had entered the equation. This was the curious phenomenon called 'untying'. In Civil Service terms, this means that no longer were individual

Departments required to go to the COI for most of their publicity services. They could still do so, if they wished. But if they preferred to go to the private sector that was their affair, provided they could justify any additional expenditure. In fact most continued to use the COI, such was its practical reputation. The COI's performance is borne out by the way it had consistently hit its targets. But the prospect of the COI relying on its commercial appeal and becoming an executive agency concentrated minds wonderfully. It placed it in an invidious position. On the one hand it was the custodian of Government rules and conventions in relation to publicity, and on the other hand it had to compete for business with the private sector. A clash of interests seemed inevitable.

The trigger for an inquiry to sort matters out was Lord Young's upwardly thrusting 'Department of Enterprise' arrow advertisements on ITV. I think it was at this stage that the Government realized that the issue really had to be looked at again. The Government was confronted with a situation in which the art of the publicist had moved so far and so fast that the political impartiality of Government publicity was in danger of being compromised. This is not to suggest that the DTI advertisements were beyond the pale. I think they kept within the bounds of propriety. But they raised some interesting questions for the conventions governing Government publicity which I have already rehearsed. After an inquiry, in which I took part, revised guidelines were placed in the House of Commons Library. They contained four interesting paragraphs which demonstrated the need to balance technique with propriety. They read:

'Government publicity (and especially advertising) campaigns have to compete for attention with other publicity. To be effective they need to be professionally presented in such a way as to register a clear message with the public. They should also impress upon the public, whether listening, viewing or participating in events such as conferences, that the Government is taking pains over the presentation of the facts and its message. Shabby and ill thought out presentation can be as much a waste of public funds as the extravagant use of resources.

'It would, however, be counter productive if the level of spending on a public campaign impeded the communication of the message it is intended to convey by itself becoming a controversial issue. To pass the test of acceptability, Government publicity should always strike a balance in spending on often expensive modern communication techniques.

'It is no less crucial, if Government publicity is to remain acceptable within the conventions, that it avoids any doubts about its purpose. Government publicity should always be directed at informing the public even where it also has the objective of influencing the behaviour of individuals or particular groups [as, for example, with road safety, crime prevention and energy saving]. It is possible that in serving the public in this way a well-founded publicity campaign can redound to the political credit of the party in Government. This is by definition a natural consequence of political office and has been accepted as such by successive Governments. But it has equally been accepted that it must not be, or be believed to be, either the primary purpose or a principal incidental purpose of a campaign.

'Ministers and Heads of Department need to be on their guard against these dangers. They can stem as much from context, treatment, style, tone and quality of presentation as from the actual text employed. Each of these will need to be examined. A publicity campaign, or individual components of it, needs to be closely scrutinized not only in detail but also for its overall effect. "Image building", whether explicit or implied and whether of Government or Minister, is not acceptable. The test is whether a campaign, taken both as a whole and in part, can be justified as an effective response to a requirement to communicate with the public, or a particular section of it on an issue of importance.'

These guidelines demonstrate the extent to which heads of information have to exercise their own judgement. They also show how far the GIS goes to ensure impartiality in Government publicity.

The review of Government publicity arrangements did not, however, stop there. It looked at the question of the potential conflict

375

of interest as between the COI as an adviser on proprieties and value for money in publicity spending and as a competitor for Departmental publicity contracts. The outcome was that the Treasury became responsible for advising Departments on the value-for-money aspects of Government publicity, and the Cabinet Office for advising on how proposed publicity campaigns squared with the proprieties as defined in the published conventions. Later, as I expected, the COI became an executive agency with responsibility for delivering publicity services to the Government, in competition with the private sector, according to defined objectives and targets. It is performing extremely well under Mike Devereau, who suceeded me as head of the GIS.

Having sorted that out, the inquiry went on to consider the future of the GIS as a separately managed service to the Government. The real questions before it were: should the GIS remain as a separate entity within the Civil Service and, if so, how should it be managed? The first question is the more interesting. The FCO argues that it gets on very well without the GIS. In fact, it cannot do without it. This is because while its news department – i.e. its press office – is manned by career diplomats, its escorting of foreign visitors and its publicity output is handled by the GIS. The fact remains that its most sensitive area – its press office – is entirely a diplomat operation – or was until Douglas Hurd imported Brian Mower, my former deputy at Number 10, from the Home Office to head the news department. For years the Treasury has used its press secretary post as a finishing school for bright young administrators on their way up such as Gus O'Donnell, who succeeded me as Chief Press Secretary at Number 10. Other Departments also from time to time polish their upwardly mobile in the top information post. This is a wonderful tribute to the importance of information work. It does not, however, make managing the GIS easy when career information staff see the top jobs apparently reserved for the administrative class.

I argued before the inquiry that, if the information role was regarded solely in terms of press relations, it might be possible to sustain a case for subsuming the GIS into the wider Civil Service. But the information role went far wider than that – indeed, twice as many people were employed on publicity tasks other than in press offices. That being so, it surely made sense to maintain a separate – and separately managed – GIS. That argument was accepted and for my pains I was asked to become head of the GIS, even though I had made it clear that I felt I had enough to do as Chief Press Secretary. I suppose the job was thrust upon me because I had been doing it in all bar name for much of the previous two years, had the seniority and had taken part in the review settling the future of the COI and the GIS.

My appointment caused much less fire and brimstone than I had expected. So did my subsequent promotion to Grade 2 (deputy secretary) in August 1989. I hoped that the wolf pack were getting bored with my brand of red meat. There was, however, one passage of arms after an account of my one and only meeting with the union representatives found its way into the press. I refused to go along with their demand for a code of ethics for information officers. Why Government information officers need a separate code of ethics when they are subject to Civil Service rules and Parliamentary control over their activities through their Minister is beyond me. In any case, I could not agree off my own bat to such a code for one tiny part of the Civil Service. And what is more, the unions knew it. I had no more trouble with union codes of ethics, though, of course, the cartoonists got to work. 'Ingham refuses code of ethics for information officers' screams the newspaper bill board. Picture of Ingham with thought bubble: 'I didn't get where I am today by having ETHICS.' I might add – and neither did some journalists.

Much though I feared the physical consequences of the additional workload, I think I can say I got job satisfaction out of being head of the GIS comparable to that given to me by promoting energy conservation fifteen years earlier. I got a terrific kick out of moving the GIS forward and bringing on talented staff. Fortunately, I acquired the services of a much strengthened and enthusiastic Information Officer Management Unit (IOMU) – the GIS's own personnel department. However, contrary to so many base and ignorant stories, I did NOT acquire responsibility for the COI, which Mike Devereau continued to manage as a separate entity, or for the Government's £150 million publicity budget. That is the responsibility of individual Government departments. It is they who

377

spend the taxpayers' money and it is they who must account for it. Neither as Chief Press Secretary nor as head of the GIS did I come anywhere near the management of – let alone accountability for – Government spending on publicity. Another journalistic fabrication comes apart at the seams.

I have never worked harder in my life than doing these two jobs during my last two years in Number 10. Mrs Thatcher contributed to the workload. She has probably never got through more work more quickly or more travelling than during this period. Four people, apart from my secretary, Anne Allan, enabled me to get through. Mike Devereau, Brian Mower and Anne Nash, head of the IOMU who made a signal contribution to professionalizing personnel management in the GIS over this period. These three formed with me the management executive of the GIS. The fourth is Terry Perks, my deputy at Number 10 (who has become head of IOMU in succession to Anne Nash). He had Mrs Thatcher's confidence as my deputy and was able to take on a substantially increased workload. But that in turn meant that the three Number 10 press officers – Sarah Charman, Philip Aylett, and first Mike Bates and then Peter Bean – and the Number 10 office manager, Ian Beaumont, each made a substantial contribution to the development of the GIS which should be acknowledged.

By the time Mrs Thatcher resigned we had substantially introduced a comprehensive system of central personnel management for the GIS covering marketing, recruitment, training and career development. I personally met more than half the 1250 members of the GIS in some fifty Government Departments and Agencies spread across Britain, at parties in my room in Number 10 and on visits to the Scottish, Welsh and Northern Ireland offices in Edinburgh, Cardiff and Belfast and to the COI's seven regional offices. I was sometimes accused of interfering in the internal affairs of organizations as when the Commissioner of the Metropolitan Police, Sir Peter Imbert, invited (repeat, invited) me over to Scotland Yard to advise on the appointment of a new director of public affairs. But I retired a happy man: morale in the GIS was high.

23

The Undefeated

Like a mighty oak, it took more than one axe to bring Mrs Thatcher down. In November 1990 they were cutting into this solid timber from all angles. The frenzy was fearsome to behold. Heaven preserve us from political axe-men in a state of panic. They would cut off their grandmas in their prime if they thought it would serve their interests. And so they cut off a grandma in her international prime by the stocking tops, to borrow one of Denis's phrases, which Mrs Thatcher often used. May God forgive them. For the road to 22 November 1990, when Mrs Thatcher resigned, was mostly paved with gold. Never have we seen such an advance in the condition of the ordinary, decent, hard-working, socially responsible and ambitious people of Britain. My kind of people. Where did it all go wrong? Why did she come a cropper?

As will be clear from all that has gone before, I am singularly unimpressed with conspiracy theory. I do not believe for a minute that Mrs Thatcher prematurely entered the history books as one of the greatest Prime Ministers Britain has known because there was a plot within her party to bring her down. Of course, some had been wanting to get rid of her from the moment she became Prime Minister, and no doubt long before that. That is politics. But I do not believe that there was a premeditated and organized coup in November 1990. Sir Anthony Meyer MP, in standing against Mrs Thatcher in 1989, had broken the long run of uncontested leadership elections during her premiership. Yet in the summer and early autumn of 1990 the betting was perhaps against another contest.

I was unimpressed with Michael Heseltine's writing of an open letter to his constituency chairman, which brought on a bout of leadership election fever. This was just 'lighting the blue touch paper and retiring to a safe distance – in his case to Amman,' I told some journalists who immediately reported the remark. (Mr Heseltine went on a tour of the Middle East after issuing his letter.) I was probably in a minority of one among my friends and colleagues in Number 10 in believing that Mr Heseltine would not fight because he knew he could not win. This judgement, which was my instinctive view, was confirmed by a number of Ministers and politicians with whom I discussed the matter. They were adamant that a majority of their Parliamentary Party would never risk splitting it worse asunder by electing Mr Heseltine. I held to the view that he would take his bat home until Sir Geoffrey Howe made his bitter, fateful resignation speech in the Commons on 13 November. A challenge to Mrs Thatcher was then, I thought, inevitable.

I would, however, be astonished if Mr Heseltine and Sir Geoffrey were some sort of 'taffia' operating out of Swansea–Port Talbot. They may both have come to breathe fire, like a pair of Welsh dragons, at the very thought of Mrs Thatcher and it may have warmed their hearts to see her fall. But they make an unlikely pair of plotters – Tarzan on Mogadon? Instead they were, in my view, mere players in a grand Shakespearian tragedy which was probably going to end in tears anyway.

Mrs Thatcher fell because of a lethal mixture of laxity and a little indulgence leading to a resurgence of inflation which, when combined with the introduction of the poll tax, gave the inevitably increasing numbers of the disappointed, the disaffected and the frustrated within her Parliamentary party the chance to wound. I suppose sex also played its part. It often does with the Tories. Some of them were fed up with being dominated by an iron-clad woman. Europe provided the implement by which the foul deed was done. Precisely how these various elements in the unmaking of a Prime Minister (and, with her, her Chief Press Secretary) inter-reacted is for maturer judgement and for someone less inhibited than me. I can merely provide the skeleton of the power play which ended a remarkable period in British post-war history.

The first – and most important – element which entered into Mrs Thatcher's demise was the economy. She came to office dedicated to the control of inflation. She got it down from 21.9 per cent in April 1980 to 2.4 per cent in July and August 1986 and she was never satisfied to allow it to rest there. Of all British politicians since the war she was the hammer of inflation. Why then in October 1990 did we end up with 10.9 per cent inflation? My answer – the product of a layman's reasoning – is complex. It is by no means explained solely by economic forces. It was also long in the making, ante-dating the arrival of John Major, Mrs Thatcher's successor, in the Treasury in 1987 as Chief Secretary. First, we experienced in the mid 1980s growing consumer and business confidence. As the nation embarked on eight years of continuous growth the public saw the dawn of a new golden age in which expansion, as it were, went on and on. After the lean, depressing years of unemployment the economy was really stoked up. And the boom was reinforced by the effects of financial liberalization and the disappearance of direct controls over credit. I have never known as many people wanting to lend me cash. Money, it seemed, was the least of anybody's problems, even if they had none.

Then came the international stock market crash on what became known as Black Monday – 19 October 1987 – immediately on the Prime Minister's return from the Vancouver Commonwealth Conference to a Britain blown over by the Great Gale. Internationally – and not merely in Britain – its effects on confidence were over-estimated and Governments over-compensated by cheapening the price of money. Nigel Lawson, the Chancellor of the Exchequer, was at this time experimenting – in the days before we had joined the European exchange rate mechanism – with shadowing the D-mark at 3DM to the £ until it became too expensive – not in supporting sterling but in holding down its level. Even though he was obliged to let the pound go above 3DM in March 1988, he continued to try to stop its rise by cutting interest rates. In a period of indulgence of her clever Chancellor – and some would say Mrs Thatcher was an excessively indulgent team manager – she left this process of Lawsonian private enterprise carry on until 17 May 1988 by which time interest rates had been brought down to 7.5 per cent.

It was at this point that I recall telling Paul Gray, the Prime Minister's economic private secretary, that – economic layman though I was – it was all getting far too loose and slack and the Government would live to regret it. Mrs Thatcher very rapidly agreed, though I never discussed the matter with her. It was now – belatedly – evident to all that the economy was roaring ahead far too fast, with the balance of payments racing into deficit and inflation set to rise. An effort was made to reassert control. Within a month the Government's relentless march to dearer money began. Its price very nearly doubled – to 13 per cent – in five months. It precisely doubled within twelve months as the Government tried somewhat desperately to slow down an economy which was frequently likened to a super-tanker. These big ships take several miles to bring from full steam ahead to dead slow. This puts a premium on the vigilance of the officer of the watch. The Prime Minister had been let down.

There is a real mystery as to how such an uncompromising inflation fighter as Mrs Thatcher should have relaxed her vigilance over those officers responsible for this crucial element in the Government's navigation. Is the clue, I wonder, Thatcher's people? That is to say, the homeowners – those with a direct bricks-and-mortar stake in their community and country? While I have never known Mrs Thatcher happy with inflation above zero or prepared to settle for anything less than honest money, meaning money of stable and lasting value, she had also made Britain a property-owning democracy. There were more than eight million people with a mortgage when she left office.

Under the influence of Thatcher's people – or, at least, a strongly felt commitment to them – her heart may for once and for a short time have ruled her head. If so, she did what no one ever felt her capable of doing: she relaxed. In doing so, she proved conclusively her own, oft repeated, view that there can be no relaxation in the fight against inflation. In doing so, she proved the effectiveness of her own measures, as events since her resignation have demonstrated. Those measures may have taken their time, but effective they are proving against inflation in 1991. The moral of the tale so far is that you have to be tough in the good times as well as in the bad. Mrs Thatcher might have been tougher – though no one else in the Government would have been as tough on inflation. She might well have been harsher but for her concern for her own people: the homeowners. Consequently, the further moral of this tale is that which is familiar to all parents: you have to be cruel to be kind. Spare the rod and you spoil the child. The Thatcher years have amply justified Victorian values. In short, the Conservative Party may have got rid of one of the toughest Prime Ministers this country has ever known for not being tough enough. It would never in a month of Sundays acknowledge that. But that could be the reality.

The second element in the complex equation which led to Mrs Thatcher departing for the backbenches was the community charge – the poll tax. There are only two ways to bring the big local authority spenders under control. Either do away with local government as we know it or make sure that everyone – but everyone – in the local community foots the bill and is armed with an annual means (election) of expressing his opinion on local budgeting. Mrs Thatcher leaned towards but did not quite reach the latter remedy. I reject the argument that the community charge is unfair. The 'rich' (of which any definition, laughably, includes me) pay vastly more, through national taxation, towards the upkeep of local government than the 'poor'. The financing of local government under Mrs Thatcher's poll tax was a progressive system of taxation, though it was difficult to present it as such. The problem was that central Government underestimated the opportunism of local government to spend and waste the public's money and blame Mrs Thatcher's 'flagship' policy for the resultant bill.

The question is whether in late 1987, in a state of post-election euphoria, the Government was politically wise to go for the 'big bang' solution and introduce the community charge in one fell swoop instead of running it alongside the rates for a phasing-in period of, say, four years. On the face of it, the Government was most unwise – and excessively overconfident – because it found itself on a slippery slope with no means of avoiding one expensive concession after another. Governments are at their most vulnerable in the immediate aftermath of being returned to power with a substantial majority in a general election. That point is, however, incidental to this argument. To repeat, I believe that with the application of suitable cushions, the community charge would have been broadly accepted – just as it has been substantially paid – had it not been introduced during a period of high mortgage rates.

None the less, the conjunction of high interest rates and mostly high poll taxes (with notable exceptions such as low-taxed Tory Wandsworth and Westminster) gave Mrs Thatcher's opponents a chance. They would not, however, have had it had Mrs Thatcher not been in office for eleven years. By then she had substantially extended beyond its natural span the life of a British Prime Minister in a Cabinet system of Government and was faced with an endless quest by journalists for something new. She was becoming a Methuselah. And Methuselahs have their critics by virtue of their longevity. Mrs Thatcher could never expect to be loved by those to whom she had declined to give office, those who felt they ought to have had higher office, those who had been sacked from office and those who disagreed with her unconsensual approach. ('What is this thing called consensus?' she used to ask. 'Consensus is something you reach when you cannot agree.') The longer a Prime Minister remains in office the longer the disaffected tail of her party becomes. And counted among this disaffected tail will be a substantial number of MPs who owe everything to the Prime Minister and who would never have come within a smell of office but for her kindness in giving them a taste of it. That makes them no less lethal.

Over and above these factors, there was unhappiness with Mrs Thatcher's stance on Europe. As I have already asserted, she had done more to reform the European Community and set it on course for development than any other single individual among a Europopulation of some 320 million. Ironically, she had also devised a policy for its pragmatic development to which the vast mass of her party could rally. This course was scarcely distinguishable from that which Mr Major took to Bonn on 11 March 1991. He was having no mad rush to European economic and monetary union. He advocated greater use of a common Community currency, the hard ECU, but he would have no imposition of a single currency by Brussels. And he supported the continued operation of collective defence under the umbrella of NATO. Mrs Thatcher's problem was not policy; it was its presentation after a decade of cuffing the Community into making something of itself. She was felt to be anti-Europe – an impression which her bold, and necessary, insistence on the Germanys taking fully into account the international ramifications of unification did nothing to dispel. But the criteria by which she came to be judged were the concepts of European political and economic and monetary union. These took as severe a battering at the hands of Saddam Hussein as did his own poor bloody infantry. Unfortunately, Mrs Thatcher's Foreign Secretary (Sir Geoffrey Howe) and her Chancellor (Nigel Lawson) also came to judge her by her Euro-credentials and more particularly by whether she was willing to join the Exchange Rate Mechanism (ERM).

For me, the ERM came to occupy the same ludicrously overrated status of a quick fix as all the earlier economic mumbo-jumbo, although there were no doubt good political reasons for entry. But worse still, it became divisive within the British Government. I have never known a worse atmosphere within the British party than at the European Council in Madrid in June 1989 when Mrs Thatcher set out the terms for British entry but not, as the Foreign Secretary and Chancellor had sought in a last minute confrontation before Mrs Thatcher left for Spain, the date by which Britain would join. Britain eventually entered on 8 October 1990 – just over a year after interest rates had peaked at 15 per cent. A year earlier Chancellor Lawson resigned, ostensibly because of competition from Sir Alan Walters, the Prime Minister's economic adviser. Less than a month after entry Sir Geoffrey Howe resigned as Lord President and Leader of the House of Commons. All his pent up frustrations of the Thatcher years, especially over Europe, came spilling out and the stage was set for the leadership challenge which saw Mrs Thatcher depart.

Gender cannot be ignored either. Mrs Thatcher's achievements stem in part from her sex. Only a woman could have done what she did because only a woman – and for most of the time the sole woman in the Cabinet – could have got away with it. Men had difficulty coping with her. It is easier for a man to have a row with a man than with a woman, especially in the superficially civilized corridors of power. It is much more difficult for men to apply pressure on a woman to conform, especially when she has a will of her own. It is well nigh impossible to bowl over, except with the most cogent arguments, a woman as fierce, dominating and aggressive in debate as Mrs T. All this may be tolerable so long as the woman in question is delivering economic and political success. But it becomes wearing and after eleven years is inclined to make for trouble when things go wrong.

The Government had not been a happy ship for some time and I had long suspected that Mrs Thatcher, in the face of all the continuing aggravation, had decided to do it her way. The tension palpably eased with the resignation of Nigel Lawson on 26 October 1989. But there was a further drain of Cabinet Ministers to the backbenches to spend more time with their families – i.e. Norman Fowler and Peter Walker – before Nicholas Ridley departed because of his candid views about our German partners in the European Community, as printed by Nigel Lawson's son, Dominic, the editor of *The Spectator*. I was beginning to dread trips abroad with the Prime Minister. I could never be sure who would resign next on our return. Nigel Lawson did so immediately after Mrs Thatcher's return from the Kuala Lumpur Commonwealth Conference. And Nicholas Ridley little more than forty-eight hours after Mrs Thatcher had flown back overnight from the Economic Summit in Houston.

If Mrs Thatcher's Ministers thought that they had a hard task-mistress, Mrs Thatcher must have felt at times that her Ministers made life impossible for her. Few were more difficult than Nigel Lawson, though I can understand how trying he must have found Sir Alan Walters. It was clear on Mrs Thatcher's return from Kuala Lumpur, via Qatar, that an article written by Sir Alan eighteen months ago (when he had no contractual relationship with the Prime Minister), and recently printed by the *Financial Times*, was still causing trouble. It was only the following day – Thursday 26 October – that I realized how much: the Chancellor resigned ostensibly on account of the competition presented by Sir Alan. This was on the day of the Cabinet after which Mrs Thatcher had to face questions in the House and then make a statement on the Commonwealth Conference. Mr Lawson first hinted at resignation when he saw Mrs Thatcher just before 9 a.m. and then tendered it just before she was to go over to the House at 2.30. He wanted to announce it at 3.10 – five minutes before the Prime Minister rose to answer questions and make her statement and before the London markets closed. He was asked to delay it until after Mrs Thatcher had finished her work in the House. I sometimes thought that, if it were not so wearing, we ought to arrange for some trauma immediately before any major performance by Mrs Thatcher. It seemed to bring out that little bit extra in her. And so it proved on this occasion – a powerful, commanding performance lasting in total seventy-five minutes on, it should be noted, her very first appearance in an experimentally televised House of Commons. Nobody could have imagined she was about to lose a Chancellor.

But lose him she did soon afterwards. Mrs Thatcher briefed me alone in her room at the House. I dashed back to Number 10 to prepare a speaking note on the resultant reshuffle which elevated John Major from Foreign Secretary to Chancellor, Douglas Hurd from the Home Office to the Foreign Office and David Waddington from the Chief Whip's Office to the Home Office. By 7.45 I had announced to the lobby the resignations of Nigel Lawson and Sir Alan and the appointments to three of the top posts in the Government below Prime Minister. It was a typical, decisive piece of Thatcher Government.

Thursday 12 July 1990 dawned burnished gold over the parched British countryside. Mrs Thatcher's party flew in from Houston in a Gulfstream on demonstration as a possible form of Prime Ministerial travel. We landed at Northolt at 6.10 and were whisked by helicopter into central London. I was not surprised to see a television crew in the pen outside Number 10. But we were all bewildered by their question: what have you to say about Mr Ridley's interview? We knew nothing of it. The BBC's 7 a.m. news solved the mystery and plunged us into further crisis. Mr Ridley, a close supporter and friend of Mrs Thatcher, had made some intemperate remarks about the Germans during a lunch with Dominic Lawson, the former Chancellor's son and, like his father before him, editor of *The Spectator*. Two days later – on Saturday 14 July – Nicholas Ridley resigned. After Andrew Turnbull, the principal private secretary, had spent hours trying to find his successor, Peter Lilley, in his constituency, I announced yet another reshuffle early in the evening. I was personally very sad to see Mr Ridley go. He had been a superb Minister to work with – and an extremely friendly and relaxed one, too. What is more, he got things moving. His resignation, even though he withdrew his remarks soon after they had appeared in print, was inevitable, reluctant though Mrs Thatcher was to see him go. It represented a further setback for the Government when its overall performance had been improving. I was beginning to have difficulty with those journalists who felt that the Government was disintegrating before their very eyes.

Mr Ridley's resignation also provided an interesting illustration of the monumental cheek which some journalists bring to their trade. I received a call on the Friday – the day after news of Mr Ridley's interview broke – from Dominic Lawson. With a disingenuousness capped only by John Palmer (*Guardian*) at every European Community press briefing at which he asked a question, Mr Lawson Jr sought an interview with the Prime Minister. He said that he had thought that, in reporting Mr Ridley's views, he was reporting the Government's views. Now, in view of all the furore, he was confused. And the only person who could unconfuse him was the Prime Minister. Could he therefore see her? Giving him full marks for chutzpah, gall and brass neck I think I conveyed the answer he was presumably expecting when I asked him: 'I suppose you won't be surprised if you don't get an interview?' He had the grace to say he wouldn't. And he didn't.

The long, hot summer brought another (planned) reshuffle, Mrs Thatcher's timely visit to Aspen, Colorado, as Iraq invaded Kuwait, the second recall of Parliament of the Thatcher years to debate the Gulf, the fiftieth anniversary of the Battle of Britain, Prime Ministerial visits to Helsinki, Czechoslovakia, Hungary, Switzerland and to New York for the UN Year of the Child summit, entry into the ERM and the appalling first of two European Councils in Rome. And then came November, ushered in by Sir Geoffrey Howe's resignation as Lord President of the Council and Leader of the House of Commons. He tendered his letter of resignation around 5.50 p.m. I announced this to the lobby at 7 p.m. and issued the exchange of letters between Mrs Thatcher and Sir Geoffrey at 8.35.

The following day – Friday 2 November – brought yet another reshuffle and some depressing intelligence. To the surprise and relief of the Government Affairs Group of the Institute of Public Relations – or GAG as it is surely inappropriately known – I managed to break off from preparing for the reshuffle to address their annual luncheon in the Commons. There a Tory MP for a marginal Midlands constituency who had strongly supported Mrs Thatcher told me that for the first time his constituents were blaming Mrs Thatcher herself for the circumstances in which they found themselves. Against that background, Sir Geoffrey's resignation and predictable calls in the *Mirror*, *Guardian* and *Independent* for Mrs Thatcher to go it was a pound to a penny that Michael Heseltine would make a move. He was well known in Number 10 for raising his head above the parapet when Mrs Thatcher was in political difficulty. News of his testing of the water with a letter to his constituency chairman broke on Saturday 3 November. My thirty-fourth wedding anniversary was spent on the telephone.

The next five weeks were the most traumatic of my professional life – and the most difficult because Mrs Thatcher's problem lay in her party. She was fighting for her life as party leader – a fight in which as a civil servant I could play no active part. Yet the outcome would determine whether she remained as Prime Minister and it was for her as Prime Minister, that I had to answer in the normal round of business and lobby briefings. Moreover, the lobby, in asking questions, did not differentiate between the party and Governmental roles; but some of its members were only too ready to expose me for party political activity – electioneering, if you like – if I put a foot wrong with my answers.

Conservative Parliamentary Party leadership elections also fall at one of the busiest periods of the year. What Mrs Thatcher, faced with a threat to her entire future, had to cope with is set out below. Interwoven are my trials and comments.

MONDAY NOVEMBER 5: Visit to Geneva to address a UN conference on the environment. I let it slip before she leaves that she had talked with Lord Whitelaw that day about the next ten years at Number 10. How's that for defiance?

– 6 NOVEMBER: Meeting in Geneva, with the snow on the Alps and Jura, with King Hussein of Jordan, no longer a favourite monarch because of his role of apologist for the Iraqis. In his speech to the UN conference he predicts ecological doom and disaster if the balloon goes up in the Gulf and oil wells are put to the torch.

—7 NOVEMBER: Speaks in the debate on the Queen's Speech, having worked on her speech on the return flight from Geneva yesterday.

—8 NOVEMBER: Autumn Statement by the Chancellor, John Major, on the outcome of the 1990 public expenditure review. This is perhaps of more marginal interest than news that Michael Heseltine is trying to dictate the terms of a TV-am interview with David Frost to exclude any references to correspondence with his constituency officers, and that Tony Benn is off to Baghdad for political and humanitarian reasons.

—9 NOVEMBER: Lunch with the BBC's top editorial team which comes out about as sweet and as illuminating as I hoped it would – and which deals mostly with issues rather than leadership elections.

—10 NOVEMBER: Mrs Thatcher feels sorry for me. She regrets that I have to put up with all the word-twisting that journalists indulge in. This time it is Anthony Bevins (*Independent*) – who else? – who has come out with the idea that the Prime Minister, according to Ingham, has endorsed Douglas Hurd as her successor. This is the usual mischief. It stems from my meeting with the Sunday lobby the previous day when they asked me who, now that Sir Geoffrey Howe had resigned, was likely to succeed Mrs Thatcher if she were knocked down by a bus. I first make Lord Carrington's point that the bus wouldn't dare. But I add that if the bus were unexpectedly brave and effective Douglas Hurd, as the senior Cabinet Minister in the Commons, would appear to be the favourite. By definition, he could not then be Mrs Thatcher's favourite. She would have no say in the matter. Five or so members of the Sunday lobby I talk to in the course of the day regret that once again the *Independent*, operating second hand, has entirely misrepresented my remarks. I am more concerned for Douglas Hurd than myself. What people never seem to understand is that I do not worry about lies, inventions, misrepresentations or inaccuracies about what I may or may not say or do. I forget about everything mundane while I watch on television a superb Great Britain *v*. Australia Rugby League Test which Australia, dammit, wins in the last minute.

—11 NOVEMBER: I talk a lot on the telephone. Mrs Thatcher does not, I suspect, agree with me that Michael Heseltine will not stand. I also get my first inkling of her thinking: if there is an election, she feels she has to win on the first round, or else she will be in potential trouble.

—MONDAY 12 NOVEMBER: The Prime Minister speaks at the Lord Mayor's Banquet in which she resorts to cricketing metaphors, written by Andrew Turnbull and Charles Powell, knocking the bowling all over the ground and for six. (I wish Yorkshire CCC would do more of this.) I decide that Mrs Thatcher does not need Sanatogen. Her nerves are good.

—13 NOVEMBER: The Prime Minister, born on the 13th and married on the 13th, thinks it is her lucky number. Not today. Sir Geoffrey Howe makes his extremely well-constructed resignation speech and cooks his goose. (As it turns out, he also cooks Mrs Thatcher's.) I reflect sadly on the tragedy of his, as well as other's relationships with Mrs Thatcher, for example, Nigel Lawson's. I have no doubt that Sir Geoffrey, with some justification, feels he has not got enough credit for the achievements of the Thatcher years. He was a pillar from 1979–83. No one, except himself, could take that away from him. But has he, I wonder, even destroyed that reputation with a speech which fell into the '*Et tu, Brute*' category.

—14 NOVEMBER: Mr Heseltine announces his candidature. I am greeted when I arrive at the *Daily Mail*'s sumptuous offices in Kensington for lunch with Sir David English and his top editorial team with the news that Mr Heseltine wants to modify the community charge. Well, of course, is my retort. Don't they all? It is the popular thing to do. But how? The lunch is wonderfully entertaining, but it gives a clue to the way their minds are turning. They see me as a potential successor to the late George Gale as a columnist. Maybe they do. But I do not regard Mrs Thatcher as finished yet. Mr Kinnock evidently thinks things are getting difficult. I am told that he telephoned David English after lunch to inquire whether I had been in the building to pray for Mrs Thatcher.

—15 NOVEMBER: The Cabinet is apparently quite robust on

the community charge. John Major is preparing himself for a nasty wisdom tooth operation at the week-end.

— 16 NOVEMBER: Arguably Mrs Thatcher's best visit to Northern Ireland. It involves eight helicopter flights down to one of the most dangerous parts of the border bandit country at Kinawley, near Enniskillen. Mrs Thatcher cuts herself in two: she performs her role as Prime Minister with distinction, and speaks as well at an evening reception at Hillsborough as she does at the beginning in Enniskillen; in between she worries about the leadership election.

— 18 NOVEMBER: Mrs Thatcher flies to Paris for the signing of the CFE agreement (Conventional Forces Reduction in Europe) and the Conference on Security and Co-operation in Europe (CSCE) which are being attended by President Bush and Mr Gorbachev. Ambassador Sir Ewan and Lady (Sara) Fergusson make us, as ever, extremely welcome. The assembled journalists, whom Brian Mower and I brief, are really only interested in one thing: the leadership campaign, on which we have nothing much to say, beyond the mechanics of timetables etc.

— 19 NOVEMBER: The CFE agreement is signed in the Elysée Palace. It is interesting that the French (of course), Russians, Americans and Germans are all on the top table and Mrs Thatcher nowhere. The FCO assure me this is the order in which the nations sit around the CFE table. How convenient! I think it is a pity that some of them are better at signing bits of paper than responding to real, live international crises – for example, the Gulf. I find it fascinating to watch Mr Gorbachev working a room for contacts. The man is a Western-style politician. Brian Mulroney, the Canadian Prime Minister, chats to me several times. He seems almost shell-shocked at the thought of Mrs Thatcher facing a leadership contest. It brings out the Irish in him. 'Jasus,' he says, 'in Canada we erect a monument to a chap who loses three elections. In Britain you threaten to get rid of your Prime Minister when she wins three. What on earth is going on?' It is the question on everyone's lips at the conference.

— 20 NOVEMBER: The fateful – leadership election-day. The Prime Minister's mind is kept off domestic affairs with meetings with Mr Gorbachev, President Mitterrand and President Özal, of Turkey; and lunch with Mr Lubbers and Mr Van den Broek, of the Netherlands. She gets back to the British Embassy at 4.45 p.m. (Paris time) for tea in the drawing-room.

It is at this point that I must break into the diary to set out the events of the evening of 20 November and its immediate aftermath in narrative form.

Mrs Thatcher, after making light of her ordeal with a good gossip about the CSCE conference, retires to her room in the residence at about 5.20 p.m. Peter Morrison, her Parliamentary Private Secretary, has arrived earlier in the afternoon. He is the keeper of the keys. He knows the truth about voting intentions – or what it is if everyone is telling the truth. I gather that Mrs Thatcher will be home and dry if every man and woman's word is his or her bond. Peter has, however, built in a 'lie factor' of 15 per cent in calculating her likely final support. If there are a lot of liars it might be dodgy. Mrs Thatcher displays an inordinate calm. We all assemble at 6.10 in Peter Morrison's room – Number 2 – in the attic. We can hear the chatter of the media down below in the residence courtyard but we cannot see the assembled hordes. Peter Morrison has an open line to the Whips' Office in the House and chatters away, seated at a corner desk, to the Deputy Chief Whip, Alastair Goodlad. Mrs Thatcher sits at a dressing-table on his left. Charles Powell lounges on one of the two beds, holding on to the other open line against the possibility of a breakdown on Peter Morrison's. The Ambassador, Mrs Crawford (Crawfie) and I pace the floor of this florally decorated room with its matching pictures of tropical birds.

We all know our parts. These were worked out last week, with supporting charts identifying Mrs Thatcher's planned responses according to the various possible outcomes. All we need are the figures. Round about 6.30, with a sudden burst of activity, Peter Morrison, who has worked himself into the ground on the Prime Minister's behalf, hands her the paper on which he has written the result, with these fateful words: 'Not, I am afraid, as good as we had hoped.'

The figures were:

- —Mrs Thatcher   204
- —Michael Heseltine   152
- —Abstentions   16

Peter Morrison's lie factor has worked to full effect. She is four votes short under the complex formula which means that she needs at least 187 votes and a 56-vote lead over her opponent. She receives the news calmly. She was always the calmest in a crisis. Then she stands up from her dressing-table and, with a sigh, says that she knows what she now has to do before she rings Denis, her family and her supporters. It is to go down and tell the press, radio and television that she intends to fight on. Her political advisers feel it is crucial that she should say this as soon as possible in order to preserve her support. In the drama of the moment, Mrs Thatcher marches relentlessly down the treacherous stairs of the residence and, without giving me time to check whether the journalists are ready, straight out through the door and down the steps into the courtyard towards the privileged pool who would have a face-to-face opportunity to ask her questions.

(As a civil servant I had no part to play in the proceedings outside. I have since been much criticized for going out with Mrs Thatcher on to a party political platform and displaying my 'bullying' presence – I attract only critical adjectives – among the journalists. The explanation is simple. Mrs Thatcher, breathing the fire of purpose, was absolutely determined to broadcast her message immediately. Unfortunately, she interrupted John Sergeant (BBC) in full spate during an outside broadcast. The outside broadcasters had also removed the central microphone which I had arranged for the benefit of all British journalists who had been admitted to the courtyard. This central microphone was essential for a good quality sound feed to the pool and also to give the much larger group of British journalists on the other side of the courtyard an opportunity to hear Mrs Thatcher's words through loudspeakers. I was damned if I was going to desert Mrs Thatcher at this hour, especially when I was trying to help the press.)

After telephoning her husband, family and friends Mrs Thatcher goes off to Versailles for an evening's CSCE entertainment to international acclaim for her 'gutsy' style. Altogether too many of her fellow summiteers are bewildered by what is happening in Britain. In our heart of hearts those of us with Mrs Thatcher know that the writing is on the wall. However narrow the margin of failure in the first ballot, a second ballot spells trouble. Has Mr Heseltine perforce turned spoiler?

Mrs Thatcher gets back late from the dinner. She goes to bed calm but subdued. The following morning George Bush, Brian Mulroney and Ruud Lubbers are shocked and very supportive. Mrs Thatcher is touched by this and feels supported but she is not the same woman in the sense, though differently, that she was not, for a time, the same woman after becoming a grandmother. But as a grandmother she was looking joyfully to the future. As a Prime Minister facing rejection she was, I suppose, looking back wistfully to what it might have been. As soon as the CSCE Treaty has been signed we leave for Orly. Charles Powell and I travel in the ambassadorial Rolls while the Ambassador accompanies Mrs Thatcher in her official car. I tell Charles that we had better enjoy the Rolls whilst it is there: we might not be in many more. In thanking Ewan Fergusson for his hospitality on the tarmac at Orly, I tell him that I do not think we [this team] will be returning to his Embassy.

Back in Number 10 the advice to the Prime Minister is inconclusive. Over a sandwich lunch in the Cabinet Room her closest advisers are unable to come up with a clear signal to fight on or to resign. Norman Tebbit and John Moore (part of her campaign team), Cranley Onslow (chairman of the 1922 Committee of Tory Backbenchers), Kenneth Baker, chairman of the party, and the Chief Whip, Tim Renton, leave it in the air. It is the worst of all worlds for me, under tremendous pressure from the lobby which is rife with rumour. When Mrs Thatcher emerges from the Cabinet Room, on her way to the House to make her statement on the CSCE summit, I tell her that such is the media pressure and speculation that if she is going to stand she must say so as she leaves. Accordingly, Mrs Thatcher repeats outside for the reporters' benefit that she intends to fight on.

But that was not the end of the story. After the inconclusive nature of the lunch-time gathering which he attended, John

Wakeham, Secretary of State for Energy and the Minister acting in Mrs Thatcher's best interests, recommended her to see her Cabinet colleagues after she had delivered her statement to the House. This she did individually. The outcome spelled the end. They told her that if she decided to stand they would back her but they feared she might lose the second round. Consequently, they advised her to open up the competition. I popped into the Cabinet Room at about 8.45 p.m. as Mrs Thatcher was preparing to start writing her speech for the confidence debate the following day. I wished her luck. She said tearfully that all support was draining away. I did not help much, though I meant well. I told her, gripping her arm, that whatever others felt, we in Number 10 were with her. It was an emotional moment.

My formal line with the press that evening was that Mrs Thatcher was considering her position. That was literally true, but I had no illusions as to what the outcome would be the following morning. Neither had the courteous Simon Walters, of the *Sun*, who rang me at 12.30 a.m. to say that they were getting the feeling that Mrs Thatcher had decided to resign. (Later that day I took Simon on one side and said that I hoped he did not think that I had misled him. Not at all, he said; they had carried some accurate, as it turned out, speculation in their last edition.)

Mrs Thatcher saw Peter Morrison and her principal private secretary, Andrew Turnbull, at 7.30 to announce her decision to resign. A little later I went up to her flat with Charles Powell to offer her our support as tearfully she read papers for the Cabinet which was to follow at 9 a.m. She worried about our futures, not about hers. We told her not to be so silly and to think about herself for a change. We also popped in to see Denis Thatcher who was breakfasting elsewhere in the flat. He was dressed in black for the memorial service of Lady Home. He was touched by our call. At 8.30 we had a meeting with the Prime Minister to prepare for questions in the House. The Prime Minister went downstairs at 9 a.m. for Cabinet. What was usually a gossipy, humming and jolly gathering in the ante-room was embarrassingly silent. There was a sense of impending doom. Mrs Thatcher found announcing her resignation to the Cabinet a traumatic experience. She broke down but recovered to conduct a businesslike meeting which decided to reinforce our troops in the Gulf. Then off Mrs Thatcher went to the Palace to tender her resignation to the Queen. On her return at 11.30 she was greeted by Sarah Charman, one of my press officers, on the doorstep. Once inside they both broke down and had a tearful effect on each other for the rest of the day. They were not the only ones who were misty-eyed.

I dreaded Prime Minister's questions in the House and the immediately following confidence debate. How could she possibly get through? But get through she did with a supreme act of will, courage, strength of character and professionalism that transcended the tears. In a moment of defiance, she even said she was enjoying it. It was a truly formidable performance. Even after eleven years she could still surprise us with her resilience and guts. For the rest much of it was a blur. I had been preparing myself for retirement in eighteen months' time. I resolved to go within the fortnight. As well as Sir Robin Butler, head of the Home Civil Service, I informed Gus O'Donnell and Brian Mower, press secretaries respectively to John Major and Douglas Hurd, that if either of their principals won I would do my best to ease them into Number 10 but I was determined that neither Mr Major nor Mr Hurd should be tainted by my entirely undeserved reputation for Ministerial assassination and leaking. Unprofessional though it may seem, if Mr Heseltine walked in the door, I would walk out. There were limits.

I recall the Sunday lobby – which had caused me so much trouble – lining up to shake me somewhat emotionally by the hand at the end of my last briefing for them on Friday, 23 November. The flood of flowers into Number 10 as the nation – indeed, the world – recognized the political passing of a phenomenon. Sir Robin Day dubbing me 'Yesterday's man' (which is true) when I met him in the Garrick before the Prime Minister's farewell party for the staff in Number 10 on Monday 26 November. My great sadness in removing from my room four water-colours by Donald Crossley, a contemporary of mine at Hebden Bridge Grammar School, which had hung there for eleven years in tribute to Donald's work and as a reminder of where I came from. Mrs Thatcher embracing John Major, her favourite political son, in Number 11 after his triumph on Tuesday 27 November.

I missed her sad departure from Number 10 the following day.

I had to drive to Halifax for the funeral of my brother-in-law, Ted O'Hara, Nancy's sister's husband. A week later – Thursday 6 December – I retired under an avalanche of expressions of good wishes and fierce expressions of anger over a Channel 4 programme about my performance as Chief Press Secretary, my style and my relationship with Mrs Thatcher. The letters were full of wonderful tributes. The Channel 4 programme was only what anyone would expect from that neck of the journalistic jungle.

At positively the last of my many farewell parties in Whitehall and Westminster, Mrs Thatcher touchingly said that she could not have gone on as long as she did without me. I believe she lasted as long as she did because she had a coherent philosophy and a programme to match. Because she had substance, weight, depth, dimension and above all guts. Because she worked at it. Because overall she was successful beyond the people's wildest hopes. Because she believed in people – and above all the British people. Because she was a patriot. Because she spoke her mind and stood for something. Because she stood for freedom and justice and was prepared to defend them. Because she wanted people to get on. Because she had the common touch. And because she didn't want to be loved. As a result she was respected beyond measure.

It is idle to speculate whether she might have won a fourth term if panic and what was described as a Heselteenie cult had not gripped the Parliamentary Tory Party. For what it is worth, I think she could have won again because she was a leader and because, when the electoral chips were down, she represented something which the British people could appreciate. But the number of ifs is seemingly endless. What matters is that, after changing so much for the better, Mrs Thatcher retired undefeated in the Commons and in the country and enhanced her already towering reputation by the impressive and dignified manner of her going.

Nor did they kill the messenger. He retired happy, fulfilled and still amazed that Mrs Thatcher chose him.

24

Fall and Decline

The messenger, still amazed at his exciting and privileged life, has had – and fortunately still has – a peculiar retirement. Indeed, twelve years after the resignation of Mrs Thatcher (now Baroness with the Orders of LG and OM to go with an honorary FRS after her name), I feel a fraud to describe myself as retired. My only qualification is a Civil Service pension which, again fortunately for me, if you are given to looking on the bright side, the Treasury and Inland Revenue have done their level best to recoup.

In those twelve years I have worked a pretty consistent seven days a week. I not only returned to journalism as a long serving columnist with the *Daily Express* and *PR Week* (with both of which I spent seven years); I also took up broadcasting and even became a pundit and programme presenter. After long stints with the BBC reviewing the newspapers on breakfast TV and presenting *The Midnight Hour* politics programme for BBC 2, I now regularly review the newspapers for BSkyB. So far, I have averaged well over one radio and one TV broadcast a week (996 TV and 739 radio broadcasts from 1991 to the end of 2002). I also still write a monthly column for the weekly newspaper on which I started my career in 1948 – the *Hebden Bridge Times*. I am delighted to say it does not seem to be good for the blood pressures of the trendy offcumdens who have colonised the district.

Latterly, I have written three books about my endless but for too long distant fascination with Yorkshire as well as one about that modern media obsession, 'spin'. I became an after-dinner speaker in response to public demand following the publication of the first edition of this book – they wanted (and still want) to hear what Lady Thatcher was really like – and, to my wife's delight, I have made with her at least two voyages a year since 1991 as a lecturer on cruise liners on the Atlantic, Pacific and Indian Oceans and the Mediterranean, Baltic and North Seas. Overall, I have given well over one thousand prepared talks and lectures since I retired.

No sooner had I finished writing this book in the 1990-1 winter than McDonald's, the hamburger people, invited me on to their UK board as a non-executive director – as did Hill and Knowlton, the international PR agency. This experience, in each case lasting more than a decade, was a rewarding insight into the way multinationals work. In fact, I am still on McDonald's board. They have been a delight to know and taught me a lot. In 1994 the British Franchise Association, the representative and regulatory body for franchising in the UK, asked me to be their president and I still am trying to promote the virtues of a sector which enables many who never thought it would be possible to go into business on their own account.

All this time I have been vice president of Country Guardian, which I helped to form in 1991 to fight against the wrecking of our upland countryside with useless, politically correct wind farms. And since 1998 I have been secretary of Supporters of Nuclear Energy, which is trying to hasten the dawn of reality in the body politic. Nuclear power is the answer to our prayers in an era of global warming since it reconciles our demand for ever more electricity with the need to cut pollution: it does not emit greenhouse gases. Nuclear and wind are not in competition and I have never seen any incompatibility in my two positions. But the professional – and unprincipled – greens and wind power industry do their best to irradiate Country Guardian because of my dual membership. So far as I know, there is only one other member of Country Guardian who is a nuclear supporter.

Perhaps inevitably, I have been called upon regularly to lecture about government and media relations which, as I shall show, have taken a serious turn for the worse since 1997. Most of my work is done in the UK but, thanks to Sir Rodric Braithwaite, our former Ambassador in Moscow, I have become closely associated over the last 10 years with a remarkable institution – the Moscow School of Political Studies – which has by now imbued more than 5,000 young Russians with democratic ideals. It is one example of the charitable work which comes the way of all who lead an active retirement. To instance another form, it was a joy to follow Ned Sherrin as president of the Television and Radio Industries Club with its remarkable record of helping a wide spectrum of charities.

I have also become involved with several universities – Newcastle upon Tyne where a unit I launched in 1989 (before my retirement) to study relations between Government and industry has evolved into the social sciences arm of a college at Westlakes, near Whitehaven in West Cumbria, specialising in communication, opinion forming and influencing policy-makers; Huddersfield, where I served for six years on the university's council; Buckingham, the independent university, where Lady Thatcher, then Chancellor, conferred upon me an honorary doctorate; and Middlesex which bestowed on me a doctorate and whose business school has even designated me as a visiting professor. I can think of nobody less like a professor than myself. I am a doer not a thinker, though I don't think much of the thoughts of too many who profess to be thinkers.

While deliberately avoiding membership of any political party, I have maintained my friendship with Margaret Thatcher, though I never call her Margaret, and was friends with her husband, whom I did call Denis. The habits of a Civil Servant die hard. In the early 1990s I often forgot myself as we sat and talked in her office and she made me work at an issue troubling her, as if she had never left office: I called her 'Prime Minister'. She didn't seem to mind nor, when, correcting myself, as I did once or twice, I described her as 'Prime Minister Emeritus'. She is now sadly not the woman she was because her memory is fading but she still mines my opinions and ideas when we meet. As ever there is no small talk, no anecdotes, at least not from her, and not much looking back. Just cross-examination and notes – her notes.

I have more often been touched by the thanks I have received from complete strangers for working for 'our greatest Prime Minister' than I have been momentarily depressed by others, similarly unknown to me, who have sidled up to me to convey their burning hatred of my former boss and myself, by association. So what's new? She always polarised opinions. 'Bring back Maggie' is, perhaps inevitably, the plaintive cry I still hear most.

I have also acquired in retirement two grandchildren, Charlotte and Tom, who make all that has gone before worthwhile.

It is fair to say that I consider myself lucky to have led such an fascinating working life and retirement. I am also astounded to have passed the allotted span of three score years and ten after being dogged, especially in childhood, by chronic asthma. But none of this good fortune makes me feel contented, however happy and fulfilled I may be, complacent or inclined to shut up if somebody gives me the floor. And that is the gift bestowed upon me by Politico's in reprinting this my first book. I shall use the floor of these pages to look at the world after 12 years out of the front line through the eyes – some would say the rheumy eyes – of an old press secretary who is libelously described as 'Britain's first spin doctor'. I cover the phenomenon of 'spin' in the final chapter.

It would be churlish of me if, before blasting off, I did not record my gratitude to all those – journalists, politicians and members of the public – who have helped to make me notorious. Notoriety is an invaluable asset in the age of ephemeral celebrity. It is quite possible that, without their attentions, my retirement would have been much less busy. In my talks, drawing on Chapter 22, I put it like this:

> The *Independent* newspaper once called me 'a mound of poisoned suet'. And the *Daily Mirror* 'an obnoxious renta-spleen'. This is what comes of spending 11 years with the wrong woman – as she was described. Indeed, I have known three kinds of abuse – journalistic, political and public.
>
> Journalists have got extremely personal about me. Craig Brown, in *The Times*, said I was loopy-looking, like one the background soldiers in *Dad's Army*. My unauthorised biographer, whose name always escapes me, but he is a friend of Peter Mandelson, said 'my eyebrows writhe and heave like a pair of lovesick squirrels'. And Peter Oborne, of the *Spectator*, said I was 'Neanderthal man' – Neanderthal man in the evolution of Number 10 press secretaries to Alastair Campbell's *homo sapiens*. Well, *homo*, maybe, though the evidence is entirely contrary. But *sapiens* certainly not, given the way his spin doctoring wrecked the Labour Government's reputation within three years.
>
> When the politicians joined in, John Biffen said I was 'a

402

rough spoken Yorkshire Rasputin' – in a moment of generosity. He also said I was the sewer but not the sewerage, presumably to indicate that I was the conduit for Mrs Thatcher's political sludge. And Sir Edward Heath said I was 'a menace to the constitution'. Well, he should know.

Finally, the public. A Chesterfield chap wrote to the *Radio Times* demanding early warning of my appearances on BBC *Breakfast News*. He said that when I appeared I frightened the children, caused the milk to go off and sent the cat missing for days. But the *piece de resistance* of all abuse came from a fellow Yorkshireman, a certain Colin Robinson FCA, of 59 Devonshire Street West in Keighley, in my native West Yorkshire just over the hill from Hebden Bridge where I was brought up.

Mr Robinson wrote to Mrs Thatcher in the following terms: 'My friend Mr Armitage knew Mr Ingham in his Hebden Bridge days. He swears that some years back he underwent a sex change and was formerly a Miss Elsie Ackroyd'. Miss Ackroyd was apparently a formidable woman in those parts, equally well known for the sharpness of her tongue and the quality of her rock cakes.

There were some pretty queer looks in the Prime Minister's study when this missive arrived. I thought I heard her say: 'Is he one of us?'. I swore I had never made a rock cake in my life. At any rate, Mrs Thatcher left Mr Robinson to my tender mercies and I think he was lucky he was not dealt with by Elsie Ackroyd.

I wish to record my thanks to all who have made me notorious. They have also made me a nice little earner in retirement.

Margaret Thatcher was also a nice little earner in retirement for, among other things, her foundation for democracy. She has flown the world on the lucrative lecture circuit. It once fell to me to brief her for one of these occasions. It was the McDonald's and Coca Cola senior management conference in West Palm Beach which the two companies take turns to organise. I had just sat through a worthy but ponderous lecture by Herr Genscher, the former German Foreign Minister, when she arrived. 'For heaven's sake,' I said, 'be lively. They need some fireworks after Herr Genscher.' She was never likely to send them to sleep but she really had their eyes popping when the chairman of Coca Cola had the honour of putting the first question. 'Say, ma'm', he asked, 'where do you see any leadership in the world?'. After what seemed an interminable pause for effect, the original executive woman drew herself up to her full height on high heels and almost spat into the microphone: 'If there were any leadership in the world today we would have sorted out Bosnia by now'. Sniff, sniff. They were deeply impressed.

In many ways I regard my old boss in retirement as the tragic figure of my declining years. After her 20-hours-a-day devotion to the interests of the UK for 11½ years she found herself on what might just as well have been the scrap heap. Cynthia Crawford, her help on Prime Ministerial trips, told me it was like 'someone coming off heroin'. Here was a woman with no interests outside politics, unable to find a satisfactory alternative role to being chief executive, UK Inc., and lauded abroad but eternally bruised by the nasty method of her domestic disposal. Fancy being stabbed in the back by those who owe almost everything to your political leadership! She soon became disillusioned with her chosen successor, John Major only then to find Tony Blair not what she had imagined him to be, leave aside his astonishingly decisive performance in backing George W. Bush over Iraq. Why is Blair 'reckless', as Labour MPs have put it, abroad and palsied at home? It is a question that will launch a thousand theses.

Lady Thatcher has never been an infallible judge of men. She certainly got it wrong with Major since he turned out not to be a political leader but a consensus man. (As someone who led her governments from seven leagues out ahead, she had an abiding contempt for consensus – it's what you get when you can't agree', she used to say.) As I have made clear, Lady Thatcher cannot deny that she nurtured and cultivated Major. She lifted him out of the Whips' Office into the Department of Social Security, which was where she began her Ministerial career, though it was then called the Ministry of Pensions and National Insurance. Then she made him Chief Secretary where he handled public expenditure very successfully, briefly Foreign Secretary and finally the Chancellor who persuaded her against her better judgement to go into the European exchange rate mechanism (ERM). And she held on in office at least partly because she thought he needed another three years to toughen and mature. It is hardly conceivable she would have persevered to this extent had she known of Major's dalliance with Edwina Currie, then a junior minister, though she was astonishingly uncensorious for one so narrowly brought up in Grantham. Needless to say the affair came as news to me more than a decade after the event.

But, to be scrupulously fair, Major, the deceptively persuasive boy from Brixton, drew the short straw. He was elected in 1990 partly because he wasn't Michael Heseltine, the instrument by which Mrs Thatcher's Deputy Prime Minister, Sir Geoffrey Howe, the real Brutus, knifed her, and partly because the panicky Conservative Parliamentary Party thought the country wanted a break from hand bagging. He inherited a tiring, largely spent force which seemed unlikely to renew itself in office and was manifestly split on the great issue of the day – Europe. At the depths of a very deep recession, he managed narrowly to win the 1992 election against Neil Kinnock who was scarcely Prime Ministerial material, though he deserves credit for taking on and defeating the militants who were killing the Labour Party. But Major never recovered from Britain's vastly expensive enforced exit from the ERM in 1992. Later he even felt obliged to resign and challenge his party to back him or sack him. They ran away from ditching Major only to find the media doing Mandelson's dirty work as Labour's campaigning genius of rubbishing the Tories for him. In what seemed to be an orchestrated series of revelations after Major had made a 'back to basics' speech, initially in the context of education, journalists traced a series of mostly obscure Tory MPs to the wrong bed. The Government party came to resemble a self-indulgent rabble and some like Jonathan Aitken paid dearly in prison for their self-indulgence. Others who took Mohamed al-Fayed's shilling at Harrod's saw their political careers terminated.

I cannot say that Lady Thatcher was invariably helpful to Major. Indeed, she was rather unhelpful on a few occasions and even threatened on one of them to be 'a backseat driver'. I taxed her about her indiscretions, especially when she gave an interview to the *European* immediately before she attended the Tory Party conference where she sat silently, having got her points over in advance. I told her that she should think twice before she thought of being difficult again, otherwise she would rapidly lose the sympathy and loyalty of her party. As one who had to put up with the curmudgeonly Sir Edward Heath, Mrs Thatcher always admired Lord Home (formerly Sir Alec Douglas-Home) for his impeccable behaviour as a former Prime Minister. Yet if she did not quite live up to his example, it could be argued she showed remarkable restraint, given her frustration, chronic lack of tact and pungent views. She was also never best served by hangers-on who were plugged into the gossip columns of an increasingly nasty media.

Lady Thatcher saw the party she had led to three consecutive election victories – the last two with majorities of more than 100 – collapse to a crushing, humiliating and humdinger of a defeat in 1997. Tony Blair, the man she rather took to and who reciprocated by consulting her on gaining office, came to power with a majority of 179 on a wave of enthusiasm and expectation she never experienced in 1979. To recap, Britons then doubted whether their country was governable any more after the unions' so-called Winter of Discontent. In 1997, the unions were in a box, or framework of law, and our economy was the best performing of the major nations in Europe. Major and Kenneth Clarke, his Chancellor, never get the credit for bequeathing to Labour the sort of financial, economic and commercial Britain that no previous post-war government had been privileged to enjoy. Until then, Governments' inheritance had been the certainty of an economic crisis of some sort.

Lady Thatcher's consolation was often to tell me: 'We [i.e. herself] showed Labour how to become electable again'. That consolation is now wearing thin. As Chancellor Gordon Brown increasingly resorts to tax and spend, he bids fair to demonstrate only that New Labour takes longer to ruin an economy than Old Labour. Perhaps that is the 'Third Way' of government which Blair professes to lead but seems incapable of defining, even after a conference in his first term to discover its fundamentals. It is certainly an improvement but it falls a long way short of a Damascene conversion from Labour's version of socialism, even if Blair did ditch Clause IV of the Labour Party's constitution requiring wholesale public ownership, distanced himself from the unions and pledged himself to prudent finance and the containment of inflation. That, a commendable early determination not to squander the Tory economic legacy and a near-useless Conservative Opposition, gave him his coveted full second term in Government, the first to be secured by Labour.

To underline the tragedy of Lady Thatcher's retirement – not to mention her frustration and astonishing restraint in the circumstances – we have only to look at the Conservatives in government and opposition since 1990. Some would say that the wilderness inevitably beckoned in 1997 after 18 years in office – an age by twentieth century British standards of government longevity. All parties find it well nigh impossible to renew themselves in Government. Indeed, I am convinced no Prime Minister, the custodian of a party's philosophy and direction, is ever as powerful as the moment he or she first steps into Number 10, though there can be periods of rejuvenation after, in Lady Thatcher's case, for example, the Falklands campaign and the 1983 election triumph. But the Conservatives were not merely worn out and decadent by 1997; they had lost their ideological compass and have not yet recovered it.

Leadership came far too early for William Hague at 36. Like Major, his party probably chose him because he was not somebody else – to wit, the europhile Kenneth Clarke. Yet however brilliantly he performed on the floor of the House – and he is probably its most natural orator – he made a number of presentational gaffes and was always struggling to contain the euro-polarisation which afflicts real British political parties as distinct from that conglomeration of local cracked-pavement opportunists called the Liberal Democrats. He also did precious little to re-think the Tory appeal and became an interlude. That should not necessarily prevent him from becoming Prime Minister when the Tories rediscover what they stand for and loyalty after their matricide and fratricide spanning three decades. He never had much of a chance between 1997 and 2001 when he resigned with considerable dignity.

His successor, Iain Duncan Smith, who was once the apple of Thatcher's eye, has endured in his short tenure since June 2001 persistent and regular rumblings of discontent, brutal criticism and threats to bring him down. Yet he is the first to be democratically elected by the whole membership. Such is the death wish of his party that it is already possible after only two years to describe him as a survivor. You need fortitude to be a Tory leader these days. If it goes on like this, it will become unleadable, to coin a word. It is true that Duncan Smith does not exude the authority of leadership, which is rather surprising in view of his military background. His baldness, like that of Hague, is even considered a handicap in this television age, even though the skinhead is the height of popular fashion in men. But he is showing signs of tackling the urgent and necessary business of re-thinking the Conservative appeal and had a very good week in May 2003 when he pledged to end the scandal of tuition fees imposed on university students who are widely reported to be starting working life with debts of £10,000-plus round their necks. Welcome though good weeks are for him, he needs good months, not to say years, to be taken seriously.

His initiative on tuition fees reminds me of a thoroughly enjoyable passage of arms I had in Huddersfield University's governing council when those fees were canvassed. It was clear that the Blairites on it simply could not understand how 'Mrs Thatcher's chap' could be against such an idea. They understood me even less when I told them that I proposed to offer my services as a shop steward to the Students' Union. I would, I said, table two fundamental demands: a reliable measure of teaching performance – students would reasonably wish to know what they were paying for – and a two-year degree to minimise their tuition costs. If Buckingham University could have two-year degree courses so could Huddersfield. In any case, it would be a selling point. I got the impression some people thought I was mad or had spat in church.

But to return to Duncan Smith. He has not been helped by his party who clearly have as much difficulty getting their knives out of their leaders as do the British media. But there is one fundamental complaint which has Thatcher's generation of Tory politicians seething with frustration: they wonder – or did until Duncan Smith scored a hit on tuition fees after the Tories had won 561 seats in the local elections – whether their party has lost its ability to oppose, to harry a Government and to make it look sick. I think I can claim some expertise in this matter after a decade performing as a speaker at Tory constituency dinners. Their frustrations are all the greater for there being plenty to oppose. The internecine warfare between Blair and Gordon Brown is a wonder to behold, especially on Europe. Taxes are beginning to pinch to no purpose. Improvements in education, the NHS, crime, transport and welfare (from the reform of which the Government long since ran away) seem as far away as ever for all the billions of pounds Gordon Brown claims to be chucking at them. Asylum and immigration stand testimony to infirmity of purpose and incompetence. The constitution has been tampered with, if not entirely wrecked, without obvious benefit and the so-called reform of the House of Lords is a scandal. For hereditary peers read Tony's cronies. And the Government's word is no longer trusted for reasons I deal with in the next chapter. In these circumstances, the Tories, Conservatives argue, should have the Government in the mincer. Instead, they haven't yet got it to the abbatoir.

For all Labour's failings we can far from rule out a third term for it. Nor will Europe necessarily do for it before 2005–6 as it did, through internecine warfare, for Mrs Thatcher, Major and Hague since Blair has effectively put off a referendum on the single European currency before the next election if he thinks he cannot win it. He may be in trouble trying to avoid a referendum on the proposed new European constitution if, as seems likely, that is resolved in 2004. But the Tories are as divided as Labour, if not more so, on our further integration into Europe and there seems no prospect of an end to a split nation until we are sunk in Europe or come out of it.

After attending thirty-one consecutive European summits in the 1980s, I have no illusions left as one who voted to confirm our membership of the Common Market in 1975. France and Germany do not want us at the heart of Europe. They mean to run it. We are valued only for our financial contribution and our respectability in the wider world. Otherwise, we are a nuisance. The case for membership of a customs union is infinitely weaker than when we joined because world trade negotiations have drastically reduced tariff barriers. The case for more voluntary international collaboration across Europe is greater now that the former satellites have emerged from the darkness of Communism. But that is not what is on offer. The latest proposals for European constitutional reform are manifestly another step along the road to a European state with its own government. Our future is a regionalised satellite of Europa, governed, if that is the right term given the prevalence of corruption and fraud at the heart of it, from Brussels. I want no truck with this kind of Europe whose capacity for treachery was fully displayed in the run up to the Iraq episode in Bush's war against terrorism.

Renegotiation of the tentacles of the EU (which Thatcher has advocated in *Statecraft*), still less cutting ourselves free of them, are not on the agenda. It's like a bad marriage. We find it difficult to live with each other but can't bring ourselves to divorce. So, there is no prospect of an end to the political nightmare that is the EU. And all the while the argument brings politicians into further contempt. This is dangerous, given the public disaffection with politics generally as demonstrated by the miserable 59.3 per cent turn out at the 2001 general election.

Thinking people feel they have been systematically misled, initially by Sir Edward Heath in negotiating our entry at any price and failing to come clean about the political nature of the enterprise. They are not now inclined to believe anybody who seeks to finesse away the latest proposed accretion of powers by the EU as mere 'tidying up' when they know that the history of our membership is one long encroachment on our right to run our own affairs within the constraints of the international market. Peter Hain made himself a laughing stock when he found great significance in the elimination of the word 'federal' from the latest Giscard d'Estaing blueprint for Europe's future. As if that makes the slightest difference after Mrs Thatcher's experience. After signing the Single European Act of 1985–6, to speed the opening up of European financial markets to British companies; her European colleagues promptly got round her carefully preserved vetoes by bringing forward legislation subject to mere majority voting. Trust is no longer a commodity to be cashed in by European supporters whose own cynical contempt for the public has bred a cynical contempt for them. The people fear the end of the UK as an independent nation. And who can blame them, given the record which has already in many respects – from trade to agriculture to law – made British Governments impotent in their own land.

Britain is not a nation content with itself. It is outwardly prosperous until you scratch below the surface of our towns and find the utter squalour of people's voyeuristic and hedonistic lives. Slums have always existed and probably always will but the excuse is wearing very thin. Graffiti appears to confirm we are the third world country some of us think we are becoming, if not we have not already become one. Educational attainment – or lack of it – is a scandal until you put yourself in the position of a teacher forced by the thought police to teach in an undisciplined environment. The police are apparently overwhelmed, even though money has been thrown at them, but one doubts the resolve of the average politically correct chief constable to concentrate on thieftaking instead of posturing. 'Lions led by donkeys' comes to mind. The ordinary copper does not get much help either from the courts where the judiciary has seldom been held in greater contempt for its feebleness. Leadership is today at a premium and is clearly not understood by the average tycoon whose creed is to reward himself ever more with both pay and pensions (while their employee pension funds are in crisis) and to protect himself with an assortment of plump financial cushions against failure. They are the best recruiting sergeants the trade unions have known since Gradgrind.

We also live under a tyranny from the sort of political correctness which makes racism, for example, the preserve of whites. It is sapping the moral fibre and will of the nation more certainly than our pale pink version of socialism ever managed. As I told Polly Toynbee, the *Guardian's* resident example of our utterly blinkered so-called intellectual elite, on a BBC programme: 'I do not want to be around when the British public wake up to the damage your kind have done to their country'. In fact, I would love to see that day dawn, but I do not think it would otherwise be pleasant. Meanwhile, my generation cry out for common sense – starting with a common sense understanding of human nature and not a hopelessly idealistic view that rewards and encourages excess and criminality.

The British media, in their various ways, chronicle and condemn or excuse all this while promoting decadence with a daily parade of so-called celebrities. Invariably, the sole qualification of these nonentities has been to appear on TV and behave badly, usually near nakedly. The worse their public performance the greater their reward in column inches and air time. The cheapening and coarsening of society gathers pace. The memory of those few heady years of the Thatcher-led revival of national pride is being swamped by a tide of tawdry mediocrity. And what has the Blair Government done? Why, contributed to the landslide. It has forfeited trust and rendered itself increasingly incredible by its peculiar method of governance – the governance of 'spin'.

25

Spinning into Oblivion

Whatever else happens before the ravages of time, Harold Macmillan's 'events, dear boy' and human frailty catch up with the Blair Government – as they do with all governments – we can already identify one certain failure. It is a failure which, in the light of circumstances, the Government's pledges and its consequently incredible performance, assumes monumental proportions. It is the failure of trust. Once lost, it is extremely difficult to recover.

New Labour, as it described itself, came to office in 1997 because after 18 years people had lost faith in the Conservatives who had also forfeited trust – first in their economic competence after the ERM debacle of 1992 and then in terms of probity. Tory 'sleaze', the charge so assiduously peddled by Labour, became an issue, if not the main issue, at the 1997 election. So, Blair came to office knowing how successful Labour had been in painting the Tories as the nasty, 'sleazy', untrustworthy party. He also knew how hard he had had to work to recover public trust in Labour after the loony tunes of the 1980s and the extended excesses of its paymasters, the trade unions. He realised, or should have realised, the value of trust as a political commodity.

Indeed, so highly did he regard its importance, that he included it as the ninth of the ten pledges in his 'contract with the people' at the 1997 election. He stated: 'We will clean up politics . . . and put the funding of political parties on a proper and accountable basis'. Against that background, Mr Blair's Government needed to be squeaky clean, sea green incorruptible and, given the political capital they made out of Tory sexual indiscretions, as unassailable as Ann Widdecombe. It rapidly became clear that the implications of his pledge – the need to follow his precepts – were either lost on Blair or that he was possessed of such an arrogantly sanctimonious view of himself that he felt he could do no wrong and people could believe no wrong of him. Perhaps the one blinded him to the need not only to be beyond reproach but also to be seen to be above it.

Within six months of coming to office Blair found his policy of banning tobacco advertising at odds with financing his party. Knowing Bernie Ecciestone, the man who made Formula 1 car racing big business, had given £1 million to the Labour Party and had been his host at Silverstone, he received Ecclestone and his team at Number 10. He then asked his Health Minister to look at ways of protecting sport in general and Formula 1 in particular. He defended his probity in a devious manner (which I shall come to later) which was bound to wreck trust. In doing so, he said on TV: 'I hope that people know me well enough and realise the type of person I am to realise I would never do anything to harm the country or anything improper. I never have. I think most people who have dealt with me think I am a pretty straight sort of guy'.

Several years later this 'pretty straight sort of guy' was assailed by the Mittal affair. Lakshmi Mittal, an Indian steel billionaire with a home in London, gave Labour £125,000 just before the 2001 election. Two months later Blair wrote favourably about Mittal's company to the president of Romania, where Mittal was trying to buy a steelworks, even though it was registered in a Caribbean tax haven, supposedly anathema to Labour, and employed only 90 people in the UK. Once again Blair had his back up against the wall of public scrutiny and defended himself in such an intricate way that newspapers were very free with the use of the word 'lies'. And then Paul Drayson, who gave £50,000 to the Labour Party, found his firm, Powderject, winning a £32m Health Department order for smallpox vaccine. This caused Bill Morris, retiring general secretary of the Transport and General Workers' Union to remark: 'It seems to a lot of people that the party is more or less abandoning its roots and the party is almost up for sale to the highest bidder'.

Interwoven with all this, Foreign Secretary Robin Cook ditched his wife at Heathrow Airport as they were about to go on holiday, apparently for presentational reasons, when his extra-marital affair was about to be exposed. Ron Davies, then Welsh Secretary, brought his political career effectively to an end by an extraordinary late night expedition to the homoerotic wastes of Clapham Common. He later used his interest in badgers to explain away his being found by the media in another compromising situation. And Peter Mandelson, the architect of New Labour's obsession with media manipulation, resigned twice from the Cabinet in one Parliament without apparently thinking he had done much wrong. First, he was found, as Secretary of State for Industry, to have kept under wraps a £373,000 loan to buy a house from a fellow Minister, Geoffrey Robinson, whose business dealings were under investigation by his Department. Then he was remarkably vague about his role, if any, in helping the wealthy Hindujah brothers, who underwrote the Faith Zone in the Millennium Dome, to secure British passports – in which the Blair Government was far more helpful than Major's had been.

This is not the full toll of Labour sleaze. It is merely the more celebrated cases that in other times, other mores, would have had Prime Ministers fighting for their very lives. I doubt whether Mrs Thatcher would have survived the Ecclestone affair since the media, who love to destroy their legends, were desperate to impugn her integrity. By any standards, the Blair Government has been lightly judged, not to say indulged, by media and public for years. But the cumulative effect has been damaging. The destruction of trust has been all the greater for the manner in which these scandals were handled and the Blair Government's approach to presentation and managing relations with the media. This brings me to 'spin', the hallmark of the Blair Government.

Labour's paranoia about the media – press, radio and television – lies deep in its history. Labour Governments have never had a happy relationship with the press primarily for ideological reasons. By contrast, both Labour and Conservative Governments – at least up to 1997 – regarded the broadcasters, and especially the BBC, with suspicion – the one as if it were a Right wing conspiracy and the other as though it were a Trotskyist cell. Who can now blame the Tories if they see anti-Conservative bias in every BBC broadcast when the chairman of its board of governors is a rich Labour crony, Gavyn Davies, and its director general, Greg Dyke, a £55,000 contributor to the Labour Party? Another case of New Labour (and the BBC) failing to understand it has not only to be impartial but also seen to be impartial in these matters.

With good and bruising reason, Labour have historically felt the dice heavily loaded against them by anti-socialist press barons. It is true that, apart from their 'socialism', their own behaviour contributed to their problems for they were, until the Conservatives latterly caught the bug, the fractious, divided party of 'splits'. After the 1978–9 'Winter of Discontent' they were in serious trouble because of their association with the trade unions and the power within their ranks of militants and what came to be dubbed the 'loony left'. It became clear that, after Mrs Thatcher's success in ending the rapidly failing post-war tax-and-spend consensus and revitalising the British economy, they would have to change if they were to remain a political force in the land.

Neil Kinnock deserves a place in the Labour hall of fame for taking on the militants. Peter Mandelson, the grandson of Herbert Morrison, a similarly unstable pillar of the 1945–51 Attlee era, modernised and revitalised Labour's campaigning force and helped to re-think its appeal to the people. A youthful looking ex-public schoolboy, Tony Blair, with a minimum of political baggage and fewer convictions, came to the fore immediately after John Smith's early death as Labour leader in 1994 to identify 'media, media and the media' as his route to the crown. He secured it over the still twitching body of Gordon Brown, his brooding Chancellor since 1997, and acquired Alastair Campbell, a former propagandist political editor of the *Daily Mirror* and the now defunct *Today* as his press secretary. Between them Blair, Mandelson and Campbell carry the can for the massive lost of trust in the Government which, according to the polls, nearly halved in the first two years of its second term. By the summer of 2003 only 29 per cent thought that on balance it had been honest and trustworthy.

Mandelson, a former researcher on LWT's *Weekend World*, came to the Labour Party's publicity directorship in 1985 as a greenhorn of 31. He was undoubtedly intelligent, energetic, driven and Machiavellian and brought with him his programme's propagandist approach. *Weekend World* was a by-word in journalism for interviewing journalists endlessly for the quote it was after to support its story line. Mandelson's business was 'creating the truth'. It was also 'control, control, control' – to keep the party 'on message' – and to suppress the all too often damaging dissent which had dogged his party in the past. He created an impressive campaigning machine, perfected after much study of American models, to propagate the message while, simultaneously, the Tories were allowing their Rolls-Royce model to decay into a 'penny-farthing' – as Harold Wilson, a former Labour Prime Minister had described Labour's 1960s publicity set-up.

Mandelson set out his stall early in the advertising industry weekly, *Campaign*: 'Of course we want to use the media, but the media will be our tools, our servants; we are no longer content to let them be our persecutors'. To this end, he correctly identified the weaknesses of journalists faced with a monopoly supplier of news in the highly competitive news business. So, he set out to create a dependency culture among them – and, of course, to terrorise those who chose independence. Trying to de-stabilise journalists with their editors seems to have been pretty routine. He even once wrote to Rupert Murdoch to try to get him to sack Trevor Kavanagh, the distinguished and influential political editor of the *Sun*.

Campbell, son of a Yorkshire vet, came to political journalism about the time Mandelson set out on his historic mission to make Labour electable again. As Number 10 press secretary, I got on with him quite well, given that he was never likely to write anything favourable about Mrs Thatcher and her Government. We come from the same part of the world and even have a mutual interest in the fortunes of Burnley AFC, though Campbell is by far the more active supporter. We were also regular reviewers of newspapers on BBC *Breakfast News* in the early 1990s. He had a colourful past after university as a soft porn writer, busking bagpiper and croupier and emerged teetotal from a breakdown in his early years as a Fleet Street journalist. He is intelligent, has a genius for tabloid journalism, and is perhaps purpose-built for the sort of 'spin politics' New Labour developed – tough, aggressive, a clever tactician and with a suitably menacing aura to go with Mandelson's more feline approach. As a journalist, Campbell formed a close, supportive bond with Kinnock and then with Blair before becoming his press secretary in 1994. The pieces were then in place to 'spin' Blair, Mandelson and Campbell into Government.

Between them they sold Blair, a consummate actor, as the

acceptable face of New Labour, leader of the celebrated 'Third Way', even though not even a conference of eggheads was able satisfactorily to define it after they had secured office. To make himself saleable, Blair ditched clause four of the Labour Party's constitution, requiring wholesale public ownership, distanced himself from the unions and pledged himself to prudent finance and the containment of inflation. The intimidation and abuse of journalists who did not write or present stories New Labour's way is chronicled in the works, for example, of Nick Jones, former BBC political correspondent, and Peter Oborne, of the *Spectator*. Yet, in spite of their methods, they managed to rally roughly two-thirds of the national press, including Murdoch's *Sun*, to New Labour's support in 1997 and to hold on to them, partly because of the lack of a viable alternative, in 2001.

May Day 1997 ended in Romanesque triumph for their project. The following day, Blair entered Number 10 – actually waved in by Labour Party workers directed to Downing Street with Union Jacks in a first deceptive act of what is called 'spin' – lord of all he surveyed, with a record majority of 179. One got the impression – for Mandelson and Campbell are not modest men – that this was a 'spin doctors' triumph. Undoubtedly, they had apparently changed the nature of their product and certainly its packaging. They had also sold it vigorously and persuasively, though by 1997 they were the only show in town, so debilitated had the Tories become. But they were not just satisfied with making it into government; they wanted to stay there. Blair coveted a second full term which Labour had never previously secured. So they started as they meant to go on in government: campaigning.

To convey any understanding of the watershed that their accession to power on May 2, 1997 represents in the manner of Britain's governance, I must delve back into history, some of which is covered in Chapters 11, 13 and 21. Relations between politicians and governments and journalists in Britain evolved with glacial slowness over the centuries. Government officials appointed to liaise with journalists appeared haltingly and haphazardly between the wars. The decisive break came in 1945 when the Attlee Government decided to disband the wartime Ministry of Information but to establish a peacetime Government Information Service (GIS) which formally came into being in 1949. The idea was controversial because MPs felt it would weaken the influence of Parliament and the Conservative Opposition that it would arm the Government with a powerful advantage. In fact, the Conservatives, however critical they had been of it in opposition, quietly accepted it when they returned to office in 1951.

By then it had had several years to bed down as a branch of the Civil Service. As such, members of the GIS were required to behave like good Civil Servants – to act only for the Government of the day, not the party in office; to remain politically impartial and above the party political battle and polemic; to deny Governments the expenditure of taxpayers' money for party political purposes; to give honest and candid advice and never to lie or mislead; to observe confidentiality – i.e. not to leak – and to respect the privileges of Parliament.

This code governed the operations of every one of my predecessors as Number 10 Chief Press Secretary from Lord Francis-Williams, Attlee's press secretary, to Major's three press secretaries after me. It was also enforced by Parliament – Tory as well as Labour MPs kept a close eye on my operations – and Permanent Secretaries, the heads of Government Departments and also their accounting officers, who had to answer for the expenditure of public money to the Commons' Public Accounts Committee. It effectively ruled out campaigning, except on such uncontroversial issues as road safety vaccination and energy conservation, and was death to what has come to be called 'spin'. So much for the claim so assiduously pursued by Labour politicians and their ignorant poodles in the media that I was the original spin doctor – the better to excuse Campbell.

We had never heard of 'spin' in the UK until just before I retired in 1990. Until then press secretaries had been in the business of presentation – putting the best possible gloss on a policy, action or circumstance within the severe constraints of the Civil Service code while at the same time ensuring that they maintained their credibility as informants. Press secretaries have only one stock in trade: their credibility. It takes time to build it up but it can be lost within seconds and incredible press secretaries are about as much use as a broken wheel. For credibility read trust.

The term 'spin doctor' had been coined, or at least put into circulation, by a *New York Times* journalist, appropriately you may feel in Orwell's 1984. His concept of the media manager spinning yarns and doctoring facts succeeded in conveying a sinister air to the whole business of government communication and everyone in the trade of media relations is a spin doctor now, regardless of any justification. It conveys the impression of unethical communication for short term advantage and therefore without restraint or judgement.

Campbell's appointment as Chief Press Secretary to the Prime Minister did not automatically qualify him for the epithet of spin doctor, even though he got the job because of his relationship and political support for Blair and was amply qualified on the basis of his track record in Opposition. Whether he would come to merit the term in Government would depend on his performance. Had he behaved like previous special adviser-press secretaries he would have escaped it. Under his status as a special adviser he was free to adopt a party political stance within certain constraints and had an exceptional dispensation (one of two in Number 10) to direct Civil Servants. This contract was not breaking new ground. Lord Francis-Williams, Douglas Clark (Sir Anthony Eden's press secretary) and Sir Trevor Lloyd-Hughes and Joe Haines (Wilson's press secretaries) had all been recruited from outside the Civil Service and so accommodated. But all of them had played their hands carefully and largely succeeded in avoiding serious controversy.

It could be argued that the Blair Government's communications system went wrong because of inexperience. Certainly Campbell and Mandelson, initially Minister without Portfolio in the Cabinet Office, were new to Government as were virtually all the members of Blair's first administration. In fact, only six of the 100 or so MPs who were invited to join the 1997 Government had been ministers eighteen years previously and then generally only on the lowest rung of the ladder. Blair and the leading members of his Cabinet were also newcomers to Government and he revealed his ignorance of what Campbell could do as a special adviser-press secretary in the Commons when he said: 'There is one reason why the Opposition attack the press spokesman: he does an effective job of attacking the Conservative Party'. The code of practice for special advisers under which Campbell was supposed to be working stated: 'They [special advisers] are employed to serve the objectives of the Government and Department in which they work. It is this which justifies their being paid from public funds and being able to use public resources, and explains why their participation in party politics is carefully limited'. In fact, Campbell has not, publicly at least, spent his time rubbishing the Tories. But if Prime Ministers are prepared to countenance that sort of behaviour on the floor of the Commons – to set the tone – is it any wonder after that Blair gaffe there is concern that about half of the eighty-one special advisers his Government employs – twice the number in Major's time – are to some extent engaged on media relations or, as others would put it, manipulation at public expense to secure Labour's perpetuation in office.

The Blair Government's inexperience or ignorance of the rules is scarcely an adequate excuse for its 'spin'. The evidence suggests that this was not a Government overly concerned about rules or conventions or people if they got in the way of their project. And that project was to secure Blair's coveted second full term which no previous Labour Government had obtained. Common sense teaches that this would have been more or less guaranteed by a record breaking majority of 179, careful husbandry of Major's golden economic legacy and workmanlike, clean Government. That was not how Mandelson and Campbell saw it. They hit the ground running on 2 May, 1997 to campaign for a full second term. Not surprisingly they ran slap bang into a GIS brought up to be impartial.

Within four days press secretaries in departments – my former colleagues – were put on warning by Mandelson and Campbell. As a former head of the GIS, I cannot say it was universally good, still less brilliant. Like most human systems, it was patchy. But it was competent at communicating the essentials of policies, handling events and maintaining relations with an increasingly difficult, arrogant and nasty media. It also had a long-term view of its role within the rules and recognised the need to maintain credibility. Properly used and encouraged it would have done a far better job for Blair than his special advisers have managed.

My former colleagues were both excited and apprehensive

(because of Labour's fearsome media reputation in Opposition) at the arrival of a new Government. Within four days they were told face to face by Mandelson and Campbell that they would be given time to prove themselves, though they did not think it would be long. Four months later Campbell told the GIS in an encyclical to 'raise its game'. By that time his assurances that there would be no great purge of GIS members were hollow. It had already begun. Within twelve months that purge helped to carry away or move on twenty-five of those occupying the top forty-four posts in the GIS. By the 2001 election only one of the eighteen Departmental press secretaries Blair inherited remained in post and he retired soon afterwards. Of course, not all of them were sacked, though some were brutally dealt with. Some retired and others left of their own volition. But no Government accidentally presides over the removal of the top echelon of its GIS in one Parliament.

It was politicisation by intimidation, as I implied when I gave evidence to the Commission on Standards in Public Life. Imagine, I said, yourself as a humble press officer who has seen his GIS bosses sacked, who knows that the Civil Service heads of their Departments have not been able to protect them, who knows the Prime Minister and Campbell are obsessed with the media and who have experienced special advisers in Departments trying to 'bend' press notices to the Government's will. What would you do in those circumstances? Answer: keep your nose clean. The Commission, a politically representative body, did not seem impressed.

So what, apart from politicisation, did Campbell, as the chief spokesman, and his spin doctors get up to? In other words, what do I define as 'spin' – unethical communication without restraint or judgement? First, there was hyperactivity. With the connivance of editors who had certainly mislaid their editorial judgement, Blair and his ministers were prolific, if boring, columnists in the early years in praise of their dynamic stewardship in 'delivering' on their promises. Another form of hyperactivity, not to mention sleight of hand, was the endless recycling of initiatives and money which they were allowed to get away with by journalists who had subjected every Thatcher announcement to the 'new money' test. 'Is it new money?' they inquired, meaning is the cost to be met out of additional funds or taken from those already set aside for such work.

Another form of 'spin', as practised notably by Gordon Brown, the Chancellor, was to exaggerate the financial provision for policies while at the same time maintaining his love affair with the virtuous Prudence. For a long time the media allowed him to get away scot-free with not double but treble counting as, for example, when he presented an additional £10 billion allocation for education over three years as £19 billion.

It became clear that Blair would promise the earth one day – even to the extent of eliminating world poverty – only to have Campbell finesse it away when his pledge came under scrutiny. If there is one area more than any other where 'spin' has damaged the Government's credibility, it is an endless succession of pledges, backed up by minutely detailed targets, which have not been fulfilled. Blair recognised on the morrow of his still huge second election victory in June 2001 that he would have to concentrate on delivery. Two years on there was precious little to show for it.

Then there is the diversionary tactic at which some senior Civil Servants concede Campbell is the master. They look for the legal-isation of cannabis being wheeled out whenever the Government is in trouble. They also saw it in the instant appointment of Baroness Amos as the first black woman Cabinet Minister to succeed Clare Short when eventually she resigned in May 2003 over Iraq. You can almost hear Campbell's mind working: how can we get them talk-ing about something else other than Short? Canvassing the legal-isation of cannabis is not spin if it is genuinely on ministers' agendas. It is spin if it is just a diversionary tactic. Similarly, Baroness Amos's appointment was not spin if she were chosen on merit rather than as a ploy. But was she a diversionary tactic? Sadly, questions are raised about her appointment because the Blair Government is known for its domination by presentation rather than substance.

That domination was confirmed by the production by Campbell and his communications staff of a 2003 published dossier on the Iraq war which relied, among other things, on a twelve-year-old US doctorate thesis without much, if any, contribution by the intelligence services. After the war was won – in military terms at least – its entire justification on the grounds of Saddam's possession of weapons of mass destruction was raised because Blair was alleged to have 'sexed up' intelligence.

Another example of spin is Campbell's instant introduction of the selective leak. No substantial announcement is now first reported to Parliament by Ministerial statement as used to be the case. It is dictated to friendly journalists or newspapers known to be 'reliable' on the issue. The implication was – and remains – that there will be more to come if the story is handled satisfactorily. The independent-minded and 'unreliable' are starved of 'exclusives' with obvious consequences for their careers in a competitive media. No wonder some journalists have admired being 'stitched up' – i.e. misled – by Campbell. What else could they do in their state of dependency? Successive Speakers of the Commons have protested about this bypassing of Parliament without any noticeable effect. The Commons continues to be treated with contempt.

Spin has also led to routine bullying and abuse of journalists and broadcasters to try to secure more favourable angles or a more advantageous place in the running order of a bulletin. It has also rendered exclusives prey to the Campbell machine. Previously, when a journalist came to a press secretary to check on an exclusive, it was a matter of honour that that story remained his property and was not to be divulged to any other journalist. The *Daily Mirror* once found its very own bright idea of a statement (which it had drafted at the behest of Campbell) by President Clinton on Northern Ireland during a visit to a London summit mysteriously handed over to the *Sun*.

The Mafia would no doubt approve of the state to which Government–media relations have been reduced in the UK. The methods employed and the deception involved explain why trust of the Government has flown out of the window. Not surprisingly, it has been trying to distance itself from 'spin' since it won its second term. Mandelson, Campbell and Charlie Whelan, Gordon Brown's thug of a spin doctor who had to resign when he became a very counter-productive story, have each entered the public confessional to admit some of their faults. They evidently convinced Clare Short since in her resignation speech she saw spin as a problem of the first term.

On 11 September 2001, within an hour of the terrorists flying their planes into the twin towers of the World Trade Centre in New York, Jo Moore, a special adviser and spin doctor in the Department of Transport, circulated an email saying this was 'a good day to bury bad news'. That revealed the utter brutal cynicism of spin. She survived the public disclosure of her email only to succumb later when she showed she had not been cured of the tactic. Her Minister, Stephen Byers also had to resign, partly because he stood by her, in an episode which revealed the Government's spin machine in all its miserable tawdriness.

Worse was to come, apart from the Iraq dossier. Just before Christmas 2002 it was revealed that Cherie Blair, the Prime Minister's wife, had used an Australian con man, boyfriend of her style guru, to help her buy two flats in Bristol where her eldest son is at university. As the press peeled this onion, the Blair Government's spinning way with crises of the Ecclestone and Mittal variety, was almost caricatured. First, the *Mail on Sunday's* allegations were denied. The messenger was a Civil Service spokesman, no doubt for greater credibility, rather than Mrs Blair's media adviser, Fiona Miller, Campbell's partner. When *the Daily Mail* stood up the story by means of leaked emails, Number 10 attacked peripheral inaccuracies rather than the substance of the charge. Then Mrs Blair went on TV with a catch in her voice to apologise for misleading the press. And then the full might of Blair cronies was unleashed on the press and airwaves to whitewash and excuse his wife whose judgement as a QC and judge had been shown to be abysmal.

Whatever the spin doctors say, spin is just as much a part of the Blair second term as it was the first. It is still destroying trust. It is what can happen when a very powerful, media-obsessed Prime Minister is not controlled by his Cabinet, by his MPs in Parliament or by the senior Civil Service, who have been steamrollered, has no credible Opposition and has a largely cowed, client media. It may be argued that mid-term into second Parliament, the Cabinet, MPs and some elements of the media are no longer 'reliable' and that Iain Duncan Smith's Opposition is showing signs of life. But there can be no disguising the crisis in our democracy when the people no longer trust their Government.

The culture of spin – an obsession with presentation which

destroys ethics, restraint and judgement – is a virus that will not be easily eradicated. And to think that less than twenty-five years ago Margaret Thatcher came to office without a press secretary!

Index

431

Quayle, Dan, 263

radio, 217
Ramelson, Bert, 72
Ramphal, Sonny, 279–80
Rampton, Sir Jack, 1–9 *passim.*, 132, 139, 144, 149
Raphael, Adam, 194, 195, 337
Reagan, Ronald, 179, 254–7, 266
Redhead, Brian, 354
Reece, Gordon, 352
Rees, Peter, 329
reform, 94
Renton, Tim, 395
Rhodesian settlement, 253
Richmond, Eric, 25, 26
Ridge, Ken, 64
Ridley, Nicholas, 331
    resignation, 387–8
Rifkind, Malcolm, 269
Riley, Bill, 37
riots (1981), 233
Robilliard, Joy, 210
Robinson, Geoffrey, 415
Rose, David, 358
Ross, Ian, 120
Routledge, Paul, 152
Rowe, Christopher, 45
Royal Ulster Constabulary, 310
'rubbishing' Ministers, 319–32
rugby league, 13, 20
Rumbold, Angela, 222
Russell, George, 357
Ryan, John, 89

sanctions, 254, 276–81, 352
Santer, Jacques, 265
Saudi Arabia, 149
Savage, Tom, 234
Save It campaign, 138, 139, 150
Scamp, Sir Jack, 117
Scanlon, Hugh, 112, 125
Scargill, Arthur, 124, 145, 239
Schlüter, Paul, 265
Schultz, George, 252
Scotsman
    joins attack on lobby system, 201
Scott, Frank, 97
Scott, Laurence, 89
Scowcroft, General Brent, 263
SDI (Strategic Defense Initiative), 257–8
Seaman, Dick, 121, 161
security and intelligence services, 316, 317, 319
Sedgemore, Brian, 145, 148, 150
Sellafield, 142
Sergeant, John, 394
Shakespeare, R. W., 72
share ownership, 231
Shea, Michael, 362
Shepherd, Gordon, *xiv*
Shepherd, John, 20, 21
Shepherd, Levi, 20

Shore, Peter, 46, 369
Sissons, Peter, 120
Sky TV, 344, 357
Smith, Dan, 62
Smith, Douglas, 115, 118, 119
Smith, Geoffrey, 257, 269
Smith, John, 139, 144
Smith, Martin, 247
Snape, Frank, 35, 42
Snowden, Alan, 49
soccer, 20, 316
soccer hooliganism, 314
social contract, 137
Social Democratic Party, 234
socialism, 17
society, 242
Solomons, Stan, 40
South Africa, 254, 276–81, 352
'spin', 418–26 *passim.*
Sri Lanka, 249
state power, 230
Steel, David, 202
Sternberg, Bill, 69
Stevas, Norman St John, 305, 328–9
Steven, Stewart, 204
Stevens, Ron, 54, 78
Strangeways prison riot, 316
strikes, 76, 82–6, 111, 118, 121
    bank employees (1981), 234
    Civil Servants (1981), 234
    General Strike (1926), 117
    miners (1972), 124, 125
    miners (1974), 135
    miners (1984–1985), 239
    seamen (1981), 234
    steelworkers (1979), 232
    water and sewage industry (1981), 234
    working days lost, 152
Sunningdale, 4, 112
Supporters of Nuclear Energy, 400
Sutcliffe, Dent, 23, 27, 30, 31
Switch Off Something campaign, 132, 134

tabloid journalists, 357
Taylor, Neville, 290, 373
Taylor, Pam, 109
Taylor, Peter, 210
Tebbit, Norman, 304, 307, 351, 395
television
    current affairs, 355, 356
    dictates, news, 188
    role during war, 284
    Soviet interview with Thatcher, 344
    televising Commons, 170, 217, 219
    transmission from Falklands impossible, 297
Telivision and Radio Industries Club 401
terrorism, 118, 304–10, 355
Terry, Walter, 154, 302
Thames
    This Week, 355
Thatcher, Denis, 248, 249, 396, 401